COGNITIVE ASSESSMENT

*An Introduction to
the Rule Space Method*

Multivariate Applications Series

Sponsored by the Society of Multivariate Experimental Psychology, the goal of this series is to apply complex statistical methods to significant social or behavioral issues, in such a way so as to be accessible to a nontechnical-oriented readership (e.g., nonmethodological researchers, teachers, students, government personnel, practitioners, and other professionals). Applications from a variety of disciplines such as psychology, public health, sociology, education, and business are welcome. Books can be single- or multiple-authored or edited volumes that (1) demonstrate the application of a variety of multivariate methods to a single, major area of research; (2) describe a multivariate procedure or framework that could be applied to a number of research areas; or (3) present a variety of perspectives on a controversial subject of interest to applied multivariate researchers.

There are currently 14 books in the series:

- *What If There Were No Significance Tests?*, coedited by Lisa L. Harlow, Stanley A. Mulaik, and James H. Steiger (1997)
- *Structural Equation Modeling with LISREL, PRELIS, and SIMPLIS: Basic Concepts, Applications, and Programming*, written by Barbara M. Byrne (1998)
- *Multivariate Applications in Substance Use Research: New Methods for New Questions*, coedited by Jennifer S. Rose, Laurie Chassin, Clark C. Presson, and Steven J. Sherman (2000)
- *Item Response Theory for Psychologists*, coauthored by Susan E. Embretson and Steven P. Reise (2000)
- *Structural Equation Modeling with AMOS: Basic Concepts, Applications, and Programming*, written by Barbara M. Byrne (2001)
- *Conducting Meta-Analysis Using SAS*, written by Winfred Arthur, Jr., Winston Bennett, Jr., and Allen I. Huffcutt (2001)
- *Modeling Intraindividual Variability with Repeated Measures Data: Methods and Applications*, coedited by D. S. Moskowitz and Scott L. Hershberger (2002)
- *Multilevel Modeling: Methodological Advances, Issues, and Applications*, coedited by Steven P. Reise and Naihua Duan (2003)
- *The Essence of Multivariate Thinking: Basic Themes and Methods*, written by Lisa Harlow (2005)
- *Contemporary Psychometrics: A Festschrift for Roderick P. McDonald*, coedited by Albert Maydeu-Olivares and John J. McArdle (2005)
- *Structural Equation Modeling with EQS: Basic Concepts, Applications, and Programming, Second Edition*, written by Barbara M. Byrne (2006)
- *Introduction to Statistical Mediation Analysis*, written by David P. MacKinnon (2008)
- *Applied Data Analytic Techniques for Turning Points Research*, edited by Patricia Cohen (2008)
- *Cognitive Assessment: An Introduction to the Rule Space Method*, written by Kikumi K. Tatsuoka (2009)

Anyone wishing to submit a book proposal should send the following: (1) author/title; (2) timeline including completion date; (3) brief overview of the book's focus, including table of contents and, ideally, a sample chapter (or chapters); (4) a brief description of competing publications; and (5) targeted audiences.

For more information, please contact the series editor, Lisa Harlow, at Department of Psychology, University of Rhode Island, 10 Chafee Road, Suite 8, Kingston, RI 02881-0808; phone (401) 874-4242; fax (401) 874-5562; or e-mail LHarlow@uri.edu. Information may also be obtained from members of the advisory board; Leona Aiken (Arizona State University), Gwyneth Boodoo (Educational Testing Services), Barbara M. Byrne (University of Ottawa), Patrick Curran (University of North Carolina), Scott E. Maxwell (University of Notre Dame), David Rindskopf (City University of New York), Liora Schmelkin (Hofstra University), and Stephen West (Arizona State University).

COGNITIVE ASSESSMENT

An Introduction to
the Rule Space Method

Kikumi K. Tatsuoka

Routledge
Taylor & Francis Group
New York   London

Routledge
Taylor & Francis Group
270 Madison Avenue
New York, NY 10016

Routledge
Taylor & Francis Group
27 Church Road
Hove, East Sussex BN3 2FA

© 2009 by Taylor & Francis Group, LLC
Routledge is an imprint of Taylor & Francis Group, an Informa business

Printed in the United States of America on acid-free paper
10 9 8 7 6 5 4 3 2 1

International Standard Book Number-13: 978-1-84872-813-4 (Softcover) 978-0-8058-2828-3 (Hardcover)

Library of Congress Cataloging-in-Publication Data

Tatsuoka, Kikumi K.
    Cognitive assessment : an introduction to the rule space method / Kikumi K.
Tatsuoka.
        p. cm.
    Includes index.
    ISBN 978-0-8058-2828-3 (hardback) -- ISBN 978-1-84872-813-4 (pbk.)
    1. Cognition--Testing. I. Title.

BF311.T295 2009
153.9'3--dc22   2008032623

Visit the Taylor & Francis Web site at
http://www.taylorandfrancis.com

and the Routledge Web site at
http://www.routledge.com

Dedication

To my late husband, Maurice,
and our sons, Kay and Curtis

Contents

Preface

The methodology portrayed in this book is central to current missions in education in the United States. The "No Child Left Behind" federal government initiative requires that each state develop diagnostic tests of basic skills that not only assess overall educational progress but also identify areas of individual student weakness that will lead to tailored educational experiences. Valuable diagnostic profiles include information about how well students perform on the underlying knowledge and cognitive processing skills required for answering problems. Measuring the underlying knowledge and cognitive skills is not an easy task because it is impossible to directly observe them; therefore, they are named *latent variables*. Statisticians and psychometricians have developed the latent trait theory, now called item response theory (IRT), to measure an underlying ability. IRT is a statistical model that tries to explain students' responses on test items by using a mathematical function on a latent variable, called IRT ability. However, the latent variables useful in cognitive diagnosis must be in the hundreds and not just one variable. For example, when we closely examined students' performances on the Scholastic Aptitude Test (SAT) Verbal test, we have frequently observed that although students may have exactly the same scores, they could have entirely different profiles of strengths and weaknesses. In the case of two students, Jason and Juliana, they had very different individual profiles, but both attained 500 on the verbal scaled score. Jason was not good at bringing together material from two passages and processing grammatically complex texts. He also did not understand the main idea when it was not explicitly stated. On the other hand, Juliana was not good at synthesizing scattered information and applying general background knowledge; however, her global understanding was passable, and she had the same IRT ability value as Jason had.

Factor analysis, cluster analysis, and traditional latent class models produce factors, clusters, and classes, but they are exploratory methods that merely group observed responses into similar classes or patterns. For this reason, they may produce solutions with no clear interpretation of the resulting groups of items or respondents. Ideally, diagnostic analyses of test results should be descriptive, objective, free from ambiguous interpretations, and uniquely express an individual's true state of knowledge. To achieve these goals, we need a new methodology that will transform many unobservable knowledge and skills variables (defined as *attributes* throughout the book) into observable and measurable attributes without losing their original meanings. The purpose of this book is to introduce one such methodology, the rule space method (RSM), that has been used since the 1980s and has made it possible to measure these unobservable latent variables and to clearly interpret the results without losing the original meaning of attributes.

The RSM transforms unobservable attributes involved in test items into observable attribute mastery probabilities that are defined as the probability of using each attribute correctly to get the correct answer for given problems. In other words, RSM converts students' item response patterns into attribute mastery probabilities.

For example, Johnny's diagnostic report will be as follows:

Scale Score of 500	
Bring together material from two passages.	Excellent: 95th percentile
Process grammatically complex texts.	Good: 80th percentile
Understand the main idea when it was not explicitly stated.	Good: 75th percentile

As long as a test shares the same set of attributes, analysis results from several tests consisting of different sets of items like the Trends in International Mathematics and Science Study (TIMSS) and several parallel forms of assessments can be combined for various secondary analyses.

The RSM, which can determine an individual's strengths and weaknesses, has been applied to Preliminary SAT (PSAT) to generate scoring reports, which inform schools, teachers, and parents exactly what the total score of 500 means. This book evolved from hundreds of journal articles, technical reports, Ph.D. theses, presentations at conferences, and book chapters in which various segments of RSM were introduced and discussed. Because RSM belongs to an approach of statistical pattern recognition and classification problems popular in engineering areas, this book will be useful to graduate students in a variety of disciplines. The book is primarily written for graduate students in quantitative and educational psychology and in instructional technology, but it is also applicable to medical diagnoses, a variety of applications in computer science, and engineering.

The conceptual framework of RSM is influenced by my early education in mathematics, in which I specialized in abstract algebra, the theories of functional space, and optimization by vector space methods, and my experience developing software to analyze students' online performance using instructional materials on the Programmed Logic for Automatic Teaching Operations (PLATO) system at the University of Illinois. These online data were so massive and extremely complex that the traditional psychometric theories, such as classical test theory and item response theories, could not be applied. New statistical methods were obviously needed for diagnosing an individual learner's state of knowledge that could be characterized by a mastered pattern of latent and unobservable cognitive processing skills, thinking skills, and content knowledge that a student possesses for solving problems. With the support of the Office of Naval Research, my late husband, Professor Maurice Tatsuoka at the University of Illinois, and I started a research project in 1979, which was aimed at developing a new statistical methodology like the one described above. I am extremely grateful to my then coordinating officer, Dr. Charles Davis, and the director of the Cognition and Psychometrics Division, Dr. Marshall Far, as well as Drs. Susan Chipman and Henry Half, for supporting us continuously until 1994. Without their long-term support, it would have been impossible to develop RSM. I am also grateful to the National Institute of Education, the National Science Foundation, the University of Illinois, Educational Testing Services (ETS), and the College Board for awarding me research grants and contracts for giving me research support.

This book has 10 chapters, starting with an introduction in Chapter 1, which provides a general overview of cognitive assessment research. Chapter 2 begins with a technical discussion of nonparametric person–fit statistics and parametric person–fit statistics zeta (ζ). Chapters 3 and 4 are devoted to the introduction of the Q-matrix theory—a Q matrix is an item and attribute matrix, knowledge states, a partially ordered network of knowledge states, and the relationship between attribute space and item space. Chapter 5 introduces rule space as a classification space. Chapter 6 discusses classification rules in general. Chapter 7 continues the discussion of rule space classification and introduces attribute mastery probabilities. Chapter 8 gives various properties of attribute mastery probabilities from the Bayesian point of view. Chapter 9 introduces the reliability theory of attributes connected to the traditional classical test theory by introducing reliability indexes derived from the attribute mastery probabilities and classification rules, as well as item response theory by introducing attribute characteristic curves. The last chapter discusses various validity topics and shows that the construct validity of a test can be clarified by using the rule space method.

Finally, I am very grateful to Professor Lisa Harlow for her kindness and patience; and to Dr. Gwyneth Boodoo, who had worked together with me at ETS and introduced me to Lisa, the editor of the Multivariate Application Series, for the contribution of writing about RSM in a book for the series, and most importantly for her friendship that developed through our hard times together. I also express my gratitude for their support of my research works to Professors Donald Bitzer at the PLATO Lab, Henry Braun, Charles Davis, Charles Lewis, and Howard Everson at

ETS and College Board, and James Corter at Teachers College, Columbia University. Many thanks to the chief editor Debra Reigert and the editorial team at Taylor & Francis especially the project editor Susan Horwitz, to Jane Hye for the developmental editing of my book, and to reviewers of Society for Multiriate Experimental Psychology (SMEP) board members for helpful comments and suggestions. Last, I still miss my late husband, Maurice, who had worked with me at the beginning stage of the project and who had developed the RSM classification procedure with me by discussing it days and nights from many angles. I am very grateful to my younger son, Curtis (a statistician); his mathematician friend, Dr. Ferenc Varadi; also my mathematician friend, Robert Baillie, for writing various computer programs essential for the development of a methodology; and my older son, Kay, who is also a statistician and mathematician, for valuable discussions.

1

Dimensionality of Test Data and Aberrant Response Patterns

1.1 General Overview of Cognitively Diagnostic Methodologies

The value of a diagnostic profile that enumerates strengths and weaknesses in individual performance has been recognized in education, and competent teachers have been using their diagnostic skills in their classrooms to teach students better. It had been common sense that only humans could do such detective work to determine what was going on inside a human brain; however, the rapid development of computer technologies in the 1970s enabled technology to accomplish what previously had been impossible for humans. As computer technologies developed rapidly, computational powers increased dramatically. Linguists worked on natural language processing, psychologists were interested in modeling human information and retrieval, mathematicians were more interested in automating the theorem-proving process, and statisticians advanced various statistical methodologies and models that were impossible to compute without the help of computers. Computer scientists Brown and Burton (1978) developed a computer program called BUGGY using a new powerful programming language suitable for processing a list of logical statements. BUGGY was able to diagnose various "bugs," or equally erroneous rules of operations committed by students in whole-number subtraction problems.

The successful diagnostic capability of the computer program BUGGY affected American education to a great extent; consequently, similar computer programs, called "expert systems" (Anderson, 1984), that are capable of diagnosing erroneous rules of operations or capable of teaching simple algebra and geometry were developed in the 1980s and 1990s. FBUG was a similar buggy system that followed the idea of the original BUGGY and was capable of diagnosing fraction, addition, and subtraction problems (Tatsuoka & Baillie, 1982). These computer programs required a prepared list of erroneous rules that were originally discovered by humans. Each erroneous rule was decomposed into a sequence of logical statements and a computer language like LISP, which could develop the diagnostic systems. If a new erroneous rule was discovered, then the program would be modified to include it. The system could not discover either new erroneous rules not listed in the initial list or common erroneous rules using a different strategy or a new method to solve a problem.

Stability and Gradient of Diagnostic Information

Sleeman, Kelly, Martink, Ward, and Moore (1989) developed a buggy system for algebra and discovered that many students changed their erroneous rules of operations so often that the buggy system was practically unable to diagnose such students. VanLehn (1983) developed "repair theory" to explain why bugs are unstable. Shaw (1984, 1986) interviewed 40 to 50 students in fraction, addition, and subtraction problems; Standiford, Tatsuoka, and Klein (1982) also interviewed many students for mixed-number operations; and so did Birenbaum (1981) for signed-number operations. They discovered that 95% of erroneous rules of operations in these domains were extremely unstable, and students kept changing their rules to something else. The students also could not answer interview questions as to why they changed their old rules to new ones. Moreover, many students could not even recall what rules they used, even when they used them only 10 seconds before. Tatsuoka (1984a) concluded it would not be wise to diagnose a micro level of performances like bugs or erroneous rules on a test. Consequently, an important question arose regarding the level of performance that would be stable enough to measure and diagnose.

Total scores of most large-scale assessments have high reliabilities, but the level of information is too coarse, and because there are too many different ways to get 50% of the items correct, total scores are not very useful for cognitive diagnosis. If a math test has 5 geometry items and 5 algebra items, then there are 252 ways to achieve a score of 5. Some students may get only the geometry items correct and all algebra items incorrect, whereas others get the geometry items incorrect and all algebra items correct. Their sources of misconceptions could be very different, and they would then need very different remediation treatments. The item score of a test is still at the macro level, and it is difficult to obtain useful diagnostic information from a single item. The question then becomes which levels of diagnostic information would be most valuable and helpful in promoting learning activities among students and whether a subscore level would be useful. The following problems, labeled Examples 1.1.1 and 1.1.2, were excerpted from the technical report to the National Science Foundation (Tatsuoka, Kelly, C. Tatsuoka, Varadi, & Dean, 2007) and coded by three types of attributes: content-related knowledge and skills (C2–C5 and Exponential and Probabilities), mathematical thinking skills (P1–P10), and special skills unique to item types (S1–S9).

Example 1.1

A water ski tow handle makes an isosceles triangle. If one of the congruent angles is 65 degrees, what is the measure of the angle?

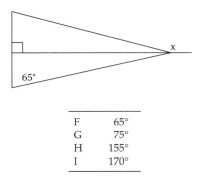

F	65°
G	75°
H	155°
I	170°

Geometric figure is given: S3.

This is a geometry problem: C4.

Have to apply knowledge about the relationships among angles to get the solution: P3.

Because the total sum of angles is 180°, the third angle becomes (180° − 130°) = 50°. Therefore, x can be obtained by subtracting half of this angle, 25°: P5.

That is, 180° − {180° − (65° + 65°)}/2 = 155°: P2.

Example 1.2

An electrician has a plastic pipe, used for underground wiring, which is 15 feet long. He needs plastic pieces that are 6.5 inches long to complete his job. When he cuts the pipe, how many pieces will he be able to use for his job?

Two thirds of the students answered this question correctly. We counted the number of words used in the stem and found 52 words; however, the problem requires translation of a word problem into an arithmetic procedure in order to solve this item: P1.

Because two different units, *feet* and *inch*, are used, we have to convert a foot to 12 inches, and then 15 feet must be 180 inches: S1.

The length of a pipe is 6.5 inches, so we need 27 pieces, 180/6.5 = 27 pieces: P2.

Dividing 180 by a decimal number, 6.5, belongs to the content domain of C2: C2.

There are two steps—the first to convert the unit to the common unit, and the second to carry out the computation: P9.

TABLE 1.1

A Modified List of Knowledge, Skill, and Process Attributes Derived to Explain Performance on Mathematics Items From the TIMSS-R (1999) for Population 2 (Eighth Graders) for Some State Assessment

Content Attributes

C1	Basic concepts and operations in whole numbers and integers
C2	Basic concepts and operations in fractions and decimals
EXP	Powers, roots, and scientific expression of numbers are separated from C2
C3	Basic concepts and operations in elementary algebra
C4	Basic concepts and operations in two-dimensional geometry
C5	Data and basic statistics
PROB	Basic concepts, properties, and computational skills

Process Attributes

P1	Translate, formulate, and understand (only for seventh graders) equations and expressions to solve a problem
P2	Computational applications of knowledge in arithmetic and geometry
P3	Judgmental applications of knowledge in arithmetic and geometry
P4	Applying rules in algebra and solving equations (plugging in included for seventh graders)
P5	Logical reasoning—includes case reasoning, deductive thinking skills, if-then, necessary and sufficient conditions, and generalization skills
P6	Problem search; analytic thinking and problem restructuring; and inductive thinking
P7	Generating, visualizing, and reading figures and graphs
P9	Management of data and procedures, complex, and can set multigoals
P10	Quantitative and logical reading (*less than, must, need to be, at least, best*, etc.)

Skill (Item Type) Attributes

S1	Unit conversion
S2	Apply number properties and relationships; number sense and number line
S3	Using figures, tables, charts, and graphs
S3g	Using geometric figures
S4	Approximation and estimation
S5	Evaluate, verify, and check options
S6	Patterns and relationships (inductive thinking skills)
S7	Using proportional reasoning
S8	Solving novel or unfamiliar problems
S9	Comparison of two or more entities

These simple problems suggest that several different attributes listed in Table 1.1 must be applied correctly in order to get the right answer. P2 is involved in both items, but the remaining attributes coded in the problems are not intersected. There are 27 attributes listed in Table 1.1 and only 45 items per test. All attributes are involved independently in different ways for each of 45 items, and none of the items involves an identical set of attributes. The attribute involvement is intertwined and complex. The problem is to determine how one can possibly separate the items into subsets based on attribute involvement, and take their subscores from each subset as the attributes' performance.

The search for the acceptable levels for helpful and reliable diagnostic information was continued in the 1980s and early 1990s. Tatsuoka (1984a) investigated by grouping erroneous rules in fraction problems into their sources of errors, and examined their stability across two parallel tests. She determined, for example, that 16 erroneous rules of operations originated from the action of making two equivalent fractions. The sources of errors or the sources of erroneous rules of operations were acceptably stable. She further investigated the changes of error types over four parallel tests of signed-number computations (Tatsuoka, 1983a; Tatsuoka, Birenbaum, & Arnold, 1990; Tatsuoka, Birenbaum, Lewis, & Sheehan, 1993), and Birenbaum and her associates (Birenbaum, Kelly, & Tatsuoka, 1993; Birenbaum & Tatsuoka, 1980) examined the stability of computational skills in algebra and exponential items by examining the agreement of a diagnostic classification from parallel subtests (Birenbaum, Tatsuoka, & Nasser, 1997). Tatsuoka and Tatsuoka (2005) tested the stability of classification results by the rule space method and found the test–retest correlations of attribute level are higher than those of item level. This series of studies confirmed that the erroneous rules are extremely unstable, but the sources of erroneous rules are acceptably stable.

When the targeted domains of cognitive diagnosis are shifted from rather small domains, such as solving simultaneous equations or subtracting mixed numbers, to a large-scale assessment such as the Scholastic Aptitude Test (SAT), the Test of English as a Foreign Language (TOEFL), the Trends in International Mathematics and Science Study (TIMSS), National Assessment of Educational Progress (NAEP), or a state assessment, appropriate levels of information about performances on items would be required. It is impossible to have attributes suitable to a small domain, such as *make two mixed fractions equivalent fractions* or *borrowing*, for a large-scale assessment, because the finer levels (still microlevel) of attributes are involved in, at most, one or two items, and the total numbers of microlevel attributes involved in the assessment will be very large. When we think about a list of "can or cannot" combinations of attributes, the volume and complexity of diagnostic information would be extremely difficult to comprehend for most humans. Human capability of handling the number of attributes in a diagnostic report is very limited. Many test users did not want to be burdened by 50 to 100 diagnosed attribute performances. In Chapter 10, we will discuss how to select the best 15 attributes from 100 candidate attributes in the SAT Writing test. If we can select only 15 attributes for a 60-item writing test, then we will need a larger gradient of attributes from micro to macro levels of diagnostic information. Note that the gradient of attributes listed in Table 1.1 for TIMSS and a state assessment is larger than the example of the attributes used in the fraction addition and subtraction test (Tatsuoka, 1984a).

Deterministic Versus Probabilistic

Valuable diagnostic profiles include information about how well test takers performed on the underlying knowledge and cognitive processing skills (termed *attributes* in the previous section) required for answering problems. The approach used by Brown and Burton (1978) and by VanLehn (1983) is deterministic, but the rule space method (RSM) developed by Tatsuoka and her associates takes account of the error of measurements and the probability of misclassifications in diagnosing individuals' misconceptions and lack of knowledge in the 1980s and the 1990s (Tatsuoka, 1983b, 1985; Tatsuoka & Tatsuoka, 1987; Tatsuoka & Tatsuoka, 1989). RSM has two phases, like a statistical pattern recognition and classification methodology, that have been one of many branches of statistical methodology. The first phase is the selection of feature variables, and then the classification stage follows. In RSM, the feature selection stage corresponds to the Q-matrix theory, which is deterministic. The Q-matrix theory generates a partially ordered set of knowledge states by applying Boolean algebra (Tatsuoka, 1990, 1991, 1993, 1995). The second stage is the statistical patterns classification stage, which is a probabilistic approach; therefore, RSM is deterministic and probabilistic.

Recently, there has been increased interest in such diagnostic testing methods, and in several new methods and models that apply various statistical techniques (e.g., Dibello, Stout, & Roussos, 1995; Gierl, 1996; Gierl, Leighton, & Hunka, 2000; Haertel & Wiley, 1993; Hunt, 2006; Junker & Sijtsma, 2001; C. Tatsuoka, 1996, 2002; C. Tatsuoka & Ferguson, 2003). C. Tatsuoka's POSET model, which is one of the most mathematically sophisticated and advanced, was developed in the context of statistical sequential analysis on the partially ordered network of knowledge states that is generated by the Q-matrix theory. Junker and Sijstma's DANA model is very similar to POSET but does not use the Q-matrix theory, which will be introduced in Chapters 3 and 4 in the detail.

History of Rule Space Methodology and Introduction to Q-Matrix Theory

Because RSM has been one of the methodologies having the longest period of development and application, the results from the RSM analyses have demonstrated that they are very useful in various educational and psychological research and decisions. Guerrero (2001) investigated the language effects of test validity in the English and Spanish versions of the SAT, and Yepes Baraya, Allen, and Tatsuoka (2000) found that students used different strategies, deductive versus experimental, to learn the hands-on tasks of NAEP Science. Birenbaum et al. (Birenbaum, Tatsuoka, & Xin, 2005; Birenbaum, Tatsuoka, & Yamada, 2004) and Xin, Xu, & Tatsuoka (2005) applied RSM to test results in the United States, Singapore, and Japan to compare the effects of their curriculum and their educational policies on attribute-level performances, and

Tatsuoka, Corter, and Tatsuoka (2004) and Tatsuoka et al. (2006) compared mathematical thinking skills of 20 countries and found the countries teaching more geometry performed better on mathematical thinking skills. Dean (2006) found that students learned mathematical thinking skills better in the seventh grade and achieved much higher scores on advanced mathematics in the 12th grade. Tatsuoka and Boodoo (2000), Kuramoto et al. (2003), Dogan (2006), and Chen et al. (2008) applied RSM to Japanese, Turkish, and Taiwanese tests to examine their constructive validities.

Knowledge and Cognitive Processing Skills: Attributes

Knowledge and cognitive processing skills will be called *attributes*, and binary attribute patterns that express mastery or nonmastery of attributes will be referred to as *knowledge states* or *latent knowledge states* hereafter. Attributes are latent variables that are impossible to observe directly. Moreover, the domains of our interest usually involve several to hundreds of attributes. Although physical objects or events in science applications are usually observable, attributes and knowledge states are not observable. Measurement of unobservable latent variables can be assessed only indirectly from observable item scores by making inferences about the misconceptions a subject most likely had, which led to incorrect responses. Given a response pattern, we want to determine the probability that a test taker's observed responses might have been drawn from a specific knowledge state. A research method, which infers a single latent variable θ in psychometrics and educational measurement, is a statistical modeling approach, item response theory (IRT). Many statistical models of test performance assume some kind of algebraic relationship with regard to a latent variable (or a few latent variables) to explain observed responses. In IRT models, logistic functions are used on the latent variable θ (ability) to explain students' item responses. The latent variable θ is viewed as an ability, or a trait, to perform well on test items.

How RSM Works

To explain how RSM works, it is helpful to relate it to statistical pattern recognition and classification problems, in which an observed pattern will be classified into one of the predetermined classification groups (Fukunaga, 1990; Ripley, 1996). Typical examples are to enable computers to recognize handwritten letters or scan X-ray images to diagnose whether or not a tumor is cancerous. For example, the letter recognition problem has 52 predetermined groups representing the lower and upper cases of 26 alphabetic characters. These letters are expressed uniquely by 52 binary patterns of features. The set of features is predesigned by examining shapes, strokes, and geometric characteristics of the 52 letters. After this design stage is done, statistical classifiers are usually estimated. The classifiers classify an observed input pattern into one of 52 predetermined groups, and compute error probabilities. The group with the smallest error probability is usually taken as the letter to which the observed input pattern would belong. This general outline of a pattern recognition system applies to cognitive diagnosis as follows: In a diagnostic analysis of a test, feature variables become attributes, and the 52 letters represented by the patterns of the feature variables are analogous to knowledge states. The predetermined groups in the letter recognition example are expressed by observable feature variables, and hence they are directly measurable, whereas attributes are feature variables that are impossible to measure directly, and knowledge states defined by patterns of attributes are also impossible to measure directly.

Therefore, RSM has to be extended to include an additional step to deal with latent feature variables (Tatsuoka, 1990, 1991, 1993). The author previously solved this difficulty by introducing an attribute Q matrix, where the cell q_{jk} in a Q matrix is coded 1 if item j involves attribute k for answering item j correctly, and 0 if not. In this instance, the Q matrix is a cognitive model for test item performance hypothesized by cognitive researchers, teachers, or other domain experts. It explains performance on the n observable test items in terms of competencies on k latent attributes. A knowledge state KS_m is defined by a latent attribute pattern of 1s and 0s. If a student can use attribute k correctly, then the kth element of KS_m is 1, and 0 if not. It is assumed that the right answer for item j is obtained if and only if all attributes involved in item j are successfully applied. Furthermore, the probability of answering item j correctly is assumed to be calculated by multiplying the probabilities of correct use of the involved attributes for item j.

Tatsuoka (1991) has described an algorithm that generates all possible knowledge states from a given Q matrix, incorporated in a program called BUGSHEL (Varadi, C. Tatsuoka, & K. Tatsuoka, 1992; Varadi & K. Tatsuoka, 1989). These possible knowledge states generate a set of expected or "ideal" item score patterns in order to differentiate them from students' observed item response patterns. The knowledge states, or equivalently the ideal item score patterns, form a set of predetermined classification groups in RSM. The unobservable attribute patterns correspond to ideal item score patterns, which are directly observable.

Classification Space: Rule Space

In the previous section, we introduced the Q-matrix theory, which corresponds to the feature extractor phase in the statistical pattern recognition and classification problems. The extracted features' presumably relevant information from the input data corresponds to our attributes and knowledge states. The classifier is used to classify the input information into one of the predetermined classification groups in a vector space. The rule space is a vector space. The third component for classification problems will be discussed later in detail in Chapters 5, 6, and 7. In this chapter, we introduce the basic concept of the rule space verbally so that the readers will get a rough idea of what will be discussed there. Rule space was designed to achieve the third stage, classification. Rule space was an n-dimensional vector space and constructed for performing the multivariate decision theory for many classification groups. The classification space could be a discrete item space—say, 59 dimensions for a 60-item test—but the knowledge states with extremely high or low total scores or unusual knowledge states did not have the covariance matrices whose determinants were not zeros (Kim, 1989). Therefore, we transformed discrete item scores to continuous variables, IRT θ and the Person–Fit Index ζ (Tatsuoka, 1984b, 1985), and used them as coordinates of the classification space. The distance in the rule space is defined by Mahalanobis distance, which is the log likelihood ratio of two density distributions in the space. Tatsuoka and Tatsuoka (1987) introduced a bug distribution whose mean vector R is given by an ideal item score pattern (a knowledge state) generated from a given Q matrix, and random variables are a slippage vector deviated from R. The distance between an individual response vector X and R are measured by the Mahalanobis distance between X and R. Given a student's observed item response pattern, statistical classifiers classify his or her response pattern by estimating a mastery probability for each attribute. This is a Bayes classification rule that is known to be the best rule. In this way, a student's observed item responses are transformed into estimated attribute mastery probabilities. In other words, RSM transforms a dataset of students by item scores into a dataset of students by attribute mastery probabilities. The benefit of this approach is that it allows for diagnosis of students' test performance in terms of very detailed content knowledge and processing skills.

One of the unique characteristics of RSM is that it entails developing a clear correspondence between a subject's observed item response pattern and the corresponding ideal item score pattern(s). By so doing, we can make an inference about how well an individual has performed on latent attributes from his or her performance on observable item responses.

Attributes derived by domain experts with the rule space procedure for large-scale assessments in past studies are almost always uncorrelated from one another (Corter & Tatsuoka, 2004; Saito, 1998; Tatsuoka, 1995; Tatsuoka et al., 2004, 2006). Indeed, the previous studies of several large-scale assessments, such as the SAT, TOEFL, Test of English for International Communication (TOEIC), TIMSS, NAEP, and Graduate Record Examination (GRE) quantitative tests, have indicated that most of their attributes are independent of principal component analyses and factor analyses (Corter & Tatsuoka, 2004; Saito, 1998; Tatsuoka, 1985; Tatsuoka & Boodoo, 2000); therefore, a space spanned by K attributes or, equally to say, a space of knowledge states is considered K-dimensional vector space. Indeed, the definition of knowledge states, as stated earlier, is given by binary attribute patterns that express mastery or nonmastery of attributes; thus, each element in a knowledge space is a vector of attribute mastery probabilities.

Any two knowledge states (e.g., C_1 and C_2) can be ordered by an inclusion relationship: $C_1 \geq C_2$ if every attribute in C_1 is larger than its corresponding attribute in C_2. With this order, knowledge states can be expressed by a network. The structure of knowledge states is a complex network, and it seems far from the traditional concept of proficiency levels expressed by scores or a unidimensional ability line. This notion of knowledge structures has been explored by several researchers (Falmagne & Doignon, 1988; Tatsuoka, 1990, 1991).

The idea of IRT and latent ability measure θ is based on a latent trait theory (Lord & Novick, 1968). The fundamental idea of a latent trait theory is that an individuals' behavior can be accounted for by defining certain human characteristics called *traits*, and hence we estimate quantitatively the individuals' standing on each of these traits, and then use the numerical value obtained to predict or explain performance in relevant situations. Estimated IRT θ values represent the individuals' trait standing to explain his/her observed total scores. Estimated IRT θ values always correlates extremely high with observed total scores of test takers.

However, it is realistic that a model or statistical method has to be able to handle multidimensional latent abilities characterized by many unobservable attributes, and although it is extremely difficult to make any inferences on such a large number of unobservable attributes, it is not impossible. This book introduces a methodology termed *rule space*, that is, a statistical tool to make inferences about several numbers of attributes from observable item responses.

A number of researchers from both sides (Chipman, Nichols, & Brennan, 1995; Bartholomew, 1987) acknowledged that combining cognitive science and psychometrics would be one of the most difficult tasks. The gap between psychometrics and cognitive science is enormously wide in several ways, and it is very difficult to find some cognitively meaningful link between existing cognitive theories and current psychometric models. For a long time, psychometric theories have been criticized by a number of cognitive psychologists and scientists as not being at all helpful in investigating learning activities necessary to understand human cognition or for developing cognitive models and theories. Abilities used in the current psychometric models are mysterious and coarse, whereas abilities in cognitive science are very detailed, practical, and specific. These differences may be due to the original motivation of those who developed various psychometric models. Psychometric models have been developed for ranking and comparing examinees by assuming that their abilities could be linearly ordered. The basic principle, in other words, is that the higher the estimated psychometric ability is, the smarter the examinee is. This is because the main purpose of the current psychometric models is to obtain accurate measures of total scores and to use the information for selection, grading, and predicting examinees' future performance; however, providing useful diagnostic information for improving teaching and learning has not been important to psychometricians. At the present time, though, many test users want testing to be an integral part of instruction so that prescribed reports can guide teachers and students to attain higher educational goals.

1.2 Dimensionality of Tests

The difference between achievement and aptitude tests is best explained by the different nature of the two types of tests. Usually, achievement tests are designed to measure an outcome of instructional activities. Especially when we are concerned with instruction or curriculum, there are two distinct purposes to which testing may be directed. One is the relatively simple task of measuring each student's overall mastery level, and the other is the more complicated matter of seeking diagnostic information concerning each student's strengths and weaknesses; however, the major thrust of the current testing practice has been focused on the measurement of proficiency levels that are assumed to be linearly ordered as points located on a continuum (Lord, 1980; Lord & Novick, 1968). Although classical test theory may not explicitly assume that students' proficiency levels can be expressed as points on a continuum, the use of total scores supports Lord's assertion as a special discrete case, not continuous values but discrete integer values. One of the essential assumptions for the IRT models used in the current assessment pertains to the unidimensionality of the data (Lord & Novick, 1968). The estimated values of IRT ability θ are lineary ordered from lower to higher values between -3 and 3. The unidimensionality used in IRT models means the factor analytic unidimensionality and not the scalability of response patterns in Guttman's sense (Wise, 1981).

Many researchers (Bejar, 1980; Birenbaum & Tatsuoka, 1982; Saito, 1998; Tatsuoka & Birenbaum, 1981; Wise, 1981) have investigated the factor analytic dimensionality of achievement tests. They found that the temporal positioning of the test—pretest, posttest, or tests administered during the learning period—affects its dimensionality as much as does the content area with which the test is concerned. Further, Tatsuoka and Birenbaum (1983) found that the unidimensional structure of the data is seriously damaged when two different teaching methods are used in the same instruction. Moreover, it has been shown that the dimensionality of a given test changes depending on the stage of the instruction in which the test is given (Kingsbury & Weiss, 1979). The dimensionality of typical large-scale assessments such as the SAT, the Preliminary SAT (PSAT), and the GRE, on the other hand, tends toward unidimensionality. It raises an interesting question about the nature of the dimensionality. What is a test really measuring? If the test measures a psychologically meaningful trait, then what is it? Saito (1998), in her Ph.D. thesis, studied the acquisition of knowledge and linguistic skills in English as a second language in Japanese students, and found that there are three main learning paths. The main path is characterized by not mastering higher cognitive skills and knowledge. The second path is affected by unfamiliarity of the topic, and the third is characterized by not mastering either the meaning of vocabulary in a given context or basic skills such as using referential expressions (e.g., *it, that, them* and *the latter*). She generated responses belonging to each learning path by controlling its sample size and proficiency level. When the sample size of one path became much larger than the remaining two paths, then the dimensionality of generated responses from three paths became one dimension. When the sample sizes of two paths were almost equally large, and twice larger than that of the remaining path, then the dimension of the dataset became two. This finding suggests that the dimensionality of assessment associates closely with a majority of students who took it and the kinds of skills and knowledge they used across different proficiency levels in taking test items.

It is known that children seek simplifying procedures that lead them to construct or invent more effective routines that might be quite different to teach directly (Resnick, 1976). Many cognitive psychologists (Birenbaum, 1981; Shaw, 1986; VanLehn, 1983) have observed independently that students' rules do not always correspond with the algorithm taught in class. When investigating the relationship between the algorithms taught and later performance, Resnick concluded that "the efficiency is a result of fewer steps and that the transformation of algorithm by learner is more general than we have thought up to now" (p. 72). The modified rules of operation sometimes happen to be incorrect as a process. Several examples of incorrect rules invented by students for solving addition problems of signed numbers are presented in Table 1.2. Erroneous rules produce various different sets of responses for a given set of items (Birenbaum, 1981).

Birenbaum (1981) observed that incorrect rules of operation could occasionally yield correct answers. For example, in addition fraction problems, the student who cross-cancels the numbers will get the correct answer for a problem such as (4/6) + (2/6). Also, in subtraction fractions, the student who always "borrows" a ten—that is, 2(3/8) − 1(7/8) = 1(13/8) − 1(7/8) = (6/8)—will get the correct answer for a problem such as 2(3/10) − 1(7/10). Birenbaum (1981) created 16 types of signed-number addition and subtraction problems. About 6% of scores (N = 125) were changed after careful examination of the application of erroneous rules, as can be seen in Figure 1.1. Then the original data and modified data were analyzed by a multidimensional scaling analysis. The modified data is termed as purified item response patterns. Figure 1.2 shows that the structure of the

TABLE 1.2

Response of Four Eighth-Grade Students Who Consistently Applied Their Erroneous Algorithms in Response to Six Addition Problems in Signed Numbers

Problem Number	Responses by Student			
	Student 1	Student 2	Student 3	Student 4
1. $3 + -7 = -4$	-4	-10	-4	$+10$
2. $7 + (-3) = +4$	$+10$	$+10$	$+4$	$+10$
3. $-6 + -15 = -21$	-21	-21	-22	-9
4. $-6 + +15 = -21$	$+9$	$+21$	$+8$	$+21$
5. $(-23) + (-9) = -32$	$+32$	-32	-31	-14
6. $(-8) + (-4) = -12$	$+12$	-12	-12	-4
Number of correct answers	3	3	3	3

Note: Rules of the four students that were validated by interviews (Birenbaum, 1981) are as follows: Student 1 treats parentheses as absolute value notation; Student 2 adds the two numbers and takes the sign of the number with the larger absolute value; Student 3 mistypes the answers to items 3, 4, and 5, or has errors in whole-number addition; and Student 4 moves the second number from the origin instead of the position of the first number on the number line.

test crystallizes into the two item types, addition and subtraction items. A scoring system that takes into consideration the process rather than relying solely on the outcome of the right or wrong scores resulted in significant improvement in the psychometric properties.

Tatsuoka et al. (2004) found that the underlying knowledge and processing skills of TIMSS showed multidimensionality, and their four factors given in Table 1.3 supported the conclusions derived independently from some other statistical analyses and background questionnaires given to teachers and schools in 20 nations.

1.3 Detection of Aberrant Response Patterns and Their Effect on Dimensionality

The arguments in the previous section seem to support the theory that aberrant response patterns (i.e., patterns deviating from a majority of response patterns) resulting from the application of erroneous rules of operation cause a dispersed scatterplot of performances on the items in signed-numbered addition and subtraction problems. "Purified item response patterns" resulted in a two-dimensional dataset, as stated in Section 1.2. Moreover, in more general settings than the micro level of erroneous rules of operations, it seems the dimensionality of assessment

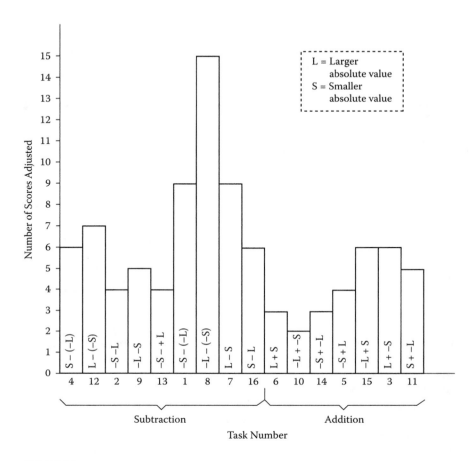

FIGURE 1.1
Number of scores adjusted in each test task.

associates closely with a majority of students who took it and the kinds of skills and knowledge they used correctly in taking test items at different proficiency levels.

It seems that detection of "aberrant response patterns" is important for data analyses. In this section, we will discuss how one can detect aberrant response patterns, which are different from "normal" item response patterns. Several indices have been developed and discussed in Meijer (1994); we will leave detailed discussion to Meijer and will introduce indices only that are closely related to cognitive perspectives.

Two indices were developed for measuring the degree of conformity or consistency of an individual examinee's response pattern on a set of items (Tatsuoka, 1981; Tatsuoka & Tatsuoka, 1980, 1982, 1983). The first, called the

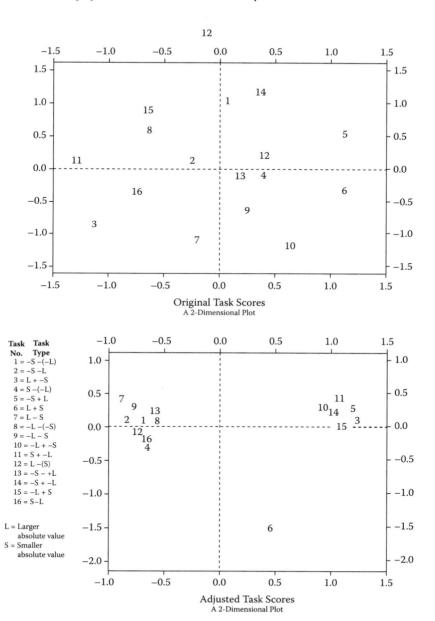

FIGURE 1.2
Analyses of multidimensional scaling for original and modified datasets.

TABLE 1.3

Rotated Component Matrix From the Principal Component Analysis of All Attributes, Performed on Mean Attribute Mastery Probability Profiles Across 20 Countries

Attribute: Description	F1	F2	F3	F4
C2: Fraction	0.66			
S3: Figure, table, and graph	0.68			
P6: Problem search and analytical thinking skills	0.73			
P1: Translate words to equations and expressions	0.76			
S11: Understanding verbally posed problems	0.54			
S10: Open0ended items	0.57	0.56		
C1: Whole numbers and integers		0.75		
C3: Elementary algebra		0.71		
C5: Data, probability, and statistics		0.75		
S6: Recognize patterns and their relations		0.62		
P2: Computational applications		0.74		
P4: Apply rules to solve equations, derive algebraic expressions		0.61		
C4: Geometry	0.57		0.65	
S7: Proportional reasoning			0.78	
P3: Judgmental applications of knowledge and concepts			0.73	
P9: Executive control, manage data, and process			0.71	
P5: Logical reasoning skills			0.65	
S2: Numerical properties and relations				0.84
S3: Figure, table, and graph	0.59			0.68
S4: Approximation and estimation				0.91
S5: Evaluate and verify options				0.75
P7: Generalize, visualize, and read graphs, figures, and tables	0.59			0.62
P10: Quantitative and logical reading				0.80

Note: Only component loadings above a cutoff of .50 are shown.

Norm Conformity Index (NCI), measures the proximity of the pattern to a baseline pattern in which all 0's precede all 1's when the items are arranged in some prescribed order. The second, called the Individual Consistency Index (ICI), measures the extent to which an individual's response pattern remains invariant when he or she responds to several waves of parallel items. We will show how these two indices, used in conjunction with test scores, can spot aberrant response patterns of students requiring detailed error diagnosis.

The possibility that an examinee obtains correct answers for the wrong reasons when responding to dichotomously scored test items has been largely ignored by psychometricians. Although scattered attempts have been made to give partial credit for partial knowledge, procedures for discrediting correct answers arrived at by incorrect reasons have typically been confined to the use of formulas for correction for guessing. This lack may not be serious for standardized ability tests, but is very important in the context of achievement testing, which is an integral part of the instructional process (Birenbaum & Tatsuoka, 1983). Here, the test must serve the purpose of diagnosing what type of misconception exists, so that appropriate remedial instruction can be given (Glaser, 1981; Nitko, 1980; Tatsuoka, 1981). This calls for the study of cognitive processes that are used in solving problems, and identifying where the examinee went astray even when the correct answer was produced. This type of diagnostic testing was pioneered by Brown and Burton (1978). Their celebrated BUGGY is essentially an adaptive diagnostic testing system, which utilizes network theory for routing examinees through a set of problems in subtraction of positive integers. Tire branching is such that each problem serves to narrow down the scope of "hypotheses" as to the type(s) of misconception(s) held by the examinee until finally a unique diagnosis is made. Baillie and Tatsuoka (1982) developed a diagnostic testing system called FBUG, which differed from BUGGY in that the test was not adaptive but "conventional" (i.e., linear). The test was constructed for use in conjunction with lessons in the addition and subtraction of signed numbers (positive and negative integers) for eighth-grade students, and consisted of four parallel subtests of 16 items each. A system of error vectors was developed for diagnosing the type(s) of error committed.

Crucial to this system of error diagnosis is the ability to tell whether and to what extent a response pattern is "typical" or "consistent." We may speak of consistency with respect to either the average response pattern of a group or an individual's own response pattern over time. To measure consistency in these two senses, two related but distinct indices are developed in this book. They are called the NCI and the ICI, respectively.

It has been or will be shown that a certain weighted average of the NCIs of the members of a group yields one of Cliff's (1977) group consistency indices, C_{tl}. The higher the value of C_{tl}, the closer the group dataset is to being unidimensional in the sense of forming a Guttman scale. This notion of unidimensionality is different from the factor analytic unidimensionality of data, and Wise (1981) created several counterexamples. One sample was highly conforming to the Guttman scale but multidimensional by factor analysis, whereas the others are unidimensional by factor analysis and principal component analysis, but they are not the Guttman scale.

Response patterns produced by erroneous rules are usually quite different from the average response pattern and not conforming to the Guttman scale; hence, removing individuals with low (usually negative) NCI values—that is, those with aberrant response patterns—will yield a dataset that is more nearly unidimensional (Tatsuoka & Tatsuoka, 1982, 1983).

The ICI, on the other hand, measures the degree to which an individual's response pattern remains invariant over time; thus, for example, in the signed-number test consisting of four parallel subtests, the ICI indicates whether an examinee's response pattern changes markedly from one subset to the next or remains relatively stable. Low ICI values, indicating instability of response pattern, would suggest that the examinee was still in the early stages of learning, changing his or her method for solving equivalent problems from one wave to the next. A high ICI value, reflecting stability of response pattern, would signal the nearing of mastery or a learning plateau.

Although the NCI and ICI can each serve useful purposes, as suggested above and illustrated in detail below, examining them jointly opens up various diagnostic possibilities, as does the consideration of each of them in combination with the total test score.

Norm Conformity Index

Cliff (1977) defined various consistency indices based on the notion of dominance and counterdominance relationships between pairs of items. Some of these are closely related to indices developed in the theory of scalability, originating in the 1930s. Although Cliff's indices are derived from the dominance matrix for the dataset of an entire group, they can be expressed as weighted averages of the corresponding indices based on constituent subgroups of examinees (Krus, 1975; Mokken, 1970; Yamamoto & Wise, 1980). Nevertheless, it should be noted that these indices are measures of *group* consistency and do not represent individual examinees' consistency of responses. Group consistency in Cliff's sense will be maximized when items are ordered by difficulty.

Consider a dataset consisting of just one person's response pattern row-vector S. The dominance matrix for this response pattern is

$$\bar{S}'S = N = (n_{ij}); \; i, j = 1,2,\ldots,n \; (= \text{number of items}) \tag{1.1}$$

where $\bar{S}'$ is the transpose of the complement of S. By construction, $n_{ij} = 1$ when the individual gets item i wrong and item j right; otherwise, $n_{ij} = 0$. Of course, the dominance matrix will be associated with ordering of the items in S. So if the ordering is changed, then the dominance matrix also is changed. Consequently, the consistency response pattern S, defined as

$$C = 2U_a/U - 1 \tag{1.2}$$

where $U_a = \sum_i \sum_{i<j} n_{ij}$ (the sum of the above-diagonal elements of N) and $U = \sum_{i,j} n_{ij}$ (the sum of the nonzero elements of N), is a function of the item order, o. To make this fact explicit, we write $C_p(o)$.

Example 1.3

Let S = (10110), for the items ordered by o, then

$$
N = \bar{S}\,'S = \begin{vmatrix} 0 \\ 0 \\ 0 \\ 0 \\ 1 \end{vmatrix} \times (10110) = \begin{vmatrix} 0 & 0 & 0 & 0 & 0 \\ 1 & 0 & 1 & 1 & 0 \\ 0 & 0 & 0 & 0 & 0 \\ 0 & 0 & 0 & 0 & 0 \\ 1 & 0 & 1 & 1 & 0 \end{vmatrix}
$$

Here, $U_a = \Sigma_i \Sigma_{i<j}\, n_{ij} = 2$ – the sum of the above—diagonal elements of N, and $U = 6$; hence, from Equation (1.2),

$$
C_p(o) = (2)(2)/6 - 1 = -1/3
$$

Example 1.4

Let S be a Guttman vector, S = (00111). Then $\bar{S}\,'S$ will be

$$
\bar{S}\,'S = \begin{vmatrix} 0 & 0 & 1 & 1 & 1 \\ 0 & 0 & 1 & 1 & 1 \\ 0 & 0 & 0 & 0 & 0 \\ 0 & 0 & 0 & 0 & 0 \\ 0 & 0 & 0 & 0 & 0 \end{vmatrix}
$$

and if S is a reversed Guttman vector, S = (11100), then

$$
\bar{S}\,'S = \begin{vmatrix} 0 & 0 & 0 & 0 & 0 \\ 0 & 0 & 0 & 0 & 0 \\ 0 & 0 & 0 & 0 & 0 \\ 1 & 1 & 1 & 0 & 0 \\ 1 & 1 & 1 & 0 & 0 \end{vmatrix}
$$

Hence, $U_a = 6$, $U = 6$, and $C_p(o) = 12/6 - 1 = 1$ for the Guttman vector S; and $U_a = 0$, $U = 6$, and $C_p(o) = 0/6 - 1 = -1$ for the reversed Guttman vector.

From the foregoing example, the first two of the following properties of $C_p(o)$ may be inferred. The other properties are illustrated by further examples, and intuitive arguments are given to substantiate them. Their formal proofs are not difficult but tedious, and therefore have been omitted.

Property 1.1: $-1 \leq C_p(o) \leq 1$.

Property 1.2: If the order of items is reversed in S, the absolute values of $C_p(0)$ remain unchanged, but its sign is reversed.

Because $U = \sum_j \sum_i n_{ij} = \sum \sum (1 - s_i)s_j$, it is invariant with respect to permutation of the elements of S. On the other hand, if the order of the elements of S is reversed, so that $s_i = s_{n-i+1}$, the U_a for the new dominance matrix becomes

$$U_a' = \sum \sum n_{ij} = \sum \sum (1 - s_i)s_j = \sum \sum (1 - s_{n-i+1})s_{n-j+1}$$

which can be shown to be equal to $U - U_a$; therefore,

$$C_p(o) = 2(U - U_a)/U - 1 = -2U_a/U + 1 = -C_p(o)$$

$$C_p(o) = (\bar{S}_1, \bar{S}_2)\begin{pmatrix} S_1 \\ S_2 \end{pmatrix} = \bar{S}_1' S_1 + \bar{S}_2' S_2$$

Property 1.3: The Consistency Index $C_p(o)$ associated with a $2 \times n$ data matrix, comprising two response pattern vectors S_1 and S_2, is a weighted average of the $C_p(o)$'s associated with S_1 and S_2, respectively.

Therefore, if we let $U_k = \sum_i \sum_j n_{ij}^{(k)}$ for $k = 1,2$, and $U_{ka} = \sum_i \sum_{j>i} n_{ij}^{(k)}$, it follows that the U and U_a are given by $U = U_1 + U_2$ and $U_a = U_{1a} + U_{2a}$. Hence,

$$C_p(o) = \{2(U_{1a} + U_{2a})\}/(U_1 + U_2) - 1$$

$$= \{U_1/(U_1 + U_2)\}\{2U_{1a}/U_1\} + \{U_2/(U_1 + U_2)\}\{2U_{2a}/U_2\} - 1$$

$$= \{[U_1/(U_1 + U_2)][2U_a/U_1 - 1]\} + \{[U_2/(U_1 + U_2)][2U_a/U_2 - 1]\}$$

$$= w_1 C_p(o)_1 + w_2 C_p(o)_2$$

This relationship can be generalized by mathematical induction. When item ordering is in descending order of difficulty for a particular group (designated the *norm group*), the Consistency Index $C_p(o)$ associated with the individual's response pattern S is called the NCI. Thus, the NCI indicates the extent to which a response vector S approximates the Guttman vector (in which all the zeros are to the left of the 1's) with the same number of 1's, when the items are arranged in descending order of difficulty for the norm group.

With this definition, plus an expanded version of Property 1.3, we state the relationship between Cliff's consistency index C_{tj} and the NCIs for the individuals in the group as the following property.

Property 1.4: Cliff's Consistency Index C_{t1} is a weighted average of the NCI_k $(k = 1,\dots,N)$, with weight $w_k = U_k/U$; in other words,

$$C_{t1} = \sum_{k=1,N} (U_k/U)NCI_k$$

where

$$U_k = \sum_i \sum_{j>i} n_{ij}{}^{(k)}$$

and

$$U = \sum_{k=1,N} U_k$$

Example 1.5

Let $S_1 = (01011)$, $S_2 = (00111)$, and $S_3 = (00001)$ be the response pattern vectors for three individuals. Then, we get (upon writing the NCI for $C_p(o)$)

$$U_{1a} = 5, U_1 = 6, NCI_1 = 2/3$$

$$U_{2a} = 6, U_2 = 6, NCI_2 = 1$$

$$U_{3a} = 5, U_3 = 4, NCI_3 = 1$$

Hence,

$$w_1 NCI_1 + w_2 NCI_2 + w_3 NCI_3 = (6/16)(2/3) + (6/16)(1) + (4/16)(1) = 7/8$$

On the other hand, with

$$X = \begin{vmatrix} 0 & 1 & 0 & 1 & 1 \\ 0 & 0 & 0 & 0 & 1 \\ 0 & 0 & 1 & 1 & 1 \end{vmatrix}$$

$$\overline{X}'X = N = \begin{vmatrix} 0 & 1 & 1 & 2 & 3 \\ 0 & 0 & 1 & 1 & 2 \\ 0 & 1 & 0 & 1 & 2 \\ 0 & 0 & 0 & 0 & 1 \\ 0 & 0 & 0 & 0 & 0 \end{vmatrix}$$

$U_a = 15$, $U = 16$, and $NCI = 30/16 - 1 = 7/8$, thus verifying Property 1.4.

In the paragraph preceding Property 1.4, the order of the items was taken to be the order of difficulty for the group of which the individual was a member, for $C_p(o)$ to be called the NCI. Actually, as evident in the formal definition of the NCI, the group need not be one to which the individual belongs. It can be any group that the researcher chooses for defining the baseline or *criterion order* of the items; hence, our referring to it as *the norm group*, and the index as the *Norm Conformity Index*. For example, we might be concerned with two groups of students with vastly different instructional backgrounds but similar abilities. It is then quite possible for the difficulties of various skills to be rather different in the two groups. We might take Group 1 as the norm group, thus arranging the items in descending

TABLE 1.4

Means of Test Scores and the Norm Conformity Index

	Group 1 ($N = 67$)	Group 2 ($N = 62$)	
Total Score			
Mean	20.06	18.36	$t = 1.90$
SD	8.30	7.88	$p > .05$
NCI			
Mean	.375	.216	$t = 3.037$
SD	.230	.292	$p = .003$

order of difficulty for this group. We could compute NCIs for members of both Group 1 and Group 2 on the basis of this criterion order and would probably find the mean NCI for the two groups to be significantly different. The following examples, based on real data, illustrate this.

Example 1.6

The seventh-grade students of a junior high school were divided at random into two groups, which were given different lessons teaching signed-number operations (Birenbaum & Tatsuoka, 1983). One sequence of lessons taught the operations by the Postman Stories Approach (Davis, 1968), whereas the other used the number line method. After addition problems had been taught, a 52-item test including both addition and subtraction problems was administered to all students.

A t-test showed no significant difference between the mean test score of the two groups, as indicated in Table 1.4; however, when NCIs were computed for all students, using the item-difficulty order in Group 1 (the Postman Stories group) as the baseline, there was a significant difference between the mean NCI of the two groups.

Example 1.7

Tatsuoka and Birenbaum (1981) demonstrated that proactive inhibition affected the performance on tests in material learned through subsequent instructions. The response patterns of students who studied new lessons written by using a different conceptual framework from that of their previous instructions showed a significantly different performance pattern. By using a cluster analysis, four groups were identified with significantly different response patterns. The NCI values were calculated for 91 students. These NCI values were based on the order of tasks determined by the proportion correct in the total sample. An analysis of variance (ANOVA) was then carried out. The F-value was significant at $p = 0.05$. Table 1.5 shows the result from statistical analysis (ANOVA) of Norm Conformity Index for Four Groups With Different Instructional Backgrounds.

TABLE 1.5

Analysis of Variance (ANOVA) of Norm Conformity Index
(NCI) for Four Groups With Different Instructional
Backgrounds

Group	N	Mean of NCIs	F
1	34	.18	3.62 with df = 3.87
2	27	.41	
3	20	.35	
4	10	.18	

Up to this point, the U_a and U in Equation (1.2) defining $C_p(o)$—and hence the NCI as a special case—were defined in terms of the numbers of dominances and counterdominances between item pairs in the dominance matrix N. We will now show that U_a can be explicitly defined in terms of the proximity of a response vector S to a Guttman vector with the same number of 1's.

Property 1.5: Let S be a response pattern vector of an examinee on an n-item test, the associated dominance matrix, and $U_a = \Sigma\Sigma n_{ij}$. Then, U_a is also the number of transpositions required to get from S to the reversed Guttman vector (all of which are preceding the zeros).

Because $n_{ij} = (1 - s_{ij})s_j$ it follows that $U_a = \Sigma\Sigma(1 - s_{ij})s_{j,}$ is the number of ordered pairs (s_i, s_j) for $i < j$ of elements of S such that $s_j = 0$ and $s_j = 1$. That is, if for each $s_i = 0$, we count the number of $s_j = 1$ to its right in S, then the sum of these numbers over the set of 0's in S is equal to U_a. This is the same as the number of transpositions (interchanges of elements in adjacent (0,1) pairs) needed to transform S, step by step, into (11...100...0); therefore, U_a is a measure of remoteness of S from the reversed Guttman vector, which is equivalently in its proximity to the Guttman vector.

Example 1.8

Let S = (01011). Then, S can be transformed into (11100) by five transitions:

$$(01011) \rightarrow (10011) \rightarrow (10101) \rightarrow (11001) \rightarrow (11010) \rightarrow (11100);$$

thus, $U_a = 5$ by the present definition. On the other hand,

$$\mathbf{N} = \begin{vmatrix} 1 \\ 0 \\ 1 \\ 0 \\ 0 \end{vmatrix}(0\ 1\ 0\ 1\ 1) = \begin{vmatrix} 0 & 1 & 0 & 1 & 1 \\ 0 & 0 & 0 & 0 & 0 \\ 0 & 1 & 0 & 1 & 1 \\ 0 & 0 & 0 & 0 & 0 \\ 0 & 0 & 0 & 0 & 0 \end{vmatrix}$$

and $U_a = \sum_i \sum_{j>i} n_{ij} = 5$ by the earlier definition. It may also be noted that if we denote the number of 1's in the lower triangle of N by U_b, that is,

$$U_b = \sum_i \sum_{j>i} n_{ij},$$

then U_b is the number of ordered pairs (s_j, s_i) for $j < i$ of elements of S such that $s_i = 0$ and $s_j = 1$. Hence, $U = \sum \sum n_{ij} = U_a + U_b$ is the number of pairs (s_i, s_j) with $s_i \neq s_j$ that can be formed from the element of S. Thus, $U = x(n - x)$, where x is the number of 1's in S, or the test score earned by a person with a response pattern S. Consequently, U_a/U and U_b/U are the proportions of (0,1) pairs and (1,0) pairs, respectively, among all possible ordered pairs (s_i, s_j) for $i < j$ of unlike elements. When S is a Guttman vector (0 0 … 0 1 1 … 1), $U_a = U$ and $U_b = 0$, because all ordered pairs of unlike elements are (0,1) pairs. Conversely, when S is a reversed Guttman vector (1 1 … 1 0 0 • … 0), $U_a = 0$ and $U_b = U$. Hence, U_a/U ranges from 0 to 1 as an increasing function of the degree to which S resembles (or is proximal to) a Guttman vector. Similarly, U_b/U measures the proximity of S to a reverse Guttman vector, or its remoteness from a Guttman vector. In fact, U_a/U was denoted by U′ and proposed as an index of "deviance" of score patterns by Van der Flier (1977, 1982).

With the above redefinition of U_a and U, the sense in which the NCI is a measure of the extent to which a response pattern approximates a Guttman vector should have become clearer.

$$NCI = 2U_a/U - 1 \qquad (1.3)$$

is a rescaling of U_a/U to have limits 1 and –1 instead of 1 and 0.

It should be noted that U_a/U, and hence also the NCI, is undefined for a person who has a test score of either 0 or n, because $U = x(n - x) = 0$ in both these cases. There are two ways (at least) in which to cope with this problem. The first is arbitrarily to set NCI = 1 when U = 0, which is analogous to setting 0! = 1. This is reasonable because U = 0 only for S = (0 0 … 0) and S = (1 1 … 1), both of which are Guttman vectors in the sense of having no zero to the right of any 1. The second solution is to redefine the NCI itself as

$$NCI = 2(U_a + 1)/(U + 1) - 1 \qquad (1.4)$$

which will automatically make NCI = 1 for the all-correct and all-incorrect response patterns.

Individual Consistency Index

In the preceding section, we defined and described various properties of an index, which measures the extent to which an individual's response pattern "conforms" to that of a norm group. In some situations, it is desirable to measure the extent to which an individual's response pattern remains unchanged or "consistent" over the passage of time. For example, it is reasonable to expect that, when a student is in the process of learning—and hence presumably modifying the cognitive processes by which he or she attempts to solve problems—his or her pattern of responses on successive sets of similar items will change considerably from one set to the next. When the student approaches mastery, or a learning plateau, his or her response pattern will probably remain relatively consistent from one set to the next. To define an index (in this case, the ICI) that will serve to measure the degree of consistency (or stability) of an individual's response pattern over time, and to investigate its properties, are the purposes of this section. In the interest of clarity and ease of exposition, we embed our discussions in the context of an actual experimental study.

A 64-item, signed-number test was administered to 153 seventh graders at a junior high school. The test comprised 16 different tasks being tested by four parallel items each. The items were arranged so that four parallel subtests were successively given to each testee. Within each 16-item subtest, the order of items was randomized. Thus, for each examinee, there are four response pattern vectors with 16 elements each.

The ICI is defined on these four applications. We shall come back to this test later, but we first introduce the ICI by a simpler example. Suppose that a person took four parallel tests—A, B, C, and D—with seven items each, and that his or her response patterns were as shown in the second column of Table 1.3.3. Also shown in this table are $U = x(7 - x)$ for each response pattern, U_j; the number U_a of transpositions needed to transform each response pattern into a reverse Guttman vector; the $C_p(o)$ for each response pattern; and the weight to be applied to each $C_p(o)$ for getting an overall index. The weighted average $\Sigma w_j C_p(o)_j = -.143$ would be Cliff's Consistency Index C_{t1} if the four response patterns of Table 1.6 were those of four individuals *and* if the items had been arranged in their difficulty order for the group.

Let us rearrange the items (or, rather, the sets of parallel items) in their order of difficulty for the person, which is (2,4,5,7,3,1,6). The response patterns and other quantities occurring in Table 1.6 now become as shown in Table 1.7, which also has a new column showing the number of transpositions t_j necessary to get from the jth response pattern in Table 1.6 to the new one here.

TABLE 1.6

Response Patterns and Various Quantities Associated With Them

Parallel Test # (j)	Response Pattern t_j	U_j	U_{ja}	$C(o')_j$	w_j
1	1010010	12	4	−.333	.286
2	0010010	10	6	.200	.238
3	1000010	10	4	−.200	.238
4	1000010	10	4	−.200	.238

TABLE 1.7

Response Patterns Resulting From Those in Table 1.6 by Arranging
the Items in Difficulty Order and Various Associated Quantities

Parallel Test # (j)	Response Pattern t_j	t_j	U_j	U_{ja}	$C(o')_j$	w_j
1	0000111	8	12	12	1.0	.286
2	0000101	3	10	9	.8	.238
3	0000011	6	10	10	1.0	.238
4	0000011	6	10	10	1.0	.238

The weighted average of the new $C_p(o)$ values is $\sum w_j C_p(o')_j = .9524$. This is what we call the ICI. We may state its definition as follows.

Definition of the Individual Conformity Index

The ICI states that given a set of response patterns shown by a single individual on a set of parallel tests, we arrange the parallel items in their overall order of difficulty for the individual and compute the $C_p(o)$ for each response pattern thus modified. If we now form a weighted average of these $C_p(o)$'s as though we were computing Cliff's C_{t1} in accordance with Property 1.4, the result is the ICI.

Note that the ICI is an index of a single individual, not of a group as is Cliff's Consistency Index. The ICI also differs from the NCI in that the latter depends on the baseline order of items (i.e., the difficulty order in some group specified as the norm group), whereas the ICI is computed for an individual with no reference to any group. Rather, the ICI requires that the individual in question has taken two or more parallel tests, and measures the consistency of his or her response patterns across these parallel tests.

Property 1.6: Because the parallel items are arranged in their order of difficulty for the individual in question when the ICI is computed, although they are arranged in their order of difficulty for a norm group when the NCI is computed, it follows that for each examinee

$$ICI > NCI \tag{1.5}$$

1.4 Nonparametric Rule Space: Spotting Erroneous Rules of Operations

We have shown in the previous section that the indices NCI and ICI are capable of giving some leads addressing some psychometric issues such as the dimensionality of achievement tests although these indices have

TABLE 1.8

Types of Students With High and Low NCI, ICI, and Total Scores

	Low ICI	High ICI
High NCI	There should be few students in this cell (none if the cutting points for the ICI and NCI are the same) because ICI ñ NCI always.	If score is **high,** all is well. If total score is **low,** a student has a serious misconception (consistently uses an incorrect rule), which leads to correct answers to easy items and wrong answers to **hard items**.
Low NCI	The errors are probably **random**.	If total score is **high,** student is merely getting **a few** of the easy items wrong. If score is **low**, student is getting **many** of the easy items wrong. The response pattern is strange, and a serious problem exists.

originally been developed to spot unusual response patterns. Because the response patterns resulting from the application of various erroneous rules of operations are often (though not always) different from typical response patterns, the indices can be used for detecting erroneous rules that are consistently used by an examinee or group of examinees. This capability is useful in aiding teaching processes by diagnosing students' problems. Table 1.8 shows a 2 × 2 contingency table based on combinations of high and low NCI and ICI values with a characterization of the status of students in each cell and dependent also on the score earned.

Birenbaum and Tatsuoka (1980) found that 1–0 scoring based on right or wrong answers caused multidimensionality of a dataset of signed-number addition and subtraction problems when erroneous rules are used by many students because some erroneous rules can lead to correct answers many times. They have identified an almost exhaustive set of 72 erroneous rules for this domain, and enumerated the number of correct answers that would result from consistently using each incorrect rule for a set of 16 items. First, using the real data from a 64-item test consisting of four 16-item subtests, Birenbaum and Tatsuoka performed a principal component analysis and found that the test was multidimensional. Second, they corrected the scores of the right answers from erroneous rules of operations to zero, and performed again principal component analysis and found that the test is unidimensional. The same phenomenon was observed by Brown and Burton (1978) in the domain of addition and subtraction of positive integers.

The indices NCI and ICI are useful for detecting erroneous rules by using total scores together that are consistently used by an examinee or a group.

Example 1.9

The summary results in Table 1.41, using the data described at the beginning of the previous section on the ICI, was the results that were thoroughly analyzed in Birenbaum and Tatsuoka (1980) with respect to error analyses. We call these data the *November data* hereafter. Table 1.9 shows the response patterns resulting from applications of some erroneous rules, and NCI and ICI values with the total scores for three students. Student 1 performed all addition problems correctly, but he failed to change the sign

TABLE 1.9

Response Patterns of Three Rules, and Their Values of the NCI and ICI

Task Number* Example	Three Responses to Four Parallel Forms Within the 64-Item Test		
	Student 1	Student 2	Student 3
6. 6 + 4 = +10	1111 (+10)	1111 (+10)	1111
15. –6 + 4 = –2	1111 (–2)	0000 (–10)	1111
3. 12 + –3 = +9	1111 (+9)	0000 (+15)	1111
5. –3 + 12 = +9	1011 (+9)	0000 (+15)	1111
10. –14 + –5 = –19	1111 (–19)	1111 (–19)	1111
11. 3 + –5 = –2	1111 (–2)	0000 (–8)	1111
14. –5 + –7 = –12	0000 (–14)	1111 (–12)	1111
7. 8 – 6 = +2	0000 (+14)	0000 (+14)	1111
8. –16 – –7 = –9	0000 (–23)	0000 (–23)	1111
16. 2 – 11 = –9	0000 (+13)	0000 (+13)	0111
13. –3 – + 12 = +9	0000 (+9)	0000 (+15)	1111
1. –6 – –8 = +2	0000 (–14)	0000 (–14)	1111
12. 9 – –7 = +16	0000 (+2)	1111 (+16)	0011
4. 1 – –10 = +11	0000 (–9)	0000 (–11)	1010
2. –7 – 9 = –16	0000 (+2)	0000 (+16)	1111
9. –12 – 3 = –15	0000 (–9)	1111 (–15)	0111
NCI value	0.9759	–0.2560	0.7073
ICI value	1.000	1.000	0.9268
Total score	27	20	58
Erroneous rules students used for answering 64 items, where?? four repeated subtests with 16 items each.	This student used an erroneous rule: If two numbers have the same sign, then add the absolute values and take the sign. If two numbers have different signs, then subtract the number with the smaller absolute value from the larger absolute value and take the sign of the number with a larger absolute value.	This student used an erroneous rule: adding the two absolute values of numbers, and taking the sign of the number with the larger absolute value.	This student used the right rule most of the time.

of the subtraction when he converted subtraction problems to addition problems. Student 2 always added the two numbers and took the sign of the larger number for her answers. She failed to discriminate subtraction problems from addition problems and applied this erroneous rule consistently to all 16 tasks. Student 3 achieved fairly well, but he occasionally mistyped or made careless mistakes. Determining the rules of operation, both right and wrong, is discussed in detail in the Tatsuoka, Birenbaum, Tatsuoka, and Baillie's Technical Report 80-3-ONR (1980).

In Table 1.9, 16 items are ordered by their proportion correct values, from the easiest item, 6 + 4, to the most difficult item, –12 – 3. The number of students who got the correct answer for this item divided by the total number of students who took this item is called *item difficulty*. Easier items have higher values, and difficult items have lower values. Because the test is composed of four parallel subtests, the scores of four parallel items for each task are four numbers (one or zero). The answers resulting from the application of each rule described in the fourth row of Table 1.9 for each student are given in the parentheses. Note that some answers are the same as the answers obtained by applying the right rule.

By looking into the NCI and ICI values given in the third row, Students 1 and 2 have the ICI value of 1, which shows they applied their rules very consistently, but the NCI values are quite different. The ICI value for Student 3 is considerably lower than 1. By pairing up the NCI values and total scores for three students, (.9759, 27), (–.2560, 20), and (.7073, 58) will give us characteristics of three students' performance on the test.

Table 1.10(a) is a 2 × 2 contingency table with .90 as the dividing point for the ICI and .60 for the NCI in the subsample of 75 students who earned scores of 53 or higher, whereas Table 1.10(b) is the corresponding table for 47 students with scores of 52 or lower. The dividing point, 52, for scores was chosen because—as shown in Figure 1.2 out of each subtest of 16 items could conceivably be answered by consistent use of an erroneous rule; 13 is the smallest number of items that cannot be done correctly in this way, which corresponds to 52 out of the entire test of four parallel subtests of 16 items each. Hence, it sees reasonable to regard 52 or less as "low scores."

TABLE 1.10

Two-Way Classifications Based on an ICI > or < .90 and an NCI > or <.60 Among Students With (a) Scores > 53 and (b) Scores < 52

(a) Scores ≥ 53			(b) Scores < 52		
ICI ≥ .90	ICI < .90		ICI ≥ .90	ICI < .90	
NCI ≥.60	8	18	26	NCI ≥ .60	3	27	30
NCI <.60	26	23	49	NCI < .60	12	5	17
	34	41	75		15	32	47

Let us see what we can say about the performances of the students represented in the November data, from the contingency tables of Table 1.10, in light of the characterizations given in Table 1.8 and with the three students' response patterns in Table 1.9 to guide us to some extent. Note first that despite the very high cutoff point of .90 for the *high ICI* category, substantially more than one half (73 out of 122) of the students have high ICI values.

This reflects the fact that the examinees were eighth graders who had already received fairly extensive instruction in signed-number operations, and hence a relatively large proportion of them showed stable response patterns over the four parallel subtests and had already approached mastery or learning plateaus—the latter being more likely in this case in view of the fact that only 75 (or 61.50/0) of them had scores over 52 out of 64. As expected, very few students (11 out of 122) had low ICIs combined with high NCIs.

Many more had low-ICI, low-NCI combinations; these are students who made more or less "random" (or at least nonsystematic) errors but who nevertheless made relatively more errors among items that were easy for the group as a whole. It is reasonable that about 70% of the low scorers who had low NCIs fell in this category, although only 53% of the high scorers with low NCIs did.

Returning to the high-ICI group, of which the three students represented in Table 1.9 are different kinds of examples, the high-ICI, high-NCI students with high scores are the "problem-free" types exemplified by Student 3. Unfortunately, there are only 18 such students, whereas there are 27 high-ICI, high-NCI students with low scores. Student 1 is an example of this type of student, and his response patterns corroborate the characterization in Table 1.8 that he has a serious misconception, but one that leads to correct answers (except for one probably careless error) to the easy items (addition) and always to wrong answers to the hard items. In the high-ICI, low-NCI category, most students (23 out of 28) are high scorers. These students can easily be "remediated," for they are probably getting only a few easy items wrong. (It is an unfortunate fact that a few easy items missed can cause the NCI to become quite low.) The students who have the most serious problems are the high-ICI, low-NCI low scorers, of whom there are fortunately only five. Student 2 in Table 1.9 exemplifies this type, and her unusual response pattern (which remains perfectly consistent over the four parallel subtests) will take quite a bit of remedial instruction to rectify.

2

Parametric Person–Fit Statistics, Zeta (ζ), and Generalized Zetas ($\zeta_1, ..., \zeta_m$)

2.1 History of Person–Fit Statistics

Several authors have shown an interest in detecting aberrant response patterns that do not fit in IRT models, and have tried to extract the information not contained in the total scores from those aberrant response patterns. Levine and Rubin (1979) and Wright (1977), for example, referred to the identification of "guessing, sleeping, fumbling and plodding" (p. 110) from the plots of residual item scores based on the differences between item responses and the expected responses for an individual based on the Rasch model. Levine and Rubin discussed response patterns that are so typical that a student's aptitude test score fails to be a completely appropriate measure (p. 269). Trabin and Weiss (1979) also investigated measures to identify unusual response patterns. Sato (1975) proposed a "caution" index, which is intended to identify students whose total scores on a test must be treated with caution. Tatsuoka and Tatsuoka (1982) and Harnisch and Linn (1981) have discussed the relationship of response patterns to instructional experiences and the possible use of item response pattern information to help diagnose the types of errors a student is making. These researchers developed various indices to detect aberrant response patterns. Later, Molenaar and his associates (Molenaar & Hoitjink, 1990; Molenaar & Sijtsma, 1984) developed an index (i.e., person–fit statistics) that is statistically capable of judging an aberrant response pattern and to what extent it deviates from average response patterns. The aim of person-fit statistics is to identify persons whose item score patterns on a test are aberrant when compared with a majority of item score patterns that are expected on the basis of some statistical or psychometric models, mainly Item Response Models. An observed pattern of item scores is called "aberrant" when it is not likely to happen, as compared with a majority of item response patterns. If a IRT parametric model can explain a set of item response patters well, then we say the model fits the data (Meijer, 1994, p.12).

There are three groups of person–fit statistics. The first group measures residual scores between the expected item scores from the model and the observed item scores (Wright & Masters, 1982). The second group uses the likelihood statistics with estimated ability θ values, and is called the Appropriateness Index (Drasgow, Levine, & Williams, 1985; Levine & Rubin, 1979). Molenaar and Hoitjink (1990) decomposed the Appropriateness Index into two parts: d_0, which is independent of item response pattern X; and M_i, which is conditional of X and called person–fit statistics after substitution of the estimated item difficulties. Statistical properties of person–fit statistics based on likelihood statistics have been further developed by Molenaar and Hoijtink (1990) and by Kogut (1987, 1988). Their person–fit statistics determine how improbable an item score pattern is for a given null hypothesis that the measurement model holds. The third trend measures the covariance of two residual functions defined on θ: one is the deviation of IRT functions from the average function $T(\theta)$ of all IRT functions, and the second is the residual functions of IRT $P_j(\theta)$ from score vector X_j (K. Tatsuoka, 1984b, 1985, 1996; Tatsuoka & Linn, 1983).

In this book, the expression *person–fit statistics* will be used to represent the indices that are developed to detect aberrant response patterns regardless of the approach used to determine them, that is, the use of likelihood of patterns (Levine & Rubin, 1979), residuals (Wright & Masters, 1982), or covariance of residuals (Tatsuoka, 1984b; Tatsuoka & Linn, 1983).

2.2 Using Person–Fit Statistics and IRT θ for Representing Response Patterns

In the previous chapter, nonparametric rule space was introduced, which is useful for diagnosing some students' item response patterns by measuring their proximities to the item response patterns resulting from applications of erroneous rules of operation. Tatsuoka (1985) has developed the ζ Index—introduced as the Extended Caution Index 4 (ECI4) in Tatsuoka (1984b), but she called it the ζ Index in a subsequent paper (Tatsuoka, 1985), in which functional properties of ζ are investigated.

Figure 2.1, also found in Tatsuoka and Linn (1983, p. 94), represents a vector space spanned by coordinates, ζ, and total scores. The figure further shows the response patterns resulting from applications of erroneous rules of operation (numerals 3, 4, and 10 in Circle A; 2 and 8 in Circle B; 9 and 12 in Circle C; and 5 and 6 in Circle D) mapped together with students' item response patterns into the space. Let us consider erroneous rule 9. If a student's response pattern is located close to erroneous rule 9, then we judge that this student would have, with high probability, used erroneous rule 9.

The purpose of defining the ζ Index is to find a continuous variable or a function of θ that is orthogonal to the first axis θ, and then define a Cartesian

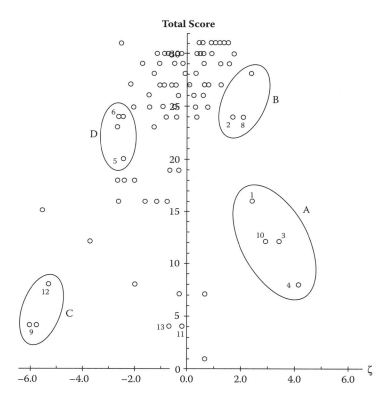

FIGURE 2.1
Plot of the rule space using total score and ζ with the erroneous rules identified in the signed-number addition and subtraction problems.

product space $\{(\theta, \zeta)\}$ as a classification space of item response patterns in which an observed item response pattern will be classified into one of the predetermined knowledge states. Tatsuoka (1983) and Tatsuoka & Tatsuoka (1987) called this Cartesian product space *rule space*. Because the IRT ability measure θ has been widely used in educational practice in the United States, a new model that has a close connection to the current psychometrics theory is desirable. Moreover, this new space has interpretable coordinates that are continuous variables; therefore, any points in the space with these coordinates will have meaningful interpretations. The points located in the lower part of the space conform better to the difficulty order of items (i.e., usual response patterns), whereas, ones in easier items and zeros, in harder items. The points in the lower part of the space have negative ζ values, which means the item response patterns corresponding to these points highly likely have the scores of ones for easier items and zeros for more difficult items. However, the points in the upper part of the space have the opposite tendency. i.e., often ones, in more difficult items and zeros, in easier items. The points in the right side of the θ-axis are associated with higher total scores and the points on the left side are associated with lower total scores. Moreover, plotting of the Rule Space coordinates will be spread almost as a circle in the two-dimensional space. The points on the right side of the ζ axis are associated with higher total scores, and the points on the left side are associated with lower total scores. Moreover, plotting of the rule space coordinates will be spread almost as a circle in the two-dimensional space. Molenaar's person–fit statistics may have similar characteristics to Tatsuoka's ζ Index, and may be used as a Cartesian product space $\{(\theta, M_j)\}$, where M_j is defined by the linear combination of item response pattern **X** and item difficulty vector **B**.

In the next section, the ζ Index will be introduced, and its statistical and functional properties will be discussed.

2.3   The Zeta (ζ) Index

Suppose a person's item response pattern is denoted by a vector **X** = $(x_1, x_2, \ldots, x_n)$, and, similarly, its corresponding logistic probabilities for n items are given by **P**(θ):

$$\mathbf{P}(\theta) = [P_1(\theta), P_2(\theta), \ldots, P_n(\theta)] \tag{2.1}$$

The test response function is also given by a vector,

$$\mathbf{T}(\theta) = [T(\theta), T(\theta), \ldots, T(\theta)] \tag{2.2}$$

where **T**(θ) is the average of n item response functions,

$$\mathbf{T}(\theta) = (1/n)\Sigma_{j=1} P_j(\theta) \tag{2.3}$$

The covariance of two residual vectors, **P**(θ)–**X** and **P**(θ)–**T**(θ), is taken and considered as a function of response pattern vector **X** as follows:

$$\mathbf{f}(\mathbf{X}) = [\mathbf{P}(\theta)-\mathbf{X}, \mathbf{P}(\theta)-\mathbf{T}(\theta)] \tag{2.4}$$

By rewriting this **f**(**X**) as a linear function of **X**,

$$f(X) = -[X, \mathbf{P}(\theta) - \mathbf{T}(\theta)] + [\mathbf{P}(\theta), \mathbf{P}(\theta) - \mathbf{T}(\theta)]$$

$$= -\sum_{j=1}^{n} (P_j(\theta) - T(\theta))x_j + \sum_{j=1}^{n} (P_j(\theta))(P_j(\theta) - T(\theta)) \tag{2.5}$$

$$= -\sum_{j=1}^{n} (P_j(\theta) - T(\theta))x_j + K(\theta)$$

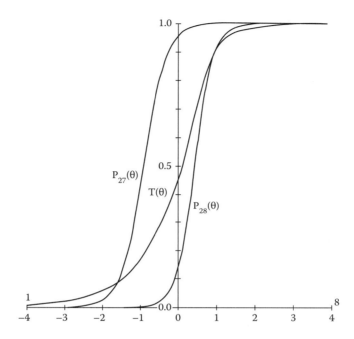

FIGURE 2.2
Average of 40-item response curves, $T(\theta)$, and IRT curves of items 27 and 28.

where $K(\theta)$ does not depend on observed item response x_j.

$$f(X) = K(\theta) - \sum_{j=1}^{n} (P_j(\theta) - T(\theta))x_j \qquad (2.6)$$

Figure 2.2 shows functions $P_j(\theta)$, $T(\theta)$, for items 27 and 28 of the 40 fraction subtraction problems. Figure 2.3 shows graphs of $P_j(\theta)-T(\theta)$ for the same items, 27 and 28. Statistical properties of **f(X)** and standardized **f(X)** are discussed below Figures 2.4 and 2.5 show the two types of graphs whose residuals $P(\theta) - T(\theta)$ are positive and negative over $T(\theta)$, respectively.

Property 2.1: The linear function **f(X)** has the expectation of zero:

$$\underset{k|i}{E}[f(X)] = 0 \qquad \text{for a fixed } \theta_i. \qquad (2.7)$$

If $X_k = (x_{k1}, \ldots, x_{kn})$, is a response pattern, whose ability level is θ_i. Then, by definition, the expectation of x_{kj} at θ_i is $P_j(\theta_i)$, which is expressed by the following equation:

$$E(x_{kj}) = P_j(\theta_i) \qquad (2.8)$$

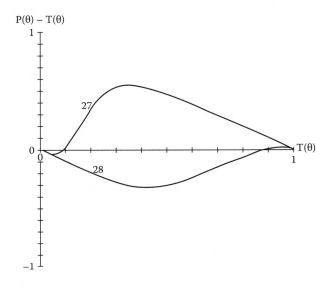

FIGURE 2.3
The curves of $P_{27}(\theta) - T(\theta)$ and $P_{28}(\theta) - T(\theta)$ over $T(\theta)$.

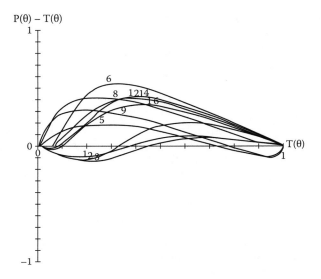

FIGURE 2.4
The curves of $P_j(\theta) - T(\theta)$ that are above the x-axis of $T(\theta)$.

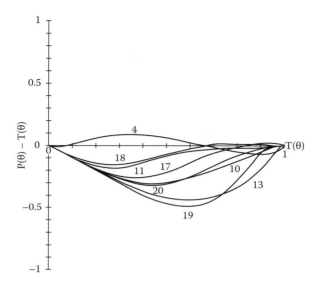

FIGURE 2.5
The curves of $P_j(\theta) - T(\theta)$ that are below the x-axis of $T(\theta)$.

Also, the expectation of $f(X_k)$ is the sum of the expectations of the first and second terms in Equation (2.5). However, the expectation of the first term becomes the same as that of the second term except for the sign; thus, Equation (2.7) is obtained (Tatsuoka, 1985).

Property 2.2: The variance of $f(X_k)$ is given by

$$\text{Var}(f(X)) = \underset{k|I}{E}[\{f(X_k) - E(f(X_k))\}^2] = \sum_{j=1}^{n} P_j(\theta_i)Q(\theta_i)(P_j(\theta_i) - T(\theta_i))^2 \qquad (2.9)$$

The derivation is given in Tatsuoka (1985, p. 59).

Property 2.3: The standardized form of $f(X)$ is the same as the standardized extended Caution Index ECI4, and is denoted by ς.

$$\varsigma = \varsigma(\theta, X) = \frac{f(X)}{\sqrt{\text{Var}(f(X))}} \qquad (2.10)$$

From now on in this book, ς will be denoted by ζ or $\zeta(\theta, X)$.

Property 2.4: The covariance matrix of the two variables θ and $f(X)$ is expressed asymptotically by a diagonal matrix with the diagonal elements

$1/I(\theta)$, the reciprocal of the information function at θ, and the variance of $f(X)$.

$$\begin{vmatrix} 1/I(\theta) & 0 \\ 0 & \sum_{j=1}^{n} P_j(\theta)Q_j(\theta)\{P_j(\theta) - T(\theta)\}^2 \end{vmatrix} \tag{2.11}$$

It will be shown that the off-diagonal elements of covariance matrix are equal to zero. For a given θ_i, covariance of θ_i and $f(X)$ is

$$\text{cov}(\theta_i, f(\mathbf{X}_i)) = E_{k|i}\left[\{\hat{\theta}_k - E(\hat{\theta}_k)\}f(\mathbf{X})\right]$$

$$= E_{k|i}\left[\sum_j (\hat{\theta}_k - \theta_i)(P_j(\theta_i) - x_{kj})(P_j(\theta_i) - T(\theta_i))\right] \tag{2.12}$$

By substituting $\theta_k - \theta_i$ by $(\partial \ln L/\partial\theta)_{\theta i}/I(\theta)$ (Kendall & Stuart, 1973, p. 46), where L is the likelihood, the last term of the above equation will be

$$\frac{1}{I(\theta_i)}E_{k|i}\left[\sum_j \left(\frac{\partial \ln L}{\partial\theta}\right)_{\theta i}(P_j(\theta_i) - x_{kj})(P_j(\theta_i) - T(\theta_i))\right] = \frac{1}{I(\theta)}E_{k|i}$$

$$\times \left[\sum_{j=1}^{n}\left\{\sum_{l=1}^{n}(x_{kl} - P_l(\theta_i)(P_j(\theta_i) - x_{kj})(P_j(\theta_i) - T(\theta_i))\right\}\right] \tag{2.13}$$

Using the assumption of local independence and the fact that expectation of x_{kl} is $P_l(\theta_i)$ (Lord, 1980), $E_{k|i}(x_{kl}) = P_l(\theta_i)$, and $E_{k|i}(x_{kj}) = P_j(\theta_i)$, the last term will be zero; hence, the covariance of θ_i and $f(x_i)$ will be zero.

It is clear from Property 2.4 that the two variables θ and $f(X)$ are mutually uncorrelated, and hence θ and ζ or $\zeta(\theta, \mathbf{X})$ are also mutually uncorrelated. It is also true that the average of $P_j(\theta)$ for $j = 1, \ldots, n$, $T(\theta)$, is orthogonal to the difference vector of $\mathbf{P}(\theta) - \mathbf{T}(\theta)$ (Tatsuoka, 1985). As a result, $T(\theta)$ and ζ are also mutually uncorrelated: therefore, a set of ordered pairs—(θ, ζ) or, equivalently, $(T(\theta), \zeta)$—forms a two-dimensional vector space with regular Euclidean distance. We will refer to this space as *rule space* hereafter. The discussion in this section was carried out for the one-parameter logistic model, but the model is applicable to the two-parameter logistic model as well, with minor modifications of conditions and proofs of the properties.

2.4 Semantic Meaning of ζ

When the items are arranged in ascending order of the proportions of individuals in a group who pass the items, this *baseline order* is used as the "norm" to define various nonparametric person–fit statistics by several researchers (Meijer, 1994; Sato, 1978; Tatsuoka, 1984b; Tatsuoka & Tatsuoka, 1982; Van der Flier, 1982). Tatsuoka's Norm Conformity Index (NCI) and Van der Flier's Index are defined as the ratios of two quantities.

The numerator is obtained by counting the number of transpositions in a response pattern as compared with the baseline order (or Guttman scale of the same total score) of this response pattern. The denominator is obtained by counting the number of transpositions in going from the reversed Guttman scale vector to the Guttman scale vector, both of which have the same total score as this particular response pattern. In short, the NCI indicates the extent to which a response vector approximates the Guttman vector with the same total score. Another famous proximity index is the correlation coefficient between the Guttman vector and a response pattern $\mathbf{X}$.

In the IRT context, Tatsuoka's ζ Index works similarly to the NCI. The ζ Index is a standardized variable that is the conditionally standardized covariance of the two residual vectors $\mathbf{P}(\theta) - \mathbf{X}$ and $\mathbf{P}(\theta) - \mathbf{T}(\theta)$ with the expectation of 0 and the variance of 1 for a given θ (Tatsuoka, 1985). It is also proportional to the conditional correlation of the two residual vectors of $\mathbf{P}(\theta) - \mathbf{T}(\theta)$ and $\mathbf{P}(\theta) - \mathbf{X}$; therefore, ζ indicates the extent to which a response vector $\mathbf{X}$ approximates the "Guttman vector" at θ. Let us restate it in simple, clear terms below.

First, the numerator of ζ, $f(\theta, \mathbf{X})$ can be rewritten into two parts: a part that is a linear function of $\mathbf{X}$, and a constant term $K(\theta)$:

$$f(\theta, \mathbf{X}) = - \sum_{j = 1,n} x_j \{P_j(\theta) - T(\theta)\} + K(\theta) \qquad (2.14)$$

where $K(\theta) = \sum_{j = 1,n} P_j(\theta)\{P_j(\theta) - T(\theta)\}$, and $K(\theta)$ is constant if θ is fixed.

Second, we need some "baseline order at a given θ." Let us assume that the values of IRT functions, $P_j(\theta)$, $j = 1, \ldots, n$ at θ, have been numbered in ascending order. Then, the quantities $P_j(\theta) - T(\theta)$, $j = 1, \ldots, n$, are written in ascending order:

$$P_1(\theta) - T(\theta) \leq P_2(\theta) - T(\theta) \leq P_3(\theta) - T(\theta) \leq \cdots \leq P_{n-1}(\theta) - T(\theta) \leq P_n(\theta) - T(\theta) \quad (2.15)$$

These inequalities indicate that at a given θ, item 1 is the most difficult item, and item n is the easiest. The items in the middle range have item response functions that are very close to the average IRT functions of the n items, $T(\theta)$, so their deviation values are nearly zero. The terms in the left part of the inequalities are negative, and those in the right part have positive values. A separate ordering may be associated with different θs. We take this order determined by $P_j(\theta) - T(\theta)$, $j = 1, \ldots, n$ at a given θ, as the baseline order or the Guttman vector at θ.

If a response pattern has 0's for the harder items (the items in the left part of the inequalities) and 1's for easier items (the right part), then $f(\theta, \mathbf{X})$ will have a negative value. That means when a response pattern conforms to the baseline order defined by the ascending order of $P_j(\theta) - T(\theta)$, then its ζ value becomes small, negative number. When a response pattern conforms to the reversed baseline order, then ζ becomes a larger, positive number. ζ measures the unusualness of the response pattern **X** with respect to the baseline order, or Guttman scale; however, it should be noted that the conditional expectation of ζ is zero, and not a negative number.

In addition to the fact that ζ measures the unusualness of the response pattern **X**, ζ has another interesting property. Tatsuoka (1984b) showed in her example that the item parameters in signed-number addition problems can be grouped into six item types. In other words, items having identical or very similar cognitive tasks have almost identical estimated IRT parameter values. This finding was also verified in the 38 fraction addition problems (Tatsuoka, 1987). That is, the items (say, L in number) requiring the same set of tasks such as *getting the common denominator* and *converting a mixed number to a simple fraction* have almost identical item parameters; therefore, these items have very similar residual functions, $P_l(\theta) - T(\theta)$ $l = 1, ..., L$ throughout θ. In the inequalities (1), items of the same type can be located within a vicinity range. New indices, called Generalized ζ Indices and given in Section 2.5 (below), that are cognitively meaningful and applicable to cognitive diagnoses were developed by exploiting this property.

Illustration With 20 Fraction Subtraction Problems

Fraction subtraction problems are constructed to include the basic skills required for solving the problems correctly, such as *borrowing, converting a whole number to a simple fraction*, and *getting the common denominator*. The 40-item test was administered to 595 junior high school students. The first set of 20 items and the second set of 20 items in this test were cognitively parallel. In other words, there were 20 pairs of items, in which each pair consisted of one from the first set and one from the second set, and in which each pair required the same set of procedures, respectively; so the first 20 items are used in this example. The 20 items are characterized by attributes as an incidence matrix given in Table 2.4.1. Tatsuoka (1990) used two strategies, Method A and Method B. Method A requires converting a mixed number into a simple fraction ($21/2 = 5/2$). Method B requires separating the whole-number part from the fraction part first, then subtracting them separately—for example, $4\,1/2 - 11/3 = (4 - 1) + (1/2 - 1/3) = 31/6$.

Items 5, 10, 11, 13, 17, 18, 19, and 20 (denoted by $L_1 = \{5, 10, 11, 13, 17, 18, 19, 20\}$) involve the *borrowing operation* to get the correct answer when students use Method B. Items 7, 9, 15, and 19 involve the skill *converting a whole number to a fraction or mixed number*. (Note that item 19 requires both of these skills.) The skill *getting the common denominator* is involved in items 1, 2, 3, 5, and 13.

For example, when a student cannot do the *borrowing operation* correctly but can do the remaining skills correctly, then he or she gets the items

TABLE 2.1

Fraction Subtraction Problems With Attributes Based on Method B

A List of Attributes

1. Converting a whole number to a fraction or mixed number
2. Separating a whole-number part from a fraction part
3. Simplifying before getting the common denominator
4. Finding the common denominator
5. Borrowing one from the whole-number part
6. Column borrowing for subtraction of the numerators
7. Reducing answer to the simplest form
8. Subtracting numerators

An Item × Attribute Incidence Matrix

		IRT Parameters			
Items	Attributes Involved in Item	a_j for Test 1	a_j for Test 2	b_j for Test 1	b_j for Test 2
1. $5/3 - 3/4$	4 6 8	1.48	1.84	.02	.23
2. $3/4 - 3/8$	4 8	1.93	2.18	−.10	.07
3. $5/6 - 1/9$	4 8	1.66	2.31	.08	.17
4. $4\,3/5 - 3\,4/10$	2 3 4 8	.63	.62	−.36	−.20
5. $3\,1/2 - 2\,3/2$	2 3 5 8	.85	1.56	−.04	.16
6. $6/7 - 4/7$	8	1.52	1.96	−1.05	−.90
7. $3 - 2\,1/5$	1 2 8	1.84	2.47	.44	.45
8. $2/3 - 2/3$	8	.65	.62	−1.24	−1.69
9. $3\,7/8 - 2$	2 8	.47	.64	−.87	−.33
10. $4\,4/12 - 2\,7/12$	2 5 6 7 8	2.10	2.89	.49	.52
11. $4\,1/3 - 2\,4/3$	2 5 8	1.79	2.56	.22	.32
12. $11/8 - 1/8$	7 8	1.30	1.26	−.77	−.57
13. $3\,3/8 - 2\,5/6$	2 4 5 8	2.32	3.59	.73	.76
14. $3\,4/5 - 3\,2/5$	2 8	1.58	1.68	−.68	−.64
15. $2 - 1/3$	1 2 8	1.98	1.86	.29	.33
16. $4\,5/7 - 1\,4/7$	2 8	1.31	1.14	−.62	−.56
17. $7\,3/5 - 4/5$	2 5 8	2.16	2.47	.35	.38
18. $4\,1/10 - 2\,8/10$	2 5 6 8	1.57	1.76	.23	.18
19. $4 - 1\,4/3$	1 2 3 5 8	3.29	3.29	.69	.67
20. $4\,1/3 - 1\,5/3$	2 3 5 8	2.33	2.62	.47	.52

involving borrowing wrong, and the other items correct. At the knowledge state of *only borrowing operation was not mastered*, the ideal response pattern **X** resulting from this misconception has the estimated θ of 0.24, and ζ of −1.19. The baseline order of the 20 items at θ = 0.24 is given in Table 2.1.

The first column of Table 2.2 indicates the label of the residual, and the second column contains the items listed in the ascending order of the values of $P_j(.24) - T(.24)$ for j = 1, ..., 20, which are given in column 3. The items having small, negative values of the residual at θ = 0.24—items 19, 13, 10, 20, 17, 18, 4, and 11—are the ones requiring the *borrowing operation* that cluster toward the left end of the inequalities Equation (2.15).

TABLE 2.2

The Items With the Ascending Order of Residuals, $P_j(\theta) - T(\theta)$ at $\theta = 0.24$

Order	Item	$P_j(.24)-T(.24)$	Ideal Response Pattern	Response Pattern 1	Response Pattern 2	Response Pattern 3
1	19	−.42	1	0	1	1
2	13	−.39	1	1	1	1
3	10	−.18	1	1	1	1
4	20	−.15	0	0	1	0
5	17	−.05	1	1	1	1
6	18	−.02	1	1	1	1
7	4	−.02	1	1	1	1
8	15	−.02	1	1	1	1
9	11	.01	1	1	1	1
10	5	.02	0	0	0	1
11	9	.05	0	0	0	1
12	3	.07	1	1	1	1
13	1	.07	0	0	0	0
14	7	.14	1	1	1	1
15	8	.17	1	1	1	1
16	2	.18	1	1	1	1
17	16	.22	0	0	0	0
18	12	.24	0	0	0	0
19	14	.25	0	0	0	0
20	6	.27	0	0	0	1
	Estimated θ		.24	.15	.28	.56
	ζ value		−1.19	−.91	−1.32	−.76

Note: Ideal response pattern corresponds to *only borrowing operation has not been mastered;* response 1 has slippage at item 1, response 2 has slippage at item 4, and response 3 has slippage at items 10, 11, and 20.

This property indicates that students' item response patterns resulting from the misconception *cannot do the borrowing operation but can do other skills* have a particular ζ value, and the response patterns with two or three slips deviated from the ideal response pattern resulting from *not-perfect performance* of the student's knowledge state have very similar ζ values. Pattern 1, shown in column 4 of Table 2.2, is the ideal pattern corresponding to this knowledge state; patterns 1, 2, and 3 are the response patterns, in which a few slips deviated from the ideal response pattens a few slips deviated from the ideal item response pattern. Their θ and ζ values are close to those of the ideal response pattern.

Let us denote two ordered pairs, $(\theta_{ks1}, \zeta_{ks1})$ and $(\theta_{ks2}, \zeta_{ks2})$, of the ideal response patterns corresponding to two knowledge states, KS1 and KS2, respectively. Suppose they are located very close to each other, and suppose a student's true knowledge state is KS1, but his or her response pattern contains several slips deviated from this state. Then, classification of the student's performance on a test will be difficult if we examine only the information obtained from the θ and ζ values computed from the student's response pattern. Separability of the classification groups (knowledge states, in this case) is one of the most important issues in the area of statistical pattern classification problems (Fukunaga, 1990). In order to separate the states KS1 and KS2 better with respect to their corresponding ordered pairs $(\theta_{KS1}, \zeta_{KS1})$ and $(\theta_{KS2}, \zeta_{KS2})$, a third variable is necessary to formulate a three-dimensional space. The third variable, a generalized ζ, is introduced in the next section.

2.5 Generalized ζ

When an achievement test is constructed to measure knowledge and cognitive processes, the items usually require the test taker to have several cognitive processes and appropriate knowledge to get the correct answers. For example, fraction subtraction problems require skills to get common denominators, convert a mixed number to a simple fraction, and borrow. The SAT Mathematics test contains arithmetic, algebra, geometry, and analytic geometry problems.

If a researcher would like to investigate an individual's performance on a subset of items such as algebra problems in SAT Mathematics, or the items requiring borrowing in fraction subtraction problems, then the generalized ζ can be computed by using only the items included in the subset of interest.

Suppose L consists of the l items of interest—for example, the algebra items in the SAT Mathematics test or the fraction subtraction items requiring borrowing. The generalized ζ_L shows the extent to which a response pattern conforms to the average performance on the subset of the items. ζ_L can be obtained in a manner parallel to the ζ Index by using only the items in L instead of using all the test items for computation (Tatsuoka, 1997).

$$\varsigma_L = \frac{\sum_{j \in L}(P_j(\theta) - x_j)(P_j(\theta) - T_L(\theta))}{\sqrt{\sum_{j \in L}P_j(\theta)Q_j(\theta)\{P_j(\theta) - T_L(\theta)\}^2}} \quad \text{where } T_L(\theta) = \frac{1}{n}\sum_{j \in L}P_j(\theta) \quad (2.16)$$

The following example shows generalized ζs computed from three subsets of items in the fraction problems described in Table 2.1.

Example 2.1 With Fraction Problems

Let L_1 be the set of items whose curves are very close to $T(\theta)$: $L_1 = \{1, 2, 3, 4, 5, 11, 18\}$; let L_2 be the complement of the items in L_1: $L_2 = \{6, 7, 8, 9, 10, 12, 13, 14, 15, 16, 17, 19, 20\}$; and let L_3 be the odd-numbered items:

TABLE 2.3

Five Response Patterns and Their θ, the Information Function Value $I(\theta)$ at Their θ and ζ, and Generalized ζs

Item Response Pattern	θ	$I(\theta)$	ζ	ζ_1	ζ_2	ζ_3
1. 11101111100101110000	0.24	30.14	−1.19	−.88	−1.72	−1.06
2. 11100111100101110000	0.20	29.38	−.90	−.81	−1.11	−.21

ζ_1 associates with $L_1 = \{1\ 2\ 3\ 4\ 5\ 11\ 18\}$.
ζ_2 associates with $L_2 = \{6\ 7\ 8\ 9\ 10\ 12\ 13\ 14\ 15\ 16\ 17\ 19\ 20\}$.
ζ_3 associates with $L_3 = \{1\ 3\ 5\ 7\ 9\ 11\ 13\ 15\ 17\ 19\}$

$L_3 = \{1, 3, 5, 7, 9, 11, 13, 15, 17, 19\}$. Three generalized ζs associated with L_1, L_2, and L_3 were computed for a fraction dataset. The response patterns of 307 students who used Method B out of 595 students were sampled as examples here, and their generalized ζs were computed. Table 2.3 summarizes the results.

Response patterns 1 and 2 have almost the same estimated θ values, .24 and .20, and very close ζ and ζ_1 values, (−1.19, −.88) and (−.90, −.81), but they have somewhat different values for ζ_2 and ζ_3: (−1.72, −1.06) and (−1.11, −.21), respectively. By comparing two sets of values for the variables θ, ζ, ζ_1, ζ_2, and ζ_3—(.24, −1.19, −.88, −1.72, −1.06) and (.20, −.90, −.81, −1.11, −.21), respectively—the two response patterns can be distinguished. Indeed, the squared Mahalanobis distance between the two points in the two-dimensional rule space (later, detailed discussion will be given) is .29, but it is 1.21 for the five-dimensional rule space. Mahalanobis distance will increase as the dimension of rule space becomes higher.

Relationship Among ζ and Generalized ζs

Property 2.1: If the items in L_1 were the geometry problems in the SAT Mathematics test, then the generalized ζ associated with L_1 accounts for the unusualness of response patterns for the geometry items. If a student's pattern is different from the baseline order, then there must be a reason for the difference. If the baseline order is defined by the order of the item difficulties, where item difficulty is the proportion correct value, then the response patterns conforming well to the baseline order can be interpreted as the average person's performance on the geometry items.

Property 2.2: Generalized ζs have the conditional expectation zero and conditional variance 1. The conditional correlation coefficient of θ and generalized ζ_1 associated with a subset of items L_1 can also be computed (Tatsuoka, 1996). Because generalized ζs are associated with subsets of items, one can select generalized ζs that are not correlated highly with ζ.

Property 2.3: If the items in L_1 are selected so that the value of the residual $P_j(\theta) - T(\theta)$ becomes close to zero for θ—in other words, if the items in L_1 whose item response functions are very close to the true score function $T(\theta)$ are selected—then the correlation between ζ and ζ_1 becomes very small (almost zero).

Property 2.4: If the items in L_1 have almost identical item parameters, then the values $P_j(\theta) - T_1(\theta)$ for θ are very close to zero where $T_1(\theta)$ is the average of the IRT functions $P_j(\theta)$ for j in L_1. Therefore, the generalized ζ_1 defined from such an L_1 has very small correlation values with ζ. Tatsuoka (1987) investigated the relationship between item parameters and the cognitive processes required in solving items correctly and found that the items requiring the same set of cognitive processes and skills have very similar item response curves in the fraction problems. Therefore, the generalized ζ associated with the items requiring the identical or almost identical set of cognitive tasks and knowledge has very small correlation values with ζ.

Property 2.5: Parallel to the properties 2.3 and 2.4 (above), the generalized ζs that correlate highly with ζ can be considered. If the items in L_1 are selected from both ends of the inequality 1—that is, if the items with larger absolute values of $P_j(\theta) - T(\theta)$ are selected—then the generalized ζ_1 correlates highly with ζ. The more items there are with high values of $P_j(\theta) - T(\theta)$ in L_1, the higher the correlation values will be with ζ and ζ_1.

Property 2.6: The correlation between two generalized ζs depends on how the two subsets of items are selected. Suppose L_1 and L_2 are sets of items, and ζ_1 and ζ_2 are the generalized ζs associated with L_1 and L_2, respectively. When the two sets L_1 and L_2 are mutually exclusive, then the correlation of generalized ζs, ζ_1 and ζ_2, becomes zero, that is, ζ_1 and ζ_2 are not correlated. Example 2.2 shows these properties using the fraction problems.

Example 2.2

The correlation matrix of generalized ζs and θ in Example 2.1 is computed. Table 2.4 summarizes this with the means and standard deviations of θ, ζ, ζ_1, ζ_2, and ζ_3.

Because the expectations and conditional standard deviations of ζs are 0 and 1, respectively, the observed means and standard deviations of ζ, ζ_1, ζ_2, and ζ_3 computed from 307 students are nearly 0 and 1. Because the correlations between θ and the ζs are asymptomatically zero (Tatsuoka, 1985),

TABLE 2.4

The Correlation Matrix of the Five Variables Given in
Example 2.5.1 and Their Means and Standard Deviations

	θ	ζ	ζ_1	ζ_2	ζ_3	**Mean**	**SD**
θ	1	.13	.13	.10	.07	.06	1.26
ζ		1	.31	.94	.70	−.02	1.05
ζ_1			1	.13	.46	.08	1.03
ζ_2				1	.62	−.05	1.00
ζ_3					1	.01	1.07

the observed correlation values are also close to zero. The correlation between ζ and ζ_1, as we have expected, is much smaller than that between ζ and ζ_2. Indeed, the ζ_2 associated with the items that have large absolute values of $P_j(\theta) - T(\theta)$ correlates very highly with ζ. The correlation between ζ_1 and ζ_2 is very small, because the two sets L_1 and L_2 are mutually exclusive.

Introduction of generalized ζs associated with various subsets of items suggests a wide applicability of person–fit statistics to cognitive diagnosis and/or detection of cheaters. If several classification groups are not well separated, then we can use several generalized ζs until our targeted separability among the groups is obtained. By applying the whitening transformation on several generalized zetas (ζ_ks, $k = 1, \ldots, K$), the normalized distance of any response pattern **Y** from a given classification group follows the gamma density function with $\alpha = 1/2$, $\beta = K/2 - 1$. This property will guide us to develop a better classification criterion for optimal results.

3

Cognitive Modeling by Developing an Incidence Q Matrix

3.1 Preparation of the Q-Matrix Theory

If new measurement models are to measure complex and dynamic cognitive processes and to be linked to instruction, then understanding knowledge structures in highly specific and detailed forms will be able to provide a rational basis for proposing and evaluating potential improvements in the measurement of general proficiency. Without this understanding, improvement remains largely a trial-and-error process.

The psychometric theories currently available express students' proficiencies by numbers that highly correlate with total scores. Suppose a 10-item fraction subtraction test consists of five types of items (listed below), and each type has two items.

Type I. Simple fraction subtraction problems with common denominators (5/7 – 2/7)

Type II. Problems requiring subtracting a simple fraction from a whole number (1 – 1/3)

Type III. Items with different denominators (5/8 – 1/4)

Type IV. Items requiring borrowing from a whole-number part (3 4/9 – 5/9)

Type V. Items requiring the combination of Type III and Type IV (3 4/9 – 1/2)

It is simple arithmetic that a total score of 4 for this 10-item test can be obtained by answering four items correctly from 210 different combinations of items. Suppose Bridget answered correctly for Type I items (simple fraction subtraction problems with common denominators), and two problems requiring subtracting a simple fraction from a whole number (Type II), but wrong for the three other item types: two items with different denominators (Type III), two items requiring borrowing from a whole-number part (Type IV), and two items from the combinations of Type III and IV (Type V). It seems she cannot get the common denominator and do borrowing from a whole-number part.

Chris answered four items correctly that are from Type I and Type III, and the other six items incorrectly. Chris can subtract simple fractions with and without the same denominators but is having trouble dealing with the whole-number part of fraction problems. However, Bridget and Chris have the same total scores although they seem to be in different knowledge states. It is extremely difficult to judge which student is more advanced.

Let us think about how these types can be expressed in a manner so that a teacher can teach her or his students fraction problems in the most efficient way. Type I must be taught before Type III because Type III requires one to make equivalent fractions before subtracting the numerators. Thus, Type I is a prerequisite skill of Type III. Type I is also a prerequisite of Type IV. Types III and IV are prerequisites of Type V, because Type V requires Types III and IV. Type II is the prerequisite of Type I. These relationships can be expressed by the diagram in Figure 3.1.

The network of five types in Figure 3.1 is created by considering which types of skills are supposed to be taught first and then which should be next in terms of optimizing effective learning activities among students. The order of Types I, III, and V are "linearly ordered," but Types III and IV are not linearly ordered. However, all types are "partially ordered" in Figure 3.1. The prerequisite relationships among skills and knowledge can be considered one of many kinds of partially ordered relations.

The types of items shown in the above example are termed *attributes*, and a new terminology called *knowledge states* will be introduced in this

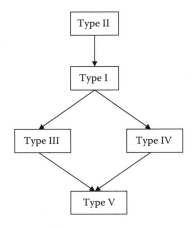

FIGURE 3.1
A flow chart of a possible teaching order of five types of fraction subtraction items.

chapter. The knowledge states consist of binary attribute mastery patterns that are defined by which attributes a student can do or cannot do. An example of a knowledge state in this example can be (1 0 0 0 0)—a student can do addition of two simple fractions, but cannot do all other attributes.

Some attributes can be observable, but most attributes are impossible to observe. For example, three problems that are coded by their involved attributes, given in Figures 3.2 and Examples 1.1 and 1.2 in Chapter 1 are from a state assessment, and Table 3.1 gives a description of these attributes.

Content variables can be measured easily because they are observable, but process-thinking skills are impossible to observe to measure. However, we would like to estimate mastery probabilities of these attributes for individuals, not a group statistics like means and medians.

An order relation to a set of attributes has been mentioned briefly in Figure 3.1 in which a psychologically meaningful structure of attributes was given. We would like to find out each student's state of learning or knowledge states: as Bridget's and Chris' example, which attributes they can do and which attributes they cannot do. A methodology that can provide us individualized information on each student's knowledge state is called a *cognitively diagnostic method*, and a test that can give us diagnostic information on a student's performance is called *diagnostic assessment*. Rule space methodology (RSM), introduced in this book, is a cognitively diagnostic methodology.

A dairy farmer is filling his cylindrical storage tank with fresh milk. The tank has been filled with 45 gallons as shown below. Which of the following is the best estimate of the number of gallons the entire tank will hold?

F. 45 gallons: G. 90 gallons: H. 180 gallons: I. 270 gallons

A geometrical figure is given._____S3 (Geometry)
This item asks for an estimation from the figure given above. This is a cylindrical storage tank and the volume must be estimated. _____C4
We estimate about ¼ of the tank is filled with milk. _____S5
We are supposed to get the "best" estimate by multiplying 4×45 ("best" is a quantitative reading)._____ P10

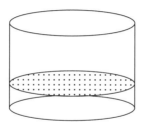

FIGURE 3.2
An example problem with a list of attributes that are involved in this problem.

TABLE 3.1

A Subset of Attributes Analyzed for Some State Mathematics Assessment

Content Attributes
C2: To be able to apply basic concepts and operations in fractions and decimals
C3: Basic concepts and operations in elementary algebra
C4: To be able to apply basic concepts and operations in two-dimensional geometry

Skill (Item-Type) Attributes
S1: To be able to do unit conversions
S3: Using figures, tables, charts, and graphs
S5: Evaluating, verifying, and checking options

Process Attributes
P1: Translate, formulate, and understand (only for seventh graders) equations and
    expressions to solve a problem
P2: Computational applications of knowledge in arithmetic and geometry
P3: Judgmental applications of knowledge in arithmetic and geometry
P4: Applying rules in algebra and solving equations (plugging-in included for seventh graders)
P5: Logical reasoning—be able to apply case reasoning, use deductive thinking skills, apply
    if-then logic, understand and use necessary and sufficient conditions, and generalize
    specific knowledge and concepts
P9: Management of data and procedures in a complex problem and ability to set multigoals
P10: Quantitative and logical reading (*less than, must, need to be, at least, best,* etc.)

RSM consists of two parts, Q-matrix theory and statistical pattern classification in a classification space named *rule space*. A Q matrix summarizes teachers' and researchers' hypotheses on what attributes would be needed for answering an item correctly and developing a matrix of items and attributes. Classification results would provide them how well their Q matrix explains the underlying attribute performances on the items of a given test. As Chipman, Nichols, and Brennan (1985) stated, RSM is a hypothesis testing of cognitive models.

One of the useful applications of the Q-matrix theory is the order relation, defined in a set of subsets (denoted by L_A) of a set (denote by Q columns) of all attribute column vectors in a Q matrix. The order relation enables us to explore the structures among attributes, items, and knowledge states. A set L satisfies the condition to be Boolean algebra.

Boolean algebra is a mathematical structure that is defined using the *meet (union or OR)* and *join (intersection or AND)* operations instead of the usual addition and multiplication operations. More explicitly, Boolean algebra is the "partial order" on a set of subsets of a set that is defined by the inclusion relation of sets. The partial order means that some elements cannot be ordered such as a network, a tree figure, or hierarchical relation figures. The set operations are *union (meet, OR), intersection (join, AND),* and *complementation (NOT).* A Boolean algebra also forms a lattice (Kolman, Busby, & Ross, 2004). The original set L_A in the Q-matrix theory is a set of the column vectors representing attributes in a Q matrix, and the set of column vectors with the set theoretic partial-order relation is called *attribute space*. An item space will be similarly defined from a given Q matrix.

The Q-matrix theory develops a mathematical connection of the two mathematical structures, the latent attribute space L_A and the observable item space L_I, by introducing a Boolean descriptive function (BDF). It expresses an unobservable knowledge state defined as an attribute mastery pattern by its equivalent ideal item score pattern. This dual space structure is very powerful because ideal item score patterns are observable and corresponding to attribute mastery patterns; it is possible to classify an incoming student's item response patterns into knowledge states represented by ideal item score patterns that were generated earlier by a BDF from a Q matrix, and yet we get cognitive interpretation of diagnoses.

This chapter discusses the Q-matrix theory and shows the development of the dual structure of knowledge states. First, we introduce other approaches developed by Falmagne and his associates (Falmagne & Doignon, 1988) and Haertel & Wiley (1993) and Wiley (2002) in Section 3.2; and then the Q-matrix theory will be introduced in Section 3.3.

3.2 Analysis of Knowledge States and Their Partially Ordered Structure

Several researchers formulated the architecture of proficiency in a tree or network of notions (Falmagne & Doignon, 1988), attributes (Tatsuoka, 1990, 1991), and microlevel abilities (Wiley, 2002), analogous to the architecture of electronic circuits. Three such studies are introduced and compared in this chapter. An individual's knowledge state in Falmagne's and Wiley's studies is defined as the set of notions that the person has mastered, or equivalently defined as the attribute mastery pattern where 1 stands for mastered and 0 for not mastered. The advantage of Tatsuoka's Q-matrix theory is that notions, microlevel abilities, and attributes can be treated as quantitative entities, and this enables us to use the computational capability of Boolean algebra, which has widely been used in the design of computers. Moreover, it is useful for analyses of knowledge structures.

Knowledge Structures Introduced by Falmagne and Doignon

Koppen and Doignon (1990) and Falmagne and Doignon (1988) formulated a knowledge structure that is defined as the collection of all possible knowledge states in abstract algebra, lattice theory. Their definition of the knowledge state of an individual is given by the set of notions this person has mastered. According to Koppen and Doignon, "The notions can be identified with a question or problem, or an equivalent class of questions or problems, testing just that notion" (p. 311). If a knowledge state includes a notion A_k or cognitively relevant attribute A_k, then it should contain all notions $A_{k-1}, A_{k-2}, ..., A_1$ that are prerequisites to A_k.

Determination of the knowledge structure for a domain relies on experts' ability to list possible states from a set of problems. However, the number of states will often be enormous.

Suppose there are five problems: a, b, c, d, and e (Koppen & Doignon, 1990). The contents of these problems were examined, and a family H of knowledge states was obtained:

$$H = \{\phi, \{c\}, \{e\}, \{b,e\}, \{c,e\}, \{a,b,e\}, \{b,c,e\}, \{c,d,e\}, \{a,b,c,e\}, \{b,c,d,e\}, \{a,b,c,d,e\}\}$$

Note that the union and intersection of any pair of sets in H are also in H. That is, the set H is closed with respect to both union and intersection. In lattice theory (Birkoff, 1970), this property is equivalently characterized by saying that H constitutes a partial order on the set of sets of the problems by prerequisite relation. In other words, if an examinee solves y correctly and the pair (x, y) is ordered as $x \leq y$, then we can infer that this student has also mastered x. Existence of the partial order between any two problems makes it easier for an expert to construct a knowledge structure of a domain in which problems are asked. The book *Knowledge Structures* (Albert & Lukes, 1999) summarizes works developed by Falmagne and his associates.

Microlevel Abilities

Haertel and Wiley (1993) also explored a similar approach. They defined a set of microlevel abilities, K, and then considered H, the set of sets of K. The set of sets of K forms a lattice H, and thus a set-theoretical partial order is introduced. This partial order is equivalent to having a prerequisite relation between any two abilities. Each combination of abilities in K is called an *ability state*, and lattice H with the prerequisite partial order is called an *ability structure*.

The abilities are always divided into two categories with respect to a specific task: those that are required to perform the given task successfully and those that are not. Haertel and Wiley (1993) also defined task structures in order to create an algebra of task combinations that can be used to create complex task structures. These structures can then be linked to ability structures, and hence the task performance state S is explained by ability performance states.

One of the primary goals of their work is to develop a framework for testing. Questions of what abilities are required for performing well on test tasks are central, and a theoretical framework for abilities and their structures facilitates content analysis of a test. Test specifications indicate precisely which ability states are confounded and which are distinguishable from these combined task performance states. A scoring rubric is considered only a further mapping of performance state patterns onto score patterns or score profiles. This specification and scoring scheme enables the resolution of two important problems. First, it clarifies the problem of constructed validity of a test what we really measure from test items. Second, the content analysis enables the use of complex tasks. Scores are not necessarily either dichotomous or graded. Any partially ordered performance states could be used in assessing ability states.

3.3   A Q Matrix as a Cognitive Model

An approach adopted by K. K. Tatsuoka (1981, 1990, 1991, 1993, 1995) to develop a framework of knowledge structures and status is slightly different from the aforementioned two approaches but it is, in fact, practical and can be easily applied to analyses of both large- and small-scale assessment data (Birenbaum, Kelly, & Tatsuoka, 1993; Buck & Tatsuoka, 1998; Dean, 2006; Dogan, 2006; Guerrero, 2001; Saito, 1998; Tatsuoka, 1995; Tatsuoka, Corter, & Tatsuoka, 2004; Tatsuoka et al., 2006; Xin, Xu, & Tatsuoka, 2004).

Tatsuoka (1990) organized the underlying cognitive processing skills and knowledge that are required in answering test items in a Q matrix, in which the columns represent cognitive tasks and the rows represent items or vice versa. The entries in each column indicate which skills and knowledge are involved in the solution of each item. The entries of a Q matrix indicate 1 or 0, in which $q_{jk} = 1$ means attribute A_k is involved in item j and $q_{jk} = 0$ means A_k is not involved in item j. This involvement is a *Boolean variable*, so a Q matrix is a Boolean matrix. Because it is different from a matrix defined on real numbers usually used in multivariate statistics, chapters 3 and 4 discuss beginning levels of mathematical properties of Boolean algebra. By reading the chapters, the readers might feel easier to accept the mathematical conceptualization of the Q-matrix theory and start seeing that it will have a wide applicability to many other domains of practice and research.

However, the cell entries in a Q matrix are not limited to cognitive tasks of skills or knowledge. You may use sex or some background variables, but use of any observable and measurable variables is not recommended in a Q matrix because Boolean computation deals with a huge number of combinations of 1s and 0s, addition of an attribute to the original Q matrix may increase computational burden to a large extent.

Let us start by introducing an example below, and then work together.

Example 3.1

Suppose that we consider three attributes, A_1, A_2, and A_3, in fraction problems:

> Attribute A_1. "Getting the common denominator of two different denominators"
>
> Attribute A_2. "Converting a whole number to a simple fraction"
>
> Attribute A_3. "Adding two fractions with the same denominator"

Suppose we have three problems:

i1. Get the common denominator of 2/3 and 1/4.

i2. Add 2/5 and 1/5.

i3. Add 2 and 1/2.

Solutions of these items are as follows:

i1. Common denominator of 2/3 and 1/4 is 12 (getting the common denominator; A_1)

i2. $2/5 + 1/5 = 3/5$ (add the numerator and get 3/5; A_3)

i3. $2 + 1/2 = 4/2 + 1/2$ (converting 2 to 4/2; A_2)
$= 5/2$ (add the numerator and get 5/2; A_3)

Then, the Q matrix for these items will be as follows:

$$Q = \begin{array}{c} \\ i1 \\ i2 \\ i3 \end{array} \begin{array}{ccc} A_1 & A_2 & A_3 \\ 1 & 0 & 0 \\ 0 & 0 & 1 \\ 0 & 1 & 1 \end{array}$$

Let us use this Q matrix for further discussions. There are three row and three column vectors in the Q matrix. Attribute A_1 is involved in item 1, attribute A_3 is required in item 2, and attributes A_2 and A_3 are required in solving item 3. In a Q matrix, the attributes are represented by vectors in which 1 is involvement, and 0 is lack of involvement. Therefore, the attributes A_1, A_2, and A_3—in other words, the column vectors of the Q matrix—are given by

$$A_1 = \begin{pmatrix} 1 \\ 0 \\ 0 \end{pmatrix} \quad A_2 = \begin{pmatrix} 0 \\ 0 \\ 1 \end{pmatrix} \quad A_3 = \begin{pmatrix} 0 \\ 1 \\ 1 \end{pmatrix}$$

We rewrite these vectors by $A_1' = (1, 0, 0)$, $A_2' = (0, 0, 1)$, and $A_3' = (0, 1, 1)$, that is, the transposed form of the former form to express attribute vectors from now on for our convenience. If we use the set theoretic notation, then $A_1 = \{i1\}$, $A_2 = \{i3\}$, and $A_3 = \{i2, i3\}$. Note that items can be expressed by vectors whose elements are attributes, $i1\{A_1\}$, $i2 = \{A_3\}$, and $i3 = \{A_2, A_3\}$. The "notions" expressed by Falmagne and Doignon (1988) and Koppen and Doignon (1990), and the "micro level abilities" discussed by Haertel and Wiley (1993), can be considered the attributes that will be represented by the column vectors of a Q matrix. What we call *attributes* are somewhat more inclusive than "notions" and "microlevel abilities"; in particular, attributes also include more general variables, latent or observable variables. Representing the item–attribute relations in a Q matrix is simply for mathematical convenience.

Example 3.2
In an identity Q matrix (k × k), each attribute A_k is involved in a single item k. The row vectors and column vectors are unit vectors with K elements, respectively.

		A_1	A_2	...	A_K
	i1	1	0	...	0
Q =	i2	0	1	...	0
	·	0	0	...	0
	ik	0	0	...	1

The columns in a Q matrix can be item types, content specifications, or even some demographic information. Similarly, the rows can be any event or objects. In our setting, analyzing cognitive performances on test items, the rows are items and the columns are cognitive processing skills and knowledge. Therefore, we call the column entries *attributes*. Chipman, Nichols, and Brennan (1995) called them "psychometric attributes." In this way, each attribute is represented by a column vector of a Q matrix for a given test. This representation enables us to introduce Boolean algebra (Davey & Priestley, 1990) to investigate various relationships among attributes, items, and knowledge states. Combinations of which attributes are mastered or not mastered define knowledge states. The identity matrix Q will have an important role in Boolean algebra; however, it is, in practice, impossible to develop a test with several attributes whose Q matrix has an identity matrix.

3.4   Stable Attributes as Knowledge and Cognitive Processing Skills

In early 1980s, Brown and Burton (1978) and VanLehn (1983) developed a computer program (the BUGGY system) by which "erroneous rules of operations" or "bugs" in whole-number subtraction problems committed by students can be diagnosed. Many studies (Mayer, 1983; Resnick, 1983; VanLehn, 1983) investigated causes of systematic errors cognitively, and other studies investigated how stable most bugs are and how often they appear (Sleeman, Kelly, Martink, Ward, & Moore, 1989; Tatsuoka, Linn, Tatsuoka, & Yamamoto, 1988). Shaw (1984) interviewed seventh graders to investigate how stable erroneous rules of fraction addition and subtraction problems are; she found that they are pretty unstable and that many students changed their reasons why they use their rules within several seconds. The attribute described earlier as *getting the common denominator* originated 15 different erroneous rules of operations (Tatsuoka, 1984a).

Chipman et al. (1995, p. 11) argued that there are two basic approaches for getting a set of attributes. One is to infer them from examinees' responses by applying various statistical analyses (Corter, 1995), and the other is to use rule space methodology, as will be described later in detail. The rule space methodology is a hypothesis testing of domain experts' cognitive models expressed by a Q matrix. We address a question of what psychometrics attributes are supposed to be.

"Bugs" Are Unstable: Then What Will Be Good for Diagnoses?

Several studies on "bug" stability suggest that bugs tend to change with "environmental challenges" (Ginzburg, 1977) or "impasses" (Brown & VanLehn, 1980). Sleeman and his associates (1989) developed an intelligent tutoring system aimed at diagnosis of bugs and their remediation in algebra. However, bug instability made diagnosis uncertain, and hence remediation could not be directed. Tatsuoka, Birenbaum, and Arnold (1990) conducted an experimental study to test the stability of bugs and also found that inconsistent rule application was common among students who had not mastered signed-number arithmetic operations. In contrast, mastery-level students show stable patterns of rule application. These studies strongly indicate that the unit of diagnosis should be neither erroneous rules nor bugs but somewhat larger components such as sources of misconceptions or instructionally relevant cognitive components.

The primary weakness of attempts to diagnose bugs is that bugs are tentative solutions for solving the problems when students don't have the right skills. As Shaw (1986) found in her thesis work, students often did not remember what erroneous rules they used and could not describe them a few seconds later.

However, two parallel subtests in which corresponding items were designed to involve identical sets of skills were developed in signed-number and fraction addition and subtraction problems (Birenbaum & Tatsuoka, 1982; Tatsuoka, 1984a), and these were administered to several hundred seventh graders in a local junior high school. Their estimated item parameters of item response curves are compared between two subtests of signed numbers and fraction tests, respectively. Both tests had almost identical true score curves for their parallel subtests, respectively, although many students used different erroneous rules of operations in two parallel subtests (Tatsuoka, 1987; Tatsuoka & Tatsuoka, 1989). Suppose that bugs and erroneous rules of operations belong to the micro level of the test performances; then, measuring total scores and true score curves in the IRT theory can be classified as the macro level of the granularity scale for the measurement of a student's performance on a test item. Attributes as knowledge and cognitive skills can be placed somewhere between the ends of the micro and macro levels.

Interestingly, diagnosed students' knowledge states are remarkably identical between two parallel fraction addition and subtraction tests (Tatsuoka & Tatsuoka, 2005). This means that bugs are unstable, but total scores are very stable. Attributes are more stable than erroneous rules. Since knowledge states are attribute vectors, they are more likely located at similar stability levels to those of attributes. Knowledge states located on the granularity levels between bugs and total scores are reasonably stable. Searching for the stable components that are cognitively relevant is an important goal for diagnostic assessment and subsequent instructions aimed at remediation of misconceptions. It seems Tatsuokas' stability research on the granularity issues of diagnoses suggests diagnosing knowledge states that are defined by "can and cannot" of attributes would be the most useful levels of stability for a practice. However, this granularity issue must be carefully investigated by many researchers from various angles in the near future.

Subscores: Are They Good Candidates of Diagnostic Components?

Use of subscores for cognitive diagnoses cannot provide test takers with precise diagnostic information. However, it seems that testing publishers like to use subscores of subtopics in a large-scale assessment. In this

TABLE 3.2

Selected 14 Geometry Items With 9 Process Attributes From the Q Matrix of 100×23 for a State Mathematics Assessment for Seventh Graders

Item	p values	C4	P1	P2	P3	P4	P5	P6	P7	P9	P10	KS A	KS B	KS C
2	0.56	1	1	1	0	0	0	0	0	0	0	0	0	1
3	0.54	1	0	1	0	0	1	0	0	0	0	0	0	1
7	0.2	1	0	1	0	0	0	0	0	0	1	0	0	0
8	0.56	1	0	0	1	0	0	1	1	1	0	1	1	0
17	0.84	1	0	0	0	0	0	0	0	0	0	1	1	1
20	0.51	1	0	0	1	0	0	0	0	0	0	1	1	1
22	0.35	1	1	1	0	0	1	0	1	1	1	0	0	0
24	0.87	1	0	0	0	0	0	0	0	0	0	1	1	1
27	0.52	1	0	1	0	0	1	0	0	1	1	0	0	0
34	0.46	1	0	0	1	0	0	0	1	0	1	1	1	0
37	0.68	1	0	0	0	0	0	0	0	1	0	1	1	1
39	0.68	1	0	0	0	0	0	0	1	1	0	1	1	0
48	0.74	1	0	0	0	0	0	0	0	0	0	1	1	1
50	0.58	1	1	1	0	0	1	0	0	0	0	0	0	1
Sum	8.09	14	3	6	3	0	4	1	4	5	4	8	8	8

* KS A: Knowledge State A, KS B: Knowledge state B., KS C: knowledge state C

section, we discuss that using subscores as feedback to test takers is not good enough for helping for the sake of optimizing learning and teaching.

Figure 3.2a and 3.2b showed four examples of coded items by attributes in some large-scale state assessment. The assessment had 100 items and was administered to 150,000 seventh graders in the United States. The following matrix is excerpted from their original Q matrix of 100×23 with content attributes and attributes representing mathematical thinking and process skills (Tatsuoka, Kelly, Tatsuoka, Varadi, & Dean, 2007). Table 3.2 describes a part of the original attributes involved in this example. All 14 geometry items in the Q matrix with their item difficulties and the attributes representing process and thinking skills are shown in the unnumbered figure. Table 3.1 describes process attributes by P1 (Translate), P2 (Computation), P3 (Judging), P4 (Solving Equations), P5 (Reasoning), P9 (Managing), and P10 (Quantitative and Logical Reading). In Table 3.3, the cell entry of 1 means attribute i1 involves attribute Pk, and 0 means not involving Pk. The column of C4 (geometry) has all 1's because we selected the geometry items. Suppose there are three hypothetical knowledge states given below:

Knowledge States	Cannot	Attributes							Can Attributes	
KS A	P1	P2	P3	P4	P5	P6	P7	P9	P10	
KS B	P2	P5	P1	P3	P4	P6	P7	P9	P10	
KS C	P7	P10	P1	P2	P3	P4	P5	P6	P9	

TABLE 3.3

Q Matrix of a Large-Scale Mathematics Test and Item Difficulties

Items	Difficulties	14 Attributes 12345678901234	Items	Difficulties	14 Attributes 12345678901234
1	−1.51	01000001000001	31	−1.18	00100010000100
2	−2.04	10000000000000	31	−1.18	00100010000100
3	−1.55	10000100000100	33	−0.22	10000110000000
4	−1.21	10000010000101	34	−0.92	00010110000100
5	−1.02	10000000000010	35	−0.51	10000110000000
6	−1.37	10000001000000	36	−0.37	10000101000000
7	−2.92	00010000000110	37	−0.22	00010110000110
8	−0.54	10000000010110	38	−1.44	10010100000100
9	−1.06	10000010000000	39	−1.25	10010100000101
10	0.16	00010000100001	40	−1.08	10000101000000
11	−0.43	11000010010100	41	0.18	10101100010001
12	−0.22	00001000010000	42	0.25	10101100010001
13	−0.45	10100001000000	43	−0.74	01000101000000
14	−1.19	00010010000100	44	−0.06	10000100001100
15	0.78	10000001000001	45	−0.10	01000101000000
16	0.33	10001000010001	46	−0.09	00010110000000
17	0.62	00010000001101	47	0.54	00100100001000
18	0.88	00010000110001	48	0.99	10000110010000
19	0.84	11001001010001	49	2.04	00010110001001
20	0.80	00101000010011	50	1.30	01000101001001
21	0.84	00100000010001	51	1.38	01100101110010
22	0.90	10011001010001	52	1.94	00010100111001
23	1.53	01001001011001	53	0.58	00011011010000
24	1.79	00010001110001	54	−0.15	11000001000110
25	1.35	11000001011001	55	1.15	00010010001001
26	−2.98	10000000000000	56	1.29	10011000011011
27	−1.89	00001000000000	57	1.60	01010001100000
28	−2.47	10000000000010	58	1.36	11000001011011
29	−1.26	10000010000010	59	1.71	11001001011101
30	−0.66	00010000000100	60	1.81	10010001111101

KS A is the knowledge state *cannot do P1 and P2 but can do the rest of the attributes*. The items involving P1 are items 2, 20, and 50. If a student in KS A answers these geometry items, then he or she answers items 2, 20, and 50 wrong with very high probabilities. Similarly, the items involving P2 would be 0 with very high probability. However, the items not involving either P1 or P2 would be correctly answered with high likelihood because the rest of the attributes are listed in the *can attributes* category. Therefore, KS A yields a response pattern (0 0 0 1 1 1 0 1 0 1 1 1 1 0) as is shown in Table 3.2. Similarly, we get the item patterns of KS B and KS C in Table 3.2. As can be seen in Table 3.2, the scores of three knowledge states are 8, but they get the same score of 8 from different knowledge states. This example shows that the use of total scores in students' reports is not informative for teaching purposes. Another example comes from an important assessment used widely in the United States.

The following list has 14 attributes identified in several studies done previously (Tatsuoka, 1995; Tatsuoka & Boodoo, 2000). Fourteen prime attributes are as follows:

A_1: Skills and knowledge in arithmetic

A_2: Skills and knowledge in elementary algebra

A_3: Skills and knowledge in advanced algebra

A_4: Skills and knowledge in geometry

A_5: Translation of word problems into algebraic expressions

A_6: Comparison item type

A_7: Recall of knowledge, rules, and theorems, then ability to do simple computations

A_8: Solving equations; substituting entities in algebraic expressions

A_9: Selection of appropriate rules and theorems from a large pool of knowledge

A_{10}: Reasoning skills and logical thinking skills

A_{11}: Analytical thinking skills

A_{12}: Comprehension of reading figures, charts, graphs, and tables

A_{13}: Spontaneous wisdom and test-taking skills

A_{14}: Setting multiple goals and solving them step by step

The incidence matrix for a 60-item large-scale mathematics test is given in Table 3.3. Examples of coding mathematics problems are similar to those in Figures 3.2a and 3.2b. Difficult items tend to involve attributes 7 (simple computations), 8 (solving equations), 9 (selection of rules and theorems), 10 (reasoning skills), 11 (analytic thinking skills), and 14 (multistep goals), which are process variables. Easy items tend to involve only a few attributes, whereas difficult items tend to involve more attributes. Tatsuoka (1995) showed that attributes 9, 10 11, and 14 were constantly strong predictors of item difficulty and total scores in her regression analyses, and the results were replicated across three parallel forms of this mathematics assessment. Table 3.4 shows the results from multiple regression analysis on Forms 1, 2, and 3. Three forms have about 80% of variances accounted for the difficulties of 60 items.

In the Q matrix in Table 3.3, 17 out of 60 items involve attribute A_{10}, and these 17 items are dispersed across four content areas designated by attributes A_1(arithmetic), A_2(elementary algebra), A_3(advanced algebra), and A_4(geometry). A_{10} is involved in 14 items in arithmetic items, 7

TABLE 3.4

Results From Multiple Regression Analysis Across Three Forms of Some
Large-Scale Mathematics Tests[a]

	Form 1	Form 2	Form 3
Analysis of variance	14.20	13.00	13.65
Prob > F	.0001	.0001	.0001
R-square	.82	.80	.81
Adjusted R-square	.76	.74	.75
Significant attributes			
A_2: Skills in algebra	**	—	—
A_3: Skills in advanced algebra	**	—	—
A_4: Skills in geometry	**	—	—
A_6: Comparison	—	—	**
A_7: Knowledge	**	**	**
A_8: Follow complex procedures	**	**	**
A_9: Selection of rules and theorems	**	**	**
A_{10}: Logical thinking skills	**	**	**
A_{11}: Analytical thinking skills	**	**	**
A_{13}: Practical, spontaneous wisdom	—	**	—
A_{14}: Solve complex problems	**	**	**

[a] Dependent variable is item difficulties, and coding of attributes in the three Q matrices is
independent variables.
** Significant at p = .95.

in elementary algebra, 5 in advanced algebra, and 5 in geometry items.
Table 3.4 shows that content attributes A_1, A_2, A_3, and A_4 are weak predictors of item difficulties but easy to make contentwise scores because can-
tant attributes are usually observable. It seems their subscores would not
tell much useful diagnostic information to teachers and students because
statistically strong predictors of scores are attributes representing mathematical processes and thinking skills, A_6 through A_{14}. For these process
attributes, the same argument used for the geometry items of the state
assessment can be applied. For example, in the SAT Mathematics tests
given in Table 3.3, we may be able to use subscores for each attribute by
counting the number of correct answers among the items involving this
attribute in the Q matrix. In other words, the subscores of items involving an attribute (say, A_{10} in the Q matrix given in Table 3.3) can be given
as a score of A_{10}. However, it does not work either. Let us list the items
involved in these four attributes given in Table 3.3:

A_{10}: {8 11 16 19 20 21 22 23 24 25 26 41 43 48 51 53 56 58 59 60}, total = 20

A_{11}: {17 23 25 44 47 49 50 52 55 56 58 59 60}, total = 13

A_{14}: {1 4 10 15 16 17 18 19 20 21 22 23 24 25 39 41 42 49 50 52 55 56 58 59 60},
     total = 25

Anybody who always can apply A_{10} correctly should get a total score of 20. Suppose Mary can do A_{10}, but cannot do A_{11} and A_{14}. Then her subscore of the set A_{10} should be 20, but she would get only 7 because items 16, 19, 20, 21, 22, 23, 24, 25, 41, 56, 58, 59, and 60 involve A_{11} and/or A_{14} also; and hence she would not be able to answer them correctly with high probability. Suppose John can do A_{10} and A_{11}, but cannot do A_{14}. Then his total score of the set A_{10} would be 7 because items 16, 19, 20, 21, 22, 23, 24, 25, 41, 56, 58, 59, and 60 would likely be answered wrong too. These two counterexamples explain why subscores could not provide accurate diagnostic information to test takers.

Macro- and Microlevel Analyses: Making Inferences on Unobservable Microlevel Tasks From Observable Item-Level Scores

Evaluating the structure or representation of cognitive skills requires response formats that are different from traditional item types. We need items that ask examinees to draw flow charts in which complex relations among tasks, subtasks, skills, and solution paths are expressed graphically, or that ask examinees to describe such relations verbally. Questions can be figural response formats in which examinees are asked to order the causal relationships among several concepts and connect them by a directed graph.

These demanding measurement objectives apparently require a new psychometric theory that can accommodate more complicated forms of scoring than just right or wrong item-level responses and can accommodate relational structures of complex task skills together with latent thinking skills. The correct response to the item is determined by whether or not all the cognitive tasks involved in the item can be answered correctly. If any of the tasks would be wrong, then the final answer would be wrong with very high probability. The item-level responses are called *macrolevel responses*, and those of the attributes and skill levels are called *microlevel responses*.

Statistical test theories deal mostly with test scores and item scores. These scores are considered to be macrolevel information in this study, whereas the underlying cognitive processes are viewed as microlevel information. Our approach uses a much finer level of *unobservable performances* than the item level or the macro level. Looking into underlying cognitive processing skills and knowledge, and speculating about examinees' solution strategies, which are unobservable, may be analogous to the situation that modern physics has come through in the history of its development. Exploring the properties and relations among microlevel objects such as atoms, electrons, neutrons, and other elementary particles led to many phenomenal successes in theorizing about physical phenomena at the macro level such as the relation between the loss and gain of heat and temperature. Easley and Tatsuoka (1968) stated in their book *Scientific Thought* that

> the heat lost or gained by a sample of any nonatomic substance not undergoing a change of state is jointly proportional to the number of atoms in the sample and to the temperature change. This strongly suggests that both heat and temperature are intimately related to some property of atoms. (p. 203)

Heat and temperature relate to molecular motion, and the relation can be expressed by mathematical equations involving molecular velocities.

This finding suggests that, analogously, it might be useful to explore the properties and relations among microlevel, invisible tasks and to predict their outcomes, which are observable as responses to test items. The approach mentioned above is not new in scientific research. Our aim is to explore a method that can explain macrolevel phenomena—in our context, item-level or test-level achievement—scientifically from microlevel tasks and objects. The method should be generalizable from specific relations in a specific domain to general relations in general domains. In order to accomplish our goal, elementary graph theory is used.

3.5 Relationship Among Attributes From the Graph Theory Approach

Graph theory (Kolman et al., 2004; M. Tatsuoka, 1986) is a branch of mathematics that has been widely used in connection with tree diagrams consisting of nodes and arcs. The main purpose of the theory is to facilitate the grasping and understanding of the relational structure represented by a complex graph through simplifying or reorganizing the graph. In practical applications of graph theory, nodes represent objects of substantive interest, and arcs show the existence of some relationship between two objects. In the task analysis setting, the objects correspond to attributes.

Determination of Direct Relations Between Attributes

Researchers determine the definition of a direct relation based on the design of their studies. For example, suppose you are asked to put gasoline in your mother's car: You would get her car key first (attribute 1), and start the car (attribute 2). Then you would drive to a gas station (attribute 3).

In this case, A_1 is the immediate prerequisite of A_2, and A_2 is the immediate prerequisite of A_3. The relationship can be expressed as follows: $A_1 \rightarrow A_2 \rightarrow A_3$. In general, $A_k \rightarrow A_l$ if A_k is an immediate prerequisite of A_l (Sato, 1978, 1990). This is called a direct graph.

Suppose a child is asked to add 1/2 and 2/3, and 1/3 and 1/3, respectively. The former is harder than the latter because it requires getting the common denominator of 2 and 3. This relation, "A is harder than B," is expressed by a direct graph: $A_k \rightarrow A_l$ if A_k is harder than A_l (Wise, 1981).

These direct relations are defined logically, but they can be determined statistically. Hubert (1974) used them by measuring the proximity of two objects, and Takeya (1981) used them for expressing dominance relations. M. Tatsuoka (1986) described various applications of graph theory in educational and behavioral research.

Adjacency Matrix

The direct relations defined above can be represented by a matrix called the adjacency matrix $\mathbf{A} = (a_{kl})$, where

$$\begin{cases} a_{kl} = 1 \text{ if a direct relation exists from } A_k \text{ to } A_l \\ a_{kl} = 0 \text{ otherwise} \end{cases}$$

Two attributes, A_k and A_l, are equivalent: If a direct relation exists from A_k to A_l and also from A_l to A_k, then A_k and A_l are said to be equivalent.

In this case, the elements a_{kl} and a_{lk} of the adjacency matrix are both one:

	A_1	A_2
Adjacency matrix A = A_1	0	1
A_2	1	0

There are many ways to define a direct relation between two attributes, but we will use a "prerequisite" relation in this book. One of the open-ended questions shown in Bennett and Ward (1993) will be used as an example to illustrate various new terminologies and concepts in this chapter.

Example 3.3

Item 1: How many minutes will it take to fill a 2,000 cubic centimeter (cc) tank if water flows in at the rate of 20 cc per minute and is pumped out at the rate of 4 cc per minute?

This problem is a two-goal problem, and the main canonical solution is as follows:

1. Net filling rate = 20 cc per minute – 4 cc per minute
2. Net filling rate = 16 cc per minute
3. Time to fill tank = 2,000 cc/16 cc per minute
4. Time to fill tank = 125 minutes

Let us define attributes involved in this problem:

A_1. First goal is to find the net filling rate.

A_2. Compute the rate.

A_3. Second goal is to find the time to fill the tank.

A_4. Compute the time.

With this example, A_1 is a prerequisite of A_2, A_2 is a prerequisite of A_3, and A_3 is that of A_4. This relation can be written by a chain, $A_1 \rightarrow A_2 \rightarrow A_3 \rightarrow A_4$. This chain can be expressed by an adjacency matrix whose cells are $a_{12} = a_{23} = a_{34} = 1$, and others are zeros.

$$\text{Adjacency matrix } \mathbf{A} = \begin{array}{c|cccc} & A_1 & A_2 & A_3 & A_4 \\ \hline A_1 & 0 & 1 & 0 & 0 \\ A_2 & 0 & 0 & 1 & 0 \\ A_3 & 0 & 0 & 0 & 1 \\ A_4 & 0 & 0 & 0 & 0 \end{array}$$

This adjacency matrix $\mathbf{A}$ is obtained from the relationships among the attributes that are required in solving item 1. These prerequisite relations expressed in the above adjacency matrix $\mathbf{A}$ in this example are item dependable. For instance, if a new item that requires the attributes A_3 and A_4 to reach the solution is added, then A_1 and A_2 are no longer prerequisites of A_3. The prerequisite relation, in practice, must be determined by a task analysis of a domain, and usually it is independent from what items are in an item pool.

Example 3.4

Suppose four attributes A_1, A_2, A_3, and A_4 are related as follows:

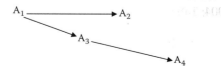

Then, the adjacency matrix is given by the following:

$$
\mathbf{A} = \begin{array}{c} \\ A_1 \\ A_2 \\ A_3 \\ A_4 \end{array} \begin{array}{cccc} A_1 & A_2 & A_3 & A_4 \\ \left|\begin{array}{cccc} 0 & 1 & 1 & 0 \\ 0 & 0 & 0 & 0 \\ 0 & 0 & 0 & 1 \\ 0 & 0 & 0 & 0 \end{array}\right| \end{array}
$$

A_1 and A_4 in Example 3.4 have a relation, but it is not direct. However, reachability matrices represent all the relations, both direct and indirect, that exist among attributes.

Reachability Matrix

Warfield (1973a, 1973b) developed a method called "interactive structural modeling" in the context of switching theory. By his method, the adjacency matrix in Example 3.4 has direct relations from A_1 to A_2, from A_2 to A_3, and from A_3 to A_4, but no direct relations other than these three. However, a directed graph (or digraph) consisting of A_1, A_2, A_3, and A_4 shows that there is an indirect relation from A_1 to A_3, from A_2 to A_4, and from A_1 to A_4. Warfield showed that we can get a reachability matrix by multiplying the matrix $\mathbf{A} + \mathbf{I}$—the sum of the adjacency matrix $\mathbf{A}$ and the identity matrix $\mathbf{I}$—by itself n times in terms of Boolean algebra operations. The reachability matrix indicates reachability in at most n steps (A_k to A_l), whereas the adjacency matrix contains reachability in exactly one step (A_k to A_l) (a node is reachable from itself in zero steps). The reachability matrix of Example 3.3 in the previous section is given below:

$$\mathbf{R} = (\mathbf{A} + \mathbf{I})^3 = (\mathbf{A} + \mathbf{I})^4 = (\mathbf{A} + \mathbf{I})^5 = \ldots$$

$$
\mathbf{R} = \begin{array}{cccc} A_1 & A_2 & A_3 & A_4 \\ \left|\begin{array}{cccc} 1 & 1 & 1 & 1 \\ 0 & 1 & 1 & 1 \\ 0 & 0 & 1 & 1 \\ 0 & 0 & 0 & 1 \end{array}\right| \end{array} \begin{array}{c} A_1 \\ A_2 \\ A_3 \\ A_4 \end{array}
$$

where the definition of Boolean operations (Davey & Priestley, 1990; Kolman et al., 2004; Tatsuoka, 1991) is as follows:

$$1 + 1 = 1, \quad 1 + 0 = 0 + 1 = 1, \quad 0 + 0 = 0 \text{ for addition; and}$$

$$1 \times 1 = 1, \quad 0 \times 1 = 1 \times 0 = 0, \quad 0 \times 0 = 0 \text{ for multiplication.}$$

The reachability matrix indicates that all attributes are related directly or indirectly. From the chain above, it is obvious that A_k and A_{k+1} relate directly but A_k and A_{k+2} relate indirectly.

This form of digraph representation of attributes can be applied to evaluation of instructional sequences, curriculum evaluation, and documentation analysis, and has proved to be very useful (Sato, 1978, 1990). Moreover, a reachability matrix can provide us with information about cognitive structures of attributes. However, application to assessment analyses requires extension of the original method introduced by Warfield (M. Tatsuoka, 1986) to more functional and computational forms of mathematical theory called Boolean algebra without losing the capability and graphically intuitive characteristics of Warfield's graph theory approach.

3.6 Partial-Order Relations Embedded in a Q Matrix: Boolean Algebra

The adjacency matrix (a_{kl}) is a square matrix of order $K \times K$, where K is the number of attributes and a_{kl} represents the existence or absence of a direct directed relation from attributes A_k to A_l. We have discussed direct and indirect relations of attributes in the previous section. Examples 3.3 and 3.4 are given in the context of a single item or without items. However, when we deal with many items in a test pool or item pool, these relations often become very complex and impossible to handle intuitively. Boolean algebra is a mathematical theory that enables us to deal with this kind of difficulty. We discuss complex relations in the context of a Q matrix instead of adjacency and reachability matrices in graph theory because Q matrices and reachability matrices are mathematically related, and the relationship expressed in an adjacency matrix is included in the corresponding Q matrix.

If new measurement models are to measure complex and dynamic cognitive processes and to be linked to instruction, then understanding knowledge structures in highly specific detail provides a rational basis for proposing and evaluating potential improvements in the measurement of general proficiency. Without this understanding, improvement remains largely a trial-and-error process.

A Q Matrix Item by Attribute Matrix Viewed From a Boolean Algebra Approach

The advantage of Tatsuoka's Q-matrix theory is that notions, micro abilities, and attributes can be treated as quantitative entities (row vectors in the Q matrix), and hence it enables us to use the computational capability of Boolean algebra, which has widely been used in the design of computers (Kolman et al., 2004). The framework of Tatsuoka's Q matrix integrates the conceptual frameworks introduced by Falmagne and Doignon (1988) and Haertel and Wiley (1993). The theory of a Q matrix conceptually includes both the lattice spaces of attributes and knowledge states, because the set of sets of its row vectors formulates a Boolean algebra (see the next section). Boolean algebra is also a lattice (Simmons, 1963). Moreover, the lattice of the Q matrix is mathematically connected through the Q matrix. Each knowledge state represents which attributes an individual has mastered, and testing for mastery or nonmastery of an attribute can be done by examining a question or an equivalent class of questions that involves this attribute.

The partial-order relationship defined by the prerequisite relation among attributes (notions and/or micro abilities) by Falmagne and Doignon (1988) and Haertel and Wiley (1993) can be equivalent to the partial-order relation defined by the set-theoretic inclusion relationship among the set of attribute vectors or the set of column vectors in a Q matrix (C. Tatsuoka, 2002; M. Tatsuoka, 1990, 1991, 1993). We explain partial-order relations in the next several sections step-by-step. However, we state mathematical properties, so if readers feel uncomfortable, they may skip them.

Boolean Algebra and Lattice

Boolean algebra and lattice comprise one branch of abstract algebra that has been widely applied to electrical engineering. The theories in Boolean algebra enable us to develop a practical computer program that creates architecture of knowledge states in partially ordered relations. Because Boolean algebra is also a lattice, we introduce lattice first.

Select a single number 1 from a set $J = \{1, 2, \ldots, K\}$, and write it $\{1\}$. Then $\{1\}$ is called a subset of J. We select further $\{2\}, \ldots, \{K\}, \{1, 2\}, (1, 3\}\ldots\{1, 2, 3, 4, 5, \ldots, K\}$. We call the set of all subsets and $\{\phi\}$, empty set by L. Let us denote these subsets by $S_1 S_2 \ldots S_K, S_0$ and set of these subset by $L = \{ S_1 S_2 \ldots S_K, S_0\}$. Then L satisfies the condition to be called lattice.

Property 3.1: Let L be a set of subsets obtained from the set of K numbers, $J = \{1, 2, \ldots, K\}$. Let L be a lattice and Boolean algebra.

The conditions to be a lattice are simple. We first define operations like addition and subtraction in a set of real numbers. We define our operations for L as union and intersection of two elements (subsets). L must have the set of two union sets, $A \cup B$, and the set of two intersections, $A \cap B$, and must have further the sets of any combinations of union and intersection of any elements in L. Like addition and multiplication of two or more real numbers, in this context, elements in a set of subsets obtained from the set of K numbers. It should be noted that the order of operation in L does not affect the result, $A \cup B = B \cup A$, $A \cap B = B \cap A$. This property is called the *commutative law*. Equally, distribution law and identity law are satisfied.

Definition of lattice L: A set of sets L is said to be a lattice if two binary compositions $\cup$ and $\cap$ are defined on its subsets (called *elements* hereafter), and they satisfy the following relations:

l_1. $A \cup B = B \cup A$, $A \cap B = B \cap A$

l_2. $(A \cup B) \cup C = A \cup (B \cup C)$, $(A \cap B) \cap C = A \cap (B \cap C)$

l_3. $A \cup A = A$, $A \cap A = A$

l_4. $(A \cup B) \cap A = A$, $(A \cap B) \cup A = A$

The above conditions are equivalent to saying that a lattice is a partially ordered set in which any two elements have a least upper bound (LUB) and a greatest lower bound (GLB). The LUB and GLB of any elements A and B in L are given by the union and intersection, $A \cup B$, and $A \cap B$, respectively.

By using our example, a set of subsets of $J = \{1, 2, \ldots, K\}$, $L = \{ S_1, S_2 \ldots S_{123}, S_0 \}$, we can draw a graph for the $K = 3$ case (see Figure 3.3). The graph in Figure 3.3 is obtained by connecting two elements that have the direct order relation such as S_0 and S_1, S_0 without arrows. The union set of S_1 and S_2 is $S_1 \cup S_2$, and it equals S_{12}. The union of S_0 and S_1 is S_1, $S_0 \cup S_1 = S_1$, the intersection of S_1 and S_2 is S_{12}, and the intersection of S_3 and S_0 is S_0, $S_0 \cap S_1 = S_0$. By tracing different combinations, unions, and intersections of the elements in L on Figure 3.3, one can find L satisfies the conditions to be a lattice L.

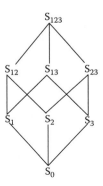

FIGURE 3.3
Lattice of a set of subsets of three numbers: 1, 2, and 3.

Lattice can be defined by Definition 2, below, which is equivalent to Definition 1. Definition 2 is sometimes easier to understand intuitively. In Figure 3.3, for example, the sets $\{S_0, S_1, S_{12}, S_{123}\}$, $\{S_0, S_2, S_{12}, S_{123}\}$, and $\{S_0, S_2, S_{13}, S_{123}\}$ are linearly ordered with respect to inclusion relation; $S_0 \subseteq S_1 \subseteq S_{12} \subseteq S_{123}$, $S_0 \subseteq S_2 \subseteq S_{12} \subseteq S_{123}$, and $S_0 \subseteq S_2 \subseteq S_{13} \subseteq S_{123}$. Or, equivalently, rewriting "$\subseteq$" to "$\leq$," we get $S_0 \leq S_1 \, S_{12} \leq S_{123}$, $S_0 \leq S_2, \, S_{12} \leq S_{123}$, and $S_0 \leq S_2 \leq S_{13} \leq S_{123}$.

However, S_1, S_2, and S_3 do not have ordered relationships, neither of S_{12}, S_{13}, and S_{23}. Therefore, lattice L is a partially ordered set. Let us look into two linearly ordered sets, $S_0 \leq S_1 \leq S_{12} \leq S_{123}$, and $S_0 \leq S_2 \leq S_{12} \leq S_{123}$. S_{123} and S_{12} in these two sets are upper bounds of S_0, S_1 and S_0, S_2 respectively, but S_{12} is the LUB of S_0, S_1 and S_0, S_2, respectively. Similarly, the lower bounds of S_{12} in both examples are S_0, S_1, and S_0, S_2, respectively, but the GLBs are S_1 and S_2, respectively.

Definition of lattice: A lattice is a partially ordered set in which any two elements have a least upper bound and a greatest lower bound. The LUB and GLB of any elements A and B in L are given by the union and intersection, $A \cup B$, and $A \cap B$, respectively. Similarly, $(A \cup B) \cup C$ is an LUB of A, B, and C, and $(A \cap B) \cap C$ is a GLB.

Let us try this relationship with our set L. $(S_1 \cup S_2) \cup S_3 = S_{123}$ by definition of creating an element in L, that is, $(S_1 \cup S_2) \cup S_3 = (\{1\} \cup \{2\}) \cup \{3\} = \{1,2,3\} = S_{123}$, and there is no element of L between S_{123}.

Similarly, for example, $(S_{12} \cap S_{23}) \cap S_1 = (\{1,2\} \cap \{2,3\}) \cap \{1\} = \{\phi\} = S_0$, so S_0 is the GLB of S_{12}, S_{23}, and S_1. We have the order $\geq$ in L as inclusion relation in L, and set theoretic inclusion relation can also be said for $A \cup B = A$ or $A \cap B = B$:

Definition of the order "$\geq$" in L: For any elements A and B in L, $A \geq B$ if and only if $A \cup B = A$ or $A \cap B = B$.

Definition of the order provides us with an equivalent condition for L to be a lattice. This order satisfies the asymmetric (if $A \geq B$ and $B \geq A$, then $A = B$) and transitivity laws (if $A \geq B$ and $B \geq C$, then $A \geq C$); thus, L becomes a partially ordered set. This definition of order is more often used in applied mathematics areas. Let us further define *identity element* i with respect to union operation and *identity element* O with respect to intersection operation as follows:

Definition of identities: $I = \cup_{k=1}^{K} A_k$ and $0 = \cap_{k=1}^{K} A_k$ where I and 0 belong to L. In our example L, I is S_{123} and 0 is S_0.

Definition of a modular lattice: If the distributive law $A \cap (B \cup C) = (A \cap B) \cup (A \cap C)$ is satisfied, then L is called a modular lattice.

Definition of a modular lattice: The modular condition has an alternative definition: if $A \geq B$ and $A \cup C = B \cup C$ and $A \cap C = B \cap C$ for any C in L, then $A = B$.

The third important operation is complementation.

Definition of complement: A complement A' of A is defined by $A' \cup A = 1$ and $A' \cap A = O$.

In our example L, we have $S_1' = S_{23}$, because $S_{23} \cup S_1 = S_{123} = I$. Similarly, we get $S_2' = S_{13}, S_3' = S_{12}, S_0' = S_{123}, S_{12}' = S_3, S_{123}' = S_0, S_{23}' = S_1$, and so on.

Because an element and its complement do not have any common element, the intersection of an element and its complement is empty, 0. The lattice of a set of subsets is complemented if the complement of a subset A is the usual set theoretic complement. One may wonder what the difference is between lattice and Boolean algebra. Boolean algebra is a special case of lattice with very convenient conditions.

Definition of Boolean algebra: A Boolean algebra is a lattice with 1 and 0, satisfying the distributive law and complementation.

This definition implies that lattice L is also a Boolean algebra. But with having 1 and 0 in L, Boolean algebra can be used as the mastery state of all attributes as 1 and nonmastery of all attributes as 0. The most important elementary properties of complements in a Boolean algebra may be stated as follows:

Theorem 1: The complement A' of any element A of a Boolean algebra L is uniquely determined. The mapping $A \rightarrow A'$ is one-to-one, onto itself. Then, the mapping satisfies conditions 1 and 2:

1. $A'' = A$
2. $(A \cup B)' = A' \cap B'$ and $(A \cap B)' = A' \cup B'$

The proof may be found in Birkoff (1970). From our example L, we have the complement of S_1 equals S_{23} (i.e., $S_1' = S_{23}$) because the union of S_{23} and S_1 equals S_{123}; that is the identity 1 with respect to union operation, $S_{23} \cup S_1 = S_{123} = I$. Taking the complement of the both terms, we get the complement of complement comes back to the original element, $S_1 (S_1')' = S_{23}' = S_1$. We call the complement of complement *idempotent*. Similarly, we get $(S_2')' = S_{13}' = S_2$.

$(S_3')' = S_{12}' = S_3, (S_0')' = S_{123}' = S_0, (S_{12}')' = S_3' = S_{12}, (S_{123}')' = S_0' = S_{123}, (S_{23}')' = S_1' = S_{23}$

For the second part of Theorem 1, the complement of the union set of A and B equals the intersection of the complement of A and B. For example, taking the complement of the union set of S_1 and S_2 becomes the intersection of the complements of S_1 and S_2. The left term of 2 in Theorem 1 is $(S_1 \cup S_2)' = (\{1\} \cup \{2\})' = (\{1, 2\})' = (S_{12})' = S_3$, and the right term of 2 in Theorem 1 is $S_1' \cap S_2' = S_{23} \cap S_{13} = S_3$. Therefore, the complement of the union of two elements equals the intersection of the complement of each element, $(S_1 \cup S_2)' = S_1' \cap S_2'$.

Similarly, $(S_1 \cap S_2)' = (\{1\} \cap \{2\})' = (\{\phi\})' = S_{123}$ and $S_1' \cup S_2' = (\{1\})' \cup (\{2\})' = \{2, 3\} \cup \{1, 3\} = \{1, 2, 3\}$; therefore, $(S_1 \cap S_2)' = S_1' \cup S_2'$.

Ring

A Boolean algebra becomes a ring with the two new operations + and ×, where + is the union set of A and B and × is the intersection of A and B. This property is extremely useful for generating all possible knowledge states from a given Q matrix.

Definition of ring: For A and B in L, the addition + of A and B is defined by $A + B = A \cup B$, and the product x is defined by $A \times B = A \cap B$. Thus, L becomes a ring.

It is obvious that L satisfies commutative law, associative law, and *identity law*: $A + O = A$, $A \times I = A$; and the idempotent law $A + A = A$ with respect to the new operations + and ×. The distributive law is also satisfied. In summary,

1. $A + B = B + A$, $A \times B = B \times A$ (commutative law)
2. $(A + B)' = A' \times B'$, $(A \times B)' = A' + B'$ (complementation)
3. $(A + B) + C = A + (B + C)$,
   $(A \times B) \times C = A \times (B \times C)$ (associative law)
4. $A + 0 = 0 + A = A$, $A \times I = I \times A = A$ (identity law)
5. $A + A = A$, $A \times A = A$ (idempotence law)
6. $(A + B) \times C = A \times C + B \times C$ (distributive law)

The set-theoretic inclusion relationship among the set of attribute vectors or the set of column vectors in a Q matrix (Tatsuoka, 1990) is described in the earlier part of this section. The attribute vectors in a Q matrix can be treated as K, numbers and a set of subsets of the attribute vectors forms a lattice and Boolean algebra. The operations in Boolean algebra that satisfy the conditions described (1 through 6) will be introduced. These operations are useful and functional for computation of generating knowledge states from a given Q matrix.

3.7 Attribute Space and Item Response Space

When a Q matrix is the identity matrix of order $K \times K$, then $\mathbf{A}_k$ will be the unit vector $\mathbf{e}_k = (0, \ldots, 1, 0, \ldots, 0)$, where kth element is 1 and the rest of the other elements are zero. A Boolean lattice L will consist of a set of attributes where attribute A_k corresponds one-to-one to item k or, equivalently, to the unit vector $\mathbf{e}_k$. Let us denote this case by L_{Id}. Therefore, L_{Id} can be considered as a set of sets of items, or equivalently as a set of sets of unit vectors $\mathbf{e}_k$, $k = 1, \ldots, K$. In order to distinguish between these two sets, the set of sets of attributes is denoted by the same notation, L_{Id}, and the set of sets of items (or sets of $\mathbf{e}_k$) is denoted by RL_{Id}, in other words, Boolean algebra of item response patterns. Both L_{Id} and R_{Id} are K-dimensional space because the incidence matrix Q is the identity of order $K \times K$.

When a Q matrix is not the identity matrix, then L, which associates with a nonidentity Q matrix, becomes a subspace of RL_{Id}. It is very difficult, in practice, to construct an item pool whose Q matrix is the identity. Each item in the identity matrix Q must contain one and only one attribute. It is very common that an item involves several attributes, and two different items usually involve two different sets of attributes. In practice, most Q matrices are usually much more complex than the identity matrix, and their columns and rows contain several nonzero elements.

Boolean Algebra in Attribute Space

Suppose L_A and L_I are lattices obtained from the attribute and item vectors from a Q matrix, respectively. Because the following discussions about L_A hold equivalently for L_I, only the attribute lattice L_A will be considered.

Addition and multiplication operations in L_A are defined by element-wise Boolean addition and multiplication of 0 and 1, $\mathbf{A}_k$ and $\mathbf{A}_l$:

Operations in L_A: $\mathbf{A}_k + \mathbf{A}_l = \mathbf{A}_k \cup \mathbf{A}_l$ and $\mathbf{A}_k \times \mathbf{A}_l = \mathbf{A}_k \cap \mathbf{A}_l$.

Partial order in L_A: For any pair of elements $\mathbf{A}_k$ and $\mathbf{A}_l$ in L_A, the partial order $\leq$ is defined by the condition "$\mathbf{B} \leq \mathbf{A}$ if and only if $\mathbf{A} \cup \mathbf{B} = \mathbf{A}$ or $\mathbf{A} \cap \mathbf{B} = \mathbf{B}$."

This inclusion relation is a partial order, as stated in Section 3.6 (Birkoff, 1970). Further, the elements **0** and **1** in L_A are defined by $0 = \prod \mathbf{A}_k$, $1 = \sum \mathbf{A}_k$, and then the complement A_k' can be defined in terms of Boolean addition and multiplication, $\mathbf{A}_k + \mathbf{A}_k' = 1$, and $\mathbf{Ak} \times \mathbf{Ak'} = 0$.

Identities 1 and 0: $0 = \prod \mathbf{A}_k$, $1 = \sum \mathbf{A}_k$

Complements: $\mathbf{A}_k + \mathbf{A}_k' = 1$, and $\mathbf{A}_k \times \mathbf{A}_k' = 0$

In order to elaborate the partial order in attribute space as Boolean algebra and lattice, we go back to Example 3.1. In this example, we used three attributes in fraction addition problems.

Example 3.5

(See Example 3.1): Suppose that we consider three attributes, A_1, A_2, and A_3, in fraction problems: Attribute A_1 is "getting the common denominator of two different denominators"; attribute A_2 is "converting a whole number to a simple fraction"; and attribute A_3 is "adding two fractions with the same denominator."

Suppose we have three problems:

  i1. Get the common denominator of 2/3 and 1/4.

  i2. Add 2/5 and 1/5.

  i3. Add 2 and 1/2.

Solutions of these items are as follows:

  i1. The common denominator of 2/3 and 1/4 is 12 (getting the common denominator; A_1).

  i2. $2/5 + 1/5 = 3/5$ (add the numerator and get 3/5; A_3).

  i3. $2 + 1/2 = 4/2 + 1/2$ (converting 2 to 4/2; A_2) $= 5/2$ (add the numerator and get 5/2; A_3).

Then, the Q matrix for these items will be as follows:

$$Q = \begin{array}{c} \\ i1 \\ i2 \\ i3 \end{array} \begin{array}{ccc} A_1 & A_2 & A_3 \\ 1 & 0 & 0 \\ 0 & 0 & 1 \\ 0 & 1 & 1 \end{array} \quad \text{and the transpose of Q matrix,} \quad Q' = \begin{array}{c} \\ A_1 \\ A_2 \\ A_3 \end{array} \begin{array}{ccc} i1 & i2 & i3 \\ 1 & 0 & 0 \\ 0 & 0 & 1 \\ 0 & 1 & 1 \end{array}$$

Then $A_1 = (1\ 0\ 0)$, $A_2 = (0\ 0\ 1)$, and $A_3 = (0\ 1\ 1)$, and $J_A = \{A_1, A_2, A_3\}$. Then a set of subsets in J_A is denoted by L_A and $L_A = (\{\phi\}, \{A_1\}\ \{A_2\}\ \{A_3\}\ \{A_1, A_2\}\ \{A_1, A_3\}\ \{A_2, A_3\}\ \{A_1, A_2, A_3\})$. Note that if you replace $\{A_j\}$ for $j = 1, 2, 3$ by $\{A_j\} = \{j\} = S_j$ by S_j, $j = 1, 2, 3$, then the argument on showing that L is a Boolean algebra can be applied to L_A. Therefore L_A is lattice and Boolean algebra. However, because A_j is a vector and not just a numeral j, let us walk through some arguments together.

The definition of Boolean algebra is (a) L_A is a lattice with the identities I and 0, and (b) it is a ring (defined at the end of Section 3.6). The identities I and 0 in L_A, "attribute lattice," are as follows:

$$0 = A_1 \cap A_2 \cap A_3 = (1\ 0\ 0) \cap (0\ 0\ 1) \cap (0\ 1\ 1) = \{\phi\} \quad \text{and}$$
$$A_1 \cup A_2 \cup A_3 = (1\ 1\ 1) = I$$

We have defined that the intersection ∩ corresponds to the multiplication ×, and the union ∪ corresponds to the addition + in the definition of *ring* in Section 3.6. We further define the addition and multiplication of two vectors by taking element-wise addition and multiplication of corresponding elements in the vectors. We defined the elements in the Q matrix as *Boolean variables* because $q_{kj} = 1$ means that attribute A_k is involved in item j, and $q_{kj} = 0$ means that attribute A_k is not involved in item j. q_{kj} takes only 1 and 0, and not any other numbers. Thus, the additions and multiplications follow the rules below:

$$1 \times 1 = 1, \quad 1 \times 0 = 0 \times 1 = 0, \quad 0 \times 0 = 0$$

$$1 + 1 = 1, \quad 1 + 0 = 0 + 1 = 1, \quad 0 + 0 = 0$$

Then $\mathbf{0} = A_1 \cap A_2 \cap A_3 = (1\ 0\ 0) \times (0\ 0\ 1) \times (0\ 1\ 1) = (0\ 0\ 0)$ and $I = A_1 \cup A_2 \cup A_3 = (1\ 0\ 0) + (0\ 0\ 1) + (0\ 1\ 1) = (1\ 1\ 1)$.

Therefore, the identities are given by $\mathbf{0} = \Pi_{k=1}^{K} \mathbf{A_k} = (0\ 0\ 0)$, and $\mathbf{1} = \Sigma_{k=1}^{K} \mathbf{A_k} = (1\ 1\ 1)$, and the complements are given by $1' = 0$ and $0' = 1$. Therefore, the complements of attribute vectors $\mathbf{A_1}$, $\mathbf{A_2}$, and $\mathbf{A_3}$ are given by $\mathbf{A_1}' = (0\ 1\ 1)$, $\mathbf{A_2}' = (1\ 1\ 0)$, and $\mathbf{A_3}' = (1\ 0\ 0)$, respectively.

Boolean algebra has an advantage over lattices, because the former is more convenient computationally. In the next section, we introduce the generation of all possible knowledge states by Boolean descriptive function, but we will spend more time to discuss the partial-order relation in L_A and its relationship to the graph theory context. By reading the following sections, you may understand intuitively that Q matrix coding reflects implicitly any hierarchical relationships among attributes and their subsets of attributes when they actually have any order relationship. Sometimes, some subsets of attributes are linearly ordered and/or there are not any noticeable structural relationships. However, you may skip to Section 3.8 directly as you wish and keep going on cognitive diagnoses in Chapter 5.

The framework of a Q matrix enables us the use of a mapping function (the BDF) between the attribute space and a set of item response patterns, called *ideal item score patterns* (Tatsuoka, 1991; Varadi & Tatsuoka, 1989). As will be discussed later, an ideal item score pattern is considered a knowledge state that is yielded by assuming a specific combination of mastery and nonmastery of K attributes.

Some Properties Related With the Partial Order in L_A

There are interesting relationships among the attribute vectors that are totally ordered. If attribute vector A_k is larger than or equal to A_l, $A_k \geq A_l$, and A_l is larger than A_m, $A_l \geq A_m$ (i.e., $A_k \geq A_l \geq A_m$), then their sum equals the largest attribute, and their product equals the smallest attribute:

$$A_k + A_l + A_m = A_k$$

$$A_k \times A_l \times A_m = A_m$$

These properties are called "degenerative relations" (Birkoff, 1970) and have an important role for reducing the number of knowledge states (Varadi & Tatsuoka, 1989; Varadi et al., 1992).

Example 3.6

Let us consider vectors $\mathbf{A_2}$ and $\mathbf{A_3}$ of Example 3.5. The sum of A_2 and A_3 is $A_2 + A_3 = (0\ 1\ 1) = A_3$, and their product is $A_2 \times A_3 = (0\ 0\ 1) = A_2$ because A_3 is larger than A_2.

If Q is a Guttman scale matrix, then the row vectors are totally ordered:

$$\mathbf{A_1 \leq A_2 \leq A_3 \leq \ldots \leq A_k}$$

Example 3.7

$$
Q = \begin{array}{c}
A_1 \\ A_2 \\ A_3 \\ A_4 \\ A_5 \\ A_6
\end{array}
\begin{vmatrix}
1 & 0 & 0 & 0 & 0 & 0 \\
1 & 1 & 0 & 0 & 0 & 0 \\
1 & 1 & 1 & 0 & 0 & 0 \\
1 & 1 & 1 & 1 & 0 & 0 \\
1 & 1 & 1 & 1 & 1 & 0 \\
1 & 1 & 1 & 1 & 1 & 1
\end{vmatrix}
$$

In this example, the identities **0** and **1** are A_1 and A_6, respectively. Note that $A_1 \neq \mathbf{0}$.

Prerequisite Relationship Among Attributes and the Inclusion Relation

Boolean algebra is a lattice with the distributive law and partial order of two vectors by an inclusion relationship. On the other hand, the prerequisite relationship, "A_k is an immediate prerequisite of A_l (A_k is required for mastering A_l)," originates from the cognitive demands unique to a content domain. This relation can be expressed by a directed graph (Sato, 1990), $A_k \rightarrow A_l$. The direct relations among the attributes can be represented by a matrix called an *adjacency matrix*, B. The element b_{kl} is given as follows:

$$
b_{kl} = \begin{cases} 1 & \text{if a direct relation exists from } A_k \text{ to } A_l \\ 0 & \text{otherwise} \end{cases}
$$

A reachability matrix R is given by computing the powers of (B + I) with respect to Boolean operations until the result becomes invariant. Reachability matrix R indicates all the relations, direct or indirect, existing among the attributes.

Let us consider a Q matrix obtained from four unrelated attributes and 15 items, which involve all possible combinations of the four attributes.

$$Q'(4 \times 15) = \begin{vmatrix} & & & & & & & & & 1 & 1 & 1 & 1 & 1 & 1 \\ 1 & 2 & 3 & 4 & 5 & 6 & 7 & 8 & 9 & 0 & 1 & 2 & 3 & 4 & 5 \\ 1 & 0 & 0 & 0 & 1 & 1 & 1 & 0 & 0 & 0 & 1 & 1 & 1 & 0 & 1 \\ 0 & 1 & 0 & 0 & 1 & 0 & 0 & 1 & 1 & 0 & 1 & 1 & 0 & 1 & 1 \\ 0 & 0 & 1 & 0 & 0 & 1 & 0 & 1 & 0 & 1 & 1 & 0 & 1 & 1 & 1 \\ 0 & 0 & 0 & 1 & 0 & 0 & 1 & 0 & 1 & 1 & 0 & 1 & 1 & 1 & 1 \end{vmatrix}$$

Note that all the column and row vectors are different, and inclusion relations among attribute vectors and among item vectors do not exist.

Next, suppose A_1 and A_2 have the prerequisite relation, $A_1 \rightarrow A_2$, but all other pairs of the combinations of attributes are unrelated. Then the adjacency matrix will be

$$B = \begin{vmatrix} 0 & 1 & 0 & 0 \\ 0 & 0 & 0 & 0 \\ 0 & 0 & 0 & 0 \\ 0 & 0 & 0 & 0 \end{vmatrix}$$

The Prerequisite Relation and the Inclusion Relation

Skill A_1 is necessary to do skill A_2, and if item i involves A_2, then item i has to involve A_1. In other words, item i may involve A_1 without involving A_2, but it is impossible for item i to involve A_2 and not involve A_1. The prerequisite relation between A_1 and A_2, $A_1 > A_2$, is expressed by the inclusion relation, $A_2 \subseteq A_1$.

Property 3.2: The prerequisite relation between **A_1** and **A_2**, **$A_1 \rightarrow A_2$**, is expressed by the inclusion relation, **$A_2 \subseteq A_1$**.

As for the $Q(4 \times 15)$ matrix, the prerequisite relation $A_1 \rightarrow A_2$ implies the relationship that any item involving A_2 must also involve A_1. Hence, the column vectors for items 2, 8, 9, and 14 become (1 1 0 0), (1 1 1 0), (1 1 0 1), and (1 1 1 1), which are identical to the column vectors for items 5, 11, 12, and 15, respectively. If two items involve the identical set of attributes, they must be parallel, so the pair may be reduced to one item. Therefore,

$\mathbf{Q}'(4 \times 15)$ will be reduced to $\mathbf{Q}'(4 \times 11)$:

$$
\mathbf{Q}'(4 \times 11) =
\begin{array}{c}
1\ 1\ 1\ 1\ 1 \\
1\ 5\ 3\ 4\ 6\ 7\ 1\ 2\ 0\ 3\ 5 \\
\left|
\begin{array}{ccccccccccc}
1 & 1 & 0 & 0 & 1 & 1 & 1 & 1 & 0 & 1 & 1 \\
0 & 1 & 0 & 0 & 0 & 0 & 1 & 1 & 0 & 0 & 1 \\
0 & 0 & 1 & 0 & 1 & 0 & 1 & 0 & 1 & 1 & 1 \\
0 & 0 & 0 & 1 & 0 & 1 & 0 & 1 & 1 & 1 & 1
\end{array}
\right|
\end{array}
$$

Comparison of the attribute vectors, $\mathbf{A}_1$ and $\mathbf{A}_2$ in $\mathbf{Q}'(4 \times 11)$, indicates that A_1 includes A_2. None of the other pairs of attribute vectors in $\mathbf{Q}'(4 \times 15)$ have the inclusion relationship. Tatsuoka (1993) showed that the pairwise comparison of the row vectors $\mathbf{A}_k$ and $\mathbf{A}_l$ in $\mathbf{Q}(k \times n)$ with respect to the inclusion relation will yield the reachability matrix $R(k \times k)$ with respect to prerequisite relations among the attributes.

Property 3.3: Pairwise comparisons of the row vectors $\mathbf{A}_k$ and $\mathbf{A}_l$ for all the pairs (k, l) in $\mathbf{Q}(k \times n)$ with respect to the inclusion relation will yield the reachability matrix $\mathbf{R}(k \times k)$ with respect to prerequisite relations among the attributes.

The pairwise comparison of the row vectors in $\mathbf{Q}(4 \times 11)$ yields the reachability matrix, $\mathbf{R}$:

$$
\mathbf{R}\ (4 \times 4) =
\begin{vmatrix}
1 & 1 & 0 & 0 \\
0 & 1 & 0 & 0 \\
0 & 0 & 1 & 0 \\
0 & 0 & 0 & 1
\end{vmatrix}
$$

It is easy to verify that $\mathbf{B} + \mathbf{I} = (\mathbf{B} + \mathbf{I})^2 = \mathbf{R}$. This shows that the partial order by the inclusion relation is equivalent to that of the prerequisite relation of notions or microlevel abilities if items are constructed under certain conditions:

Definition of a sufficient Q matrix: Suppose K attributes have a prerequisite relation with a reachability matrix $\mathbf{R}$, and their involvement relationships with n items are expressed by a $\mathbf{Q}$ matrix. If the pairwise comparison of attribute vectors in the $\mathbf{Q}$ matrix with respect to the inclusion relation yields the reachability matrix R, then the $\mathbf{Q}$ matrix is said to be *sufficient* for representing the cognitive model of a domain of interest.

Definition of a sufficient item pool: The item pool associated with a sufficient $\mathbf{Q}$ matrix is called a *sufficient item pool*.

In other words, this condition will navigate processes of item construction and test design toward achieving the goal of measuring the intended objectives (Tatsuoka, 1991, 1993). As a result, the construct validity of a test will improve. It is important to note that a sufficient **Q** matrix is the core of a knowledge structure, and the partial order induced by the inclusion relation makes the **Q**-matrix theory capable of representing the prerequisite relationships among the attributes.

3.8   Universal Set of Knowledge States and Ideal Item Score Patterns

The original purpose of formulating a Boolean algebra from a **Q** matrix is to determine the universal set of knowledge states. As long as the **Q** matrix represents well the underlying cognitive processes of a domain, all possible combinations of attribute patterns will generate an appropriate set of ideal item score patterns in which a majority of students' misconception states can be captured.

Ideal Item Score Patterns as Knowledge States

Wrong answers for an item usually have reasons. Suppose there are three items whose underlying cognitive processes are identified, and two attributes, A_1 and A_2, that are cognitively relevant are found. Let the transpose of the **Q** matrix of the order 2×3 be as follows:

$$\mathbf{Q'} = \begin{array}{c} \quad\; i1 \;\; i2 \;\; i3 \\ \begin{vmatrix} 1 & 0 & 1 \\ 0 & 1 & 1 \end{vmatrix} \begin{array}{l} A_1 \\ A_2 \end{array} \end{array}$$

This means item 1 involves A_1, item 2 involves A_2, and item 3 involves both A_1 and A_2. There are 2^3 possible item response patterns: (1 1 1), (1 1 0), (1 0 1), (0 1 1), (1 0 0), (0 1 0), (0 0 1), and (0 0 0); and 2^2 possible mastery patterns: (1 1), (1 0), (0 1), (0 0). It is obvious that attribute pattern (11) suggests the item score pattern of all ones for three items, (1 1 1). Similarly, attribute pattern (0 0) suggests the corresponding item score pattern to be (0 0 0). How about (1 0) and (0 1)?

Space of Knowledge States

Definition of knowledge states: For a given set of attributes, their combination of attribute patterns is called *knowledge states*.

Assumption 3.1: Item j is correctly answered if and only if all attributes involved in item j are correctly applied. In other words, item j = 1 if $A_k = 1$ for k that are involved in item j.

This assumption implies that the score of item j will be 0 even if at least one attribute A_m is wrongly applied. Suppose item j involves L attributes; then, $2^L - 1$ attribute patterns will yield a score of 0 for item j, and the attribute vector whose elements are only 1s, (1 1...1), yields a score of 1 for item j. This is the multiplicative relationship between item scores and attribute scores. This multiplicative relationship enables us to generate item score patterns by applying all the combinations of attribute patterns to a given **Q** matrix. Tatsuoka (1991) related this assumption with item scores and total score. It is important to realize that this assumption will not provide you the situation that one can predict the scores of the items involving attribute A_k, even if A_k is mastered. If any attributes coexisting with A_k would not be mastered, then the items involving such attributes should have the score of 0 even if A_k is mastered. The sufficient condition of Assumption 3.8.1 requires attribute patterns of the existing set of attributes to determine item scores for a given test.

Applying the attribute pattern of (10), attribute A_1 is correct, but attribute A_2 is wrong—to the **Q** matrix, we get (100) because items 2 and 3 involve attribute 2, but item 1 does not involve attribute A_2. Similarly, applying (01) to the Q matrix yields (010). Now we have a correspondence between attribute space and item space:

$$(00) \rightarrow (000), (01) \rightarrow (010), (10) \rightarrow (100), (11) \rightarrow (111)$$

However, only four of these are cognitively meaningful ones. Item pattern (010) results from attribute pattern (01)—a subject cannot do A_1 but can do A_2 correctly. Item pattern (100) results from attribute pattern (10)—a subject can do A_1 but cannot do A_2 correctly. Similar arguments hold for (111) and (000). The other item patterns (110), (101), (011), and (001) cannot be interpreted in this manner; they are considered to be perturbations from the former four item patterns due to slips. Therefore, in this simple example, there are four classification groups. We call the item patterns resulting from the lack of knowledge or misunderstanding of underlying cognitive tasks clearly explained by the two attribute performances without slippage *ideal item response patterns*. Note that the word *ideal* does not connote *desirable*, but rather suggests perfect fit with an underlying theory, analogous to the notion of "ideal gas" in physics.

Ideal Item Score Patterns

Definition of ideal item score patterns: Item patterns generated from attribute patterns and a **Q** matrix are called *ideal item score patterns*. Sometimes, we refer to knowledge states in both ways: as ideal item score patterns or attribute patterns.

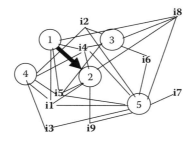

FIGURE 3.4
The incidence matrix Q and influence diagram for nine fraction addition problems and their five attributes.

Example 3.8

The **Q** matrix of fraction addition problems (Tatsuoka, 1993) is expressed by the inference diagram in Figure 3.4. The pairwise comparison of the row vectors in a **Q** matrix leads to a reachability matrix if the **Q** matrix is sufficient. Similarly, the pairwise comparison of the column vectors leads to an item tree, as shown in Figure 3.5 (Tatsuoka, 1990).

Example 3.9

Let us use the same **Q** matrix given in the previous section.

$$
Q(4 \times 11) = \begin{matrix}
 & & & & & & & & 1 & 1 & 1 & 1 & 1 \\
 & 1 & 5 & 3 & 4 & 6 & 7 & 1 & 2 & 0 & 3 & 5 \\
\hline
 & 1 & 1 & 0 & 0 & 1 & 1 & 1 & 1 & 0 & 1 & 1 \\
 & 0 & 1 & 0 & 0 & 0 & 0 & 1 & 1 & 0 & 0 & 1 \\
 & 0 & 0 & 1 & 0 & 1 & 0 & 1 & 0 & 1 & 1 & 1 \\
 & 0 & 0 & 0 & 1 & 0 & 1 & 0 & 1 & 1 & 1 & 1 \\
\end{matrix}
$$

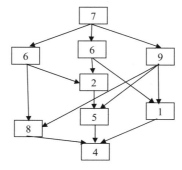

FIGURE 3.5
An item tree for nine fraction addition problems in Figure 3.4

TABLE 3.5

Output of the Computer Program BUGLIB, Applied to the Fraction Addition Problems With Four Attributes in Figure 3.4 (Correspondence Between Attribute Patterns and Ideal Item Score Patterns)

Knowledge States	Attribute Patterns				Corresponding Ideal Item Score Patterns										
	A1	A2	A3	A4	i1	i2	i3	i4	i5	i6	i7	i8	i9	i10	i11
1	1	1	1	1	1	1	1	1	1	1	1	1	1	1	1
2	1	1	1	0	1	1	1	0	1	0	1	0	0	0	0
3	1	1	0	1	1	1	0	1	0	1	0	1	0	0	0
4	1	1	0	0	1	1	0	0	0	0	0	0	0	0	0
5	1	0	1	1	1	0	1	1	1	1	0	0	1	1	0
6	1	0	1	0	1	0	1	0	1	0	0	0	0	0	0
7	1	0	0	1	1	0	0	1	0	1	0	0	0	0	0
8	1	0	0	0	1	0	0	0	0	0	0	0	0	0	0
9	0	*	1	1→0 0 1 1	0	0	1	1	0	0	0	0	1	0	0
10	0	*	1	0→0 0 1 0	0	0	1	0	0	0	0	0	0	0	0
11	0	*	0	1→0 0 0 0	0	0	1	0	0	0	0	0	0	0	0
12	0	*	0	0→0 0 0 0	0	0	0	0	0	0	0	0	0	0	0

The computer program BUGLIB, which was developed by Varadi and Tatsuoka (1989) and Varadi et al. (1992), yielded 11 ideal item response patterns corresponding to the 16 attribute mastery patterns given in Table 3.5.

The attribute mastery patterns 9, 10, 11, and 12 are affected by indeterminacy of mastery or nonmastery of A_2. The nonmastery of A_1 corresponds to the assignment of the score of zero for the set of items {1, 5, 6, 7, 11, 12, 13, 15} involving A_1 in the Q matrix. The nonmastery of A_2 corresponds to the assignment of the score of zero for the set of items involving A_2, which is {5, 11, 12, 15}, and which is a subset of the set associated with A_1. Because we assumed that A_1 is a prerequisite of A_2, it is natural to assume that the nonmastery of A_1 implies the nonmastery of A_2. Therefore, * in Table 3.5 implies the score of 0. The attribute patterns 9, 10, 11, and 12 become (0 0 1 1), (0 0 1 0), (0 0 0 1), and (0 0 0 0), respectively.

Summary

Rule space methodology (RSM) belongs to a branch of statistical pattern recognition and classification problems in statistics. This approach has two phases: First is the feature variables selection phase, and second is the statistical pattern classification phase. This chapter is the first phase of RSM for the introduction of Q-matrix theory, which will be continued in chapter 4. In the feature selection phase, we determine feature variables that in RSM are knowledge and cognitive or thinking skills called *attributes*, and then classification groups as knowledge states defined by which attributes a student can or cannot do. Note that attributes and knowledge states are impossible to measure directly because they are latent variables. In the second phase, an observed input will be classified into one of the predetermined groups. A Q matrix is an involvement matrix of attributes into items, and coding of the matrix should be carefully done with domain experts and cognitive researchers. Uniqueness of the Q-matrix theory is to create the dual spaces of knowledge states consisting of attributes and of items, respectively, and yet two spaces have the correspondence by sharing the same knowledge states. The Q matrix can be interpreted as a bridge between the attribute part and the item part of knowledge states; and this bridge, the Q matrix, enables us to connect interpretable knowledge states expressed by attribute mastery patterns and measurable, observable knowledge states expressed by ideal item score patterns. Since the knowledge states represented by items are observable and any observable response item patterns can be classified into one of the most plausible knowledge states; then, from the classified knowledge states, one can get its corresponding attribute mastery pattern, which is interpretable and can be used as diagnostic information of student's latent knowledge state.

This chapter has formulated the conceptual foundation of the space of knowledge states in Boolean algebra and introduced the dual spaces of knowledge states with latent attributes and observable items, respectively. The connection between psychologically interpretable, but latent attributes, and observable item scores is a Q matrix. Moreover, the partial order relation was defined in the space of knowledge states and so did in the attribute Boolean algebra L_A and item Boolean algebra Li. This dual relationship of knowledge states enables us to provide test users cognitively diagnostic results.

4

Knowledge Space Generated
From a Q Matrix

Both an error analysis and a task analysis are tremendously laborious and time-consuming. Tatsuoka (1991) developed a new technique utilizing Boolean algebra to generate a list of item response patterns corresponding to psychologically meaningful knowledge states. However, if we have identified 17 attributes for a domain of our interest, then the profiles of mastery or nonmastery on the 17 attributes have the combination of $2^{17} = 131,072$ patterns, which is a very large number. We need some clever techniques to deal with the combinatorial computational problems for handling enormously large numbers of knowledge states, and to classify a student response into one of these knowledge states. The traditional statistical decision theory (Kendall & Stuart, 1973; M. Tatsuoka, 1990) handles only a small number of classification groups.

Several statistical methodologies were developed in the late 19th century, such as fraction addition or subtraction or whole-number operations, that can be used for diagnoses in small domains. These methodologies have been used mostly for medical diagnoses and are very difficult to apply to a large-scale assessment in education and psychology. Moreover, they require training sets to prepare a classification system. What we need most is to create a training set to prepare the classification system. In medical areas, their diagnostic system uses previously diagnosed data by doctors as a training set. Let us introduce such systems used in psychometrics.

Neural networks (Riply, 1996) were derived from analogies with models of the way that a human might approach the acquisition of new knowledge and skills. This approach has had a great impact on the practice of pattern recognition in engineering and science. Once a good training set is obtained, the trained neural network can perform either better than or equally well as human experts. Hayashi (2002) trained a neural network using the rule space results in a fraction subtraction domain (Klein, Birenbaum, Standiford, & Tatsuoka, 1981), and confirmed that the trained neural network worked very well for diagnosing fraction errors committed by individual test takers. Leighton and Hunka (2000) tamed a neural network using simulated responses. One of the weaknesses of a neural network approach is instability, because if new inputs following a totally different cognitive model from the initial training set are used for taming coefficients and are fed to the system, the coefficients of nodes in the networks would be altered and lose the capability of original diagnostic power.

Similarly, by using the rule space results as a training set, Mislevy (1995) created a Bayesian influence network that is capable of diagnosing fraction errors. As long as training sets are available, we can use either a neural network or Bayesian influence network to replace human decision-making processes.

A natural question arises: Is it possible to develop training sets without going through laborious and painstaking task analysis or collecting descriptive hand-recorded data such as medical records? The rule space method developed by Tatsuoka and her associates (Tatsuoka, 1983, 1985, 1990, 1991, 1993, 1995; K. Tatsuoka & M. Tatsuoka, 1998, 1987; M. Tatsuoka & K. Tatsuoka, 1989) is designed to generate a training set without relying on a human's judgment. The methodology adapts one of the statistical approaches used in the statistical pattern recognition and classification approach (Fukunaga, 1990; Riply, 1996). Statistical pattern recognition and classification theory is known as a methodology for assignment of a physical object or event to one of several predetermined categories. Having a computer recognize handwritten letters or describe the shape of a figure has been one of the most popular applications of this theory. Predetermined categories correspond to knowledge states in our context. In this chapter, we discuss the generation of knowledge states.

4.1   More About Attribute Space and Item Response Space

In Chapter 3, we discussed the identities 0 and 1 in Boolean algebra. For example, a Boolean algebra generated from a Q matrix (3×5), given below, has the identity elements 0 and 1. Let us repeat briefly an excerpt of the discussion given in Chapter 3 here. You may also skip to the next section without loss of understanding.

Review of Foundations in Boolean Algebra

Suppose we have a Q matrix of five items with three attributes, given below.

Q' =	Item 1 (i1)	Item 2 (i2)	Item 3 (i3)	Item 4 (i4)	Item 5 (i5)
A_1	1	0	1	0	1
A_2	0	1	0	0	1
A_3	0	1	1	1	1

Three row vectors correspond to attributes A_1, A_2, and A_3 for given items i1 through i5 and can also be expressed set theoretically: $A_1 = (1\ 0\ 1\ 0\ 1)$

corresponds to set $A_1 = \{1, 3, 5\}$, $A_2 = (0\ 1\ 0\ 0\ 1)$ to $A_2 = \{2, 5\}$, and $A_3 = (0\ 1\ 1\ 1\ 1)$ to $A_3 = \{2, 3, 4, 5\}$.

The union set of A_1 and A_2, $\{1, 2, 3, 5\}$, corresponds to the addition of $A_1 + A_2 = (1\ 1\ 1\ 0\ 1)$ in terms of element-wise Boolean addition. Boolean addition is defined by $1 + 1 = 1$, $1 + 0 = 1$, $0 + 1 = 1$, and $0 + 0 = 0$.

Definition of Boolean addition: $1 + 1 = 1$, $1 + 0 = 1$, $0 + 1 = 1$, and $0 + 0 = 0$.

The intersection of A_1 and A_2, $\{5\}$, corresponds to the product of $A_1 \times A_2 = (0\ 0\ 0\ 0\ 1)$ in terms of element-wise Boolean multiplication of 0 and 1. Boolean multiplication follows the rules $0 \times 0 = 0$, $1 \times 0 = 0$, $0 \times 1 = 0$, and $1 \times 1 = 1$.

Definition of Boolean multiplication: $0 \times 0 = 0$, $1 \times 0 = 0$, $0 \times 1 = 0$, and $1 \times 1 = 1$.

Property 4.1: The union set of A_1 and A_2 corresponds to the element-wise Boolean addition of A_1 and A_2. The intersection of A_1 and A_2 corresponds to the element-wise multiplication of A_1 and A_2.

It is clear that these operations satisfy the commutative laws, associative laws, and distribution laws. The complement of A_k is A'_k, whose elements are obtained by switching the elements of A_k to the opposite; thus, complements are $A_1' = (0\ 1\ 0\ 1\ 0)$, $A'_2 = (1\ 0\ 1\ 1\ 0)$, and $A'_3 = (1\ 0\ 0\ 0\ 0)$.

Definition of complement of A_j: The complement of A_k is A'_k, whose elements are obtained by switching the elements of A_k to the opposite.

It is also clear that $A_k + A'_k$ is equal to 1.

Property 4.2: Boolean addition of A_k and its complement becomes 1. $A_k + A'_k = 1$.

If A_k, $k = 1, \ldots, K$ are the row vectors of such a general incidence matrix (Q matrix), and L_A is a set of sets of the attribute vectors, then L_A becomes a sublattice of RL, which is derived from a set of all the response patterns.

A subset L_A of RL is called a *sublattice*, if it is closed with respect to the binary compositions $\cap$ and $\cup$. A *Boolean algebra* is a lattice with 1 and 0, in which the distribution law is satisfied and the complement of an element is defined. Further, L_A is called a *subring* if any of the elements A and B in L_A, addition (+) and multiplication (×), are defined and closed. Property 4.1 shows that L_A becomes a subring of RL.

Property 4.3: A set L_A of sets of row vectors of an incidence matrix Q is a Boolean algebra with respect to the element-wise Boolean addition and multiplication of 0 and 1.

Element-wise Boolean addition and multiplication of any two attribute vectors satisfy the associative laws and distribution laws with respect to the example shown below:

$$(0 + 1) \times 0 = 1 \times 0 = 0 \text{ and } (0 \times 1) + 0 = 0 + 0 = 0$$
$$(0 + 1) \times 1 = 1 \times 1 = 1 \text{ and } (0 \times 1) + 1 = 0 + 1 = 1$$
$$(0 + 1) + 0 = 0 + (1 + 0) \text{ and } (0 \times 1) \times 1 = 0 \times (1 \times 1)$$

Further, L_A satisfies $0' = 1$ and hence $1' = 0$; thus, L_A is a Boolean algebra. If any elements of L_A, $\mathbf{A}_k + \mathbf{A}_l$, is defined by element-wise Boolean operations of $+$ and $\times$, then any elements $\mathbf{A}_k$ and $\mathbf{A}_l$ of L_A satisfy the lattice conditions given below:

l_1 $\mathbf{A}_k + \mathbf{A}_l = \mathbf{A}_l + \mathbf{A}_k$ and $\mathbf{A}_k \times \mathbf{A}_l = \mathbf{A}_l \times \mathbf{A}_k$

l_2 $(\mathbf{A}_k + \mathbf{A}_l) + \mathbf{A}_m = \mathbf{A}_k + (\mathbf{A}_l + \mathbf{A}_m)$ and $(\mathbf{A}_k \times \mathbf{A}_l) \times \mathbf{A}_m = \mathbf{A}_k \times (\mathbf{A}_l \times \mathbf{A}_m)$

l_3 $\mathbf{A}_k + \mathbf{A}_k = \mathbf{A}_k$ and $\mathbf{A}_k \times \mathbf{A}_k = \mathbf{A}_k$

l_4 $(\mathbf{A}_k + \mathbf{A}_l) \times \mathbf{A}_k = \mathbf{A}_k$ and $(\mathbf{A}_l \times \mathbf{A}_m) + \mathbf{A}_l = \mathbf{A}_l$

Let us define the identities **0** and **1**:

Definition of identities 0 and 1: If for any $\mathbf{A}_k$, $\mathbf{A}_k + \mathbf{0} = \mathbf{0} + \mathbf{A}_k = \mathbf{A}_k$, and $\mathbf{A}_k \times \mathbf{1} = \mathbf{1} \times \mathbf{A}_k = \mathbf{A}_k$, then **0** and **1** are called identities with respect to addition and multiplication, respectively. They are given by

$$\mathbf{0} = \prod_{k=1}^{K} A_k \quad \text{and} \quad \mathbf{1} = \sum_{k=1}^{K} A_k \tag{4.1}$$

Property 4.4: The complement $\mathbf{A}'_k$ is defined by $\mathbf{A}_k + \mathbf{A}'_k = \mathbf{1}$ and $\mathbf{A}_k \times \mathbf{A}'_k = \mathbf{0}$ with element-wise Boolean operations of $+$ and $\times$. The distribution laws are also satisfied as shown above, that is, $\mathbf{A}_k \times (\mathbf{A}_l + \mathbf{A}_m) = \mathbf{A}_k \times \mathbf{A}_l + \mathbf{A}_k \times \mathbf{A}_m$; therefore, L_A becomes a Boolean algebra.

In the example of our 3×5 incidence matrix, the elements 0 and 1 are given by

$$\mathbf{0} = (0\ 0\ 0\ 0\ 1) \text{ and } \mathbf{1} = (1\ 1\ 1\ 1\ 1)$$

Example 4.1

$$Q' = \begin{vmatrix} 1 & 0 & 1 & 0 & 1 \\ 0 & 1 & 0 & 0 & 1 \\ 0 & 1 & 1 & 1 & 1 \end{vmatrix}$$

$0 = (0\ 0\ 0\ 0\ 1)$, $1 = (1\ 1\ 1\ 1\ 1)$, and the complements are $\mathbf{A}'_1 = (0\ 1\ 0\ 1\ 1)$, $\mathbf{A}'_2 = (1\ 0\ 1\ 1\ 1)$, and $\mathbf{A}_3 = (1\ 0\ 0\ 0\ 1)$.

Useful Applications of Cognitively Diagnostic Assessment in Boolean Algebra

The final part of Chapter 3 and the previous section have established the foundation of Boolean algebra for L_A, where L_A is a set of subsets of the column vectors of a Q matrix $\{A_k\}$. Further, L_A is not only a Boolean algebra but also a ring. Computations in psychometrics and statistics are built upon a set of real numbers, and we use commutative law, associative law, distribution law, identity law, and the law of complementation in the real numbers. Because a set of real numbers is a ring, we take advantage of these convenient properties of real numbers without realizing the foundations of mathematics. In other words, because the Q-matrix theory is built on Boolean variables, and not on the real numbers, it is extremely important to clarify the mathematical foundation of L_A. Once it is clarified that L_A is a ring like the set of real numbers, one can use the same advantages of real numbers for L_A.

Presented below are several extremely useful properties, which aid in the understanding of a variety of information that a Q matrix implicitly contains.

Property 4.5: L_A is a subset of all possible response patterns and is closed with respect to the Boolean operations.

Addition and multiplication of two real numbers are also real numbers. This property assures us that we can add and multiply two elements in L_A safely, and we are still talking about L_A.

The identity Q matrix is a special case: The number of items and the number of attributes are the same, and each item includes a different attribute; however, in this case, a test becomes very easy and unrealistic. Many difficult problems involve several different attributes.

Property 4.6: If $\mathbf{Q}$ is the $n \times n$ identity matrix, then $L_A = RL$.

Because the Q matrix is identity, n attribute vectors (the column vectors of the Q matrix) are unit vectors, that is, $e1 = (1\ 0\ ...\ 0)$, $e2 = (0\ 1\ 0\ ...\ 0)$, $e3 = (0\ 0\ 1\ 0\ ...)$, ... $en = (0\ 0\ 0,\ ...\ 0\ 1)$. This is the basis of the item space with n dimensions, and any response patterns can be expressed by $\sum s_j ej$, where s_j is the item score of item j.

Property 4.7: If $\mathbf{A}_k \geq \mathbf{A}_l$, then $\mathbf{A}_k + \mathbf{A}_l = \mathbf{A}_k$ and $\mathbf{A}_k \times \mathbf{A}_l = \mathbf{A}_l$.

Because the partial order is defined by set theoretic inclusion relation, A_k is included in more items than A_l is, and the items including A_l are a subset of the items including A_k; therefore, the union of A_k and A_l equals the larger set A_k, and their intersection becomes the smaller A_l. Example 4.2 explains this relation with the Q matrix in Example 4.1

Example 4.2

Because $A_3 \geq A_2$, $A_2 + A_3 = A_3$ and $A_2 \times A_3 = A_2$.

Property 4.8: If $A_k \geq A_l$, then $A'_k \leq A'_l$, $(A_k + A_l)' = A'_k$ and $(A_k \times A_l)' = A'_l$.

In Example 4.2, $A_3 \geq A_2$ means $A_3 = (01111) \geq A_2 = (01001)$, and $A_3' = (10001)$ and $A'_2 = (10111)$, so $A'_3 \leq A'_2$ $(A_3 + A_2)' = (01111) = A'_3$ and $(A_k \times A_l)' = (01001) = A'_l$.

Property 4.9: If **Q** is a Kxn lower triangle matrix (or Guttman scale matrix), then L_A becomes the set of K row vectors.

If **Q** is a Guttman scale matrix, then the row vectors are totally ordered, $A_1 \leq A_2 \leq \cdots \leq A_K$. For any **k** and **l** like $k \geq l$, or equivalently $A_k \geq A_l$, we have the relation, $A_k + A_l = A_k$ and $A_k \times A_l = A_l$ from Property 4.7. Moreover, the identity 1 will be A'_k and the identity 0 will be A_l.

Any Q matrices having this form are often seen in attitude tests where measures are coded by ratings. Models such as Samejimàs (1972) graded response model or Masters' (1982) partial credit model will be suitable to this form of incidence matrices. These models were developed to measure an ordered trait. For such a trait, linearly ordered levels or categories within an item exist. Table 3.2 showed a Q matrix coded for the SAT Mathematics test by a group of item developers and mathematics educators. The matrix is not obviously a Guttman scale matrix.

The following example shows a Guttman scale matrix in a fraction addition problem.

Example 4.3

Let us consider three problems in fraction addition problems:

1. Add 2/3 and 2/3, then reduce the answer to its simplest form.
2. Add 1/3 and 1/3.
3. What is the common denominator of 1/3 and 1/5?

Then the attributes are as follows:

A_1: Simplify to the simplest form.
A_2: Get the numerator.
A_3: Get the common denominator.

The transposed Q matrix and Q matrix are as follows:

$$\mathbf{Q'} = \begin{array}{c} \\ A_1 \\ A_2 \\ A_3 \end{array} \begin{array}{ccc} i1 & i2 & i3 \\ \hline 1 & 0 & 0 \\ 1 & 1 & 0 \\ 1 & 1 & 1 \end{array} \qquad \mathbf{Q} = \begin{array}{c} \\ i1 \\ i2 \\ i3 \end{array} \begin{array}{ccc} A_1 & A_2 & A_3 \\ \hline 1 & 1 & 1 \\ 0 & 1 & 1 \\ 0 & 0 & 1 \end{array}$$

There are three levels of performances: Levels 1, 2, and 3 (below). Moreover, we have $A_3 \geq A_2 \geq A_1$.

Level 1. Can do A_3.
Level 2. Can do A_3 and A_2.
Level 3. Can do all.

Property 4.10: The complement of the sum of $\mathbf{A_k}$ and $\mathbf{A_l}$ with respect to Boolean addition is the product of the complements of $\mathbf{A_k}$ and $\mathbf{A_l}$, $(\mathbf{A_k} + \mathbf{A_l})' = \mathbf{A'_k} \times \mathbf{A'_l}$.

Property 4.11: The complement of the product of $\mathbf{A_k}$ and $\mathbf{A_l}$ with respect to Boolean product is the sum of the complements of $\mathbf{A_k}$ and $\mathbf{A_l}$ (i.e., $(\mathbf{A_k} \times \mathbf{A_l})' = \mathbf{A_k}' + \mathbf{A_l}'$).

Definition: A chain is a subset of L_A in which all the elements are totally ordered with respect to $\geq$ or $\leq$.

Because L_A is a partially ordered set, there is more than one chain. Any Q matrices with a Guttman scale have only one linearly ordered set of attributes, like the previous example given after Property 4.9.

A Network of Attributes

The order relation is not applicable to two different elements coming from two different chains. Moreover, two chains may contain the same elements in common; therefore, connecting the elements in chains would result in a tree graph (Tatsuoka, 1990). The following example shows how the relation works.

Example 4.4

A large-scale state assessment has been analyzed, and its Q matrix was developed. The Q matrix in Figure 4.1 is excerpted from a large Q matrix of 100 items with 27 attributes, and it includes only three content attributes,

	a1	b21	b29	t40	a2	a4	b23	t44	t41			
item	1	2	3	4	5	6	7	8	9	sum	pval	attribute invovement
1	1	0	0	1	0	0	0	0	0	2	.31	{1 4}
2	1	0	0	1	1	0	1	0	0	4	.33	{1 4 5 7}
3	0	0	0	0	1	0	0	0	0	1	.51	{5}
4	0	0	0	0	0	1	0	0	0	1	.63	{6}
5	1	0	1	1	1	1	1	1	1	8	.60	{1 3 4 5 6 7 8}
6	1	0	1	0	0	0	0	0	0	2	.53	{1 3}
7	1	0	1	0	0	1	0	1	1	5	.42	{1 3 6 8 9}
8	1	1	1	0	0	0	0	0	0	3	.60	{1 2 3}
9	0	0	0	0	1	1	1	0	0	3	.88	{5 6 7}
10	1	0	0	0	0	1	0	1	1	4	.40	{1 6 8 9}
11	1	1	1	1	0	1	0	1	0	6	.42	{1 2 3 4 6 8}
12	1	0	0	0	0	1	0	1	0	3	.70	{1 6 8}
13	1	0	0	1	1	1	0	1	1	6	.45	{1 4 5 6 8 9}
14	1	0	0	1	1	1	1	1	1	7	.38	{1 4 5 6 7 8 9}
15	1	0	0	0	0	0	0	0	0	1	.24	{1}
16	1	0	0	1	1	1	0	1	0	5	.45	{1 4 5 6 8}

Contents: Knowledge of concepts, operations, properties, relations	
a1	Mixed and simple fraction numbers, concept, operations, relations %
a2	Geometry, areas of shapes, angles, relation of angles
a4	Geometry, symmetric, parallel, intersections
Special and action skills	
b21	Conversion of numbers, to make comparable, to convert mixed to decimals
b23	Compare two or three geometric figures,
b24	Comprehend geometric figures
b29	Understand percentages as decimal or fractions
Thinking skills	
t40	Quantitative reading of "not," less than, greater than, must be, at least, "off from
t41	Translating words into arithmetic relationship,"implicitly req. %"
t44	Use reasoning to find the next step or get answers

FIGURE 4.1

Excerpt from a Q matrix analyzed for some state assessment and the set theoretic representation of column and row vectors with description of attributes.

four special skills, and three mathematical thinking skills. They are given in Figure 4.1.

The column vectors of the Q matrix in Figure 4.1 are rewritten by set theoretic expressions because the order relation can be understood intuitively. Attribute b21 is expressed by {8 11}, and items 8 and 11 involve attribute b29, so b29 ⊇ b21. We rewrite it by the order notation "b29 ≥ b21." Similarly, we get five chains below.

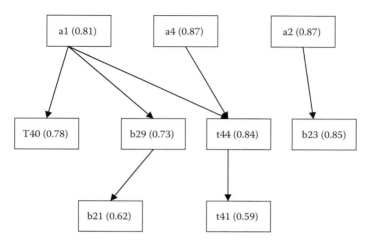

FIGURE 4.2
Partially ordered network of attributes with their estimated attribute mastery probabilities,
N = 150,000 sixth graders.

a1 ⊇ b29 ⊇ b21 or a1 ≥ b29 ≥ b21,

a1≥ t44 ≥ t41,

a1 ≥ t40,

a2 ≥ b23, and

a4 ≥ t44 ≥ t41.

These chains share some attributes, so we can connect them and draw a partially ordered network in Figure 4.2.

Some chains may be interpreted, for example, "The items from content geometry dealing with symmetric figures, parallel lines, and perimeter of shapes (a4) require reasoning (t44), and reasoning is connected to translation of verbal expressions to arithmetic relations (t41)"; or "The items involving attribute (a1) that deals with areas, angles, and relation of angles tend to require skills of percentages that also require conversion of numbers to comparable ones in this assessment."

Item Tree

This section will discuss the twin counterpart of a Boolean algebra L_I that is a set of subsets of row vectors of a Q matrix with the same Boolean operations and order structure as L_A. All properties discussed in Chapter 3 and the subsection, A Network of Attributes, will be applicable to L_I

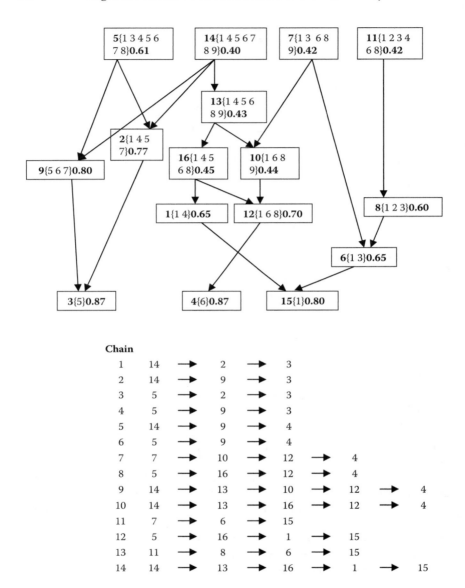

FIGURE 4.3
An item tree of the Q matrix given in Figure 4.1. Each box has item with boldface, row vector corresponding to the item number, and proportion correct computed from N = 150,000 sixth graders, and the chains included in the item tree.

without loss of generality. An item tree is especially useful in item construction and test assembly for cognitive diagnostic assessment. How it is useful will be explained in Chapter 4.

Let us use Example 4.4, and the Q matrix in Figure 4.1. We rewrite 16 items with set theoretic notations of involved attributes in the figure. Item 1 involves attributes a1(mixed numbers, fractions, concept, operations, and percentages) and b21 (conversion of numbers to make comparable), and the above list writes attributes with assigned numbers in the Q matrix. Item 2 involves a1, t40 (quantitative reading), a2 (geometry, areas of shapes, angles, and relation of angles), and b23 (compare two or three geometric figures). By looking into set theoretic inclusion relations between two items, one can create chains or a totally ordered sequence of items. There are 14 chains shown in Figure 4.3.

These 14 chains can be connected through common items and can be developed to a partially ordered network in Figure 4.3. The boxes in the network given in Figure 4.3 is first item j with boldface, the attributes involved in this item inside of the parentheses, and then item difficulties. Tatsuoka (1990) called it an "item tree" and introduced some interesting relationships between item difficulties and the number of attributes involved in items. This item tree also shows that the items located in the upper part of the tree are more difficult than the items located in the lower part of the network. Because this Q matrix is only an excerpt from the original larger Q matrix, the multiplicative relationship of attribute mastery probabilities that would be closer to the item proportion correct is not very clear from the example, but some tendencies are still observable.

The next section introduces a new function by which all possible ideal item score patterns (or all possible states of knowledge) are obtainable from an incidence matrix and gives their descriptive meanings. The description of states is given by a list of combinatorial *can* or *cannot* attributes.

4.2   Boolean Description Function (BDF): Determination of Ideal Response Patterns as Error-Free States of Knowledge and Capabilities

Let L_A be a sublattice and also Boolean algebra whose elements consist of various combinations of K independent attributes. Let A_k be the kth row vector of the incidence matrix Q. Addition of A_k and A_l, $A_k + A_l$ with respect to Boolean addition + defined in L_1 produces the binary item pattern in which the elements of one indicate that their corresponding items are included in the union set of A_k and A_l. The sum of any attributes, A_{kg}, belongs to L_K. $A_k \times A_l$ with respect to the Boolean multiplication operation $\times$ contains 1's for the items that belong to both attribute vectors A_k and A_l.

Let e_k, $k = 1, \ldots, K$ be the unit vectors of K-dimensional space. $\{e_k, k = 1, \ldots, K\}$ is called *basis*. Any vector space has basis, and any element in the space can be expressed by a linear combination of basis. There are several interesting relationships between the K-dimensional unit vector e_k and A_k. Because e_k is a vector with 1 at the kth element and zeros elsewhere, the mapping e_k to A_k is one-to-one and the expression "onto" is every A_k can be expressed by a linear combination of basis, e_j, $j = 1, \ldots, K$. (Hoffman & Kumze, 1971). In other words, the following property holds:

Property 4.12: The unit vector e_k of the latent variable space uniquely corresponds to attribute vector A_k, and the Boolean sum of e_k and conversely e_k corresponds to the sum of A_k, A_k. Similarly, the Boolean product of the elements of e_k, e_k uniquely corresponds to that of A_k, A_k.

One can always find a linear transformation T to orthogonalize K attribute vectors. This is an important notion not only in the theory of linear algebra (Hoffman & Kumze, 1971) but also in rule space methodology. RSM is a classification space, and later we have to compute multivariate covariance matrices and their inversions for individuals. Orthogonalized rule space coordinates will help computational time tremendously because a large-scale assessment such as the Preliminary Scholastic Aptitude Test (PSAT) has to process a few million students in a short period of time.

Tatsuoka (1991) discussed "atoms" in L_A that can be generated by the elements of L_A as follows:

$$A_s = (\cap A_k) \cap (\cap A'_k)$$

for all possible subsets of J, $J = (1, 2, \ldots, K)$. The set of atoms is the basis of L_A, and hence any element B of L_A can be expressed by the atoms. Considering atoms has a great advantage in investigating the mathematical properties of L_A, but the interpretability of attributes will be diminished.

Hypotheses as Combinatorial Combinations of Attribute Patterns

Because our goal is to draw some inferences about unobservable latent variables from observable information of item response patterns, it is necessary to introduce a series of hypotheses that convert the latent but interpretable information into observable and interpretable information. The observable information in our context is obtainable only from item responses.

Definition: A hypothesis H_k is the statement that *one cannot do attribute A_k correctly but can do the rest of the attributes.* H_k will produce the item pattern that is the complement of A_k and represent an interpretable state of knowledge.

H_k is *cannot do A_k but can do the rest of the attributes.* Or, equivalently, $H_k = (h_1, h_2, ..., h_k, ..., h_K)$ where $h_k = 1$, and $h_j = 0$ for $j \neq k$.

It is clear that if a student cannot perform A_k correctly but can do the rest of the attributes right, then the items involving attribute A_k will have the score of zero but the items not involving A_k will have the score of ones.

Definition: The hypothesis $H_{k1+...kl}$ is *one cannot do attributes $A_{k1}, A_{k2}, ..., A_{kl}$ correctly but can do the rest of the attributes.*

H_{K1+k2} is *cannot do A_{k1} and A_{k2}, but can do the remaining attributes.* Or, equivalently, $H_k = (h_1, h_2, ..., h_k, ..., h_K)$, where $h_{k1} = 1$ and $h_{k2} = 1$, but $h_{kj} = 0$ for $k_j \neq k_1, k_2$.

We can develop 2^K hypotheses from K attributes by taking combinatorial combinations of K elements in vectors H_m, $m = 1, ..., 2^K$. A set of H_m is equivalent to the attribute space introduced in Chapter 3 using Property 4.13.

Boolean Descriptive Function

We now have a set of hypotheses expressed by K-dimensional vectors with psychological interpretation, because if jth element of a vector is 1, then a student can do attribute A_j; if it is 0, then the student cannot do attribute A_j.

Definition: A hypothesis H_k is called a *knowledge state*, and a set of hypotheses is called a *knowledge space*. An element of the knowledge space is an *attribute pattern*. Hereafter, we will call H_k an *attribute pattern k*, and knowledge space an *attribute space*.

A knowledge space is still unobservable, and everything is in a black box. If researchers have already developed a Q matrix with K attributes and n items, then the Boolean description function enables us to establish a correspondence between the attribute space of K attributes and the item score patterns of n items.

Example 4.5

Let us consider the same Q matrix we used in Example 4.1. There are three attributes, so we can have $2^3 = 8$ binary attribute patterns.

$$
Q' = \begin{array}{c} \\ A1 \\ A2 \\ A3 \end{array}
\begin{array}{ccccc}
i1 & i2 & i3 & i4 & i5 \\
1 & 0 & 1 & 0 & 1 \\
0 & 1 & 0 & 0 & 1 \\
0 & 1 & 1 & 1 & 1
\end{array}
\qquad \text{where } \mathbf{A2 < A3}
$$

Attribute patterns are given below:

1. (1 1 1) can do A1, A2, and A3.
2. (1 1 0) cannot do A3 but can do A1 and A2.
3. (1 0 1) cannot do A2 but can do A1 and A3.
4. (0 1 1) cannot do A1 but can do A2 and A3.
5. (1 0 0) cannot do A2 and A3 but can do A1.
6. (0 1 0) cannot do A1 and A3 but can do A2.
7. (0 0 1) cannot do A1 and A2 but can do A3.
8. (0 0 0) cannot do A1, A2, and A3.

Now let us consider attribute pattern 2, (1 1 0), in which A3 is not mastered. Item 1 involves 1 only, and A_1 is *can do*, so the score of i1 will be 1. Item 2 involves A2 and A3, but A3 is *cannot do*, so the score of i2 will be 0 because we assumed item j becomes 1 if all attributes involved in item j are mastered. i3 has the vector of (1 0 1), which involves A1 and A3 so the score of i3 will be 0. Item i4 is (0 0 1), and because A3 is *cannot*, the score of i4 will be 0. Item i5 involves all attributes, so the score of i5 will be 0. In summary, items involving *cannot* attributes have the score of 0. Let us now define Boolean description function.

Definition of Boolean description function (BDF): A mapping function from an attribute space to item patterns defined by the following manner is called a *Boolean description function* (BDF):

$$
\begin{cases}
X_j = 0 & \text{if } q_{mj} = 1 \text{ and } A_m \text{ is cannot do for at least one attribute } A_m \\
& \text{among the attributes involving in item j} \\
X_j = 1 & \text{if all attributes involving in item j are can do.}
\end{cases}
$$

TABLE 4.1

Boolean Descriptive Function: Attribute Patterns and Ideal Item Score Patterns

Hypothesis	Interpretation	Attribute Pattern	Ideal Item Score Pattern
H_0	Cannot do any	(0 0 0)	(0 0 0 0 0)
H_1	Cannot do A_1, can do A_2 and A_3	(0 1 1)	(0 1 0 1 0)
H_2	Cannot do A_2, can do A_1 and A_3	(1 0 1)	(1 0 1 1 0)
H_3	Cannot do A_3, can do A_1 and A_2	(1 1 0)	(1 0 0 0 0)
H_{1+2}	Cannot do A_1 and A_2, can do A_3	(0 0 1)	(0 0 0 1 0)
H_{1+3}	Cannot do A_1 and A_3, can do A_2	(0 1 0)	(0 0 0 0 0) (= H_0)
H_{2+3}	Cannot do A_2 and A_3, can do A_1	(1 0 0)	(1 0 0 0 0) (= H_3)
H_{1+2+3}	Can do A_1, A_2, and A_3	(1 1 1)	(1 1 1 1 1)

Knowledge States

A BDF determines knowledge states from a given Q matrix by assuming all possible combinations of "can do and cannot do" of all attributes. The examples of these hypotheses are listed with a simple example of 3 attributes and 5 items in Table 4.1 Applying H_i to the Q matrix and using the BDF in Definition 4.8, one can generate an item pattern from an attribute pattern of H_i.

Definition of ideal item score patterns, we call this generated item pattern from H_i and DBF, ideal item score parttern: The images of a BDF from the attribute patterns are called *ideal item score patterns*.

Let us consider the Q matrix (3 × 5) in the example given in the previous section. Table 4.1 shows eight hypotheses consisting of all combinations of three attributes with respect to *can do* and *cannot do*. Each attribute pattern corresponds to an ideal item score pattern. Each attribute pattern and its corresponding ideal item score pattern together are called a *knowledge state*. In other words, a knowledge state can be an attribute pattern or, equivalently, its corresponding ideal item score pattern. Hypotheses associate with attribute patterns, in which 1 means *can do* and 0 means *cannot do*.

Figure 4.4 represents this important relationship. Because knowledge states are impossible to observe, we make correspondence between latent but interpretable attribute space and observable item space by a BDF and Q matrix. When a student's item response comes in, we take the ideal item score pattern most closely matched to the input from the predetermined list of ideal item score patterns. Then we will get the corresponding attribute pattern that is interpretable. In other words, if **X** is an observable response pattern of a test, then by examining which ideal item score pattern most closely matches a predetermined list of ideal item score patterns, we can make an inference regarding which attribute pattern most likely represents **X**'s underlying performance.

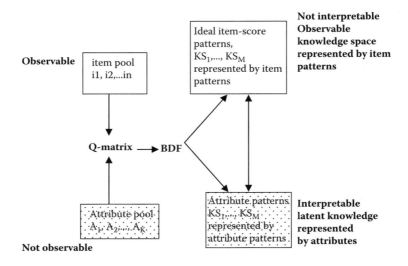

FIGURE 4.4
Correspondence between latent knowledge states and observable knowledge states.

A BDF constructs a bridge that connects unobservable and observable worlds. This connection enables us to make inferences about the underlying cognitive processing and knowledge influencing the performance of observable item responses. This relationship is explained graphically in Figure 4.4. A computer program, BUGLIB, was developed by Varadi, Tatsuoka, and Tatsuoka (1992), which computes Boolean descriptive functions and constructs the knowledge space in Figure 4.4 (Tatsuoka & Hayashi, 2001).

4.3 Prerequisite Relationships in a Q Matrix

A close examination of attribute patterns and their corresponding ideal item score patterns reveals that the correspondence between two spaces is not one-to-one. In the subsection, A Case When Attributes Are Lineary Ordered, we will discuss this problem.

A Case When There Is No Relation Among the Attributes

Suppose there are four attributes in a domain of testing, and the universal set of items 2^4 is constructed. None of the row vectors in its incidence matrix Q of 16 items is included in any others.

$$Q(4 \times 16) = \begin{array}{cccccccccccccccc} 1 & 2 & 3 & 4 & 5 & 6 & 7 & 8 & 9 & 10 & 11 & 12 & 13 & 14 & 15 & 16 \\ 0 & 1 & 0 & 0 & 0 & 1 & 1 & 1 & 0 & 0 & 0 & 1 & 1 & 1 & 0 & 1 \\ 0 & 0 & 1 & 0 & 0 & 1 & 0 & 0 & 1 & 1 & 0 & 1 & 1 & 0 & 1 & 1 \\ 0 & 0 & 0 & 1 & 0 & 0 & 1 & 0 & 1 & 0 & 1 & 1 & 0 & 1 & 1 & 1 \\ 0 & 0 & 0 & 0 & 1 & 0 & 0 & 1 & 0 & 1 & 1 & 0 & 1 & 1 & 1 & 1 \end{array} \begin{array}{l} \\ A_1 \\ A_2 \\ A_3 \\ A_4 \end{array}$$

The hypothesis "This subject cannot do A_1 but can do $A_1, \ldots, A_{1-1}$, $A_{1+1}, \ldots, A_k$ correctly" corresponds to the attribute pattern $(1 \ldots 1\,0\,1 \ldots 1)$. If we denote this attribute pattern as H_k, then it will be mapped to the item pattern X_1 by a BDF, where $x_j = 1$ if item j does not involve A_k, and $x_j = 0$ if item j involves A_k for $j = 1, \ldots, n$. Sixteen possible attribute patterns and the images of a BDF, 16 ideal item score patterns, are summarized in Table 4.2. If we consider, for instance, attribute response pattern No. 10, which indicates that a subject cannot do A_1 and A_3 correctly but can do A_2 and A_4, then from the incidence matrix $Q(4 \times 16)$ shown above, we see that the scores of items 2, 4, 6, 7, 8, 9, 11, 12, 13, 14, and 16 must become zero, whereas the scores of 1, 3, 5, and 10 must be 1.

Table 4.2 indicates that any response to the 16 items can be classified into one of the 16 predetermined groups. They are the universal set of knowledge and capability states that are derived from the incidence matrix $Q(4 \times 16)$ by applying the properties of Boolean algebra. In other words, 16 ideal item patterns exhaust all the possible patterns logically compatible with the constraints imposed by the incidence matrix $Q(4 \times 16)$. By examining

TABLE 4.2

A List of 16 Ideal Item Response Patterns Obtained From 16 Attribute Response Patterns by a BDF

Attribute Response Patterns	Ideal Item Response Patterns
1. 0000	1000000000000000
2. 1000	1100000000000000
3. 0100	1010000000000000
4. 0010	1001000000000000
5. 0001	1000100000000000
6. 1100	1110010000000000
7. 1010	1101001000000000
8. 1001	1100100100000000
9. 0110	1011000010000000
10. 0101	1010100001000000
11. 0011	1001100000100000
12. 1110	1111011010010000
13. 1101	1110110101001000
14. 1011	1101101100100100
15. 0111	1011100011100010
16. 1111	1111111111111111

and comparing a subject's responses with these 16 ideal item patterns, one can infer the subject's performance on the unobservable attributes. As long as these attributes represent the true task analysis, response patterns to the above 16 items, which are different from the 16 ideal item patterns, are regarded as fuzzy patterns or perturbations resulting from lapses or slips on one or more items, reflecting random errors.

A Case When There Are Prerequisite Relations Among the Attributes

So far, we have not assumed any relations among the four attributes in Table 4.2; however, it is often the case that some attributes are directly related to one another.

Suppose A_1 is a prerequisite of A_2, A_2 is a prerequisite of A_3, and A_1 is also a prerequisite of A_4. If we assume that a subject cannot do A_1 correctly, then A_2 and A_3 cannot be correct because they require knowledge of A_1 as a prerequisite. Let us consider the following example:

$$Q(4 \times 11) = \begin{array}{r} & 1\ 2\ 3\ 4\ 5\ 6\ 7\ 8\ 9\ 10\ 11 \\ A_1 & 1\ 1\ 0\ 0\ 1\ 1\ 1\ 1\ 0\ \ 1\ \ 1 \\ A_2 & 0\ 1\ 0\ 0\ 0\ 0\ 1\ 1\ 0\ \ 0\ \ 1 \\ A_3 & 0\ 0\ 1\ 0\ 1\ 0\ 1\ 0\ 1\ \ 1\ \ 1 \\ A_4 & 0\ 0\ 0\ 1\ 0\ 1\ 0\ 1\ 1\ \ 1\ \ 1 \end{array}$$

There is the set theoretic inclusion relationship among A_1, A_2 by $A_1 \supseteq A_2$ in $Q(4 \times 11)$. The reachability matrix of $Q(4 \times 11)$ indicates this is the only relation existing in $A(4 \times 11)$ given above. Hand calculation yielded 11 ideal item score patterns corresponding to the 16 attribute patterns.

Table 4.3 shows that the second element of attribute patterns A_2 cannot be determined uniquely when the dominant attribute A_1 is

TABLE 4.3

A List of Attribute Patterns and Corresponding Ideal Item Score Patterns

Knowledge States	Attribute Patterns	Ideal Item Score Patterns
1	1 1 0 1	1 1 1 1 1 1 1 1 1 1 1
2	1 1 1 0	1 1 1 0 1 0 1 0 0 0 0
3	1 1 0 1	1 1 0 1 0 1 0 1 0 0 0
4	1 1 0 0	1 1 0 0 0 0 0 0 0 0 0
5	1 0 1 1	1 0 1 1 1 1 0 0 1 1 0
6	1 0 1 0	1 0 1 0 1 0 0 0 0 0 0
7	1 0 0 1	1 0 0 1 0 1 0 0 0 0 0
8	1 0 0 0	1 0 0 0 0 0 0 0 0 0 0
9	0 * 1 1	0 0 1 1 0 0 0 0 1 0 0
10	0 * 1 0	0 0 1 0 0 0 0 0 0 0 0
11	0 * 0 1	0 0 0 1 0 0 0 0 0 0 0
12	0 * 0 0	0 0 0 0 0 0 0 0 0 0 0

*Can be 1 or 0.

hypothesized as *cannot do.* (0 1 1 1) and (0 0 1 1) correspond to a single ideal item score pattern (0 0 1 1 0 0 0 0 1 0 0). Similarly, two attribute patterns (0 1 1 0) and (0 0 1 0) correspond to the ideal item score pattern (0 0 1 0 0 0 0 0 0 0 0).

4.4 Equivalent Classes of Attribute Patterns

When one of the degenerative relationships exists among attributes, then several different attribute patterns correspond to a single ideal item score pattern. These attribute patterns are "indeterminate" elements, and they form a module with respect to their corresponding single ideal item score patterns. In Property 4.13 (below), they are called *equivalent attribute patterns.* The ideal item score patterns resulting from the application of two different hypotheses, whose attribute patterns come from the same module, are always the same, and indeed there is a systematic relation when two hypotheses produce the same ideal item score pattern. Property 4.14, needless to say, implies that any element $\mathbf{A}_l$ smaller than $\mathbf{A}_k$ with respect to the order $\geq$ degenerates so that addition of $\mathbf{A}_k$ and $\mathbf{A}_l$ becomes $\mathbf{A}_k$. Because a BDF starts creating a series of hypotheses for assuming *can do* or *cannot do* of attributes, the dominant attribute $\mathbf{A}_k$ ordered directly by inclusion relations with others such as $\mathbf{A}_k \geq \mathbf{A}_l$ incapacitates the recessive attribute $\mathbf{A}_l$. If the hypothesis H_k (cannot do $\mathbf{A}_k$) is created, then either hypotheses H (cannot do $\mathbf{A}_k$ and cannot do $\mathbf{A}_l$) or H (cannot do $\mathbf{A}_k$ but can do $\mathbf{A}_l$) will not produce one-to-one correspondence between attribute patterns and ideal item score patterns. Let us restate Property 4.13 as a "degenerative" property with respect to BDF.

Degenerative Property

We have discussed earlier in Properties 4.7 and 4.8 that when two attributes are ordered, their addition and multiplication yield one of them, respectively. Let us call these properties *degenerative properties.*

Degenerative Property 4.14: If $\mathbf{A}_k \geq \mathbf{A}_l$, then $\mathbf{A}'_k \leq \mathbf{A}'_l$, $(\mathbf{A}_k + \mathbf{A}_l)' = \mathbf{A}'_k$ and $(\mathbf{A}_k \times \mathbf{A}_l)' = \mathbf{A}'_l$.

In other words, a BDF degenerates "receptive" attributes, so a number of attribute patterns having *cannot do or 0* for the dominant attribute correspond to a single ideal item score pattern. We call these attribute patterns *equivalent with respect to A_k* (Tatsuoka, 1991, 1993, 1995).

A Case When Three Attributes Are Linearly Ordered

Suppose we have a chain, $A_1 \geq A_2 \geq A_3$, with n items. From three attributes, eight attribute patterns can be created. If Y_k is the ideal item score pattern, then correspondence can be pictorially presented below. Modules 1 and 2 express two sets of equivalent attribute patterns with respect to a BDF. Attribute patterns (100) and (101) in Module 1 correspond to the ideal item score pattern Y_3, because A_2 is denied and is not *cannot do*, so A_3 becomes recessive. Attribute patterns (011), (010), (001), and (000) in Module 2 correspond to Y_3. This relation can be also explained by *cannot do A_1*, implying that A_2 and A_3 are smaller than A_1 and thus become recessive. In Module 2, there are four attribute patterns.

Degenerative Property 4.15: If Q' is a Guttman scale matrix, then the row vectors are totally ordered, $A_1 \leq A_2 \leq \cdots \leq A_K$.

For any k and l like $k \geq l$, $A_k + A_l = A_k$ and $A_k \times A_l = A_l$ from Property 4.15. Moreover, the identity 1 will be A_k, and 0 will be A_l. This case is described in Figure 4.5.

If none of the K attributes are related in terms of the prerequisite relationship; none of the row vectors are totally ordered by the inclusion relation in a Q matrix; and it is possible to construct a pool of $2^K - 1$ items, in which the items involve all $2^K - 1$ attribute mastery patterns, then we will have 2^K distinguishable attribute mastery patterns, and their corresponding 2^K ideal item response patterns will be different.

If one could construct K items whose **Q** matrix is a $K \times K$ identity matrix, then the 2^K attribute mastery patterns would correspond one-to-one to 2^K ideal item patterns, and hence the indeterminacy of attribute mastery patterns would not occur. It is almost impossible to construct K items for K attributes whose **Q** matrix is an identity matrix, because most questions usually involve at least two attributes (cognitive tasks) unless the questions are extremely easy and simple; consequently, **Q** matrices usually do not have very simple forms.

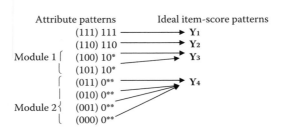

FIGURE 4.5
Modules of equivalent attribute patterns.

An Equivalent Class of Attribute Mastery Patterns

Suppose that the attribute mastery patterns α_1, ..., α_t are in the same module because of attribute(s) A_ks, and they correspond to the same ideal item response pattern R, as defined in the previous subsection, A Case When Three Attrbutes Are Linearly Ordered, and defined in K. Tatsuoka and Varadi (1989), Varadi, C. Tatsuoka, & K. Tatsuoka (1992). We will refer to them as Γ. Because the equivalent attribute mastery patterns are not distinguishable from their ideal item pattern, it is necessary to introduce a measure to differentiate the attribute mastery patterns in an equivalence class.

Let us define the maximum and minimum of Γ as follows:

α_{max} = when all indeterminate attribute(s) take(s) on the value 1

α_{min} = when all indeterminate attribute(s) take(s) on the value 0

Similarly, the average (or weighted average) $\bar{\alpha}$ of the indeterminate attributes in Γ, α, can be taken. It will allow us to choose either α_{max} or α_{min} as the need arises. These parameters can be chosen probabilistically to take the most plausible choice after the classification of all examinees is completed. The classification of examinees, as can be seen in the following section, is determined by item response patterns and knowledge states, which are expressed by ideal item response patterns, so indeterminate attributes do not influence the classification results. When an individually diagnosed result is to be used for remediation or curriculum guidance, the minimum, α_{min}, would be the most appropriate choice. When adaptive testing algorithms are to be developed, selection of an optimum subset of items so as to minimize the problem of attribute indeterminacy would be an important constraint. Tatsuoka (1991) discussed the importance of constructing items so as to minimize the problem of attribute indeterminacy.

Example 4.6

In Table 4.2, attribute mastery patterns 3, 9, 10, and 15 have the indeterminate attribute 2. The maximum, minimum, and average of these equivalent attribute patterns are as follows:

	Maximum	Minimum	Average	Weighted Average
3	0 1 0 0	0 0 0 0	0.5 0 0	0 w 0 0
9	0 1 1 0	0 0 1 0	0.5 1 0	0 w 1 0
10	0 1 0 1	0 0 0 1	0.5 0 1	0 w 0 1
15	0 1 1 1	0 0 1 1	0.5 1 1	0 w 1 1

where w is a number such as the mean value of attribute mastery probability of the individuals in a population, and it will be in [0,1].

A Scoring Matrix Associated With a Q Matrix

Binary Multiplicative Scoring Formula

Because a set of sets of attributes (or, equivalently, L_A) is Boolean algebra, which has been used widely in the theory of combinatorial circuits of electricity and electronics, unobservable performances of the attributes may be viewed as unobservable electric currents running through various switches if they are closed. A closed switch corresponds to an attribute that is answered correctly, and an open switch corresponds to an attribute that is answered incorrectly. All the switches in a circuit must be closed for the current to go through it. An item can be answered correctly if and only if all the attributes involved in the item can be answered correctly. This is an intuitive analogy between electricity and the cognitive processes of answering the items, whereas Boolean algebra, which is used for explaining various properties of electricity and combinatorial circuits, can be applied to explain the underlying cognitive processes of answering the items. With this analogy, the scoring formula will be defined as follows: Examinee i has the score of 1 on item j only when he or she uses every attribute involving item j correctly. In other words, score S_{ij} is defined as follows:

$$S_{ij} = 1 \text{ if and only if } p_{ikj} = 1 \text{ for all k such that } q_{kj} = 1$$

where i is an examinee, j is an item, k is an attribute, q_{kj} is the (k,j) element of a **Q** matrix, and p_{ikj} is the probability that examinee i will answer correctly attribute k involved in item j. Attribute mastery scores occur when $p_{ikj} = 1$. In this case, the elements of the scoring matrix **S** coincide with those in the **Q** matrix.

Additive Scoring Formula: Ideal Item Response Patterns for Partial Credit Scores

The items used in classroom assessments or performance assessments usually involve open-ended or constructed responses. Typical scoring rubrics for such items are partial credit, graded, or rating scores. In this section, we discuss the use of a Q-matrix theory for developing a scoring rubric.

Suppose a Q matrix for a test of constructed-response items is defined, and its scoring rubric is defined so as to take the number of right scores for the attributes for each item:

$$s_{ij} = \text{the number of correct attributes for which } q_{kj} = 1$$

For some other scoring rubrics, s_{ij} can be a weighted sum of numbers of right attributes, or in general some rational number between 0 and 1.

Suppose M is a l × k matrix of attribute patterns, where l is the number of possible attribute patterns for a Q matrix, and k is the number of attributes. Suppose G is a matrix of all possible ideal item score patterns, with order m × n, where m is the number of the ideal item score patterns, and n is the number of items. We assume that l = m. Let us consider the following hypothetical scores u_{lk}, l = 1, ..., L and k = 1, ..., K.

$$u_{lk} = \sum m_{lk} q_{kj}, \quad j = 1, ..., n$$

Then, u_{lk} is the same as the number of right attribute scores s_{lk} defined above, except that u_{lk} are scores for ideal item score patterns and not for examinees. But l is the index for the number of attribute patterns, whereas k is an attribute. Let us call the row vectors of matrix U *ideal item score patterns for partial credit scores*.

Completeness of Attributes in a Q Matrix

After we classify examinees into one of a predetermined set of knowledge states derived from a Q matrix, we may find that a high percentage of individuals could not be classified. We then may have to reconsider the appropriateness of the Q matrix for representing the underlying cognitive tasks of that domain, even if the Q matrix is sufficient. A sufficient Q matrix is not necessarily an *appropriate* Q matrix. If the Q matrix is a good cognitive model and it represents well the underlying cognitive processes for a population, then the classification rate would be very high. A set of attributes used in such a Q matrix is said to be *complete*. Dibello, Stout, and Roussos (1995) also discuss a complete Q matrix in their model. If our sufficient Q matrix is, indeed, a good cognitive model, and the classification rate is very high (say, 90% or more), then the classified examinees' item response patterns are converted to the attribute mastery patterns. We should be able to estimate density functions or conditional distributions of attributes. A cluster analysis, factor analysis, and/or analysis of influence networks could be applied to investigate further properties of attributes or their relationships.

4.5 Item Construction

The degenerative properties introduced in the previous subsection, Degenerative Property, suggest that it is necessary to develop an item construction method, by which useful and desired knowledge states for diagnosis will be created by a BDF from a given Q matrix. Understanding what knowledge states will be important to diagnose can be determined by a task analysis. In the following section, we discuss a procedure to develop a useful item pool for diagnosis.

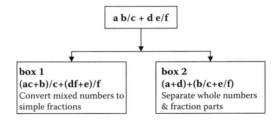

FIGURE 4.6
Task specification, part 1: two different methods in fraction addition problems.

Task Specification Charts and Attributes

If we would like to develop a fraction addition test, then teachers and domain experts draw a task specification chart.

Boxes 1 and 2 in Figure 4.6 present two different ways to add two mixed numbers, a b/c + d e/f: Box 2 represents Method B, by which a student separates the whole-number and fraction parts; and Box 1 represents Method A, by which a student converts mixed numbers to simple fractions. The two attributes are summarized in the boxes as *convert mixed numbers to simple fractions* and *separate whole numbers from fraction parts*.

Then, there are cases: Two denominators are the same number, and they are different numbers. A student must check this condition, and if the denominators are different, the student has to get the common denominator. After the common denominator is obtained, the student has to make equivalent fractions to add the numerators. Three more attributes are written in the boxes in the chart in Figure 4.7.

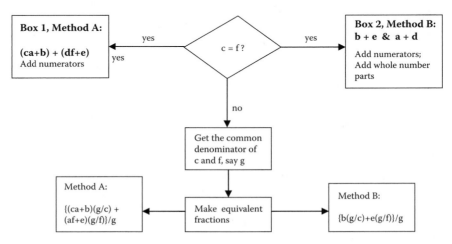

FIGURE 4.7
Task specification, chart 2: case of the same denominator in fraction addition problems.

Problem: a b/c + d e/f		Method A	Method B
A_1	Convert a b/c to (ac+b)/f	used	not used
A_2	Convert d e/f to (df+e)/f	used	not used
A_3	Simplify before getting common denominator	used	used
A_4	Find the common denominator of c and f	used	used
A_5	Make equivalent fractions	used	used
A_6	Add numerators	used	used
A_7	Reduce answers to the simplest form	used	used
B_1	Separate a and d, and b/c and e/f	not used	used
B_2	Add the whole number part and 0	not used	used
Attributes A_k are for Method A, B_k are for Method B.			

FIGURE 4.8
List of attributes used in Methods A and B in fraction addition problems.

It is obvious that Method B becomes computationally much simpler when making equivalent fractions. If Method A is used, the numerators become larger numbers than when Method B is used, and multiplication and addition of these large numbers may cause more frequent computational errors. Alternatively, some students may simplify fractions before getting their common denominators to ease computational burdens. After adding the two numerators of equivalent fractions, the answers can be simplified to simpler fractions or mixed numbers; therefore, we add the attributes *simplify before adding* and *reduce answers to the simplest form*. Let us summarize the attributes we have found in the tasks in Figure 4.8.

The tasks are summarized and named A_1 through A_7, and B_1 and B_2. The last two columns show *used* and/or *not used* for each method.

Developing Items

We discuss the item construction of Method A and Method B separately.

Method A

Let us start with the items for Method A users. There are $2^7 = 128$ ways to make combinations of seven attributes, so we develop items by referring to the task flow chart, Figure 4.7.

To find out whether or not a student can do attribute A_1, *convert a mixed number to a fraction*, we need two items, one involving A_1 and the other not involving A_1. i1 = 7/4 + 5/4, and i2 = 2 8/6 + 3 10/6. A_3 is asking about the possibility of applying *simplify before getting the common denominator of two denominators*. Item i1 is not applicable, but i2 is because 8 and 6, and 10 and 6, are multiples of 2, so we need an item not involving A_3. We create i3, which does not have multiples of their denominators and numerators; this is not applicable to A_3. i3 = 1 4/7 + 1 12/7. Then we go down to the node of checking whether or not the denominators are the same. So, we make an item with different denominators, i4 = 3/4 + 1/2 and i5 = 3 1/6 + 2 3/4. For A_7, i1, i2, i3, and i4 involve A_7. So we need an item not involving A_7. i5 = 3/5 + 1/5, and i6 = 3 1/6 + 2 3/4. Now we have developed six items involving attributes A_1, A_3, and A_7. Because A_3 is involved in only one item with a mixed-number addition problem, we develop an item with a fraction type that requires simplification before getting its common denominator. So, i7 = 2/5 + 12/8. Figure 4.5.4 gives the Q matrix and its reachability and adjacency matrices. It is ideal if the entries of the Q matrix are balanced in a way that the marginal sums of rows and columns are at least larger than 2.

Reachability matrix R in Figure 4.9 suggests that Attributes A_1 and A_2, and A_4 and A_5, are equivalent, respectively. Attributes A_3 and A_7 have the direct relationship, $A_3 \subseteq A_7$, which means we cannot diagnose a particular combination, A_7 *cannot do but A_3 can do*. A_6 is involved in all items, and $A_k \subseteq A_6$.

The structure of knowledge states is drawn in Figure 4.5. In this figure, pairs of attributes 1 and 2, and 4 and 5, appear in the same node because they are equivalent. The BUGLIB program generated all possible knowledge states from the Q matrix and generated knowledge states are listed in Figure 4.10. It is clear that there is no such case A_7 *cannot do but A_3*

			i1	i2	i3	i4	i5	i6	i7
$Q7_A =$	A_1	Convert a b/c to (ac+b)/f	0	1	1	0	0	1	0
	A_2	Convert d e/f to (df+e)/f	0	1	1	0	0	1	0
	A_3	Simplify before take CD.	0	1	0	0	0	0	1
	A_4	Find the common denominator	0	0	0	1	0	1	1
	A_5	Make equivalent fractions	0	0	0	1	0	1	1
	A_6	Add numerators	1	1	1	1	1	1	1
	A_7	Reduce answers to the simplest form	1	1	1	1	0	0	1

Adjacency and reachability matrices of the incidence matrix Q will be

$$A = \begin{matrix} 1 & 1 & 0 & 0 & 0 & 1 & 0 \\ 1 & 1 & 0 & 0 & 0 & 1 & 0 \\ 0 & 0 & 1 & 0 & 0 & 1 & 1 \\ 0 & 0 & 0 & 1 & 1 & 1 & 0 \\ 0 & 0 & 0 & 1 & 1 & 1 & 0 \\ 0 & 0 & 0 & 0 & 0 & 1 & 0 \\ 0 & 0 & 0 & 0 & 0 & 1 & 1 \end{matrix} \qquad R = \begin{matrix} 1 & 1 & 0 & 0 & 0 & 1 & 0 \\ 1 & 1 & 0 & 0 & 0 & 1 & 0 \\ 0 & 0 & 1 & 0 & 0 & 1 & 1 \\ 0 & 0 & 0 & 1 & 1 & 1 & 1 \\ 0 & 0 & 0 & 1 & 1 & 1 & 0 \\ 0 & 0 & 0 & 0 & 0 & 1 & 0 \\ 0 & 0 & 0 & 0 & 0 & 1 & 1 \end{matrix}$$

FIGURE 4.9

Q_{7A} matrix for seven attributes and seven items, and the adjacency and reachability matrices.

		i1	i2	i3	i4	i5	i6	i7	i8	i9	i10	i11
$Q_{11A} =$	A$_1$ Convert a b/c to (ac+b)/f	0	1	1	0	0	1	0	**0**	**0**	**0**	**1**
	A$_2$ Convert d e/f to (df+e)/f	0	1	1	0	0	1	0	**0**	**0**	**1**	**0**
	A$_3$ Simplify before take CD.	0	1	0	0	0	0	1	**1**	**1**	**0**	**0**
	A$_4$ Find the common denominator	0	0	0	1	0	1	1	**1**	**0**	**1**	**0**
	A$_5$ Make equivalent fractions	0	0	0	1	0	1	1	**1**	**0**	**1**	**0**
	A$_6$ Add numerators	1	1	1	1	1	1	1	**1**	**1**	**1**	**1**
	A$_7$ Reduce answers to the simplest form	1	1	1	1	0	0	1	**0**	**0**	**1**	**1**

		i1	i2	i3	i4	i5	i6	i7	i8	i9	i10	i11
$Q_{11B} =$	A$_1$ Convert a b/c to (ac+b)/c	0	0	0	0	0	0	0	0	0	0	0
	A$_2$ Convert d e/f to (df+e)/f	0	0	0	0	0	0	0	0	0	0	0
	A$_3$ Simplify before taking CD.	0	1	1	0	0	0	1	1	1	1	0
	A$_4$ Find the common denominator	0	0	0	1	0	1	1	1	0	1	0
	A$_5$ Make equivalent fractions	0	0	0	1	0	1	1	1	0	1	0
	A$_6$ Add numerators	1	1	1	1	1	1	1	1	1	1	1
	A$_7$ Reduce answers to the simplest form	1	1	1	1	0	0	1	0	0	1	1

FIGURE 4.10
The Q matrix with seven attributes and 11 items.

can do. However, in reality, we would like to diagnose this combination of A_7 *cannot do but* A_3 *can do*. We need to add more items to the original seven-item pool in order to diagnose A_3.

Let us construct items involving A3 but not A7. They are i8 = 2/4 + 1/9 and i9 = 15/35 + 10/35. We add these two items to our Q matrix, with the entries being written in boldface in Figure 4.10.

Attributes A1 and A2 are equivalent as long as we do not add more items. So, we develop the following new items: One is the type of *fraction + mixed number*, and the other is the type of *mixed number + fraction*. The 10th and 11th items are i10 = 1/2 + 1 10/7 and i11 = 1 2/5 + 3/5, and their attribute involvement is entered in the Q matrix above in Figure 4.10 with boldface letters. The other pair of equivalent attributes is *get common denominator* and *make equivalent fractions*. This problem is difficult to solve unless we create a new item type such as asking students to make two equivalent fractions after giving a common denominator of a b/c + d e/f.

Attribute A_6 is involved in all items as long as we restrict item types in our scope; therefore, we have to give up diagnosing attributes A_6 and A_5, as long as we restrict the format of our item types and tasks to the test.

A new Q matrix for seven attributes and 11 items, Q_{11A}, is given in Figure 4.10. The new Q_{11A} matrix clearly improved with 11 items because the original undesirable direct relation between A_3 and A_7 is eliminated, and each attribute is involved in at least three items. In summary, a list of 11 items is given in Table 4.4. The Q matrix with seven items is given in Figure 4.10, and its knowledge states are given in Figure 4.11.

The knowledge states generated from Q_{11A} and their structure are given in Figure 4.12 The figure of the knowledge structure in Figure 4.12 clearly

TABLE 4.4

Eleven Items Constructed by Considering Attribute Involvement

Items		Items		Items	
i1	7/4 + 5/4	i5	3/5 + 1/5	i9	15/35 + 10/35
i2	2 8/6 + 3 10/6	i6	3 1/6 + 2 3/4	i10	1/2 + 1 10/7
i3	1 4/7 + 1 12/7	i7	2/5 + 12/8	i11	1 2/5 + 3/5
i4	3/4 + 1/2	i8	2/4 + 1/9		

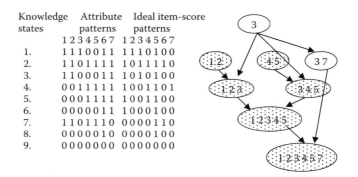

Knowledge states	Attribute patterns	Ideal item-score patterns
	1 2 3 4 5 6 7	1 2 3 4 5 6 7
1.	1 1 1 0 0 1 1	1 1 1 0 1 0 0
2.	1 1 0 1 1 1 1	1 0 1 1 1 1 0
3.	1 1 0 0 0 1 1	1 0 1 0 1 0 0
4.	0 0 1 1 1 1 1	1 0 0 1 1 0 1
5.	0 0 0 1 1 1 1	1 0 0 1 1 0 0
6.	0 0 0 0 0 1 1	1 0 0 0 1 0 0
7.	1 1 0 1 1 1 0	0 0 0 0 1 1 0
8.	0 0 0 0 0 1 0	0 0 0 0 1 0 0
9.	0 0 0 0 0 0 0	0 0 0 0 0 0 0

FIGURE 4.11

Knowledge states for seven items.

KS	Attribute Patterns	Ideal Item-score Patterns
	1 2 3 4 5 6 7	1 2 3 4 5 6 7 8 9 0 1
1	1 1 1 0 0 1 1	1 1 1 0 1 0 0 0 1 0 1
2	1 1 0 1 1 1 1	1 0 1 1 1 1 0 0 0 1 1
3	1 1 0 0 0 1 1	1 0 1 0 1 0 0 0 0 0 1
4	0 1 1 1 1 1 1	1 0 0 1 1 0 1 1 1 1 0
5	1 0 1 1 1 1 1	1 0 0 1 1 0 1 1 1 0 1
6	0 0 1 1 1 1 1	1 0 0 1 1 0 1 1 1 0 0
7	0 1 0 1 1 1 1	1 0 0 1 1 0 0 0 0 1 0
8	1 0 0 1 1 1 1	1 0 0 1 1 0 0 0 0 0 0
9	0 0 0 1 1 1 1	1 0 0 1 1 0 0 0 0 0 0
10	1 0 1 0 0 1 1	1 0 0 0 1 0 0 0 1 0 1
11	0 0 1 0 0 1 1	1 0 0 0 1 0 0 0 1 0 0
12	1 0 0 0 0 1 1	1 0 0 0 1 0 0 0 0 0 1
13	0 0 0 0 0 1 1	1 0 0 0 1 0 0 0 0 0 0
14	1 1 1 1 1 1 0	0 0 0 0 1 1 0 1 1 0 0
15	1 1 0 1 1 1 0	0 0 0 0 1 1 0 0 0 0 0
16	0 0 1 1 1 1 0	0 0 0 0 1 0 0 1 1 0 0
17	0 0 1 0 0 1 0	0 0 0 0 1 0 0 0 1 0 0
18	0 0 0 0 0 1 0	0 0 0 0 1 0 0 0 0 0 0
19	0 0 0 0 0 0 0	0 0 0 0 0 0 0 0 0 0 0

Structure of Knowledge States in Attributes

FIGURE 4.12

Knowledge states and their structure for 11 items by Method A.

shows that attributes A_1 and A_2, and A_4 and A_5, are separated so we can diagnose the capability of attributes better. However, the structure of knowledge states derived from 11 items in Figure 4.12 becomes more complicated than that of seven items in Figure 4.11.

Method B

Using Method B, a student separates whole-number parts from fraction parts, thus significantly simplifying computation of making equivalent fractions. This method is usually seen in advanced students, whereas Method A users are somewhat less advanced than Method B users. Let us create a Q matrix for 11 items by applying this method and shown in Figure 4.10.

Note that this matrix is quite different from Q_{11A}, which is based on Method A strategy. By looking into the entries of Q_{11B}, we find all attributes are involved in at least two items. Because A_9 is a subset of A_7, $A_9 \subseteq A_7$, and this relationship is not desirable, we add a new item, with *not reduce answers* but also involving A_9 *separate one whole-number part*: i12 = 2 1/7 + 3/7. The new entries in Q_{12B} are coded with boldface. The direct-order relation between A_9 and A_7 does not exist with the new item i12 in Q_{12B}; therefore, one can diagnose the state characterized by *cannot do A_7 but can do A_9*.

Let us modify the matrix Q_{11A} to be Q_{12A} by adding the involvement relationship for item 12, which is given in Figure 4.13. Possible knowledge states from the matrices Q_{12A} and Q_{12B} are generated and listed in Tables 4.8 and 4.9. Because the items in both Q matrices are the same; attributes A_3, A_4, A_5, A_6, and A_7 are the same; and the item type of a fraction plus a fraction shares the identical set of attributes, some ideal item score patterns overlap between Methods A and B. A close investigation reveals that 18 ideal item score patterns, including all 0s and all 1s, are identical across the two sets of ideal item score patterns. Table 4.5 summarizes the two Q matrices, Q_{12A} by Method A and Q_{12B} by Method B, in which coding of the new item, i12, is written with boldface. A_1 and A_2 are unique to Method A, but A_8 and A_9 are unique to Method B only. Item construction is also discussed in detail by Tatsuoka and Hayashi (2001).

Diagnosing Which Method Is Used

We further add two items that may differentiate Method A users from Method B users, i13 = 3 + 10/5 and i14 = 12/8 + 1. Item i13 involves attributes A_1, A_6, and A_7 for Method A, and A_3 for Method B. Item i14 involves A_2, A_3, A_6, and A_7 for Method A, and A_3, A_7, and A_9 for Method B. These two items are expected to be very easy for Method B users, but would be extremely difficult for Method A users. Method A users are usually weak in understanding the concept of the number line (Shaw, 1986), that is, converting whole numbers to fractions in these items requires a search for appropriate denominators, and this task may not be easy for them. Therefore, we

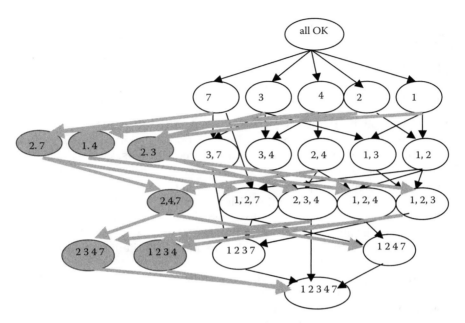

FIGURE 4.13
The structure of knowledge states of 14 items for method a where grey lines indicate new additions to that of 11 items in Figure 4.7.

TABLE 4.5

The Q Matrices Q_{12A} and Q_{12B} for 12 Items of Fraction Addition Problems

			i1	i2	i3	i4	i5	i6	i7	i8	i9	i10	i11	i12
$Q_{12A} = A_1$		Convert a b/c to (ac + b)/c.	0	1	1	0	0	1	0	0	0	0	1	1
	A_2	Convert d e/f to (df + e)/f.	0	1	1	0	0	1	0	0	0	1	0	0
	A_3	Simplify before taking common denominator (CD).	0	1	0	0	0	0	1	1	1	0	0	0
	A_4	Find the common denominator.	0	0	0	1	0	1	1	1	0	1	0	0
	A_5	Make equivalent fractions.	0	0	0	1	0	1	1	1	0	1	0	0
	A_6	Add numerators.	1	1	1	1	1	1	1	1	1	1	1	1
	A_7	Reduce answer to the simplest form.	1	1	1	1	0	0	1	0	0	1	1	0

			i1	i2	i3	i4	i5	i6	i7	i8	i9	i10	i11	i12
$Q_{12B} = A_1$		Convert a b/c to (ac + b)/c.	0	0	0	0	0	0	0	0	0	0	0	0
	A_2	Convert d e/f to (df + e)/f.	0	0	0	0	0	0	0	0	0	0	0	0
	A_3	Simplify before taking CD.	0	1	1	0	0	0	1	1	1	1	0	0
	A_4	Find the common denominator.	0	0	0	1	0	1	1	1	0	1	0	0
	A_5	Make equivalent fractions.	0	0	0	1	0	1	1	1	0	1	0	0
	A_6	Add numerators.	1	1	1	1	1	1	1	1	1	1	1	1
	A_7	Reduce answer to the simplest form.	1	1	1	1	0	0	1	0	0	1	1	0
	A_8	Separate two whole-number parts.	0	1	1	0	0	1	0	0	0	0	0	0
	A_9	Separate one whole-number part.	0	0	0	0	0	0	0	0	0	1	1	1

TABLE 4.6

Fourteen Items Determined by Applying Rule Space Analysis

i1 7/4 + 5/4	i5 3/5 + 1/5	i9 15/35 + 10/35	i13 3 + 10/5
i2 2 8/6 + 3 10/6	i6 3 1/6 + 2 3/4	i10 1/2 + 1 10/7	i14 12/8 + 1
i3 1 4/7 + 1 12/7	i7 2/5 + 12/8	i11 1 2/5 + 3/5	
i4 3/4 + 1/2	i8 2/4 + 1/9	i12 2 1/7 + 3/7	

constructed two items that are very easy for Method B users but very difficult for Method A users: modifying Q_{12A} and Q_{12b} to Q_{14A} and Q_{14B}, respectively, and generating all possible knowledge states for Q_{14A} and Q_{14B}. They are given in Tables 4.7 and 4.8. With the 12 items, 25 possible knowledge states for Q_{14A} and 26 for Q_{14B} are generated. A close examination of the two sets of ideal item score patterns revealed that seven ideal item score patterns are identical, but most of their sources of differences come from the attributes commonly used across two methods such as A_3, A_4, A_5, and A_7; therefore, these knowledge states are thought to belong to fraction computation problems, in general, regardless of the method a student uses. Both Method A and B users can have these knowledge states.

Note that our purpose of measurement is to obtain individuals' cognitive diagnosis and not to rank or select individuals based on their proficiency

TABLE 4.7

Q Matrices of 14 Items and 9 Attributes Using Methods A and B

	i1	i2	i3	i4	i5	i6	i7	i8	i9	i10	i11	i12	i13	i14
Q_{14A} = A_1 Convert a b/c to (ac + b)/c.	0	1	1	0	0	1	0	0	0	0	1	1	1	0
A_2 Convert d e/f to (df + e)/f.	0	1	1	0	0	1	0	0	0	1	0	0	0	1
A_3 Simplify before taking common denominator (CD).	0	1	0	0	0	0	1	1	1	0	0	0	0	1
A_4 Find the common denominator.	0	0	0	1	0	1	1	1	0	1	0	0	0	0
A_5 Make equivalent fractions.	0	0	0	1	0	1	1	1	0	1	0	0	0	0
A_6 Add numerators.	1	1	1	1	1	1	1	1	1	1	1	1	1	1
A_7 Reduce answers to the simplest form.	1	1	1	1	0	0	1	0	0	1	1	0	1	1
A_8 Separate two whole-number parts.	0	0	0	0	0	0	0	0	0	0	0	0	0	0
A_9 Separate one whole-number part.	0	0	0	0	0	0	0	0	0	0	0	0	0	0

	i1	i2	i3	i4	i5	i6	i7	i8	i9	i10	i11	i12	i13	i14
Q_{14B} = A_1 Convert a b/c to (ac + b)/c.	0	0	0	0	0	0	0	0	0	0	0	0	0	0
A_2 Convert d e/f to (df + e)/f.	0	0	0	0	0	0	0	0	0	0	0	0	0	0
A_3 Simplify before taking CD.	0	1	1	0	0	0	1	1	1	1	0	0	1	1
A_4 Find the common denominator.	0	0	0	1	0	1	1	1	0	1	0	0	0	0
A_5 Make equivalent fractions.	0	0	0	1	0	1	1	1	0	1	0	0	0	0
A_6 Add numerators.	1	1	1	1	1	1	1	1	1	1	1	1	0	0
A_7 Reduce answer to the simplest form.	1	1	1	1	0	0	1	0	0	1	1	0	0	1
A_8 Separate two whole-number parts.	0	1	1	0	0	1	0	0	0	0	0	0	0	0
A_9 Separate one whole-number part.	0	0	0	0	0	0	0	0	0	1	1	1	0	1

TABLE 4.8

All Possible Knowledge States Generated From Q_{14B} Using Method A

Knowledge States	Attribute Patterns									Ideal Item Score Patterns													
	1	2	3	4	5	6	7	8	9	1	2	3	4	5	6	7	8	9	0	1	2	3	4
1	1	1	1	1	1	1	1	0	0	1	1	1	1	1	1	1	1	1	1	1	1	1	1
2	1	1	1	0	0	1	1	0	0	1	1	1	0	1	0	0	0	1	0	1	1	1	1
3	1	1	0	1	1	1	1	0	0	1	0	1	1	1	1	0	0	0	1	1	1	1	0
4	1	1	0	0	0	1	1	0	0	1	0	1	0	1	0	0	0	0	0	1	1	1	0
5	0	1	1	1	1	1	1	0	0	1	0	0	1	1	0	1	1	1	1	0	0	0	1
6	1	0	1	1	1	1	1	0	0	1	0	0	1	1	0	1	1	1	0	1	1	1	0
7	0	0	1	1	1	1	1	0	0	1	0	0	1	1	0	1	1	1	0	0	0	0	0
8	0	1	0	1	1	1	1	0	0	1	0	0	1	1	0	0	0	0	1	0	0	0	0
9	1	0	0	1	1	1	1	0	0	1	0	0	1	1	0	0	0	0	0	1	1	1	0
10	0	0	0	1	1	1	1	0	0	1	0	0	1	1	0	0	0	0	0	0	0	0	0
11	1	0	1	0	0	1	1	0	0	1	0	0	0	1	0	0	0	1	0	1	1	1	0
12	0	1	1	0	0	1	1	0	0	1	0	0	0	1	0	0	0	1	0	0	0	0	1
13	0	0	1	0	0	1	1	0	0	1	0	0	0	1	0	0	0	1	0	0	0	0	0
14	1	0	0	0	0	1	1	0	0	1	0	0	0	1	0	0	0	0	0	1	1	1	0
15	0	0	0	0	0	1	1	0	0	1	0	0	0	1	0	0	0	0	0	0	0	0	0
16	1	1	1	1	1	1	0	0	0	0	0	0	0	1	1	0	1	1	0	0	1	0	0
17	1	1	0	1	1	1	0	0	0	0	0	0	0	1	1	0	0	0	0	0	1	0	0
18	1	0	1	1	1	1	0	0	0	0	0	0	0	1	0	0	1	1	0	0	1	0	0
19	0	0	1	1	1	1	0	0	0	0	0	0	0	1	0	0	1	1	0	0	0	0	0
20	1	0	1	0	0	1	0	0	0	0	0	0	0	1	0	0	0	1	0	0	1	0	0
21	0	0	1	0	0	1	0	0	0	0	0	0	0	1	0	0	0	1	0	0	0	0	0
22	1	0	0	0	0	1	0	0	0	0	0	0	0	1	0	0	0	0	0	0	1	0	0
23	0	0	0	0	0	1	0	0	0	0	0	0	0	1	0	0	0	0	0	0	0	0	0
24	0	0	0	0	0	0	0	0	0	0	0	0	0	0	0	0	0	0	0	0	0	0	0

levels. Traditional techniques of item analysis may not be applicable and not useful for selecting items for diagnostic purposes. In item analysis, we select items with high discriminating powers, and discard items with low correlations with total scores. By so doing, the unidimensionality of a test may be created. However, Tatsuoka (1987) showed that the items involving important tasks often have to be deleted from the parameter estimation of IRT models.

Table 4.6 summarizes 14 items we constructed. Table 4.7 lists the two Q matrices, Q_{14A} and Q_{14B}, respectively.

The knowledge states listed in Tables 4.8 and 4.9 are logically generated from Q_{14A} and Q_{14B}, and hence they are not real. After classification of students' responses into one of the predetermined knowledge states, some knowledge states may not have anybody classified. We select only the knowledge states in which at least one student is classified. The nonempty knowledge states will form a partially ordered network that is called *progressive paths* or *learning paths*.

TABLE 4.9

All Possible Knowledge States Generated From Q_{14B} Using Method B

Knowledge States	Attribute Patterns									Ideal Item Score Patterns													
	1	2	3	4	5	6	7	8	9	1	2	3	4	5	6	7	8	9	0	1	2	3	4
1	0	0	1	1	1	1	1	1	1	1	1	1	1	1	1	1	1	1	1	1	1	1	1
2	0	0	1	1	1	1	1	1	0	1	1	1	1	1	1	1	1	1	0	0	0	1	0
3	0	0	1	0	0	1	1	1	1	1	1	1	0	1	0	0	0	1	0	1	1	1	1
4	0	0	1	0	0	1	1	1	0	1	1	1	0	1	0	0	0	1	0	0	0	1	0
5	0	0	0	1	1	1	1	1	1	1	0	0	1	1	1	0	0	0	0	1	1	0	0
6	0	0	0	1	1	1	1	1	0	1	0	0	1	1	1	0	0	0	0	0	0	0	0
7	0	0	1	1	1	1	1	0	1	1	0	0	1	1	0	1	1	1	1	1	1	1	1
8	0	0	1	1	1	1	1	0	0	1	0	0	1	1	0	1	1	1	0	0	0	1	0
9	0	0	0	1	1	1	1	0	1	1	0	0	1	1	0	0	0	0	0	1	1	0	0
10	0	0	0	1	1	1	1	0	0	1	0	0	1	1	0	0	0	0	0	0	0	0	0
11	0	0	1	0	0	1	1	0	1	1	0	0	0	1	0	0	0	1	0	1	1	1	1
12	0	0	1	0	0	1	1	0	0	1	0	0	0	1	0	0	0	1	0	0	0	1	0
13	0	0	0	0	0	1	1	0	1	1	0	0	0	1	0	0	0	0	0	1	1	0	0
14	0	0	0	0	0	1	1	0	0	1	0	0	0	1	0	0	0	0	0	0	0	0	0
15	0	0	1	1	1	1	0	1	1	0	0	0	0	1	1	0	1	1	0	0	1	1	0
16	0	0	1	1	1	1	0	1	0	0	0	0	0	1	1	0	1	1	0	0	0	1	0
17	0	0	0	1	1	1	0	1	1	0	0	0	0	1	1	0	0	0	0	0	1	0	0
18	0	0	0	1	1	1	0	1	0	0	0	0	0	1	1	0	0	0	0	0	0	0	0
19	0	0	1	1	1	1	0	0	1	0	0	0	0	1	0	0	1	1	0	0	1	1	0
20	0	0	1	1	1	1	0	0	0	0	0	0	0	1	0	0	1	1	0	0	0	1	0
21	0	0	1	0	0	1	0	0	1	0	0	0	0	1	0	0	0	1	0	0	1	1	0
22	0	0	1	0	0	1	0	0	0	0	0	0	0	1	0	0	0	1	0	0	0	1	0
23	0	0	0	0	0	1	0	0	1	0	0	0	0	1	0	0	0	0	0	0	1	0	0
24	0	0	0	0	0	1	0	0	0	0	0	0	0	1	0	0	0	0	0	0	0	0	0
25	0	0	1	0	0	0	1	0	1	0	0	0	0	0	0	0	0	0	0	0	0	1	1
26	0	0	1	0	0	0	0	0	0	0	0	0	0	0	0	0	0	0	0	0	0	1	0
27	0	0	0	0	0	0	0	0	0	0	0	0	0	0	0	0	0	0	0	0	0	0	0

In this chapter, the first section showed that Boolean algebra L_A and also L_I are very similar to a set of real numbers, and that one could add or multiply two elements, take their complement, and have the identities 0 and 1 with respect to the Boolean operations. The chapter also introduced useful properties for understanding various relationships and useful information implicitly embedded in a given Q matrix. Partially ordered networks of attributes and items are shown with an example of data (i.e., a state assessment administered to 150,000 students).

Ideal item score patterns that are generated from a Q matrix by a BDF are discussed as latent knowledge states, and their relationship to attribute mastery patterns is introduced. Whether or not there are prerequisite relationships among attributes, their Q matrices have different forms.

The former is characterized by a Guttman scale, a triangle form, whereas the latter has no obvious relationships.

The correspondence between the dual spaces of knowledge states (one is represented by attribute mastery patterns, and the other by ideal item score patterns) may not be one-to-one, and often several to one depend on Q matrices. When a Q matrix forms a Guttman scale, the degenerative property discussed in Section 4.4 becomes valid. The chapter discusses solutions for this problem, and the equivalent classes of attribute patterns and their degenerative properties.

Last, application to item construction for cognitively diagnostic assessment is discussed with fraction addition problems. It is interesting to note that the fraction addition problems were developed to include the item patterns generated from all the erroneous rules of operations discovered (Tatsuoka, 1984a; Tatsuoka & Tatsuoka, 2005), but when using the space of knowledge states, it was concluded that we would need a few more items to be able to diagnose all possible ideal item score patterns generated from their Q matrix.

5

A Classification Space: Rule Space as a Cartesian Product of the Person Parameter θ in Item Response Theory, ζ, and Generalized ζs

This chapter introduces the classification space called rule space and its coordinates, emphasizing their practical characteristics. The first coordinate is the ability measure obtained from item response theory (IRT); therefore, it is sensitive to how high each student's score in a test is. The second coordinate is the index that measures unusualness of response patterns called *person–fit statistics*. In Chapter 4, determination of all the possible knowledge states from a Q matrix that is viewed as a set of hypotheses generated by domain experts was discussed. Each knowledge state consists of mastered or nonmastered attributes. The rule space enables us to interpret which knowledge states are commonly populated and, moreover, to tell the test users that different ability levels, high or low scores of students, would be located in different knowledge states.

Section 5.1 discusses the sensitivity of IRT curves to underlying cognitive processing and knowledge required in answering items correctly. Sections 5.2 and 5.3 introduces an item tree by which cognitive requirements for the items in a test are expressed graphically, and Sections 5.4 and 5.5 construct probabilistic bases for applying the Bayes decision rules in a multivariate space with many classification groups. The last section discusses the extension of the two-dimensional rule space to a multidimensional space.

5.1 Cognitive Sensitivity for Item Response Curves

This section seeks a way to examine whether item response curves are influenced systematically by the cognitive processes underlying solution of the items in a procedural domain of fraction addition problems. Starting from an expert teacher's logical task analysis and investigating various sources of misconceptions using an error diagnostic computer program, Tatsuoka (1987) tackled this problem. This section introduces her work briefly, but more detailed information on cognitive research done on the domain of fractions is not discussed. They can be found in the following materials: Tatsuoka (1984a, 1987); Klein, Birenbaum, Standiford, and Tatsuoka (1981); Shaw and Birenbaum (1985); Shaw and Tatsuoka (1984); and Tatsuoka K.K and Tatsuoka C. (2005).

Items and Tasks

A 38-item fraction addition test was carefully constructed (Klein et al., 1981) such that the 19 pairs of parallel items involving various combinations of tasks: Items 20 to 38 were the parallel counterparts of items 1 to 19. Each item was of the form $a(b/c) + d(e/f)$, where a, b, d, and e were nonnegative integers and c and f were positive integers. The notation $a(b/c)$ stands for a mixed number composed of an integer "a" and a proper fraction "b/c." There were four basic item types: (I) $a = d = 0$ and $c = f$, (II) $a = d = 0$ and $c \neq f$, (III) a and/or $d \neq 0$ and $c = f$, and (IV) a and/or $d \neq 0$ and $c \neq f$. Item types I and II were referred to as the F + F (fraction + fraction) type, and III and IV were referred to as M + M (mixed number + mixed number), M + F (mixed number + fraction), or F + M (fraction + mixed number) types. The numerals used in the items were carefully selected from small numbers to minimize the effects of computational difficulty on test performance.

The task analysis, as described in Section 4.5, identified the four types of items that require different solution paths and different combinations of subtasks for correct solutions. In addition to the different types of items, there were two distinct methods for reaching correct solutions. Method A converted the mixed numbers to two improper fractions and added the two fractions. Method B separated the whole-number parts (a, d) from the fraction parts (b/c, c/f), added the two whole numbers and the two fractions separately, and then combined the answers for the two parts and got the final answer. For example, an M + M problem of type c or d such as $2\ 1/5 + 5\ 1/5$ can be solved by either

$$\text{Method A } [2\ 1/5 + 5\ 1/5 \Rightarrow 11/5 + 26/5 \Rightarrow 37/5 \Rightarrow 7\ 2/5]$$

or

$$\text{Method B } [2\ 1/5 + 5\ 1/5 \Rightarrow (2 + 5) + (1/5 + 1/5) \Rightarrow 7\ 2/5]$$

Using Methods A and B requires different skills. For Method A, a student has to convert a mixed number to an improper fraction, and thus he or she has to carry out computations correctly. Method B requires a deeper understanding of the number system but less computational skill.

The tasks needed in the correct solutions of fraction addition problems were classified into seven subtasks (c_1, ..., c_7), which are summarized in Table 5.1. The first task, c_1, asked the student to distinguish between the two item types, F + F and M + M. If the students had little knowledge of fractions, then he or she used seriously ill-composed, erroneous rules. Their error types were basic, often due to having trouble understanding the meaning of numerators and denominators. The rules in this category usually did not discriminate one item type from another. The erroneous rules disregarding task c1 were usually applied to the 38 items regardless of item type, F + F, M + M, F + M, or M + F. A typical example of such a wrong rule was to add corresponding parts respectively (Shaw & Birenbaum, 1985; Tutsuoka, 1984a). The second task, c2, was to determine whether the denominators are same. If the denominators were not the same, then the common denominator had to be obtained (task c4). Task c3 was relevant only to Method A users and involved conversion of a mixed number to an improper fraction. Tasks c5 and c6 were computational operations: Make fractions equivalent, and then add the numerators. The last task, c7, was relevant to Method B users. That is, students often forgot to combine two parts of the answers after adding the whole-number and fraction parts separately. The seven subtasks characterize each item in the test.

Classification of Items Into Categories

Table 5.2 shows a summary list of item characteristics (Q matrix) expressed by a table of binary numbers in which $X_{ij} = 1$ if item i tests subtask j, and $X_{ij} = 0$ if not. For example, items 1 and 20 involved subtasks c2, c3, c6, and c7, so that the entries of X_{12}, X_{13}, X_{16}, and X_{17} equaled one and the others in that row equaled zero.

The items are divided into four categories based on the subtask required by each item. Items 1, 6, 9, 11, 16, and their parallel counterparts are classified in category 1; items 2, 8, 11, 15, and 18 and their parallel items are in category 2; items 3, 7, 10, 14, 17, and 19 and their parallel counterparts are in category 3; and the remaining items are in category 4. The categories are listed in the ninth column of Table 5.2. These categories happened to be identical to the four item types, but they were not usually the same if subtasks were decomposed to finer subcomponents.

IRT Analysis: Relationships Between Attributes and IRT Parameters

Item difficulties and discriminations for the two-parameter logistic model for the 38 items were estimated by GETAB (Baillie & Tatsuoka, 1980).

TABLE 5.1

Description of Seven Subtasks Needed in the Correct Solution of Fraction Addition Problems of the Forms $a(b/c) + d(e/f)$, $a \neq 0$ and/or $d \neq 0$, and 38 Problems

Subtasks	Descriptions
c_1	Determine if the item is of type $F^1 + F$.
c_2	Determine if $c = f$.
c_3	Convert a mixed number, M^2, to the improper fraction F if Method A^3 is used.
c_4	Get the common denominator.
c_5	Make equivalent fractions.
c_6	Add numerators.
c_7	Combine the whole-number part with the fraction part if Method B is used.

1. If $a = 0$, then b/c is denoted by F (e.g., $3/4$, $1/2$).
2. If $a \neq 0$, then a (b/c) is denoted by M (e.g., $2\ ¾$).
3. $d(b/c) \rightarrow (ac + b)/c$.

1. $2\ 8/6 + 3\ 10/6$	20. $3\ 10/4 + 4\ 6/4$
2. $2/5 + 1\ 2/8$	21. $2/7 + 18/12$
3. $8/5 + 6/5$	22. $9/7 + 11/7$
4. $2\ 1/2 + 4\ 2/4$	23. $1\ 1/3 + 2\ 4/6$
5. $1/2 + 1\ 10/7$	24. $1/5 + 2\ 5/3$
6. $3\ 5/7 + 4\ 6/7$	25. $3\ 4/5 + 5\ 3/5$
7. $3/5 + 7/5$	26. $7/4 + 5/4$
8. $1/3 + 1/2$	27. $1/5 + 1/4$
9. $1\ 4/7 + 1\ 12/7$	28. $1\ 3/5 + 1\ 8/5$
10. $3/5 + 1/5$	29. $4/7 + 1/7$
11. $3/4 + 1/2$	30. $5/6 + 1/3$
12. $2\ 5/9 + 1\ 1/9$	31. $3\ 5/8 + 1\ 1/8$
13. $3\ 1/6 + 2\ 3/4$	32. $2\ 1/8 + 3\ 5/6$
14. $15/35 + 10/35$	33. $16/36 + 10/36$
15. $1/2 + 3/8$	34. $1/3 + 4/9$
16. $1\ 2/5 + 3/5$	35. $2\ 5/7 + 2/7$
17. $1/4 + 3/4$	36. $1/5 + 4/5$
18. $4/15 + 1/10$	37. $5/6 + 1/8$
19. $4/5 + 3/5$	38. $6/7 + 3/7$
(20). $3 + 10/5*$	(44). $5 + 8/4*$
(21). $1\ 3/9 + 2*$	(45). $1\ 2/6 + 2*$
(22). $3 + 1\ 5/2*$	(46). $2 + 1\ 7/3*$
(23). $12/8 + 1*$	(47). $18/12 + 3*$
(24). $2\ 1/3 + 3\ 1/4 + 2\ 2/6*$	(48). $2\ 1/3 + 1\ 2/9 + 3\ 1/2*$

*These items were not used.

TABLE 5.2

Classification of Items Into Categories on the Basis of Their Required Subtasks

	Subtask							
Items	c_1	c_2	c_3	c_4	c_5	c_6	c_7	Categories
1, 20	0	1	1	0	0	1	1	1
2, 21	1	0	0	1	1	1	0	2
3, 22	1	1	0	0	0	1	0	3
4, 23	0	0	1	1	1	1	1	4
5, 24	0	0	1	1	1	1	1	4
6, 25	0	1	1	0	0	1	1	1
7, 26	1	1	0	0	0	1	0	3
8, 27	1	0	0	1	1	1	0	2
9, 28	0	1	1	0	0	1	1	1
10, 29	1	1	0	0	0	1	0	3
11, 30	1	0	0	1	1	1	0	2
12, 31	0	1	1	0	0	1	1	1
13, 32	0	0	1	1	1	1	1	4
14, 33	1	1	0	0	0	1	0	3
15, 34	1	0	0	1	1	1	0	2
16, 35	0	1	1	0	0	1	1	1
17, 36	1	1	0	0	0	1	0	3
18, 37	1	0	0	1	1	1	0	2
19, 38	1	1	0	0	0	1	0	3
Total number of items	22	22	16	16	16	38	16	

Table 5.3 summarizes the means and standard deviations of item difficulties and discriminations in the four categories. The means and standard deviations of the discriminations for the items in category 2 were substantially larger than those in the other categories because item $1/5 + 1/4$ had an extraordinary large p-value compared to the other items in category 2. This item and its parallel counterpart were deleted from the following analysis.

TABLE 5.3

Means and Standard Deviations of the Item Difficulties and Discriminations in Four Groups

		Discrimination		Difficulty	
Group	N	Mean	SD	Mean	SD
1	10	.96	.24	−.64	.18
2	10	3.05	1.16	.24	.23
3	12	1.12	.20	−.84	.23
4	6	2.56	.57	.29	.14
Total	38	1.82	.66	−.33	.21

Dissimilarity of the response curves for each pair (i and j) was measured by the area between the IRT curves, given in the following statistic:

$$\Delta_{km}(i,j) = \int_{-\infty}^{\infty} |P_i(\theta) - P_j(\theta)|^2 \, d(\theta) \qquad (5.1)$$

where $P_i(\theta)$ is predicted performance on item i as a function of ability level θ using the two-parameter logistic model (Lord, 1980), and k and m represent the categories for items i and j, respectively. Equation (5.1) is often used as a standard distance measure between two functions in mathematics (Simmons, 1963). The mean delta value for item pairs within Category k was calculated as

$$\Delta_{kk} = \frac{1}{n_k(n_k - 1)/2} \sum_{i=1}^{n_k} \sum_{j=i+1}^{n_k} \Delta_{kk}(i,j) \qquad (5.2a)$$

where there were n_k items in category k. The mean delta value for all pairs of items for which one of the items appeared in category k and the other appeared in category m is given below:

$$\Delta_{km} = \frac{1}{n_k n_m} \sum_{i=1}^{n_k} \sum_{j=i}^{n_m} \Delta_{km}(i,j) \qquad (5.2b)$$

Standard deviations for delta values calculated within and between categories were found in a similar fashion. These means and standard deviations appear in Table 5.4. In Table 5.4, all means on the diagonal were smaller than those in the off-diagonal, indicating that items in the same category

TABLE 5.4

Means and Standard Deviations of $\Delta_{km}(i,j)$ Values

	Category Means			
	1	2	3	4
1	.16	.59	.20	.62
2		.12	.68	.18
3			.17	.72
4				.14

	Standard Deviations			
1	.09	.10	.10	.11
2		.07	.13	.09
3			.10	.14
4				.09

had more similar item response curves than items in different categories. Furthermore, the squared areas between item response curves for parallel items for the 18 pairs were also computed. Their mean and standard deviation were .13 and .05, respectively. The values of .13 and .05 are much closer to the values on the diagonal in Table 5.4 than those in the off-diagonal.

Tatsuoka (1987) formulated two null hypotheses from the observations mentioned above:

1. The squared areas of the curves for items within the same category are not significantly different from those of the items in different categories (H_0: mean of Δ_{kk} = mean of Δ_{km}).

2. The squared areas between the item response curves in different categories are not significantly different from those of the pairs of the parallel items (H_0: mean of $\Delta_{km} = \Delta_{kk}$; in other words, the mean of different categories equals the means of parallel items).

Each null hypothesis was tested by a one-way analysis of variance (ANOVA) using the values of Δ_{km}, obtained from the 10 possible pairs of categories and the parallel group as cells. Analyses of the one-way ANOVA rejected both the null hypotheses ($F = 430.70$ and $p < .0001$ for the first, and $F = 319.47$ and $p < .0001$ for the second, where the degree of freedom [df] is 598), and hence it was concluded that the item response curves of the two-parameter logistic model were influenced by the subtasks underlying cognitive processes in the fraction addition problems.

These findings imply that cognitive processes underlying students' performances on tests influenced the IRT curves in a well-defined procedural domain, fraction arithmetic. The items requiring the same set of cognitive subtasks underlying the correct solutions had similar curves; items requiring different subtasks tended to produce dissimilar curves. Although this conclusion was based on the study of fraction addition problems, the same result has also been obtained from other well-defined domains such as fraction subtraction and signed-number subtraction problems (Tatsuoka, 1984a, Tatsuoka, Birenbaum, M. Tatsuoka, & Baillie, 1980; Standiford, Klein, & Tatsuoka, 1982).

5.2 Clustering Item Response Functions Into Homogeneous Categories and the Relationship Among Categories

In Section 5.1, it was shown that cognitive processes underlying the performance on test items influence item response curves in arithmetic domains. Similar findings were observed in several other domains (Tatsuoka, 1987). This property of item response curves enables us to group item response curves into one of several categories. The items in the same category have almost identical item response functions when examining the item attribute involvement. In other words, for a given incidence matrix of a test, we can make several categories of homogeneous items by grouping items based on their attribute involvement in a test. If two items involve the same set of attributes, then the two items are classified into the same categories.

Grouping of IRT Curves

The items in the same category have almost identical item response functions and hence identical item parameters. The fraction addition test described in the previous section has four categories. Category 1 contains items 1, 6, 9, 12, and 16 that require tasks c_2, c_3, c_6, and c_7 (mixed fractions with an equal denominator); category 2 contains items of simple fractions with different denominators; category 3 contains items of simple fractions with the same denominators; and category 4 contains items of mixed numbers with different denominators. Figure 5.1 is a plot of the four categories where the x-axis (the horizontal axis) is *item difficulties* and the y-axis (the vertical axis) is *item discrimination powers*. Categories 1 and 3 are located in the vicinity of each other in the second quadrant, whereas categories 2 and 4 are located in the upper part of the first quadrant. It is obvious that the task of getting a common denominator of two different denominators affects item difficulties, and then dealing with two mixed numbers affects item difficulties and discriminating powers. Conversely, if two items have very similar IRT curves, then they have very similar set of tasks that are involved in such items.

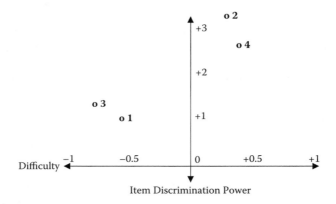

FIGURE 5.1
Clustering of items into four categories: 1, 2, 3, and 4.

5.3 Representing Items in a Tree Based on the Underlying Tasks

In this section, we described the hierarchical relationship among items ordered by the attribute involvement. If item j involved two easy attributes, whereas item k involved 10 harder attributes, then it would be much harder to get the correct answer for item K. By looking into what and how many attributes were involved in the items in a test, one could structure the items in a tree form as shown in Figure 3.5 in Chapter 3 or in Tatsuoka (1990).

This structure would provide an intuitive understanding of how the test would work on students, would give us a better idea of assembling appropriate items for a desired test, and further would give us useful hints to construct items. Structuring a tree of items would be illustrated with fraction subtraction problems in the next section.

Fraction Subtraction Test

Fraction subtraction problems (a b/c – d e/f) also have two strategies, Methods A and B. Method A converted the mixed numbers to two improper fractions and subtracted the second from the first. Method B separated the whole-number parts (a, d) from the fraction parts (b/c, and c/f), subtracted the two whole numbers and the two fractions separately, and then combined the answers for the two parts to get the final answer.

$$\text{Method A } [5\ 2/5 - 2\ 1/5 \Rightarrow 27/5 - 11/5 \Rightarrow 16/5 \Rightarrow 3\ 1/5]$$

or

$$\text{Method B } [5\ 2/5 - 2\ 1/5 \Rightarrow (5 - 2) + (2/5 - 1/5) \Rightarrow 3\ 1/5]$$

Item Tree

Tatsuoka (1990) showed two incidence matrices, **Q**s, developed for fraction subtraction problems. They are based on two different strategies for answering the problems with the identical set of attributes. Method A converts mixed numbers to simple fractions, and subtracts the second from the first. On the other hand, Method B uses borrowing—to borrow 1 from the whole-number part of the first fraction until its numerator becomes large enough to perform subtraction by the numerator of the second fraction number. Their tasks and Q matrices are described in Figure 5.2. The two matrices show quite a difference in involvement of attributes.

For Method A, the number of categories is 16, and they are {1}, {2, 3}, {4}, {5}, {6, 8}, {7}, {9}, {10, 11}, {12}, {13}, {14}, {15}, {16}, {17}, {18, 20}, and {19}. For Method B, the number of categories is 14, and they are {1}, {2, 3}, {4, 11, 20}, {5}, {6, 8}, {7, 15}, {9}, {10}, {12}, {13}, {14, 16}, {17}, {18}, and {19}. The inclusion

Method A (Always convert a mixed number to an improper fraction.)

Attributes	1	2	3	4	5	6	7	8	9	10	11	12	13	14	15	16	17	18	19	20
A1. Convert a whole number to a fraction	0	0	0	0	0	0	1	0	1	0	0	0	0	0	0	1	0	0	0	1
A2. Convert 1st mixed number to a fraction	0	0	0	1	1	0	1	0	1	1	1	0	1	1	0	1	1	1	1	1
A3. Convert 2nd mixed number to a fraction	0	0	0	1	1	0	0	0	0	1	1	0	1	1	0	1	0	1	0	1
A4. Simplify before subtracting	1	0	0	1	1	0	0	0	0	1	1	1	0	0	0	0	0	1	1	1
A5. Find a common denominator & make equivalent fractions	1	1	1	0	1	0	0	0	0	0	0	0	0	1	0	0	0	0	0	0
A6. Column borrow to subtract numerators	1	0	0	0	1	0	0	0	1	0	0	0	1	0	0	0	0	1	1	1
A7. Reduce answer to the simplest form	0	0	0	0	1	0	0	0	1	1	1	1	0	0	1	1	1	1	1	1

Method B (Separate mixed numbers into whole and fraction parts.)

Attributes	1	2	3	4	5	6	7	8	9	10	11	12	13	14	15	16	17	18	19	20
A1. Convert a whole number to fraction or mixed number	0	0	0	0	0	0	1	0	1	0	0	0	0	0	0	1	0	0	0	1
A2. Separate whole number from fraction	0	0	0	1	1	0	1	0	1	1	1	0	1	1	1	1	1	1	1	1
A3. Simplify before subtraction	0	0	0	1	1	0	1	0	0	1	1	1	0	0	1	0	0	1	1	1
A4. Find a common denominator & make equivalent fractions	1	1	1	0	1	0	0	0	0	0	0	0	0	1	0	0	0	0	0	0
A5. Borrow 1 from whole number part, change numerator	0	0	0	1	0	0	0	0	0	0	1	1	0	1	0	0	0	1	1	1
A6. Column borrow to subtract 2nd numerator from 1st	1	0	0	0	0	0	0	0	0	0	1	0	0	0	0	0	0	0	1	0
A7. Reduce answer to the simplest form	0	0	0	0	1	0	0	0	0	1	0	1	0	0	0	0	0	0	0	0

FIGURE 5.2
The incidence matrices Q_A and Q_B based on Methods A and B in 40-item fraction subtraction problems.

relation of attributes can order each item that is represented by a column vector of Q. That is, if item j includes all the attributes involved in item i, then item j requires no fewer tasks than item i. Thus, we consider item j to be included ($j \subseteq i$) in item i. This relation satisfies the reflexive and transitive laws that are necessary to form an order relationship. Therefore, column vectors $q_1, q_2, \ldots, q_n$ in **Q** are partially ordered with respect to the inclusion relation of attributes involved in the items. Figures 5.3a and 5.3b, which are called *item trees*, depict the partial order relation among the items in Methods A and B (Tatsuoka, 1990). The items connected by directed arrows are totally ordered.

Conditional Probabilities in an Item Tree

There are 2^7 possible response patterns obtainable from the attribute item matrix in each method. However, the item trees in Figures 5.3a and 5.3b enable us to select a smaller number of rules and bugs that are substantially important in designing and evaluating lessons. The numbers shown near the directed arcs of Figures 5.3a and 5.3b are conditional probabilities,

$$\text{Prob} (X_i = 1|_{Xi-1} = X_{i-2} = \cdots X_1 = 1)$$

where $i - 1, i - 2, \ldots, 1$ are antecedent items of i, and X is the score of item i.

Because $q_i \geq q_{i-1}$ (i.e., item i includes all the attributes involving item $i - 1$), a drastic decrease in the value of the conditional probability implies that a newly added attribute (or attributes) causes the change. For instance, for Method B, the new attribute added to item 17 is indeed a difficult subtask—borrowing. If a student cannot do this new attribute but can do the other attributes perfectly well, then subsequent items not including the borrowing attribute can be answered correctly. Thus, a binary response pattern corresponding to the student's performance would be zero (0) for the items that involve borrowing and would be one (1) for nonborrowing items. This conjecture with respect to borrowing may be confirmed by examining the arc between items 12 and 10.

Next, the conditional probability value between items 9 and 7 is .60, which is low enough to merit attention. The new attribute in the second box is *w to f or m*—converting whole numbers to fractions or mixed numbers. Therefore, the second response pattern resulting from this case is zero (0) for the items with whole numbers in their first position such as $3 - \frac{1}{2}$, and one (1) for the items not including whole numbers in their first position. By proceeding in this manner, we would obtain a set of response patterns that are logically interpretable. Thus, representing the structural relationships among the items with respect to their underlying cognitive attributes facilitates error analysis.

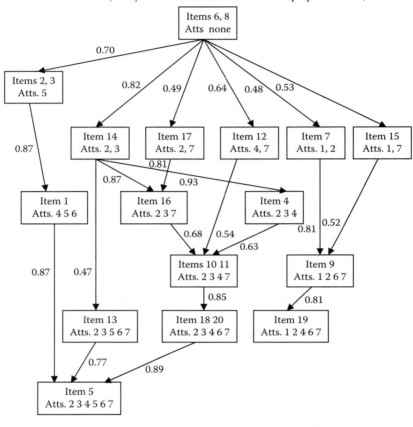

Method A (Always convert mixed numbers to an improper fractions)

Items

1. 5/3 – ¾	11. 4 1/3 – 2 4/3
2. 3/4 – 3/8	12. 11/8 – 1/8
3. 5/6 – 1/9	13. 3 3/8 – 2 5/6
4. 3 1/2 – 2 3/2	14. 3 4/5 – 3 2/5
5. 4 3/5 – 3 4/10	15. 2 – 1/3
6. 6/7 – 4/7	16. 4 5/7 – 1 4/7
7. 3 – 2 1/5	17. 7 3/5 – 4/5
8. 2/3 – 2/3	18. 4 1/10 – 3 8/10
9. 3 7/8 – 2	19. 4 – 1 4/3
10. 4 4/12 – 2 7/12	20. 4 1/3 – 1 5/3

FIGURE 5.3a

Item tree of Method A for fraction subtraction problems with conditional probabilities between two boxes connected by the inclusive relation of attributes.

Method B (Separate a mixed number into whole and fraction parts)

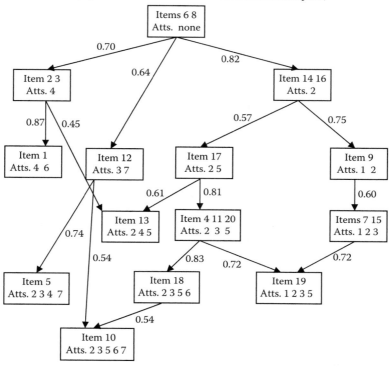

Items

1. 5/3 – ¾
2. 3/4 – 3/8
3. 5/6 – 1/9
4. 3 1/2 – 2 3/2
5. 4 3/5 – 3 4/10
6. 6/7 – 4/7
7. 3 – 2 1/5
8. 2/3 – 2/3
9. 7/8 – 2
10. 4 4/12 – 2 7/12

11. 4 1/3 – 2 4/3
12. 11/8 – 1/8
13. 3 3/8 – 2 5/6
14. 3 4/5 – 3 2/5
15. 2 – 1/3
16. 4 5/7 – 1 4/7
17. 7 3/5 – 4/5
18. 4 1/10 – 3 8/10
19. 4 – 1 4/3
20. 4 1/3 – 1 5/3

FIGURE 5.3b
Item tree of Method B for fraction subtraction problems with conditional probabilities between two boxes connected by the inclusive relation of attributes.

However, when we consider a larger scale of assessment such as the SAT Verbal or Mathematics tests, then very few items have the same set of attributes.

5.4 Rule Space as the Cartesian Product of Two Variables, IRT θ and ζ

Most models for pattern recognition and classification problems consisted of three components called a transducer, a feature extractor, and a pattern classifier. The transducer sensed the input and converted it to a form suitable for machine processing. The feature extractor extracted presumably relevant information from the input data. The classifier used the information to classify the input to one of the predetermined classification groups. However, the last two components were relevant to our goals of cognitive diagnosis. Because feature extraction was discussed in the earlier chapters, the third component for classification problems will be discussed in this chapter and Chapter 2. Rule space was designed to achieve the third stage, classification. Rule space was an n-dimensional vector space and was constructed for performing the multivariate decision theory for many classification groups. The classification space could be a discrete item space (say, 60 dimensions for a 60-item test), but the knowledge states with extremely high or low total scores or unusual knowledge states did not have the covariance matrices whose determinants were not zeros (Kim, 1989). Therefore, we transformed discrete item scores to continuous variables, IRT θ and person–fit index ζ (Tatsuoka, 1984b, 1985), and used them as coordinates of the classification space.

Rule Space (Classification Space)

The IRT models assume the local independence of responses to the items. Therefore, the likelihood of each knowledge state can be computed by Equation (5.3). For each ideal item response pattern R_i,

$$L_{R_i} = \prod_{j=1}^{n} P_j(\theta)^{R_{ij}}[1 - P_j(\theta)]^{1-R_{ij}} \tag{5.3}$$

It is known that the likelihood correlates very highly with ζ defined in Chapter 6. (Birenbaum, 1985; Harnisch & Tatsuoka, 1983). Index ζ is defined by the standardized covariance of two residuals: $P(\theta) - x$, and

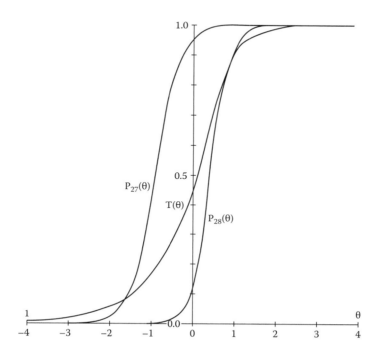

FIGURE 5.4
Average of 40-item response curves, T(θ), and IRT curves of items 27 and 28.

$P(θ) - T(θ)$ denoted by $f(X)$. Then, $f(x)$ is a linear function of x, as follows:

$$f(x) = P(θ) [P(θ) - T(θ)] - x [P(θ) - T(θ)] \qquad (5.4)$$

Because IRT curves are sensitive to the underlying cognitive processes, as mentioned earlier (Tatsuoka, 1987), the deviation of $P_j(θ)$ denoted by $P_j(θ) - T(θ)$ also reflects the underlying cognitive processes. But the shapes of the function $P_j(θ) - T(θ)$ are different from those of the original logistic function. Figure 5.4 shows three curves where the difficulty of item 27 is smaller than the average function $T(θ)$ and that of item 28 is greater than $T(θ)$. Let us take $T(θ)$ as the horizontal axis and the value of $P_j(θ)$ as the vertical axis and draw the deviations of item response curves. Then, graphs of deviations $P_j(θ)$ would given in Figure 5.5.

Easier items are located in the upper half of the space, whereas more difficult items are in the lower half. If a student with ability 0 takes the score of 1 for easier items and 0 for harder items, then the value $f(x)$ would be smaller. If the student scores 0 for easier items and 1 for harder items, then the values of $f(x)$ tend to become larger. The same relation holds for Equation (5.2), the likelihood function.

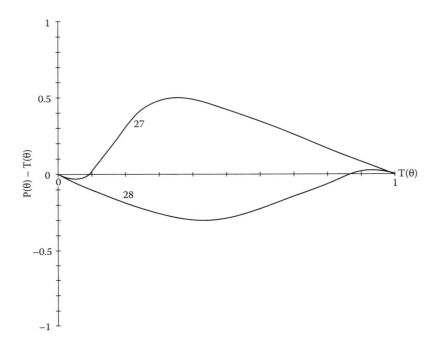

FIGURE 5.5
The curves of $P_{27}(\theta) - T(\theta)$ and $P_{28}(\theta) - T(\theta)$ over $T(\theta)$.

The rule space is defined as the Cartesian product of the IRT θ and zeta value for response pattern **X** where zeta depends on **X**, and is defined by Equation (5.5):

$$\mathbf{X} = (x_1, x_2, \ldots, x_n) \rightarrow (\theta_x, \zeta_x) \tag{5.5}$$

where $\zeta_x = f(\mathbf{X})/\text{sqrt}\{\text{var}(f(\mathbf{X})), \text{ and } \text{var}(f(\mathbf{X})) = [\sum_{j=1,n} \{(P_j(\theta_x) - T(\theta_x))(P_j(\theta_x) - x_j)\}]/[\sum_{j=1,n} \{P_j(\theta_x) Q_j(\theta_x) (P_j(\theta_x) - T(\theta_x))\}]$. Equation 5.5 will be discussed more in Section 5.6.

This representation of response patterns—mapping a response pattern into a vector space as a point—implies useful interpretation of the nature of responses. Although various statistical properties will be discussed in detail in Chapters 6 and 7, we mention that the points in space enable us to interpret the nature of response patterns with respect to which knowledge states or erroneous rules are commonly observed or unusual across the different levels of abilities. Table 5.5 shows the summary of the points (θ_x, ζ_x) of 39 rule classes called *knowledge states* introduced in Chapters 3 and 4 (for detailed descriptions of the 39 patterns, see Baillie

TABLE 5.5

The 39 Centroids Representing 39 Erroneous Rules of Operation (in Other Words, 39 Centroids of the Density Distribution of Latent Knowledge States)

KS	θ	ζ	Number of 1s	I(θ)⁻¹	KS	θ	ζ	Number of 1s	I(θ)⁻¹
1	−2.69	−.80	1	.85	21	.24	−.89	22	.01
2	−1.22	−.69	4	.08	22	−.22	−1.23	14	.02
3	−.75	−.68	8	.05	23	.62	−1.55	32	.01
4	−.46	.75	10	.03	24	1.04	−.61	38	.03
5	.11	.91	18	.02	25	.75	−.05	34	.01
6	.64	1.74	30	.01	26	−.51	−1.62	10	.04
7	−.17	1.48	13	.02	27	−.87	−.56	6	.05
8	.40	−.16	25	.01	28	−1.99	1.01	2	.29
9	.60	−.43	31	.01	29	−.19	1.53	12	.02
10	.57	−.24	29	.01	30	−.24	2.74	10	.03
11	.99	.72	37	.03	31	−1.18	1.46	4	.07
12	1.19	.86	39	.05	32	−1.45	.58	4	.11
13	−.60	−1.58	10	.04	33	.57	−.66	31	.01
14	−.44	−2.31	12	.03	34	.59	−1.39	30	.01
15	−.18	.67	14	.02	35	−1.66	−1.96	4	.16
16	−.08	−1.81	16	.02	36	−.52	−.94	10	.04
17	.16	−.86	20	.02	37	−.32	−1.26	14	.03
18	−.01	−2.12	18	.02	38	−.41	−2.57	13	.03
19	.09	−2.26	20	.02	39	.17	−2.34	22	.01
20	.29	−1.51	24	.01					

& Tatsuoka, 1984). These points expressed by a set of ordered pairs (θ, ζ) in Table 5.5 are plotted in Figure 5.6, which shows the 39 centroids of these 39 patterns in the rule space.

The Interpretation of the Points in the Rule Space

Figure 5.6 indicates that the points in the upper-right side correspond to the high total scores and unusual response patterns. The upper-left side symbolizes that low-ability students are committing unusual errors. The lower part of the rule space in the figure indicates that students' errors are commonly observed. Moreover, the black squares in Figure 5.6 stand for the knowledge states using Method B, whereas the circles with "+" sign inside are the knowledge states using Method A (Tatsuoka, Linn, Tatsuoka, & Yamamoto, 1988). Figure 5.6 shows that Method A users are located in the upper part of the rule space and Method B users are located in the lower part of the rule space. Method B users have lower values of zeta as compared with Method A users. It implies that Method B is a more typical strategy than Method A for this sample (Tatsuoka, 1990).

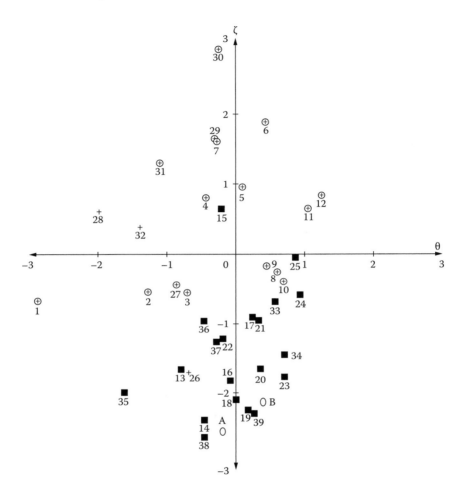

FIGURE 5.6
The centroids of 39 bug distributions; in other words, the density distribution of 39 latent knowledge states.

The rational of atypicality and typicality will be explained by a fraction subtraction example. If a student has a wrong rule for the borrowing operation in fraction subtraction, then that student's response pattern consists of 1s for the items that do not require borrowing and 0s for those requiring borrowing. Figures 5.7 and 5.8 show two sets of strikingly different curves of the deviation of $P_j(\theta)$.

The first set of items, in Figure 5.7, contains items 4, 10, 11, 13, 17, 18, 19, and 20, which require borrowing before subtraction of the numerators is

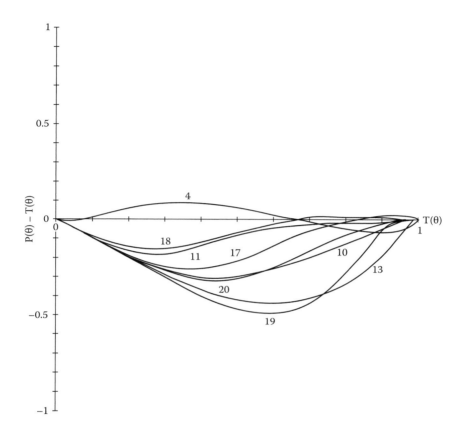

FIGURE 5.7
The curves of eight items requiring borrowing.

carried out. The second set of items, in Figure 5.8, includes nonborrowing items 1, 2, 3, 5, 6, 8, 9, 12, 14, and 16; items 7 and 15 are excluded. Items 7 and 15 need conversion of a whole number to an improper fraction or mixed number. All the items in Figure 5.7 (except item 4) have the functions $P_j(\theta) - T(\theta)$ that are below the x-axis. The x-axis represents the average function of $P_j(\theta)$, $T(\theta)$. The functions in Figure 5.8 all have curves above the horizontal axis.

Let us consider the borrowing error (called "G19" in Tatsuoka, 1984a). This error makes the responses wrong for the items involving the borrowing attribute in Method B in Figure 5.4. Thus, the items not containing this attribute become 1, and those involving borrowing become 0. The response pattern associated with the borrowing error G19 has the ideal item score

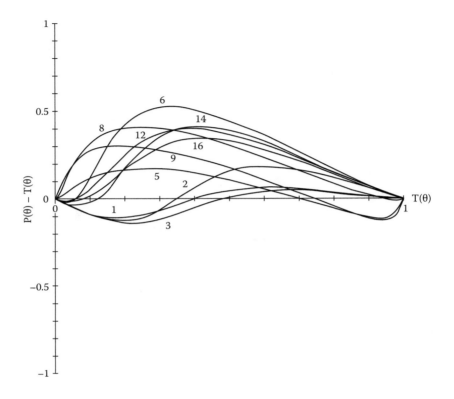

FIGURE 5.8
The curves of items *not* requiring borrowing.

pattern of G19 = (11101101100111010000111011011100111010000), and the maximum likelihood estimate of the latent variable θ is .09. The value of T(θ) for G19 is obtained by substituting θ = .09 into the item response functions and yields T(.09) = .48. Next, let us examine the values of the functions Pj(θ) – T(θ) at T(θ) = .48. The functions Pj(θ) – T(θ) at T(θ) = .48 have clearly different values for borrowing items than for nonborrowing items. Because the value of Equation (5.5) at a given θ depends on the item score of 1 or 0, the ζ value of G19 is a negative number. By dividing the value of f(G19) by the standard deviation at 0, the value of ζ is obtained, G19 = (.09, –2.26) in the rule space. It is interesting to see that the two sets of knowledge states derived from the two entirely different structures of the item trees, based on Methods A and B, partition the rule space and yet spread evenly over the θ-axis. Because the points below the θ-axis conform better to the order of item difficulties, they are more typical performances on the test items. If a rule is very unusual, then the location of the rule is in the upper part of the space. Thus, the location within the space tells whether or not the rule is atypical with high scores or low scores. In this example, Method B is a more typical strategy than Method A.

5.5 Variability of Response Errors and a Cluster of Response Patterns Around a Knowledge State (or, Equivalently, Ideal Item Score Patterns)

If we perform perfectly consistently on a test, then our responses to the test items will be perfectly matched to one of the ideal item score patterns generated from its Q matrix when it is assumed to be true. If a student answers perfectly consistently to test items, then we can identify the student's knowledge state (KS) by matching it to a list of the ideal item score patterns. The mastery state will, by definition, produce the right answer to all the items. Although wrong rules such as those we found in the study of signed-number operations (Birenbaum & Tatsuoka, 1980) sometimes may produce the right answer to some subset of the test items, it is very unlikely that they will produce the right answer to all the items. We further assume that the test items are carefully constructed so that the important, predicted common knowledge states can be expressed by unique item response patterns of ones and zeros. Therefore, KS R can be represented by a binary vector $R = (r1\ r2, \ldots, rm)$. However, actual student performance on the test items is unlikely to be perfectly consistent, and is subject to random errors or slips due to carelessness or uncertainty that always affects the outcomes of performances on a test. Even if a student possesses some systematic error, it is rare to have the response pattern perfectly matched with the pattern theoretically generated by its algorithm (Tatsuoka, 1984a; VanLehn, 1983). Some systematic errors may have a tendency to produce more slips, whereas other rules produce fewer slips. Some items may be prone to produce more slips than other items. Thus, it would not be realistic to assume that all the items have equal slip probabilities.

Any diagnostic methods must be capable of taking the variability of response errors into account. The methods must be able to diagnose responses that are affected by random errors (sometimes called *slips*) or that are produced by novel ways of thinking that are not taken into account by the current models. It is very difficult to develop a computer program whose underlying algorithms for solving a problem represent a wide range of individual differences (Sleeman, Kelly, Martink, Ward, & Moore, 1989). Yet, when diagnostic systems (Brown & Burton, 1978) are used in educational practice, they must be capable of evaluating any responses on test items, including inconsistent performances and those yielded by creative thinking. Developments in cognitive psychology and science point out that students repeatedly test and evaluate hypotheses until learning advances. As stated by VanLehn (1983),

> If they are unsuccessful in an attempt to apply a procedure to a problem they are not apt to just quit, as a computer program does. Instead they will be inventive, invoking certain general purpose tactics to change their current process state in such a way that they can continue the procedure. (p. 10)

Birenbaum and Tatsuoka (1980) showed that inconsistent and volatile applications of skills and erroneous rules in signed-number arithmetic were a common phenomenon among nonmasters.

Clustering Similar Response Patterns

Tatsuoka (1985) described why one of the zeta indices, ζ_2, has the property of clustering the points in the rule space that correspond to the response patterns originating from similar kinds of performances on test items. Tatsuoka and Baillie (1982) simulated such clusters in the context of signed-number arithmetic. Similarly, various cluster points in the rule space that correspond to different kinds of response patterns and their neighboring patterns in fraction addition and subtraction problems are shown in Tatsuoka (1984a). The simulation study by Tatsuoka and Baillie showed that the response patterns yielded by less than perfect application of a specific erroneous rule of operation in a procedural domain form a cluster around the rule. This useful result is due to the use of f(**x**) as a mapping function, and this property is summarized below as Property 5.1 of f(**x**).

Figure 5.9 is obtained by mapping four different response patterns (24 items) resulting from the four erroneous rules of operations in signed-number problems to the rule space (Birenbaum & Tatsuoka, 1982; Tatsuoka, 1985). Four sets of 24 patterns that are deviated from the original four rules of patterns by one slip are generated and mapped into the same rule space. The 24 points (marked x) in each set are swarmed around their original response pattern (marked blank square), respectively. In Figure 5.9, we used T(θ) as the horizontal axis instead of using θ, but using θ produces the same results.

Property 5.1: Similar response patterns are mapped into neighboring points in the rule space. The similarity of patterns is measured by counting the different responses on the items. We call the number of different responses on the items *Hamming distance*. If two response patterns x_1 and x_1 are

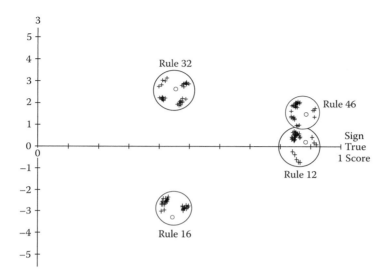

FIGURE 5.9
The four clusters of the response patterns deviated from the four erroneous rules with a few slippages in the signed-number problems are plotted in the space spanned by ζ and $T(\theta)$, which are computed in a sample dataset scored by the correct use of signs.

close with respect to Hamming distance, then their images $\{\theta_1, f(x_1)\}$ and $\{\theta_2, f(x_2)\}$ are also close and fall into neighboring points in the rule space.

More importantly, some studies found empirically that the two random variables, θ and ζ, obtained from those response patterns in the cluster follow an approximate multivariate normal distribution. This cluster around a rule will be called a *bug distribution* hereafter. The theoretical foundation of this empirical finding will be discussed in the Section 5.6. First, a brief description of the probabilistic model introduced in Tatsuoka (1985) will be given. Then the connection of each bug distribution to this model will be discussed in conjunction with the theory of statistical pattern classification and recognition.

5.6 Bug Distributions: Distribution of Responses Around an Ideal Item Score Pattern

We here assume that a set of knowledge states or erroneous rules that one wishes to diagnose is given a priori. Indeed, it is possible to predict a set of erroneous rules by carrying out a detailed, logical task analysis

(Klein et al., 1981). Further, we assume that each KS or rule yields its unique response pattern(s) to the test items.

The responses that are produced by not perfectly consistent applications of a rule or a knowledge state to the test items form a cluster around the response pattern yielded by consistent application of the rule or the knowledge state. They include responses that deviate, in various degrees, from the response generated by the rule or from a Q matrix. When these discrepancies are observed, they are considered random errors. These random errors are called *slips* by cognitive scientists (VanLehn, 1983). The statistical properties of such responses around a given erroneous rule were investigated (Tatsuoka & Tatsuoka, 1987). We introduce their work in this section.

Bug Distribution

The distribution of observations plays an important role in statistical theories. When we deal with students, random errors or slips due to careless errors or uncertainty always affect the outcomes of performance on a test. A slip on item j occurs when a student does not use his or her rule exactly on item j, and as a result, the response to item j does not match the response yielded by the rule. The response that deviated from the rule-based response may, of course, be the correct response. Even if a student possesses some systematic error, it is very rare to have the response pattern perfectly matched with the patterns theoretically generated by its algorithm (Tatsuoka, 1984b; VanLehn, 1983). Figure 5.10 shows the outcome of a deterministic buggy system for fraction addition problems. Figure 5.10 shows the erroneous rules used by 149 students on the 38 items of fraction addition problems. The entries of the dataset were sorted by the total scores and item difficulties given by the proportion correct. The entry of 1 represents the correct answers, and the entry of –1 means some erroneous rules yield correct answers coincidentally, and 99 in the table represents missing data. The numbers in the table indicate that most students use their erroneous rules fairly systematically. However, most students use two or three erroneous rules throughout the 38-item test. The entry of "0" is considered random errors or unknown erroneous rules. Erroneous rule 11 (students add the numerators and denominators independently for their answers) is seen systematically, especially for the lower scored students. Figure 5.11 shows the probability distribution (bug distribution) of rules 15, 17, 33, 32, and 43.

stu	sc	17	18	7	12	16	6	19	14	9	3	1	11	15	8	4	13	18	2	5
1	38	1	1	−1	1	1	1	1	1	1	1	1	−1	−1	−1	1	1	−1	1	1
152	37	1	1	−1	1	1	1	1	1	1	1	43	−1	−1	−1	1	1	−1	1	1
95	36	1	1	−1	1	1	1	1	1	1	1	43	−1	−1	−1	1	0	−1	1	1
195	36	1	1	−1	1	1	1	1	1	32	1	1	−1	−1	−1	1	1	−1	1	1
223	36	1	1	−1	1	1	1	42	1	1	1	1	−1	−1	−1	1	1	−1	1	1
257	36	1	1	−1	1	1	1	1	1	43	1	1	−1	−1	−1	1	1	−1	1	1
310	36	1	1	−1	1	1	1	1	1	1	1	43	−1	−1	−1	1	1	−1	1	1
311	36	1	1	−1	0	1	1	1	1	43	1	1	−1	−1	−1	1	1	−1	1	1
546	25	1	0	7	11	1	1	1	1	1	57	43	−1	−1	−1	1	1	−1	1	1
560	25	1	1	0	1	1	1	42	0	1	1	0	−1	−1	−1	1	1	26	99	0
99	24	1	1	−1	1	1	0	1	1	1	1	1	58	−1	58	1	0	11	0	11
326	22	1	1	1	0	1	99	1	0	1	1	1	12	1	1	99	1	1	99	1
117	21	1	1	−1	1	1	1	1	1	1	1	1	0	0	56	0	40	0	65	0
127	21	1	1	−1	1	1	1	1	1	1	33	1	15	0	1	0	0	0	0	0
242	21	1	1	−1	1	1	1	1	1	1	1	1	11	11	11	99	11	11	0	99
284	21	1	1	−1	1	1	1	1	1	1	1	1	11	11	11	99	11	11	11	99
294	21	1	1	−1	1	0	1	1	1	1	1	1	99	99	15	99	99	99	99	99
300	21	1	1	−1	1	1	1	1	1	1	1	0	11	11	11	99	11	99	11	99
317	21	1	1	−1	1	1	1	1	1	1	1	43	99	99	99	99	99	99	99	99
332	21	1	1	−1	1	1	1	1	1	1	1	1	11	11	11	99	11	99	11	99
425	21	1	1	−1	1	1	1	1	1	1	1	0	99	0	12	48	0	54	0	99
558	21	1	1	1	1	1	1	1	1	1	1	1	63	0	63	0	0	64	0	0
239	20	1	1	−1	1	1	1	1	1	1	1	0	48	15	15	48	11	11	66	99
261	20	1	1	7	1	1	1	1	1	1	1	1	63	15	15	15	0	11	0	0
334	20	1	1	−1	1	1	1	1	1	1	1	0	51	21	51	1	51	51	0	51
351	20	1	1	−1	1	1	1	1	0	1	1	0	63	1	63	0	0	0	0	7
418	20	1	1	−1	1	1	1	1	1	1	1	1	15	15	15	15	47	17	15	15
482	20	1	1	−1	1	1	1	1	1	1	1	1	11	11	0	15	67	11	15	67
506	20	1	1	−1	1	1	1	1	1	1	1	1	0	15	15	17	0	0	15	15
448	3	0	45	45	0	0	0	45	0	0	7	0	45	45	0	45	45	45	0	99
578	3	1	11	99	11	11	99	99	99	99	99	99	11	11	11	0	11	99	11	99
26	2	11	1	28	11	0	11	0	38	11	38	51	11	11	11	11	0	11	11	11
65	2	11	11	11	11	67	2	11	0	15	67	11	11	11	0	0	67	11	67	67
68	2	11	11	−1	11	1	11	0	11	11	11	11	11	11	11	0	11	11	11	11
82	2	11	11	0	11	11	11	0	11	11	33	0	11	11	11	11	11	0	11	11
98	2	1	99	99	11	99	99	99	11	99	0	1	11	99	99	99	99	17	99	10
131	2	10	10	0	67	0	10	67	67	10	1	10	10	14	67	67	10	0	10	67
222	2	11	11	11	1	11	11	11	0	11	11	11	11	11	11	0	11	11	0	11
305	2	11	11	0	11	1	0	11	11	11	11	11	11	11	11	11	11	11	11	11
370	2	11	11	11	11	11	1	11	11	11	11	11	11	11	11	0	11	11	11	11
440	2	11	11	11	11	11	11	99	0	11	11	0	11	11	11	0	11	99	11	99

FIGURE 5.10
A data matrix of students and items in which each cell is filled with erroneous rules of operation, which the students have used in solving the items listed on the first row.

7	The whole number multiplied by the numerator equals the new numerator. Then add the fractions correctly.
10	Append a one to all fractions and convert the mixed fraction to an improper fraction. Apply an addition procedure error by corresponding parts.
11	Addition procedure error, add corresponding parts.
14	Change mixed numbers to improper fractions, cancel factors common to the numerator of one 21 fraction and the denominator of the other fraction. Multiply denominators if different after cancelling.
15	Change mixed numbers to improper fractions then add numerators and multiply denominators.
19	Use the denominator by the denominator of the other fraction to get the new numerator. The least common denominator must be less than the denominators multiplied together. Then add correctly.
32	When adding mixed numbers, add a one to the whole number part of the answer.
33	When adding mixed numbers add the fractions correctly but omit the whole number.
42	Multiply the numerators. Add the whole numbers.
43	Addition procedure error: multiply the whole numbers.
45	Add the denominator of the first fraction to the numerator of the second fraction to obtain the numerator. Add the numerator of the first fraction to the denominator of the second fraction to obtain the denominator.
48	Multiply both numerator and denominator, add the whole numbers.
51	Change mixed numbers to improper fractions, invert second fraction and multiply corresponding parts.
57	Cancel common factors from one numerator to the other denominator. Add numerators, multiply denominators, and add whole numbers.
63	Add the numerator and denominators of both fractions to obtain the numerator. Multiply the denominators.
66	Add the numerator and denominator of the second fraction to obtain the numerator. The denominator is the least common denominator.
67	Mixed numbers are converted to improper fractions, corresponding parts are added.
99	Missing, they did not try this item.
−1	There are erroneous rules produce the correct answer.

FIGURE 5.10
(Continued)

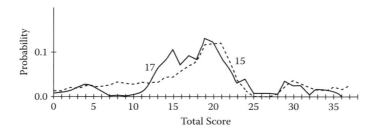

FIGURE 5.11
Probabilities of the occurrences of erroneous rules 11 and 15 in fraction addition problems.

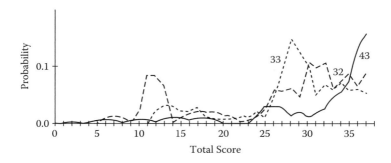

FIGURE 5.12
Fifteen ellipses representing 15 knowledge states that are randomly chased from the original 39 knowledge states given in Table 5.1.

Slips From Rules or Knowledge States

Some systematic errors may produce more slips, whereas others have a small number of slips. Also, some items may be prone to produce more slips than other items. It is very important that we are able to predict the probability of having slips on each item for each systematic error (or rule). Knowing the theoretical distribution of observed slips of a rule enables us to see and predict statistical properties of observed responses yielded by the rule. The argument using rules can be applied to knowledge states without loss of generality. A rule will be an ideal item score pattern generated by belonging to a particular knowledge state.

First, the probability of having a "slip" on item j (j = 1, 2, ..., n) is assumed to have the same value, p, for all items and to have the slips occur independently across items. This will be called *slip probability* in this book. Let us denote an arbitrary rule for which the total score is r by rule R, and let the corresponding response pattern be

$$
R = \begin{vmatrix} X_1 \\ X_2 \\ \cdot \\ X_r \\ X_{r+1} \\ X_{r+2} \\ \cdot \\ \cdot \\ X_n \end{vmatrix} = \begin{vmatrix} 1 \\ 1 \\ \cdot \\ 1 \\ 0 \\ 0 \\ \cdot \\ \cdot \\ 0 \end{vmatrix}
\tag{5.6}
$$

The response patterns existing "one slip away" from rule R are of two kinds: x_j going from one to zero for some j between 1 and r and x_j going from zero to one for some j between $r + 1$ and n. The first r elements in Equation (5.6) are 1s and starting from $r + 1$, $n - r$ elements from X_{r+1} to X_n are 0s. The number of response patterns having one slip has two cases: (1) one of X_1 through X_r changed to 0, and none of X_{r+1} through X_n changed or (2) none of X_1 through X_r changed to 0, and one of X_{r+1} through X_n changed to 1. The selection of a slip "1 to 0" from $X_1,\ldots, X_r$ has r ways, and expressed by $_rC_1 \frac{r!!}{1!(r-1)!} = r$ (Kolman, Busby, & Ross, 2004; Stuare & Ord, 1987). Similarly, the selection of a slip "1 to 0" from $X_{r+1}, \ldots, X_n$ ha $n-r$ ways and expressed by $_{n-r}C_1 = \frac{(n-r)!}{1!(n-r-1)!} = n - r$. The probability of having a slip on item is the multiplication of $p(1 - p)$ and the number of ways to have a slip on X_1 through X_n, so Equation (5.7),

$$
\text{Prob (having a slip on an item)} = \left\{ r + (n - r) \right\} p^1 \left(1 - p \right)^{n-1} = np^1(1-p)^1
\tag{5.7}
$$

For k slips, there are k different ways to have k slips from 2 set of items, X_1 through X_r and X_{r+1} through X_n. The partition of k will be $\{1, k-1\}, \{2, k-2\},\ldots ,\{k - 1, 1\}$. We have to count separately how many ways an item has a slip by each of k partioned set and sum up them. Therefore, we express it by $\Sigma_{k_1+k_2=k}$. Having k_1 slips among X_1 through is $_rC_{k1}$ and having k_2 slips X_{r+1} through X_n is $r_{n-r}C_{k2}$ where $_rC_{k1} = \frac{r!}{k_1!(r-k_1)}$ and $_{n-r}C_{k2} = \frac{(n-r)!}{k_2!(n-r-k_2)!}$, respectively. Since having the slips of k_1, "1 to 0" and having the slips of k_2 "0 to 1" are independent event, having the slips of $k_1 + k_2$ can be obtained by multiplying and $_rC_{k1\ n-r}C_{k2}$. The probability of having k slips on the items is given by the following:

$$\text{Prob (having k slips on the items)} = \left\{ \sum_{k_1+k_2=k} (_rC_{k1})(_{n-r}C_{k2}) \right\} p^k (1-p)^{n-k}.$$

(5.8)

The probability of having no more than k slips will be given by Equation (5.9):

$$\text{Prob (having up to k slips)} = \sum_{s=0}^{k} {}_nC_s p^s (1-p)^{n-s}.$$

(5.9)

Therefore, a cluster around rule R that consists of response patterns including various numbers of slips (not-perfectly-consistent applications of KS R) has a probability distribution of the binomial form if all items have the same slip probability p. If, on the other hand, we assume each item to have a unique slip probability, then the cumulative binomial distribution expressed above will become a compound binomial distribution, as in Equation (5.10).

The probability of having up to k slips is given by

$$\text{Prob (having up to k slipes)} = \sum_{s=0}^{k} \left[\sum_{\sum xj=s} \left\{ \prod_{j=1}^{n} p_j^{xj} (1-p_j)^{1-x_j} \right\} \right]$$

(5.10)

The bug distribution of KS R is a function defined on the slip random variable u_j, and it relates algebraically to the conditional probability that a subject in the state of processing rule R would respond correctly to item j (Tatsuoka & Tatsuoka, 1987).

Building the Rule Space for Classification

The rule space model begins by mapping all possible binary response patterns into a set of ordered pairs $\{(\theta, \zeta)\}$, where θ is the latent ability variable in IRT and ζ is one of the IRT-based caution indices (Tatsuoka, 1984b; Tatsuoka & Linn, 1983). As stated in Section 5.5, ζ is the standardized form of a mapping function $f(x)$, which is the inner product of two residual vectors, $P(\theta) - x$ and $P(\theta) - T(\theta)$, where elements of $P(\theta)$, $P_j(\theta)$, $j = 1, ..., n$ are the one- or two-parameter logistic-model probabilities; X is a binary response vector; and $T(\theta)$ is the mean vector of the logistic probabilities.

f(**X**), the numerator of ζ, is a linear mapping function between **X** and ζ at a given level of θ, and the response patterns having the same sufficient statistics for the maximum likelihood estimate θ-hat of θ are dispersed to different locations on the vertical line $\theta = \theta$-hat.

$$\zeta = f(\mathbf{X})/\text{squared}(\text{var}(f(\mathbf{X}))) \tag{5.11}$$

For example, on a 100-item test, there are 4,950 different response patterns having the total score of 2. The ζs for the 4,950 binary patterns will be distributed between ζ_{min} and ζ_{max}, where ζ_{min} is obtained from the pattern having ones for the two easiest items and zeros elsewhere, and ζ_{max} is from the pattern having ones for the two most difficult items.

Tatsuoka (1985) showed that f(X) has expectation zero and variance given in Equation (5.12).

$$E(f(X)) = 0 \text{ at given } \theta,$$
$$\text{var}(f(X)) = \sum_{j=1,n} P_j(\theta) Q_j(\theta) \{P_j(\theta) - T(\theta)\}^2 \tag{5.12}$$

Because the conditional expectation of the random variable x_j, given θ, is $P_j(\theta)$, the expectation of response vector x is **P**(θ), whose jth component is $P_j(\theta)$. The vector **P**(θ) will be mapped to zero, as shown in Equation (5.12). Thus, the expected pattern (given θ) corresponds to (θ, 0) in the rule space.

$$f(E(X|\theta)) = f(\mathbf{P}(\theta)) = 0 \tag{5.13}$$

As for an erroneous rule R, the response vector **R** given by Equation (5.6) will be mapped onto (θ_R, f(**R**)), where the f(**R**) value is $\sum_{j=1,n}(P_j(\theta_R) - X_j)$ ($p_j(\theta_R) - T(\theta_R)$), and rewritten by Equation (5.14).

$$f(\mathbf{R}) = \sum_{j=1,n} P_j(\theta_R)\{P_j(\theta_R) - T(\theta_R)\} - \sum_{j=1,n} X_j\{P_j(\theta_R) - T(\theta_R)\} \tag{5.14}$$

Equation (5.14) is actually Equation (5.3) obtained by substituting θ by θ_R.

Similarly, all the response vectors resulting from several slips around rule R will be mapped in the vicinity of (θ_R, f(**R**)) in the rule space and from a cluster around R.

In particular, rule R itself will be mapped as

$$\mathbf{R} \rightarrow (\theta_R, f(\mathbf{R})) \tag{5.15}$$

where f(**R**) is given by Equation (5.14).

The variance of the cordinates of the cluster around R can be expressed by using the slip probabilities of the items p_j and $q_j = 1 - p_j$,

$$\text{Var(the cluster around R)} = \sum_{j=1,n} p_j q_j (P_j(\theta_R) - T(\theta_R))^2 \tag{5.16}$$

The variance of θ in any cluster, on the other hand, is given by the reciprocal of the information function at θ_R,

$$\text{Var } (\theta \text{ in the cluster around R}) = 1/I(\theta_R) \tag{5.17}$$

The variances, along with the fact that $f(x)$ and θ-hat are uncorrelated (Tatsuoka, 1985), plus the reasonable assumption that they have a bivariate normal distribution, allow us to construct any desired percent ellipse around each point R. If all erroneous rules and the correct one were to be mapped into the rule space along with their neighboring response patterns representing random slips from them, the resulting topography would be something like what is seen in Figure 5.9. That is, the population of points would exhibit modal densities at many rule points such that each forms the center of an enveloping ellipse, with the density of points getting rarer as we depart farther from the center in any direction. Furthermore, the major and minor axes of these ellipses would—by virtue of the uncorrelatedness of ζ and θ—be parallel to the vertical (ζ) and horizontal (θ) reference axes of the rule space, respectively (Tatsuoka, 1985).

Recalling that for any given percentage ellipse, the lengths of the major and minor diameters are fixed multiples of the respective standard deviations $1/[I(\theta)]^{1/2}$ and $[\Sigma_{j=1,n} \, P_j(\theta)Q_j(\theta)\{p_j(\theta) - T(\theta)\}^2]^{1/2}$, respectively. Because once these ellipses are given, any response pattern point can be classified as most likely being a random slip from one or another of the erroneous rules (or correct one). We have only to imagine letting all the ellipses "grow" in size at the same rate in terms of percent coverage. Then the point will, in most instances, be found to lie on just one of the ellipses (unless, with probability zero, it happens to be one of the points of intersection of two ellipses). Therefore, we may assert that the set of ellipses gives a complete characterization of the rule space.

The variance of the ordinates of the cluster of points around R is given as follows:

$$\text{Var(the cluster around R)} = \sum_{j=1,n} P_j(\theta)Q_j(\theta)(P_j(\theta_R) - T(\theta_R))^2 \tag{5.18}$$

$$\text{Var(the cluster around R)} = 1/I(\theta_R)$$

The variance and covariance matrix Σ_R is given by

$$\begin{bmatrix} \dfrac{1}{I(\theta_R)} & 0 \\[2em] 0 & \displaystyle\sum_{j=1}^{n} P_j(\theta_R)Q_j(\theta_R)(P_j(\theta_R) - T(\theta_R))^2 \end{bmatrix} \tag{5.19}$$

Slip Probabilities When a Cluster Around R Is Conditioned on θ Only

Slip probability of item j for a knowledge state R can be estimated by assuming the latent class model. The latent class model assumes that the state probability of **R** follows a multivariate normal distribution. However, in this chapter, we show that a slip probability for item j can be roughly approximated from item response theory functions, $P_j(\theta)$. Although the approximation from IRT functions is not recommended because there are better ways to estimate slip probabilities, it will give an intuitive insight into how IRT, latent class modelings, and the rule space method relate mathematically.

Suppose p_j is the slip probability of item j, and $p_j \neq p_l$ for items l different from j, $j \neq l$. Then, the probability density function of a cluster around R will be a compound binomial distribution. The conditional probability that x_j, the response to item j, is not equal to the jth element $(x_R)_j$ of rule R but $1 - (x_R)_j$ will be either $P_j(\theta)$ or $Q_j(\theta)$ depending on whether the jth element $(x_R)_j$ of x_R is zero or one, respectively. That is,

$$\text{Prob}(x_j \neq x_{Rj} \mid \theta_R) = \begin{bmatrix} \text{Prob}(x_j = 1 \mid \theta_R) = p_j(\theta_R) & \text{if } (x_R)_j = 0 \\ \text{Prob}(x_j = 0 \mid \theta_R) = Q_j(\theta_R) & \text{if } (x_R)_j = 1 \end{bmatrix} \quad (5.20)$$

Therefore, the slip probability of item j will be expressed by the logistic function $p_j(\theta)$ whose parameters are estimated from a sample. After mapping the distribution function g(R), the compound binomial distribution of the cluster around rule R is given by the term of the expansion of the generating function,

$$g(R) = \Pi_{j=1,n}\,(p_j(\theta_R) + Q_j(\theta_R)) \quad (5.21)$$

The mean and variance are given by the following:

$$\mu_R = \sum_{j=1,n} P_j(\theta_R) + \sum_{j=1,n} Q_j(\theta_R),$$

$$\sigma_R^2 = \sum_{j=1,n} P_j(\theta_R)Q_j(\theta_R) \quad (5.22)$$

After mapping the distribution function g(R) of rule R, the centroid becomes $(\theta_R,\ f(R))$ and the covariance matrix is given by the slip variable U_j, which is related to the item scores X_j on item j:

$$S_j = 1 \text{ if a slip occurs, and hence } X_j \neq X_{Rj}$$

$$S_j = 0 \text{ if a slip does not occur, and hence } X_j = X_{Rj} \quad (5.23)$$

or, equivalently,

$$U_j = |X_{Rj} - X_j| \tag{5.24}$$

The conditional probability of having a slip on item j for a given rule R is

$$\text{Prob}(U_j = 1|R) = \text{Prob}(X_j \neq X_{Rj}|R) \tag{5.25}$$

This relationship can be rewritten in the context of IRT models in the rule space:

$$\text{Prob}(X_j \neq X_{Rj}|R) = \text{Prob}(X_j \neq X_{Rj}|\theta_R, f(\mathbf{x})) \tag{5.26}$$

Because the expectation of $f(\mathbf{x})$ is zero, the rules that are used by many students have small values of $f(\mathbf{x})$. The conditional probability of having a slip on item j for such a rule will be very close to the conditional probability on θ only,

$$\text{Prob}(X_j \neq X_{Rj}|\theta_R, f(\mathbf{x})) \sim \text{Prob}(X_j \neq X_{Rj}|\theta_R) \tag{5.27}$$

Therefore, we get the expression

$$S_j(\theta) = (1 - X_{Rj})P_j(\theta_R) + X_{Rj}Q_j(\theta_R) \tag{5.28}$$

Relationship Between Bug Distribution and the Item Response Theory Model

Bug distribution was formulated by taking the notion of slips and slip probabilities into account. It was assumed that the occurrence of slips was independent across the items, and the probability of a slip occurring for each item was denoted by $P_{j|R}$, $j = 1, \ldots, n$. Each item j has its unique chance of having a slip away from Rj, and different values of slip probabilities are assumed across the items. Then, the probabilities of having some finite number of slips away from R was given by Equation (5.9) with the slip variable u_j.

Derivation of the compound binomial distribution in Equation (5.9) is applicable to any rules or knowledge states—where a set of response patterns resulting from inconsistent application of rule R was introduced as a cluster around rule R in Tatsuoka and Tatsuoka (1987) and was denoted by {R}. Tatsuoka and Tatsuoka (1987) discussed the bug distribution in the context of erroneous rule R, but the notion could be applicable to knowledge state R without loss of generality. When an erroneous knowledge state produces wrong answers for all the items in a test, it corresponds to the null vector, $\mathbf{0} = (0,0, \ldots, 0)$. In this case, the random variable u_j is the same as the random variable of item score x_j, so $\text{Prob}(u_j = 1 | \theta_0) = \text{Prob}(x_j = 1 | \theta_0)$, where θ_0 is the latent ability level of rule $\mathbf{0}$, and the slip probabilities of n items become the logistic functions $Pj(\theta)$ of IRT models. Therefore, it can be said that the IRT model is equivalent to the latent class model associated with the rule that produces the null vector, $\mathbf{0}$.

A sample whose response patterns are well described by the IRT model (i.e., an *IRT sample*) may contain clusters around many rules, including the cluster around the correct rule $\mathbf{1}$. Tatsuoka and Tatsuoka (1989) proposed a conjecture that the IRT model can be obtained by the finite number of a union set of latent class samples. They technically demonstrated that the likelihood functions of IRT expressed by IRT functions $Pj(\theta)$ and item response pattern $\mathbf{X}$ can be transformed to the likelihood functions of slippage probability functions $S_j(\theta_R)$ and patterns of slippages of several latent class samples. Let us state Tatsuokas' conjecture as follows:

Conjecture: Suppose that a sample {IRT} fits the IRT model well, then it contains K + 2 subsamples where each subsample is a latent class sample. The sample of latent class R_k is the clusters of responses around Rule R_k denoted by {R_k} that includes Rule $\mathbf{0}$ and Rule $\mathbf{1}$, denoted by {0} and {1}; then the IRT sample must be the union set of K + 2 samples of latent classes R_k, K = 1, ..., K

$$\{IRT\} = \{0\} \cup \{R_1\} \cup \{R_2\} \cdots \cup \{R_k\} \cup \{1\} = \overset{K+1}{\underset{k=0}{U}} \{R_k\}. \tag{5.29}$$

Yamamoto's hybrid model (1987) deals with this conjecture. He combined latent class modeling and item response theory in a single statistical model. Later, C. Tatsuoka developed the POSET model in the context of sequential analysis on a partially ordered network of knowledge states logically derived from a given Q matrix. He solved this issue in a general mathematical framework and proved that one can always converge to his or her true knowledge state with the optimum rate by selecting the next item based on his algorithm (Tatsuoka, 2002; Tatsuoka & Ferguson, 2003).

5.7   Expanding the Rule Space to a Multidimensional Space

Rule space was obtained by transforming a response pattern of n items into a Cartesian product of two continuous variables θ and ζ. One of several advantages of this approach was to provide the interpretability of knowledge states, and other advantages were also discussed in the previous section. One of the most important contributions was that it would help us to overcome some computational problems in decision theory. The conversion of a large number of binary item scores into a smaller number of continuous variables would ease computational burden. Then, more importantly, it would enable us to compute the inverse of a variance–covariance matrix, and thus the statistical pattern classification approach will be applicable for our classification problems. However, when we deal with a large-scale assessment, the number of knowledge states to be considered becomes several thousand. Therefore, the rule space with all the possible knowledge states mapped in the space would be too crowded. This situation would lead us to some problems.

Why We Need a Multidimensional Rule Space

Two important issues arise from this approach. The first issue is whether or not similar response patterns are mapped into two very close points in the space, and the second is that two points in the close vicinity in the space have similar response patterns. Let us define the similarity of two response patterns by the most intuitive manner, the number of different items in the patterns.

Definition of Hamming distance between two response patterns: The similarity of two response patterns X_1 and X_2 is given by their element-wise differences. The difference is measured by Hamming distance,

$$d = |X_1 - X_2| = \sum_{j=1,n} |x_i - x_i| \tag{5.30}$$

Property 5.1: Two similar response patterns will be mapped into two points close to each other in the rule space.

Let $P_j(\theta), j = 1, \ldots, n$ be the item response curves for n items, and R and X be similar response patterns. The meaning of *similar* is defined by Hamming distance, which is the number of nonmatched elements between R and X, $d = |R - X| = \sum_{j=1,n} |r_j - x_j|$. If d is a small integer value, then R and X are similar. If d = 2, then two elements in the response patterns R and X are different.

Because the rule space is a Cartesian product of θ and ζ, the proximity of estimated θ_R and θ_x is examined first. Estimated θ values are obtained iteratively from the likelihood function,

$$\sum_{j=1,n} a_j x_j = \sum_{j=1,n} a_j P(\theta_i) \tag{5.31}$$

for the response pattern of person i.

Graphical Estimation of θ Values

The relationship between the θ_R and the estimated θ_i is shown in Figure 5.13: The graph shows that the distance between estimated θ_R and estimated θ_i, $|\theta_R - \theta_i|$, depends on the difference between the two weighted total scores of $\Sigma_{j=1,n} a_j x_j$ and $\Sigma_{j=1,n} a_j r_j$. If the total scores of two response patterns are close, then their estimated θ values will be close too.

The numerator of the second coordinate ζ in the rule space is written by $f(X, \theta)$ and the absolute value of the difference between $f(X, \theta_X)$ and $f(R, \theta_R)$ is given by

$$|f(X, \theta_X) - f(R, \theta_R)| = | \sum_{j=1,n} \{P_j(\theta_X)(P_j(\theta_X) - T(\theta_X)) - P_j(\theta_R)(P_j(\theta_R) - T(\theta_R))\}$$

$$+ \sum_{j=1,n} \{x_j(P_j(\theta_X) - T(\theta_X)) - r_j(P_j(\theta_R) - T(\theta_R))\}|$$

$$= |K(\theta) + \sum_{j=1,n} \{x_j(P_j(\theta_X) - T(\theta_X)) - r_j(P_j(\theta_R) - T(\theta_R))\}| \quad (5.32)$$

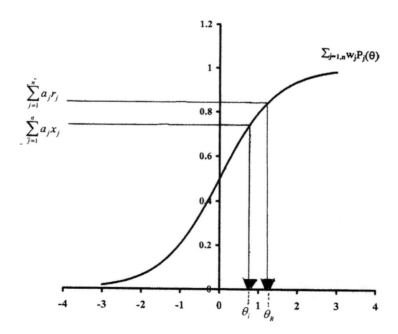

FIGURE 5.13
Graphical estimation of estimated θ_i and θ_R for a response pattern X for person i and Rule R, where $w_j = a_j/(\Sigma_{j=1,n} a_j)$.

$K(\theta)$ is not a function of response patterns X and R, so if we have a fixed θ value, then it can be considered a constant value. The second term can be rewritten by applying a Taylor expansion as follows:

$$\sum_{j=1,n} \{x_j(P_j(\theta_X) - T(\theta_X)) - r_j(P_j(\theta) - T(\theta_R))\}$$

$$= \sum_{j=1,n} \{(x_j - r_j)((P_j(\theta_R) - T(\theta_R)) + (\theta_R - \theta_X)[\partial(P_j(\theta_R))/\partial\theta - \partial(T(\theta_R))/\partial\theta]\}$$

$$\leq | \sum_{j=1,n} \{(x_j - r_j)((P_j(\theta_R) - T(\theta_R))| + | \sum_{j=1,n} (\theta_R - \theta_X)[\partial P_j(\theta_R)/\partial\theta - \partial T(\theta_R)/\partial\theta]\}|$$

(5.33)

Therefore, we get Equation (5.7.5),

$$|f(X, \theta_X) - f(R, \theta_R)| \leq \{|\theta_R - \theta_X| \ | \sum_{j=1,n} (\partial K(\theta)/\partial\theta + \partial P_j(\theta_R)/\partial\theta - \partial T(\theta_R)/\partial\theta)|\}$$

$$+ | \sum_{j=1,n} \{|(x_j - r_j)| \ |((P_j(\theta_R) - T(\theta_R))|\}$$

(5.34)

Hamming Distance and Mahalanobis Distance

If X and R have the Hamming distance of 1, the difference in the total scores is 1, and hence $|\theta_R - \theta_X|$ becomes a small number, where the Hamming distance is defined by the number of discrepancies in two corresponding columns of X and R. Therefore, $|f(X, \theta_X) - f(R, \theta_R)|$ becomes a small number.

The squared Mahalanobis distance D^2 between X and R in the rule space D^2 is given by $(\theta_R - \theta_X)^2/I(\theta_R)^{-1} + (f(R,\theta_R) - f(X,\theta_X))^2/var(f(\theta_R))$.

$$D^2 = (\theta_R - \theta_X)^2/I(\theta_R)^{-1} + \{f(R, \theta_R) - f(X, \theta_X)\}^2/var(f(\theta_R))$$ (5.35)

If X and R are close, then the squared Mahalanobis distance D^2 also becomes small because the two terms $(\theta_R - \theta_X)$ and $\{f(R,\theta_R) - f(X,\theta_X)\}$ in Equation (5.35) become small. The difference between X and R for ζ is the standardized version of $f(X,\theta_X)$ and $f(R,\theta_R)$, so both ζ values, ζ_X and ζ_R, must be close to each other in the rule space with respect to their Mahalanobis distance.

Example 5.1

The 20-item fraction subtraction problems have the following IRT item parameters. The response patterns R and the 20 patterns $X_1, X_2, ..., X_{20}$ are deviated by one element from R—in other words, their Hamming distance to R is 1, as given below.

IRT θ and ζ values for $\mathbf{R}$ and $\mathbf{X_1}$ through $\mathbf{X_{20}}$ are computed and listed in Table 5.6. This table also contains the 20 Mahalanobis distances, values of $P_j(\theta_R)$ and $P_j(\theta_R) - T(\theta_R)$. Then, the rule space coordinates for 20 patterns and $\mathbf{R}$ are plotted in the rule space in Figure 5.14.

We have shown that a response pattern similar to $\mathbf{R}$ was located in the vicinity of the point corresponding to $\mathbf{R}$ in the rule space. However, the next issue—whether or not any points closer to the point of $\mathbf{R}$ in the rule space would have the response patterns similar to $\mathbf{R}$ with respect to the Hamming distance $\mathbf{d}$—must be examined. There are, unfortunately, counterexamples. In order to find out the nature of counterexamples, we investigate what factors will contribute to them.

The difference between ζ_R and ζ_X comes mainly from the difference between $f(X, \theta_x)$ and $f(R, \theta_R)$:

$$
\begin{aligned}
|f(X, \theta_x) - f(R, \theta_R)| \leq \Bigg\{ & |\theta_R - \theta_x| \left| \sum_{j=1,n} (\partial K(\theta)/\partial \theta \right. \\
& \left. + \partial P_j(\theta_{Rj})/\partial \theta - \partial T(\theta_{Rj})/\partial \theta) \right| \Bigg\} \\
& + \left| \sum_{j=1,n} \{ |(x_j - r_j)| \ |((P_j(\theta_R) - T(\theta_R))| \} \right|
\end{aligned}
\tag{5.36}
$$

From the above inequality, it is clear that the factors contributing to the difference are $|\theta_R - \theta_x|$ and $|(x_j - r_j)| \ |((P_j(\theta_R) - T(\theta_R))|$. Suppose $\mathbf{X_j}$ is a pattern with the total score of 11, and item j deviates from the jth component of R. Table 5.7 clearly indicates that $|\theta_R - \theta_x|$ and the product of $|(x_j - r_j)|$ and $|((P_j(\theta_R) - T(\theta_R))|$ are the factors influencing the difference between Mahalanobis distances of the rule space points for R and X. The quantities $|(P_j(\theta_R) - T(\theta_R)|$ at θ_{Rj} become proportionally larger as the item discrimination powers a_j, $j = 1, \ldots, n$ get larger. When the total scores of response patterns are about the same, such as in our example in Table 5.6, the items with larger discriminating powers a_j influence the magnitude of the quantities $|\theta_R - \theta_x|$, for X_j. Hence, the Mahalanobis distance of the two response patterns may become larger for those of which the items with differences in their discriminating powers. Therefore, generally speaking, the items with larger discriminating powers influence the magnitudes of the Mahalanobis distances more than the items with smaller discriminating powers. The argument is summarized in Property 5.2.

Property 5.2: The items with larger values of $|(P_j(\theta_R) - T(\theta_R)|$, and hence the larger discriminating powers, have a tendency to influence the magnitude of Mahalanobis distance more seriously than the items with smaller values of $|(P_j(\theta_R) - T(\theta_R)|$, or smaller discriminating powers.

TABLE 5.6

The IRT Item Parameters for 20 Fraction Subtraction Items, Response Pattern R, and 20 Simulated Item Patterns X_k Deviated From R by One Slip

a_j	1.48	1.93	1.66	.85	.63	1.52	1.84	.65	.47	2.10	1.79	1.30	2.32	1.58	1.98	1.31	2.16	1.57	3.29	2.33
b_j	.02	-.10	.08	-.04	-.36	-1.05	.44	-1.24	-.87	.49	.22	-.77	.73	-.68	.29	-.62	.35	.23	.69	.47
Item	1	2	3	4	5	6	7	8	9	10	11	12	13	14	15	16	17	18	19	20
R	1	1	1	0	1	1	1	1	1	0	0	1	0	1	1	1	0	0	0	0
X_1	0	1	1	0	1	1	1	1	1	0	0	1	0	1	1	1	0	0	0	0
X_2	1	0	1	0	1	1	1	1	1	0	0	1	0	1	1	1	0	0	0	0
X_3	1	1	0	0	1	1	1	1	1	0	0	1	0	1	1	1	0	0	0	0
X_4	1	1	1	1	1	1	1	1	1	0	0	1	0	1	1	1	0	0	0	0
X_5	1	1	1	0	0	1	1	1	1	0	0	1	0	1	1	1	0	0	0	0
X_6	1	1	1	0	1	0	1	1	1	0	0	1	0	1	1	1	0	0	0	0
X_7	1	1	1	0	1	1	0	1	1	0	0	1	0	1	1	1	0	0	0	0
X_8	1	1	1	0	1	1	1	0	1	0	0	1	0	1	1	1	0	0	0	0
X_9	1	1	1	0	1	1	1	1	0	0	0	1	0	1	1	1	0	0	0	0
X_{10}	1	1	1	0	1	1	1	1	1	1	0	1	0	1	1	1	0	0	0	0
X_{11}	1	1	1	0	1	1	1	1	1	0	1	1	0	1	1	1	0	0	0	0
X_{12}	1	1	1	0	1	1	1	1	1	0	0	0	0	1	1	1	0	0	0	0
X_{13}	1	1	1	0	1	1	1	1	1	0	0	1	1	1	1	1	0	0	0	0
X_{14}	1	1	1	0	1	1	1	1	1	0	0	1	0	0	1	1	0	0	0	0
X_{15}	1	1	1	0	1	1	1	1	1	0	0	1	0	1	0	1	0	0	0	0
X_{16}	1	1	1	0	1	1	1	1	1	0	0	1	0	1	1	0	0	0	0	0
X_{17}	1	1	1	0	1	1	1	1	1	0	0	1	0	1	1	1	1	0	0	0
X_{18}	1	1	1	0	1	1	1	1	1	0	0	1	0	1	1	1	0	1	0	0
X_{19}	1	1	1	0	1	1	1	1	1	0	0	1	0	1	1	1	0	0	1	0
X_{20}	1	1	1	0	1	1	1	1	1	0	0	1	0	1	1	1	0	0	0	1

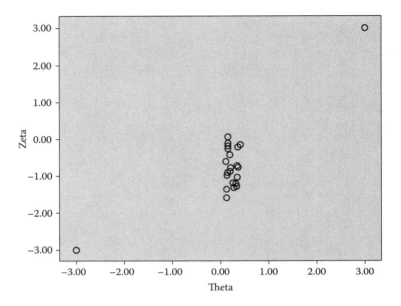

FIGURE 5.14
The 20 patterns in Table 5.7 that are mapped in rule space.

Suppose that we select items 1, 3, 4, 5, and 15 because they have substantially small values of $|(P_j(\theta_R) - T(\theta_R)|$ from Table 5.6, and then modify the elements of **R** associated with these items by adding one slip to them. Then, we get a new pattern, $\mathbf{X}_{21}$ as (01010111100101010000). The rule space coordinate of $\mathbf{X}_{21}$, $(\theta_{X21}, \zeta_{X21})$, has the squared Mahalanobis distance of $D^2 = 2.615$, which is pretty close to the rule space coordinate of (θ_R, ζ_R) for R. However, the number of slips is 5, which is the Hamming distance is 5, d = 5, because Hamming distance is the number of columns whose entries do not match in **R** and $\mathbf{X}_{21}$—in other words, the number of pairs of (1 0) and (0 1). This example suggests that response patterns that deviated substantially from **R** with respect to Hamming distance can have a smaller Mahalanobis distance.

Figures 5.7 and 5.8 in the previous section (Section 5.4) have shown the residual curves, $P_j(\theta) - T(\theta)$, j = 1, ..., n, for fraction problems. Some items in these figures such as items 1, 3, 4, and 5 are almost flat, and hence they are very close to the horizontal axis of $T(\theta)$ as compared with the other items. From the above property, these items might not be able to contribute to differentiate zeta values of response patterns from one another at any θ values. In other words, ζ values of response patterns are more strongly affected by the items with larger residual values $|(P_j(\theta_R) - T(\theta_R)|$ than the items having smaller residual values. Although some response patterns are different at the flat items having small residual values, their ζ values can be almost identical. This weakness must be remediated by adding a new dimension to the two-dimensional rule space. Generalized ζ is designed for solving this weakness.

Generalized Zetas

In short, a generalized zeta is defined on a subset of items, as compared with zeta, which is defined on all the items in a test as the covariance of two residuals $P_j(\theta) - T(\theta)$ and $X_j - P_j(\theta)$. Suppose S is a subset of items; then, generalized zeta will be the covariance of residuals over the summation of items in S,

$$\text{Generalized } \zeta \text{ for S,} \quad \zeta_S = \sum_{j \text{ in } S} \{P_j(\theta) - T_S(\theta)\}\{X_j - P_j(\theta)\} \quad (5.37)$$

where $T_S(\theta)$ is the average of $P_j(\theta)$ over j in S.

Suppose S to be a set of items that have fairly flat curves of $Pj(\theta) - T(\theta)$. Let us compute generalized zeta ζ_S for S, and take ζ_S as the third coordinate of the three-dimensional rule space. Then the rule space coordinates of **R** and X_{21} are computed and given below in Table 5.7. The squared

TABLE 5.7

Various Statistics for 21 Response Patterns Given in Table 5.6

	Score	d^2	Slip Item j	$I(\theta)$	θ	Zeta	D^2	$|\theta_R - \theta_x|$	$|(P_j(\theta_{Rj}) - T(\theta_{Rj})|$
R	12	0	0	30.17	0.25	−1.20	0.00	0.00	N.A.
X_1	11	1	1	20.29	0.15	−0.92	0.29	0.10	0.065
X_2	11	1	2	27.65	0.12	−0.61	0.71	0.13	0.167
X_3	11	1	3	28.04	0.14	−0.99	0.32	0.11	0.038
X_4	13	1	4	31.09	0.28	−1.33	0.09	0.03	0.035
X_5	11	1	5	29.41	0.20	−0.90	0.12	0.05	0.069
X_6	11	1	6	28.23	0.15	0.02	1.71	0.10	0.395
X_7	11	1	7	27.78	0.13	−1.61	0.51	0.12	0.191
X_8	11	1	8	29.38	0.20	−0.43	0.62	0.05	0.271
X_9	11	1	9	29.61	0.21	−0.79	0.19	0.04	0.142
X_{10}	13	1	10	32.21	0.35	−0.72	0.63	0.10	0.097
X_{11}	13	1	11	31.96	0.34	−1.28	0.30	0.09	0.060
X_{12}	11	1	12	28.54	0.16	−0.19	1.18	0.09	0.330
X_{13}	13	1	13	32.38	0.36	−0.21	1.47	0.11	0.394
X_{14}	11	1	14	28.15	0.15	−0.11	1.43	0.10	0.347
X_{15}	11	1	15	27.58	0.12	−1.38	0.42	0.13	0.069
X_{16}	11	1	16	28.52	0.16	−0.28	1.01	0.09	0.296
X_{17}	13	1	17	32.26	0.35	−1.06	0.45	0.10	0.140
X_{18}	13	1	18	31.77	0.32	−1.21	0.23	0.07	0.051
X_{19}	13	1	19	32.98	0.41	−0.15	2.07	0.16	0.426
X_{20}	13	1	20	32.38	0.36	−0.77	0.68	0.11	0.232

Mahalanobis distances between $\mathbf{R}$ and $\mathbf{X}_{21}$ becomes larger than that in the two-dimensional rule space, that is, $3.5 > 2.615$.

On the Selection of New Coordinates of a Multidimensional Rule Space

The above example shows that a generalized zeta, ζ_S, associated with S can distinguish $\mathbf{X}$ from $\mathbf{R}$ in the three-dimensional rule space (θ, ζ, ζ_S) better than in the two-dimensional rule space with respect to the Mahalanobis distance. There are several ways to select generalized zetas that would separate "undesirable" points in the rule space. *Undesirable* means that they do not have similar response patterns but have very close rule space coordinates, and hence their Mahalanobis distance becomes a very small number. If the items in L_1 are selected so that the value of the residual $P_j(\theta) - T(\theta)$ becomes close to zero for θ—in other words, if the items in L_1 whose item response functions are very close to the true score function $T(\theta)$ are selected—then the correlation between ζ and ζ_{L1} becomes very small (almost zero; Tatsuoka, 1997).

Generalized Zetas Uncorrelated With ζ

Several properties of the generalized zetas have been discussed in Chapter 2. Because generalized ζs are associated with subsets of items, one can select generalized ζs that are not correlated highly with ζ. By so doing, the coordinates almost uncorrelated from one another can be selected because both ζ and generalized ζ are uncorrelated with θ (Tatsuoka, 1985) as long as we assume local independence of item responses.

If the items in L_1 have almost identical item parameters, then the values of $P_j(\theta) - T_{L1}(\theta)$ for ζ_{L1} are very close to zero, where $T_{L1}(\theta)$ is the average of the IRT functions $P_j(\theta)$ for j in L_1. Therefore, the generalized zeta, ζ_{L1}, defined from such an L_1, has some constant value and thus very small correlation values with ζ.

Generalized Zetas Associated With Different Sets of Cognitive Tasks

We discussed the relationship between item parameters and the cognitive processes required in solving items correctly earlier in Section 5.1. The conclusion was that the items requiring the same set of cognitive processes and skills have almost identical item response curves in the fraction problems. It is highly likely that the generalized ζs associated with the items requiring the identical or almost identical set of cognitive tasks and knowledge have very high correlation values.

Generalized Zetas Associated With Mutually Exclusive and Disjoint Subsets of Items

The correlation between two generalized ζs depends on how the two subsets of items are selected (Tatsuoka, 1997). Suppose L_1 and L_2 are two sets of items, and ζ_1 and ζ_2 are the generalized ζs associated with L_1 and L_2, respectively. When the two sets L_1 and L_2 are mutually exclusive, then the correlation of generalized ζs, ζ_1, and ζ_2 becomes zero, that is, ζ_1 and ζ_2 are not correlated. This relationship can be generalized to any subsets of items, $L_k, k = 1, \ldots, K$, that are mutually exclusive and totally together.

Suppose $\zeta_1 \zeta_2, \ldots, \zeta_k$ are generalized zetas obtained from k subsets of items that are mutually exclusive and totally together, for which the items in the same set L_k require the identical set of attributes. In other words, we divide the items in a test to homogeneous sets of items based on the underlying cognitive processing skills and knowledge needed for answering each item as stated in Section 5.2. Then, such subsets $\{L_k\}$ are mutually exclusive and totally together for a test. We can define generalized zetas $\{\zeta_{Lk}\}$ for L_k, $k = 1, \ldots, K$. Then, ζ_ks are uncorrelated.

Example 5.2

We classified 38 items for fraction addition problems into four categories based on the underlying seven tasks in Table 5.2. They are as follows:

Category 1, L_1.	1, 6, 9, 12, 16, 20, 25, 28, 31, 35: (0110011)
Category 2, L_2.	2, 21, 8, 27, 11, 30, 15, 34, 18, 37: (1001110)
Category 3, L_3.	3, 22, 7, 26, 10, 29, 14, 33, 17, 36, 19, 38: (1100010)
Category 4, L_4.	4, 23, 5, 24, 13, 32: (0011111)

where the seven tasks are as follows:

c_1: Determine if the item is of type F + F.

c_2: Determine if the two denominators are the same.

c_3: Convert a mixed number, M, to the improper fraction, F.

TABLE 5.8

The Coordinates of Two Response Patterns R and X_{21}, and Squared Mahalanobis Distance Between R and X_{21} in the Three-Dimensional Rule Space

Item	1	2	3	4	5	6	7	8	9	10	11	12	13	14	15	16	17	18	19	20	Rule Space Point	D^2
R	1	1	1	0	1	1	1	1	1	0	0	1	0	1	1	1	0	0	0	0	(.25, –1.20, –1.28)	0
X_{21}	0	1	0	1	0	1	1	1	1	0	0	1	0	1	0	1	0	0	0	0	(–.08, –1.04, –.36)	3.5

TABLE 5.9

The Correlation Matrix of θ, ζ, ζ_{L1}, ζ_{L2}, ζ_{L3}, and ζ_{L4}

	θ	ζ	ζ_{L1}	ζ_{L2}	ζ_{L3}	ζ_{L4}
θ	1	−.03	−.00	.00	−.04	.01
ζ		1	.17	.11	.08	.03
ζ_{L1}			1	.06	.09	.01
ζ_{L2}				1	.05	.07
ζ_{L3}					1	.02
ζ_{L4}						1

c_4: Get the common denominator.

c_5: Make equivalent fractions.

c_6: Add numerators.

c_7: Combine the whole-number part with the fraction part.

Four generalized zetas—ζ_{L1}, ζ_{L2}, ζ_{L3}, and ζ_{L4}—are computed, and the correlation matrix M is given in Table 5.9. As can be seen in Table 5.9, θ, ζ_{L1}, ζ_{L2}, ζ_{L3}, and ζ_{L4} are mutually uncorrelated.

When the coordinates of the rule space are almost orthogonal, then the Mahalanobis distance between two points will be maximized. In other words, if two ideal item score patterns are mapped into the multidimensional rule space having orthogonal coordinates, then the Mahalanobis distance between the knowledge states will be larger than the distance computed from using not-orthogonal coordinates (Tatsuoka, 1997). However, further research for the optimum selection of coordinates will be needed.

5.8   Conceptual Framework of the Rule Space Methodology

The conceptual framework of the RSM may not be easy to grasp intuitively. Figure 5.15 summarizes complicated and abstract relationships among attributes, item responses, Q matrices, ideal item score patterns, and attribute mastery patterns and probabilities, then the rule space as a classification space. In this figure, the shaded square represents *impossible to observe directly*, and white shapes represent *observable variables*.

The item pool in an oval shape is connected to the attribute pool in a shaded box representing latent variables through a Q matrix, or equivalently to an incidence matrix. By applying the Boolean descriptive function to the Q matrix, we can connect an ideal item score pattern in a white box

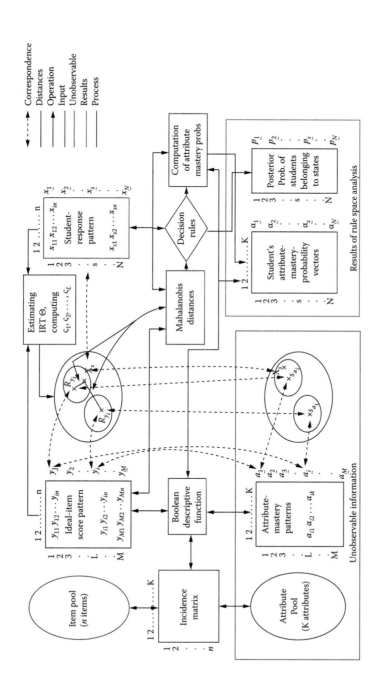

FIGURE 5.15

The conceptual framework of the rule space methodology.

to an attribute mastery pattern in a shaded box. Because invisible attribute mastery patterns are connected to ideal item score patterns, one can make inferences about the performances on attributes from performances on the observable items.

Suppose we have a student's item response pattern, and want to find out from which knowledge states this student is coming. The easiest way is that we start matching the student's response pattern one by one to the entire ideal item score patterns in a list of ideal item score patterns in a white box. Then, we can find several ideal item score patterns similar to the student's response pattern. The classification space, the rule space, determines the membership probabilities of the student to these closest ideal item response patterns, and estimates each posterior probability to the closest ideal item score patterns. Then attribute mastery probability vector will be given as this student's diagnosis.

In sum, this chapter introduced a new method to diagnose individuals' latent knowledge states. This approach described as the *rule space method* has two components: first, the mathematical component called the *Q-matrix theory*; and, second, statistical pattern classifications in a vector space called *rule space*. This approach is similar to statistical pattern recognition and classification problems. Their feature variable selection part corresponds to our Q-matrix theory. An important difference is that the feature variable selection deals with mainly observable variables, but the Q-matrix theory deals with latent variables.

6

Classification Rules

Most of the classification procedures fall into one of the four types—partitioning methods, hierarchical methods, geometrical methods, and clumping methods.

Partitioning methods aim to partition the set of n objects into a specified number of disjoint groups so that each object belongs to one and only one group. Latent classes modeling is one of these procedures. The value of a g partition has to be specified by researchers, and analyses are usually undertaken for several different values, and for each value of g, a partition must be optimal with respect to a given clustering criterion (Bartholomew, 1987).

Hierarchical methods are used to investigate the structure in data at several different levels, and to express in a tree diagram or a nested set of partitions. A hierarchical cluster analysis is one of these procedures. A more recent development, C. Tatsuoka's POSET model, deals with sequential classification on partially ordered sets, and this is one of the most mathematically sophisticated methodologies in psychometrics (C. Tatsuoka, 1996, 2002; Tatsuoka & Ferguson, 2003).

In geometrical methods, each object is represented by a point in a low-dimensional space. This geometric representation is arranged to have the property that objects, which are similar to one another, are represented by points, which are close together. The rule space is one of these geometrical methods, and another well-known example is multidimensional scaling methods (Riply, 1996).

In clumping methods, the groups are allowed to overlap. Hence, it is possible for a word to have more than one meaning. Such overlapping groups are called *clumps*, and a division of the set of n objects into clumps, such that each object belongs to at least one clump, will be called a *covering of the dataset*.

In this chapter, our focus will be on geometric methods.

6.1 Intuitive Classification Using Generalized Distance

The purpose of the IRT models is focused on measuring the amount of ability or knowledge that an individual possesses, but the assumption used in the modeling was that the ability of the individual can be located on the unidimensional real number line θ. Therefore, only two classes, mastery and nonmastery groups, can be considered, and they are obtained by partitioning the line into the two parts: $\theta \geq \theta_0$ and $\theta_0 < \theta$ for a given cutoff point θ_0. A threshold called a cutoff score θ_0 is determined first, and then anybody who obtained the estimated ability level θ that is larger than θ_0 is classified in the mastery group. This is the one-dimensional distance decision rule.

Assessing the Similarity or Dissimilarity of Individuals or Groups

A recurring problem in several branches of psychological and educational research such as clinical diagnosis, personnel guidance, study of personality types, and recent problems of cognitive diagnosis is that of assessing the similarity or dissimilarity of individuals or groups based on the number of attributes. The purpose may be to ascertain which of several groups an individual's performance most closely resembles or matches so that the individual may be "classified as a member of that group." This requires that there exist several well-defined mutually exclusive groups, to one of which the individual in question must belong. One of the most intuitive classification procedures is to use the distances defined among individuals.

Suppose that four students took the SAT I Mathematics and Verbal tests and got scores as follows:

	SAT I Mathematics	SAT I Verbal
Student 1	500	630
Student 2	700	650
Student 3	520	450
Student 4	600	530

The difference between Students 1 and 3 for SAT I Mathematics is only 20 and between Students 1 and 2 for SAT Verbal is also 20. However, Students 1 and 4 have a difference in score of 100 each for both tests. Which student is similar to Student 1? One way to measure proximity of the four students is to compute the distance among them. By taking SAT Mathematics as the horizontal line and SAT Verbal as the vertical line, the students are located in points 1, 2, 3, and 4 in Figure 6.1. Suppose their coordinates are given by (x_1, y_1), (x_2, y_2), (x_3, y_3), and (x_4, y_4), then Euclidean distances between 1 and 2, 1 and 3, and 1 and 4 are given by the following:

Euclidean Distance	
Students 1 and 2	$\{(x_1 - x_2)^2 + (y_1 - y_2)^2\}^{1/2} = 201$
Students 1 and 3	$\{(x_1 - x_3)^2 + (y_1 - y_2)^2\}^{1/2} = 181$
Students 1 and 4	$\{(x_1 - x_4)^2 + (y_1 - y_4)^2\}^{1/2} = 141$

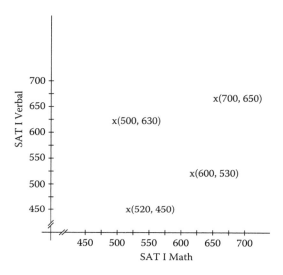

FIGURE 6.1
Plotting four students' SAT scores.

The Euclidean distance gives the proximity among three pairs differently from that of SAT Mathematics or SAT Verbal alone. Euclidean distance places Student 4 the closest to Student 1. In general, Euclidean distance for X_i and X_j is expressed by

$$D^2 = (X_{i1} - X_{j1})^2 + (X_{i2} - X_{j2})^2 + \cdots + (X_{im} - X_{jm})^2 = (X_i - X_j)S^{-1}(X_i - X_j) \quad (6.1)$$

where $X_i = (X_{i1}, X_{i2}, \ldots, X_{im})$, $X_j = (X_{j1}, X_{j2}, \ldots, X_{jm})$, S is a diagonal matrix of order m, and S^{-1} is the inverse of S.

$$S = \begin{vmatrix} 1 & 0 & \cdots & 0 \\ 0 & 1 & \cdots & 0 \\ 0 & 0 & \cdots & 1 \end{vmatrix} = S^{-1}$$

It is known that the scores of SAT I Mathematics and Verbal correlate highly, and their variances are usually different. Substituting the diagonal matrix by a variance–covariance matrix will provide some adjustment for Euclidean distance. This weighted Euclidean distance is called *generalized distance* (M. Tatsuoka, 1970), and the matrix S is the covariance matrix of the two tests. Generalized distance, D^2, measures the "distance"—in other words, the dissimilarity—between a pair of individuals. Hence, it may be used in taxonomic problems for forming clusters of similar individuals— that is, individuals separated by similar values of D^2 among themselves than from individuals outside the clusters. To use the distance measure in classification problems, the formula for D^2 has to be modified slightly from that given in Equation (6.1). Instead of the D^2 between the points in p-dimensional space representing two individual profiles, we need to calculate the D^2 between the point representing the individual to be classified and that representing the mean of each group of which the individual may possibly be a member. The latter point is known as the *centroid* of the group. The square of the generalized distance of an individual given from the centroid of the mth group is rewritten by Equation (6.2),

$$D^2 = (X_i - \mu_k)^T \sum_K{}^{-1} (X_i - \mu_k) \qquad (6.2)$$

where $\mu_k = (\mu_{1k}, \mu_{2k}, \ldots, \mu_{mk})$ and Σ_k^{-1} is the inverse of the covariance matrix of the kth group.

The idea is to compute the individual's generalized distance from the centroid of each of the K groups to which the individual might belong, and to classify the individual into that group for which the D^2 value is the smallest. In practice, we do not know the population Σ_k, but they may be estimated from samples from K populations, respectively. We denote the centroid and covariance matrix of the sample from the kth population by μ_k, Σ_k^{-1}.

$$D^2 = (X_k - \mu_k)' \sum_K{}^{-1} (X_k - \mu_k) \qquad (6.3)$$

Although we have shown above that the generalized distance reduces to ordinary Euclidean distance in the special case of uncorrelated tests with unit standard deviations, one may still be curious as to just what D^2 means in the general case. This is best explained by examining what the locus of equal D^2 from a group centroid consists of. The equation obtained by setting the right side of Equation (6.3) to a constant, in the case of two variables, we get the equation of an ellipse centered at the group center point μ_k. Such an ellipse is shown in Figure 6.2, along with points P_1, P_2, ..., P_5 representing five individuals. These five individuals are all "equivalent" from the centroid μ_k in the generalized distance sense, even though the ordinary distance from μ_1 to P_1 is longer than that from μ_k to P_2. Any point inside the ellipse is said to be "closer" to μ in generalized distance than is any point on the ellipse, whereas any point outside it is said to be "farther" than any point on it. Thus, P_4 is "closer" to μ_k than P_1, even though the ordinary distance is not. Figure 6.2 shows an isodensity contour of the bivariate normal distribution with the centroid and covariance matrix of Σ_K in Equation (6.3). Hence, when sampling at random from this bivariate normal distribution, it is more likely to get an individual whose score combination defines a point on or inside the ellipse than

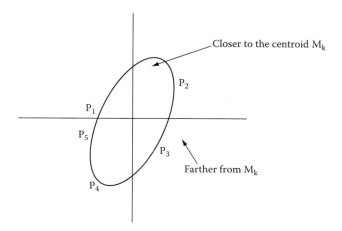

FIGURE 6.2
Isodensity contour of bivariate normal distribution.

it is to get any individual outside the ellipse. Thus, generalized distance D^2 from a population centroid is really a measure of "how probable it is to have drawn an individual with a particular score combination by sampling randomly from the population." The less likely a score, the "farther" it is said to be from the centroid.

In the next section, the relationship of the generalized distance to probabilistic concepts will be discussed, and it will be shown that when the variables follow the normal distribution, the generalized distance indeed provides a natural basis for classification procedures.

6.2   Conditional Density Function of Group π_k

Classification procedures in statistical practice consider predominantly normal populations, so the conditional density functions of classification groups are assumed to associate with multivariate normal distributions with the mean vector μ_i, $i = 1, ..., m$ and the covariance matrices $\Sigma_1, ..., \Sigma_m$. In the rule space context, group π_K corresponds to latent knowledge states $\pi_1, ..., \pi_m$. The conditional density function for a p-variate normal population with centroid μ_i and Σ_i is

$$p(X \mid \pi i) = \frac{1}{(2\pi)^{m/2}(|\Sigma_i|)^{1/2}} \exp\left\{ -.5(X - \mu_i)\sum_i^{-1}(X - \mu_i) \right\} \qquad (6.4)$$

The meaning of this expression is as follows: If a single observation is drawn at random from the indicated population, then the probability that the scores will fall within a specified distance from the elements X is very nearly proportional to $p(X|\pi_i)$. Because $p(X|\pi_i)$ itself is not a probability, it is often called the *likelihood function*.

In the next section, we introduce some important concepts for classification procedures such as conditional probabilities and the Bayes theorem in the probability theory.

6.3   Conditional Probabilities and the Bayes Theorem

Independent Events

Suppose C_1 consists of people who speak English, and C_2 of those who speak Spanish. The joint set of C_1 and C_2, $C_3 = C_1 \cap C_2$, consists of people who speak both English and Spanish. The probability of the joint set is given by

$$P(C_1 \cap C_2) = \frac{\text{number of elements in } C_1 \cap C_2}{\text{total number of elements}} \tag{6.5}$$

In other words, any event that is the intersection of two or more events is called a joint event and is written by $C_1 \cap C_2$. A member of set $C_1 \cap C_2$ is a member of set C_1 and also of set C_2.

The probability of the occurrence of the event C_1, C_2, or both $(C_1 \cup C_2)$ is given by the probability of C_1 plus the probability of $P(C_2)$ minus the probability of the joint event C_1 and C_2,

$$P(C_1 \cup C_2) = P(C_1) + P(C_2) - P(C_1 \cap C_2) \tag{6.6}$$

When C_1 and C_2 are mutually exclusive, the joint event has the probability of zero. So the probability of $C_1 \cup C_2$ is the sum of the probabilities of C_1 and C_2. For the m mutually disjoint set, $C_1, ..., C_m$, the probability of the union set $C_1 \cup ... \cup C_m$ is given by the sum of the probabilities of $C_1, ..., C_m$.

$$P(C_1 \cup C_2 \cup C_3 \cup \cdots \cup C_m) = P(C_1) + P(C_2) + \cdots + P(C_m) \tag{6.7}$$

For any event, its complement is written by C^c, and the sum of their probabilities is one.

$$P(C) + P(C^c) = 1 \tag{6.8}$$

Conditional Probability

A test was taken by the eighth graders in a school district. The sample consists of males (denoted by A) and females (A^c), but we would like to restrict our observations to only females. Among the female sample, some are enrolled in algebra class (say, B), and the rest are not (B^c). Then, the probability of observing the students enrolled in algebra class is

$$P(\text{enrolled in algebra among females}) = \frac{\text{Number of algebra students}}{\text{Total number of females}}$$

(6.9)

The males enrolled in algebra class are denoted by C_{21}, and those who are not by C_{22}. The probability, P(enrolled in algebra among males) is obtained by replacing females by males in the above definition. Suppose the total number of females is $n_{1.}$, the total number of males is $n_{2.}$, and the total sample is given by n, then the sum of the total numbers of female and males, $n_{1.} + n_{2.}$.

	Algebra	Nonalgebra	Total
Females	n_{11}	n_{12}	$n_{1.}$
Males	n_{21}	n_{22}	$n_{2.}$
Total	$n_{.1}$	$n_{.2}$	$n_{..}(=n)$

From the above table, it can be easily seen that the probability of female algebra students among the total sample is given by n_{11}/n, and the probability of male algebra students among the total sample is given by n_{21}/n. The probability of females is $n_{1.}/n$. Therefore, the ratio of P(female algebra students among students) and P(female among total sample) is $(n_{11}/n)/(n_{1.}/n)$ becomes $n_{11}/n_{1.}$ which is the probability of algebra students among females.

$$P(C_{11}/C_{1.}) = \frac{P(\text{in algebra class and female})}{P(\text{females})} = \frac{P(C_{11} \cup C_{1.})}{P(C_{1.})} \qquad (6.10)$$

In general, the value $n_{11}/n_{1.}$ is called the conditional probability of C_{11} given $C_{1.}$. Similarly, we get the conditional probability of C_{21} given $C_{2.}$.

$$P(C_{21}/C_{2.}) = \frac{P(\text{in algebra class and male})}{P(\text{males})} = \frac{P(C_{21} \cap C_{2.})}{P(C_{2.})} \qquad (6.11)$$

Now we think about the probability of females among the students, n_{11}/n. The probability of algebra students among the total sample is $n_{.1}/n$. The ratio is $n_{11}/n_{.1}$, the probability of female algebra students in algebra class.

$$P(C_{11}/C_{.1}) = \frac{P(\text{in algebra class and female})}{P(\text{algebra students})} = \frac{P(C_{11} \cup C_{.1})}{P(C_{.1})} \tag{6.12}$$

Because $P(C_{11} \cap C_{1.}) = P(C_{11} \cap C_{.1})$, $P(A|B)P(B) = P(B|A)P(A)$. By rewriting it, we get Equation (6.13),

$$\frac{P(A|B)}{P(B|A)} = \frac{P(A)}{P(B)} \tag{6.13}$$

Bayes Theorem

The Bayes theorem is a very useful property for the probability theory. Suppose $C_1, \ldots, C_m$ are mutually disjoint sets, and each has a nonzero probability. If C is a subset of the union of $C_1 \cup C_2 \cup C_3 \cup \ldots \cup C_m$, then Equation (6.14) is true.

$$P(C) = P(C_1)P(C|C_1) + P(C_2)P(C|C_2) + \cdots + P(C_m)P(C|C_m) \tag{6.14}$$

If $P(C) > 0$, then we get Equation (6.15).

$$P(C_i|C) = \frac{P(C_i)P(C|C_1)}{P(C_1)P(C|C_1) + P(C_2)P(C|C_2) + \cdots + P(C_m)P(C|C_m)} \tag{6.15}$$

for $i = 1, \ldots, m$.

When $m = 2$, the conditional probability of C_i given C is shown by

$$P(C_i|C) = \frac{P(C_1)P(C|C_1)}{P(C_1)P(C|C_1) + P(C_2)P(C|C_2)} \tag{6.16}$$

This relationship can be proved inductively. From the definition of the conditional probabilities,

$$P(C_1|C) = \frac{P(C_1)P(C|C_1)}{P(C)} \tag{6.17}$$

Because $P(C_1)P(C|C_1) = P(C)P(C_1|C)$, and $P(C_2)P(C|C_2) = P(C)P(C_2|C)$, replacing the terms in the denominator by the right side of the above terms leads to Equation (6.18):

$$P(C)\{P(C_1|C) + P(C_2|C)\} = P(C)\{P(C_1 \cup C_2|C\} = P(C|C) = P(C) \tag{6.18}$$

By applying the induction method, we can have the general form of the Bayes theorem given in Equation (6.15) (Gelman, Carlin, Stern, & Rubin, 1995; Tatsuoka, 1988).

6.4 Classification Into One of Two Groups (Knowledge States)

We assume now that each population has a normal distribution and that the means and the covariance matrices are different. Then the density function $p(X|\pi_i)$ is given by Equation 6.19,

$$p(X|\pi_i) = \frac{1}{(2\pi)^{m/2}(|\Sigma_i|)^{1/2}} \exp\left\{-.5(X-\mu_i)^T \sum_i^{-1} (X-\mu_i)\right\} \qquad (6.19)$$

where μ_i and Σ_i are the mean and covariance matrix of population π_i, and m is the dimension of X, $X = (X_1, X_2, ..., X_m)$. The most plausible classification rule is to use the posterior probabilities, sometimes called the membership probabilities.

Classification Based on the Posterior Probabilities

Posterior probability, $p(\pi_K|X)$, requires one further assumption that is not required in considering probabilities of the type $p(X|\pi_K)$: The eventuality that the individual belongs to *none* of the predetermined groups is prohibited. In the case of two knowledge states, the decision rule based on the probabilities of an observation vector X, whether X belongs to π_1 or π_2, is given by the rule that if the posterior probability of π_1 for X is larger than the posterior probability of π_2 for X, then X is classified to π_1. The rule is summarized in Equation (6.20).

$$\text{If } p(\pi_1|X) > p(\pi_2|X), \text{ then X belongs to } \pi_1;$$
$$\text{if } p(\pi_1|X) < p(\pi_2|X), \text{ then X belongs to } \pi_2. \qquad (6.20)$$

The posterior probability $p(\pi_i|X)$ is obtained from the prior probability of π_i, P_i, and the conditional density function of π_i, $p(X|\pi_i)$, by applying the Bayes theorem,

$$p(\pi_i|X) = \frac{P_i p(X|\pi_i)}{P_i p(X|\pi_i) + P_i p(X|\pi_i)} \qquad (6.21)$$

Therefore, the decision rule of Equation (6.21) is restated by using the conditional density functions of π_i as follows:

$$\text{If } P_i p(X|\pi_i) > P_j p(X|\pi_j), \text{ then X belongs to } \pi_i;$$

$$\text{if } P_j p(X|\pi_j) > P_i p(X|\pi_i), \text{ then X belongs to } \pi_j. \tag{6.22}$$

We have stated the maximum likelihood rule. Rewriting Equation (6.22), we get Equation (6.23).

$$\text{If } l(X) = \frac{p(X|\pi_i)}{p(X|\pi_j)} > \frac{P_j}{P_i}, \text{ then X belongs to } \pi_i;$$

$$\text{if } l(X) = \frac{p(X|\pi_i)}{p(X|\pi_j)} < \frac{P_j}{P_i}, \text{ then X belongs to } \pi_j. \tag{6.23}$$

Discriminant Functions h(X)

Further, if we replace $p(X|\pi_i)$ by the normal density function of Equation (6.19), and then take the minus log of $l(X)$, then we get the ratio of the conditional density functions of π_i and π_j.

$$\text{If } h(X) = -l(X) = .5\left\{ (X-\mu_i)' \sum_I^{-1} (X-\mu_i) - (X-\mu_j)' \sum_j^{-1} (X-\mu_j) \right\}$$

$$+.5 * \ln\left\{ \frac{|\Sigma_i|}{|\Sigma_j|} \right\} > \ln\left\{ \frac{P_i}{P_j} \right\}, \text{ then X belongs to } \pi_i;$$

$$\text{if } h(X) = -l(X) = .5\left\{ (X-\mu_j)' \sum_j^{-1} (X-\mu_j) - (X-\mu_i)' \sum_I^{-1} (X-\mu_i) \right\} \tag{6.24}$$

$$+.5 * \ln\left\{ \frac{|\Sigma_i|}{|\Sigma_j|} \right\} < \ln\left\{ \frac{P_j}{P_i} \right\}, \text{ then X belongs to } \pi_i;$$

The first term of the discriminant function h(X) is considered the generalized distance of X from the centroid of the distribution of knowledge state π_i, and so is the second term from the centroid of the distribution of knowledge state π_j. h(X) is called the quadratic discriminant function, and the decision rule is given by a quadratic boundary (Lachenbruch, 1975; Tatsuoka, 1988). Figure 6.3 shows a graphical example of h(x).

If the covariance matrices Σ_i and Σ_j are alike, $\Sigma_i = \Sigma_j = \Sigma$, then the third term of the quadratic discriminant function h(x) will be zero, and the difference of two generalized differences, X from the centroid of π_i and π_j,

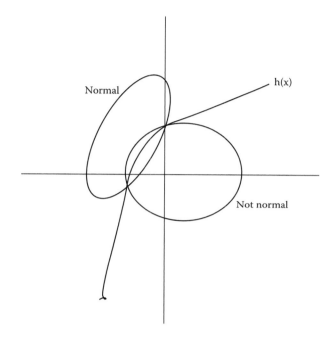

FIGURE 6.3
Quadratic discriminant function h(x).

will be simplified to a linear form as

$$(X-\mu_i)' \overset{-1}{\sum_i}(X-\mu_i)-(X-\mu_j)' \overset{-1}{\sum_j}(X-\mu_j)$$

$$= (\mu_j-\mu_i)' \overset{-1}{\sum}X+.5\left(\mu_i \overset{-1}{\sum}\mu_i-\mu_j \overset{-1}{\sum}\mu_j\right)$$

$$(6.25)$$

Therefore, the boundary becomes a linear function of X,

$$\text{If } h(X) = (\mu_j-\mu_i) \overset{-1}{\sum}X+.5\left(\mu_i \overset{-1}{\sum}\mu_i-\mu_j \overset{-1}{\sum}\mu_j\right) > \ln\left\{\frac{P_i}{P_j}\right\}, \text{ then X is in } \pi_i;$$

$$\text{If } h(X) = (\mu_j-\mu_i) \overset{-1}{\sum}X+.5\left(\mu_i \overset{-1}{\sum}\mu_i-\mu_j \overset{-1}{\sum}\mu_j\right) < \ln\left\{\frac{P_i}{P_j}\right\}, \text{ then X is in } \pi_j;$$

$$(6.26)$$

The decision rule of Equation (6.26) is explained by Figure 6.4.

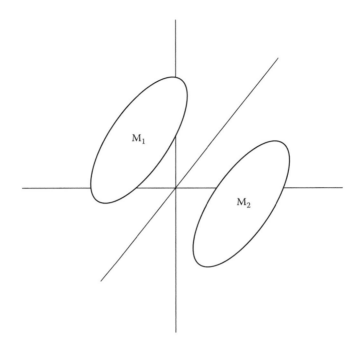

FIGURE 6.4
Linear discriminant function h(x).

When the prior probabilities P_i and P_j are equal, then the right side of Equation (6.26), $\ln(P_i/P_j)$, will be 0 because the logarithm of 1 is zero.

$$\text{If } h(X) = (\mu_j - \mu_i) \sum{}^{-1} X + .5 \left(\mu_i \sum{}^{-1} \mu_i - \mu_j \sum{}^{-1} \mu_j \right) > 0, \quad \text{then } X \text{ is in } \pi_i;$$

$$\text{If } h(X) = (\mu_j - \mu_i) \sum{}^{-1} X + .5 \left(\mu_i \sum{}^{-1} \mu_i - \mu_j \sum{}^{-1} \mu_j \right) < 0, \quad \text{then } X \text{ is in } \pi_j;$$

$$(6.27)$$

Rewriting Equation (6.27) by using the expression of the generalized distance, we get

$$\text{If } (X - \mu_i)' \sum_i{}^{-1} (X - \mu_i) < (X - \mu_j)' \sum_j{}^{-1} (X - \mu_j) \text{ then } X \text{ is in } \pi_i. \qquad (6.28)$$

Suppose the squared generalized distances of X from two groups, π_i and π_j—that is, $D_i^2 = (X - \mu_i)'\Sigma_i^{-1}(X - \mu_i)$ and $D_j^2 = (X - \mu_j)'\Sigma_j^{-1}(X - \mu_j)$—are computed and compared. In the two-dimensional case, the observation vector X belongs to whichever group is closer in terms of the generalized distance. Equation (6.4.10) indicates the linear equation $aX + b$, where $a = (\mu_j - \mu_i)\Sigma^{-1}$ and $b = .5(\mu_i\Sigma^{-1}\mu_i - \mu_j\Sigma^{-1}\mu_j)$, is the classification boundary: the X that is located above $aX + b$ belongs to π_i, and that located below belongs to π_j. An observed vector that is on the boundary line gives the equal generalized distance from the centroids of two groups. Given the decision rules for the case of two groups, the generalized distances can be very large numbers. The classification conclusion is still the same: X belongs to whichever is lesser.

When X_ks are mutually independent and exponentially distributed,

$$p(X|\pi_i) = P(1/\alpha_{ik})\exp[(-1/\alpha_{ik})X_k]\,\mu(X_k) \quad (i = 1, 2) \tag{6.29}$$

where α_{ik} is the parameter of the exponential distribution for X_i and $P(1/\alpha_{ik})$ and $\mu(X_k)$, $k = 1, \ldots, n$ is constant for each k. Then the $h(X)$, the minus log of the likelihood ratio, becomes

$$h(X) = \sum_1^n [(1/\alpha_{1k}) - (1/\alpha_{2k})]X_k + \sum_1^n \ln(\alpha_{1k}/\alpha_{2k}) \tag{6.30}$$

which is the linear function of X_k. Therefore, the Bayes decision rule becomes a linear function in this case. When we discuss classification of two-group cases, quadratic or linear classifiers have wide applications. However, when we have to handle three or more groups, a single quadratic or linear discriminant function cannot be used effectively.

6.5 Classification Into One of Several Groups

Bayes Classification Rule

It is well known (Fukunaga, 1990; Gelman et al., 1995; M. Tatsuoka, 1988) that the multihypothesis test for multigroup problems in the Bayes sense gives the best classification results with respect to minimizing the classification errors. The rule is to assign X to the group with the maximum value of posterior probability among K groups. It is stated in Equation (6.31):

$$\text{If } p_k p(X|\pi_k) = \max\{p_j\,p(X|\pi_j)\}, \text{ then X belongs to } \pi_k. \tag{6.31}$$

For K groups' case, their prior probabilities and the conditional density functions are required to formulate the Bayes decision rule in addition to Equation (6.31). However, by imposing conditions, Equation (6.31) reduces to simpler rules. Some applications use density functions as a classification rule when the prior probabilities p_k and p_j are reasonably close. This case is called the *maximum likelihood rule*, and is explained below.

Maximum Likelihood Rule

We now have K different centroid M_k and covariance matrices Σ_k, $k = 1, ...K$, which gives K conditional density functions $p(X|\pi_k)$, $k = 1, ...K$. Each of these tells us how likely it is that the person would have this score if he or she were a randomly selected member of Population 1, of Population 2, ..., and of Population K. So we look for the largest of these likelihood values, and classify the person in that group to which this likelihood value refers. That is, if $p(x|\pi_k)$ is the largest of K likelihood values, he or she is placed in group K. This rule is called the maximum likelihood rule for classification.

> *Maximum likelihood rule*: If $p(X \mid \pi_k)$ is the largest of K likelihood values, then the person is placed in group K. (6.32)

This case obviously assumes that the prior probabilities in Equation (6.31) are equal, $p_1 = p_2 = \cdots = p_K$.

When the Conditional Density Functions for the Groups Are Normal

When the conditional density functions for the multigroups are normal, then the Bayes classification rule can be replaced by Equation (6.33):

$$\text{If } \mu_k \text{ gives } \min_j \{1/2(X - \mu_j)' \sum_j^{-1} (X - \mu_j) + 1/2 \ln \left| \sum_j \right| - \ln P_j \},$$

(6.33)

$$\text{then X belongs to } \pi_k.$$

The Quadratic Discriminant Function

Note that *max* is changed to *min* because we took the minus-log operation to Equation (6.32). The expression in Equation (6.33) is called the quadratic discriminant function. When the population means and covariance matrices are unknown, they can be replaced by the sample means, M_j, and sample covariance matrices, S_j.

$$1/2(X - M_j)'S_j^{-1}(X - M_j) + 1/2\ln|S_j| - \ln P_j \qquad (6.34)$$

The Minimal Generalized Distance Rule for Many Groups

If we examine the expression in Equation (6.34) and compare it with the expression of normalized distance of X from the centroid of each group π_k, $D^2 = (X_i - \mu_k)^T \Sigma_k^{-1} (X_i - \mu_k)$, then we find that it is equal to $-(1/2) D_k^2$ by adjusting two constant terms $1/2\ln|\Sigma_j|$ and $\ln p_j$.

$$-(1/2) D_K^2 + 1/2 \ln \left| \sum_j \right| - \ln p_j = -(1/2) D_K^2 + \text{constant terms} \qquad (6.35)$$

Thus, there is a close relationship between generalized distance and the concept of likelihood of group membership. The relationship becomes even closer in the special case when all K populations have the same covariance matrix Σ.

When the Covariance Matrices Are Equal, $\Sigma_1 = \Sigma_2 = \cdots = \Sigma_j = \cdots = \Sigma_K$

The covariance matrix Σ_K in the above expression Equation (6.35) for D_K^2 is replaced by the common covariance matrix regardless of the different k's. This tells us that the magnitude of $p(x|\pi_K)$ for different k's depends only on that of D^2, because nothing else in the right-hand side of the density functions varies with k. The smaller the value of D_K^2, the larger the value of $p(x|\pi_K)$. We thus see that when the K covariance matrices are equal, the maximum likelihood rule of classification just described is mathematically equivalent to the minimum generalized distance rule outlined in discriminant function h(x) in Section 6.4.

The covariance matrices Σ_j in the expression $(X - M_j)'\Sigma_j^{-1}(X - M_j) + 1/2\ln|\Sigma_j|$ can be replaced by the common Σ, then reduced to $(X - M_j)'\Sigma^{-1}(X - M_j) + 1/2\ln|\Sigma| - \ln p_j$. When the K population covariance matrices are not equal, the two rules are not identical but will nevertheless lead to fairly similar classification results, provided the matrices are not drastically different. We may replace Σ by the average covariance. The summary of the classification rule becomes as follows:

> *Minimum generalized distance rule:* When the covariance matrices are the same, X belongs to the group having the smallest value of D_K^2. (6.36)

Piecewise Linear Classifiers When $\Sigma_1 \neq \Sigma_2 \neq \cdots \neq \Sigma_K$

When covariance matrices are not close to each other, an alternative rule is to set a linear discriminant function for each pair of groups and to optimize the coefficients. This rule is called piecewise classifiers

(Fukunaga, 1990). This method gives the optimal classification rule in the Bayes sense with respect to the probability of misclassification. Suppose the linear discriminant function for groups i and j is

$$h_{ij}(X) = B'_{ij}X + c_{ij0} \quad (i, j = 1, \cdots, K: i \neq j) \tag{6.37}$$

The sign of the coefficient B_{ij} is chosen such that the distribution of π_i is located on the positive side of h_{ij}, and that of π_j is on the negative side. Suppose the region for each group is convex; then the region of group j can be determined by Equation (6.38):

If $h_{j1}(X) > 0, \ldots, h_{jK}(X) > 0,$ then X belongs to π_j where h_{ij} is not considered.
$$\tag{6.38}$$

When piecewise classifiers such as given in Figure 6.5 are used, any observation vector X must belong to one of K groups.

Prior Probability

The Bayes likelihood ratio test has been shown to be optimal in the sense that it minimizes the cost or the probability of errors (Box & Tao, 1975; Gelman et al., 1995). In order to get the optimum classification rule, we need the posterior probability that a person with the score vector X is a member of group k, for each k = 1, 2, ..., K, and prior probabilities. Prior probability is traditionally considered as a person's prior belief about the

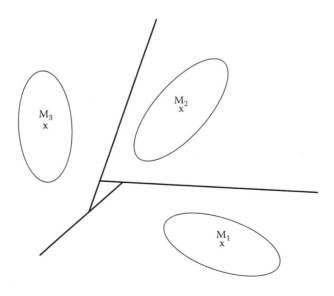

FIGURE 6.5
Piecewise classification boundaries.

membership probability of X before classification is performed. We often have a rough idea of what the relative sizes of the various occupational groups have been in the past. These estimates may be taken as prior probabilities. In the cognitive diagnosis, a teacher may have a rough idea about which errors were more commonly observed in the past. These estimated frequencies for various error states may be used as prior probabilities. However, such a procedure has sometimes been criticized for its tendency to "perpetuate the status quo" by keeping traditionally large groups large, and small ones small. This criticism would be justified to the extent that the "traditional" sizes of various vocational and curricular groups have been arbitrary determined by policy or expediency considerations (M. Tatsuoka, 1988, p. 359). M. Tatsuoka showed in his example that the role played by prior probabilities sometimes affects classification results in favor of oversupplying small groups and undersupplying large ones.

Without any information about prior knowledge, the uniform distribution will be used. Otherwise, the normal distribution is often used as the prior probability. A good classification procedure should result in few misclassifications, and therefore, the probabilities of misclassification should be small. For example, latent knowledge state p_A may have more students than another latent knowledge state p_B because the tasks associated with state A are less difficult than those with state B. An optimal classification rule should take this information about "prior probabilities of occurrence" into account. Another important aspect of classification is cost.

Cost

Suppose a student belonging to π_A is classified into π_B, and consequently the student could not get his or her necessary remedial instruction. On the other hand, a student belonging to π_B is classified into class π_A, and the necessary remedial instruction was given to the student. The first misclassification has more serious implications to the students' future work than the second classification error. The cost is defined by zero for the correct classification, but the costs of misclassifications are more complicated. The costs of misclassification are explained by the (2 × 2) table below such that $C(j|i) - X$ is really in group i but classified in group j and $C(i|j) - X$ is from group j but classified in group i, respectively.

Classification results:

	π_i	π_j
True state π_i	0	$C(j|i)$
π_j	$C(i|j)$	0

The optimal classification procedure should account for the cost associated with misclassification.

Expected Loss and Classification Rules

Suppose $p(X|\pi_i)$ is the conditional density functions of X, a random variable (a student response pattern) from one of M populations, and P_i is a priori probabilities of π_i. We wish to divide the space of X (rule space or classification space) into m mutually exclusive and exhaustive regions, $R_1, \ldots, R_m$. If student response pattern X falls in region R_i, then we say X comes from π_i. The cost of misclassification, X is from π_i as coming from π_j, is given by $C(j|i)$. The probability of this misclassification is given by

$$P(j|i, R_j) = \int_{Rj} p(X|\pi_j)dX. \qquad (6.39)$$

From the Bayes theorem, the posterior probability of p_j given X, or the conditional probability of an observation coming from π_j given the value of the vector X, is given by

$$p(\pi_j|X) = \frac{P_j(X|\pi_j)}{\Sigma_{k=1,m}P_k(X|\pi_k)} \qquad (6.40)$$

If student response is classified into p_j, then the expected loss is

$$\sum_{i=1}^{m} \frac{P_i p(x|\pi_i)}{\Sigma_{i\neq j}^{k=1,m} P_k p(x|\pi k)} C(j|i). \qquad (6.41)$$

In order to minimize Equation (6.41), we minimize Equation (6.42) after omitting the denominator:

$$\sum_{\substack{i=1,m \\ i\neq j}}^{} P_i p(x|\pi_i) C(j|i). \qquad (6.42)$$

We select region R_j, which gives the expected loss (Equation (6.42)) minimum. The classification rule is given by

$$\text{If} \sum_{\substack{i=1,m \\ i\neq j}}^{} P_i p(x|\pi_i)C(j|i) > \sum_{\substack{i=1,m \\ i\neq j}}^{} P_i p(x|\pi_i)C(k|i) \quad \text{then X belongs to } \pi_k. \qquad (6.43)$$

The decision rule, Equation (6.43), minimizes the expected cost.

When Costs Are Equal

Although the misclassification of a cancer patient to normal may have a drastic damaging effect, in educational applications, it may not be true that the misclassification becomes a matter of life or death. Therefore, the cost can be set to equal to the educational situation. Then the decision rule, Equation (6.43), is restated by

$$\text{If} \sum_{\substack{i=1,m \\ i\neq j}} P_i p(x|\pi_i) > \sum_{\substack{i=1,m \\ i\neq j}} P_i p(x|\pi_i), \text{ then } X \text{ belongs to } \pi_k. \tag{6.44}$$

The rule (Equation (6.44)) is equivalent to saying as follows:

$$\text{If } p_k p(X|\pi_k) > p_j p(X|\pi_j) \quad \text{for all } j \neq k, \text{ then } X \text{ belongs to } \pi_k. \tag{6.45}$$

The rule (Equation (6.45)) is identical to the one that maximizes the posterior probability, $p(\pi_k|X)$, by dividing the constant term, which is the mixture probability expressed by $\sum_{k=1,m} P_k p(x|\pi_k)$.

If posterior probabilities for π_i, $i = 1, \ldots, m$ are equal to one, then the decision rule becomes the same rule (the maximum likelihood rule) as stated earlier before the posterior probabilities are introduced.

$$\text{If } p(X|\pi_k) > p(X|\pi_j) \text{ for all } j \neq k, \text{ then } X \text{ belongs to } \pi_k. \tag{6.46}$$

If the likelihood value of X becomes the largest for π_k, then X belongs to π_k.

Summary of Classification Rules

These several decision rules are summarized in Table 6.1.

TABLE 6.1

Summary of Classification Rules

Classification to One of Two Groups	
Bayes decision rule:	
If $p(\pi_1|X) > p(\pi_2|X)$, then X belongs to π_i.........(0 0 0 0)*	(6.20)
If $P_i p(x|\pi_i) > P_j p(x|\pi_j)$, then X belongs to π_i.........(0 0 0 0)	(6.22)
If $l(X) = \dfrac{p(X|\pi_i)}{p(X|\pi_j)} > \dfrac{P_j}{P_i}$, then X belongs to π_i.........(0 0 0 0)	(6.23)

(Continued)

TABLE 6.1 (Continued)

Summary of Classification Rules

Classification to One of Two Groups

$$\text{If } h(X) = -l(X) = .5\left\{(X-\mu_i)'\sum_I^{-1}(X-\mu_i) - (X-\mu_j)'\sum_j^{-1}(X-\mu_j)\right\}$$

$$+.5*\ln\left\{\frac{|\Sigma_i|}{|\Sigma_j|}\right\} > \ln\left\{\frac{P_i}{P_j}\right\}, \text{ then X belongs to } \pi_i; \qquad ....(1\ 0\ 0\ 1) \qquad (6.24)$$

$$h(X)\ (X-\mu_i)'\sum_i^{-1}(X-\mu_i) - (X-\mu_j)'\sum_j^{-1}(X-\mu_j)$$

$$= (\mu_j - \mu_i)'\sum^{-1}X + .5\left(\mu_i\sum_i^{-1}\mu_i - \mu_j\sum^{-1}\mu_j\right) \qquad ....(1\ 1\ 0\ 0) \qquad (6.25)$$

$$\text{If } h(X) > \ln\left\{\frac{P_i}{P_j}\right\}, \text{ then X is in } \pi_i \text{ ....}(1\ 1\ 0\ 0) \qquad (6.26)$$

$$\text{If } (X-\mu_i)'\sum_i^{-1}(X-\mu_i) < (X-\mu_j)'\sum_j^{-1}(X-\mu_j) \text{ then X is in } \pi_i \text{ ....}(1\ 1\ 1\ 0) \qquad (6.28)$$

Classification to One of Many Groups

Bayes decision rule:
$$p_k p(X|\pi_k) = \max\{p_j p(X|\pi_j)\} \text{ then X to } \pi_k \text{.........}(0\ 0\ 0\ 0) \qquad (6.31)$$
Maximum likelihood rule: If $p(X|\pi_k)$ is the largest of K likelihood values,
then it is placed in group K.........(0 0 0 0) $\qquad (6.32)$

$$\text{If } \mu_i \text{ gives min}_j\left\{1/2(X-\mu_j)'\sum_j^{-1}(X-\mu_j) + 1/2\ln\left|\sum_j\right| - \ln P_j\right\},$$

then X belongs to π_i.........(1 0 0 0) $\qquad (6.333)$

$-(1/2)\ D_K^2 + 1/2\ln|\Sigma_j| - \ln p_j = -(1/2)\ D_K^2 + \text{constant terms.........}(1\ 1\ 0\ 0) \qquad (6.35)$

Minimum generalized distance rule: When the covariance matrices are the same, X belongs

to the group having the smallest value of D_K^2, $D_K^2 = (X-\mu_K)'\sum_K^{-1}(X-\mu_K)$.........(1 1 1 1) $\qquad (6.36)$

*Condition $C_j = (c_1, c_2, c_3, c_4)$ is defined as follows:

c_1: Density distributions are multivariate normal.
c_2: Covariance matrices are equal.
c_3: Prior probabilities are almost equal.
c_4: Costs are almost equal.
$c_k = 1$ if a rule requires the condition c_k.

For example, (1 0 1 1) means the density functions are normal, the covariance matrices are not equal, and the prior probabilities and costs are same.

6.6 Error Probabilities or Misclassification Probabilities

It is important to evaluate the performance of any classification procedures. When forms of the conditional density functions are known, then misclassification probabilities can be computed without problems. However, if the density functions are not known, then estimating misclassification probabilities becomes a very difficult task. In this section, we discuss only simple cases.

The discriminant function h(X) is defined as the minus logarithm of the likelihood ratio of the conditional density functions $p(X|\pi_i)$, i = 1, 2. When the prior probabilities P_i and P_j are equal and costs are equal, the discriminant function h(X) becomes

$$h(X) = -\ln p(X|\pi_i) + \ln p(X|\pi_j) \tag{6.47}$$

The conditional error given X, r(x) is given by

$$r(X) = \min(\text{the posterior probability of } \pi_i \text{ or } \pi_j) = \min\{p(\pi_i|X), p(\pi_j|X)\} \tag{6.48}$$

The total error that is called the Bayes error is the expectation of r(X) and is given by

$$\varepsilon = E[r(X)] = \int_R r(X)p(X)dX = P_i \int_{Rj} p(X|\pi_i)dx + P_j \int_{Ri} p(X|\pi_j) \tag{6.49}$$

where the regions R_i and R_j are defined as follows: If X falls in R_i, then X belongs to π_i; and if X falls in R_j, then X belongs to π_j. This is the Bayes decision rule.

Prior Probabilities, Covariance Matrices Are Alike

When three conditions are met: (1) prior probabilities are alike, (2) costs are assumed to be one, and (3) covariance matrices Σ_i and Σ_j are also alike; then the discriminant function becomes a linear function. The decision boundary is set at x = t where the posterior probabilities are equal, and x < t is for the region L_1 and x > t is for the region L_2. In this simplest case, the misclassification probabilities are illustrated by Figure 6.6. The resulting errors are $P_1 \varepsilon_1 = B + C$ and $P_2 \varepsilon_2 = A$, and $\varepsilon = A + B + C$. Bayes decision rule provides with the smallest probability of error. Suppose that the boundary is moved from t to t', setting up the new p_1' and p_2', then the resulting error are $P_1 \varepsilon_1' = C$ and $P_2 \varepsilon_2' = A + B + D$, and $\varepsilon' = A + B + C + D$. Note that

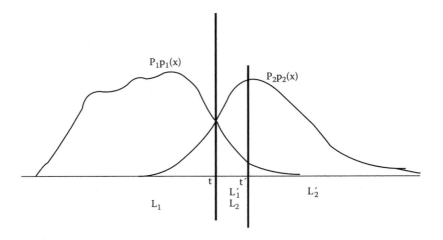

FIGURE 6.6
Bayes decision rule for minimum error.

ϵ' is larger that ϵ by D. This argument can be extended to more general cases (Fukunaga, 1990). This relationship is summarized in the following matrix:

	Classification of X	
	π_1	π_2
True state π_1	$p(\pi_1\mid X)$	ϵ_1
π_2	ϵ_2	$p(\pi_2\mid X)$

The total error is given by $\epsilon_1 + \epsilon_2$.

When There Are Many Classes

When there are many classes, the decision rule based on the probabilities is to allocate an observed vector X to group π_k if the posterior probability of π_k given X is the maximum among the groups. By applying the Bayes theorem, this rule is restated as follows: If the product of the prior probability P_k and the conditional density function $p(X\mid\pi_k)$ is the maximum among the groups, then X is allocated to group π_k. In the region R_k, $P_k p(X\mid\pi_k) > P_j p(X\mid\pi_j)$, and $r(X) = \{P_j p(X\mid\pi_j)\}/p(X)$. Because X belongs to the other group π_j with the probability of $p(p_j\mid X)$, the probability of errors or misclassification is obtained by summing up the posterior probabilities of the groups for $j \neq k$. Therefore, $1 - p(\pi_k\mid X)$ is the conditional probability of misclassification for a given X. The Bayes error is obtained by taking the expectation over X.

$$r(X) = 1 - \max_k \{p(\pi_k | X)\} \tag{6.50}$$

$$\varepsilon = E\{r(X)\}, \quad \text{where expectation is taken over X} \tag{6.51}$$

When Costs are Involved, the Decision Rule Becomes

$$\text{If min} \sum_{i,j=1}^{m} C(j|i)p(\pi_j | X) \text{ for k,} \quad \text{then X belongs to } \pi_k. \tag{6.52}$$

The resulting conditional cost given X and the total cost are given by

$$r(X) = \min_i \{ri(X)\} \quad \text{and} \quad r = \underset{X}{\text{Exp}}[r(X)] \tag{6.53}$$

When $C(i|i) = 1$, $C(i|j) = 0$, then the above equation becomes the Bayes error, the total error without considering costs. That is, $r = \varepsilon$.

6.7 Distribution of D^2

We have discussed a bug distribution consisting of some erroneous rule R and a cluster of points deviated by slips from R, but they can be easily replaced by a knowledge state consisting of some ideal item score patterns derived from a given Q matrix and a cluster of points deviated from R by various numbers of slips. A bug distribution discussed above can be replaced by a distribution of knowledge states without any loss of generality. In latent classes modeling, the distribution of a knowledge state is often assumed to be a unit normal distribution.

Let us consider a distribution of D^2 with the expected vector of M_K and the covariance matrix Σ_K as a fixed quantity where $D^2 = (X - M_K)' \Sigma_K^{-1} (X - M_K)$. When X is close to M_K, the value of D^2 is small, but D^2 increases as X is farther apart from M_K. D^2 can be transformed (called the *whitening transformation*; Fukunaga, 1990) by a linear transformation A to $Z = A(X - M_K)$ that has the expectation of zero and the covariance matrix of the identity matrix I, so D^2 becomes an orthonormal form, $Z'Z = \Sigma_{i=1,p} z_i^2$. If Z_i is normally distributed and independent, then D^2 follows a chi-square distribution with the expectation of p (the dimension of X) and $p\gamma$, where γ is given by $E(Z_i^2) - 1$.

In general for normal variables Z_is, the density function of D^2 is known as the gamma density function with the parameters $\alpha = p/2 - 1$, $\beta = 1/2$.

Let us denote D^2 by Y; then the gamma function will be

$$p(Y) = \frac{1}{2^{p/2}\Gamma(p/2)} Y^{(p-2)/2} e^{-Y/2} \qquad \text{for } 0 < Y < \alpha$$

$$= 0 \qquad\qquad\qquad\qquad\qquad \text{elsewhere.}$$

(6.54)

The expected value and variance of the gamma distribution are given by

$$E(D^2) = (\beta + 1)/\alpha = p \tag{6.55}$$

$$Var(D^2) = (\beta + 1)/\alpha^2 = 2p \tag{6.56}$$

When the density functions of groups are multivariate normal, and when costs and prior probabilities can be considered alike, then the Bayes decision rule is reduced to a simple form of using the Mahalanobis distances in the rule space. The boundary of this decision rule becomes a hyperplane, and the decision rule is that if X lies in the same side of space that is divided by the boundary as π_i, then it belongs to group π_i.

However, we have advantages and disadvantages unique to the rule space classification problems for applying these classifiers without modification. The uniqueness to our situation is characterized by at least two points: (a) The number of knowledge states usually ranges from a few hundred to several thousand, and (b) two groups (knowledge states) that are closely situated in the rule space usually have very similar ideal item score patterns. That means the two ideal item score patterns have very similar attribute mastery patterns. The separation among the ideal item patterns (or knowledge states) resulting from similar attribute mastery patterns is poor, the proximity of such ideal item score patterns is very high, and, indeed, they cluster within a small neighborhood, $D^2 < a$ small number, α from one another. This issue will be discussed again in Chapter 7.

7

Rule Space Decision Rules and Attribute Mastery Probabilities

7.1 Classification Rule for Two Groups in Two Dimensional Rule Space

Review From Chapter 5

In the rule space, one of the motivations to express both the observed and ideal item score patterns by a set of ordered pairs of (θ, ζ)—this is a classification space—is to have a connection to the current psychometric theories, especially item response theory. Additionally, having discrete variables such as item scores as the coordinates in a classification space may cause computational problems. Kim (1989) used a discriminant analysis for a 20-item algebra test, in which binary item scores are independent variables and form a space with 19-dimensional item response space as a classification space. Kim classified a student response pattern into one of 12 predetermined knowledge states. He generated 1,200 response patterns from the 12 knowledge states, and classified observed item responses into one of the 12 knowledge states by using three different methods: discriminant analysis, RSM, and the Kth nearest method. Kim found that the covariance matrices for some knowledge states became singular, and he could not compute the inverses of these covariance matrices. The knowledge states having very high scores and very low scores often have singular covariance matrices. However, converting discrete variables (item scores) into continuous variables avoids this computational problem. Kim found that the rule space performed as well as the discriminant analysis, and much better than the Kth nearest method when the covariance matrices are not singular and hence invertible. Because the variables in the rule space are continuous, it is always possible to compute the squared Mahalanobis distances. In other words, classification results are always available. This is one of advantages for using RSM.

The two variables θ and the numerator of ζ, denoted by $f(X,\theta)$, are not only continuous variables but also mutually uncorrelated, as has been shown (Tatsuoka, 1985). An ideal item score pattern $\mathbf{R}$ associated with knowledge state π_R can be mapped to an ordered pair of the estimated IRT ability value of θ_R and the covariance of two residuals, $f(R, \theta_R)$, that is denoted by $\mathbf{Y_R} = (\theta_R, f(R, \theta_R))$. The response patterns deviating from $\mathbf{R_1}$

with different numbers of slips will cluster around $\mathbf{Y}_{RI}$ and are assumed to follow a multivariate normal distribution with the centroid $\mathbf{Y}_{RI}$ and the covariance matrix Σ_{RI} (Tatsuoka & Tatsuoka, 1987).

$$\sum_{RI} = \begin{vmatrix} Var(\theta_{R1}) & 0 \\ 0 & var(f(\theta_{R1})) \end{vmatrix} = \begin{vmatrix} \dfrac{I}{I(\theta)} & 0 \\ 0 & \displaystyle\sum_{j=1}^{n} P_j(\theta_{R1})Q_j(\theta_{R1})\{P_j(\theta_{R1}) - T(\theta_{R1})\}^2 \end{vmatrix}$$

(7.1)

where $I(\theta)$ is the information function of the test and is given by

$$\sum_{j=1}^{n} P_j(\theta_{R1})Q_j(\theta_{R1})\{P_j(\theta_{R1}) - T(\theta_{R1})\}^2$$

for the one-parameter logistic model, and

$$\sum_{j=1}^{n} a_j^2 \, P_j(\theta_{R1})Q_j(\theta_{R1})\{P_j(\theta_{R1}) - T(\theta_{R1})\}^2$$

for the two-parameter logistic model.

From now on, we use the shorter notation $\mathbf{R}_l$ for $l = 1, \dots, K$, instead of $\mathbf{Y}_{RI}$, to express the rule space coordinates. Because ζ is the standardized variable of $f(X, \theta)$ divided by its standard deviation, Equation (7.2),

$$SD^2 \text{ of } f(X, \theta) = \left[\sum_{j=1}^{n} P_j(\theta_{R1})Q_j(\theta_{R1})\{P_j(\theta_{R1}) - T(\theta_{R1})\}^2 \right]^{1/2} \quad (7.2)$$

the covariance matrix Σ of θ and ζ is given by a simple diagonal matrix, Equation (7.3):

$$\sum = \begin{vmatrix} \dfrac{1}{I(\theta)} & 0 \\ 0 & 1 \end{vmatrix} \quad (7.3)$$

The following example shows numerical examples of knowledge states and their coordinates (θ_R, ζ_R) and covariance matrices.

Example 7.1

The two knowledge states are used to show how ideal item score patterns and their corresponding attribute patterns relate to each other. Then, their rule space coordinates and the covariance matrices are given.

KS R	$I(\theta_R)$	θ_R	ζ_R at θ_R	Ideal Item Score Patterns (20 Items)	Attribute Patterns
5	32.06	0.3427	2.0239	1 1 1 0 0 1 1 1 1 0 0 1 0 0 1 0 1 0 1 0	1 1 0 1 1 1 1 1
6	18.40	−0.273	2.4041	1 1 1 0 0 1 1 1 0 0 0 0 0 0 0 0 0 0 0 1	1 0 1 1 1 1 0 1

This example has two knowledge states, KS 5 and KS 6, in the 20 fraction addition problems. Their IRT person parameter θ_R is estimated, and ζ_R is computed using ideal item score patterns. Their covariance matrix will be Σ_5 and Σ_6, respectively, and given as below:

$$\sum_5 = \begin{vmatrix} 1/32.06 & 0 \\ 0 & 1 \end{vmatrix} \quad \sum_6 = \begin{vmatrix} 1/18.40 & 0 \\ 0 & 1 \end{vmatrix}$$

Since ideal item score pattern, KSR 5, corresponds to attribute pattern (1 1 0 1 1 1 1 1), the point in rule space (0.3427, 20239) now has the diagnostic information. The following section discusses more about ζ:

ζ as the Second Coordinate Orthogonal to θ

Researchers have named ζ a person–fit statistic (Drasgow, 1982; Meijer, 1994), but measuring the degree of person–fit was not our original intention. The original purpose of the index ζ is for solving three problems:

1. To find a variable that is orthogonal to IRT θ, and spans a classification space with θ
2. To reduce the dimension of a classification space (usually the number of items minus 1) to a much smaller number of continuous variables
3. To map similar item score patterns into neighboring points in space so that they form a cluster

These characteristics, along with the fact that $f(\mathbf{X}, \theta)$ and θ are uncorrelated (Tatsuoka, 1985, 1995), suggest using this variable, $f(\mathbf{X}, \theta)$, to create a Cartesian product space of IRT ability measure θ and ζ. Figure 5.6 in chapter 5 shows that the coordinates θ and ζ of 39 knowledge states for fraction subtraction problems are not correlated, and indeed the correlation value of θ and ζ with this dataset is .053 at $p = .008$, $N = 595$.

The variances of θ and $f(\mathbf{X}, \theta)$, plus the reasonable assumption that they have a bivariate normal distribution (K. Tatsuoka & M. Tatsuoka, 1987; M. Tatsuoka & K. Tatsuoka, 1989), allow us to construct any desired ellipse around each rule point $\mathbf{R}_l$. The upshot is that if all knowledge states (erroneous rules) were to be mapped onto the rule space along with their neighboring response patterns representing random slips from them, the resulting topography would be something like that seen in Figure 7.1.

That is, the population of points would exhibit modal densities at many rule points, such that each forms the center of an enveloping ellipse, with the density of points getting rarer as we depart farther from the center in any direction. Furthermore, the major and minor axes of these ellipses would—by virtue of the uncorrelatedness of ζ and θ—be parallel to the vertical ζ and horizontal θ reference axes of the rule space, respectively.

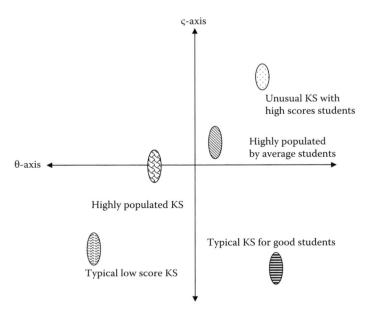

FIGURE 7.1
Interpretation of various locations in the rule space.

Recalling that for any given percentage ellipse, the lengths of the major and minor diameters are fixed multiples of the respective standard deviations:

$$\left[\sum P_j(\theta_{R1})Q_j(\theta_{R1})\{P_j(\theta_{R1}) - T(\theta_{R1})\}^2\right]^{1/2} \quad \text{and} \quad \{I(\theta_{R1})\}^{-1/2}, \tag{7.4}$$

We may assert that the set of ellipses gives a complete characterization of the rule space. In other words, once these ellipses are given, any response pattern point can be classified as most likely being a random slip from one or another of the knowledge states. We have only to imagine letting all the ellipses "grow" in size at the same rate in terms of percent coverage. Then the point will, at some instant, be found to lie on just one of the ellipses (unless, with probability zero, it happens to be one of the points of intersection of two ellipses). The geometric scheme outlined in Figure 7.1 for classifying any given response pattern point as being a "perturbation" from one or another of the rule points has a certain intuitive appeal. However, it is obviously difficult, if not infeasible, to put it into practice. We therefore now describe the algebraic equivalence of the foregoing geometric classification decision rule, which is none other than the well-known minimum D^2, Mahalanobis' generalized squared distance. Next, the Bayes decision rule for minimum error will be discussed in the context of the rule space.

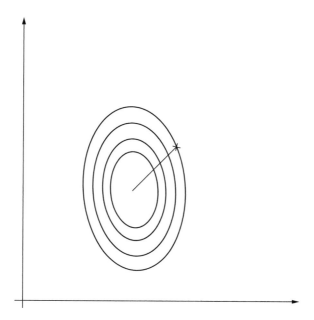

FIGURE 7.2
The density function of a knowledge state in the rule space.

Without loss of generality, we may suppose that a given response pattern point, **X**, has to be classified as representing a random slip from one of two knowledge states, π_1 and π_2. Let **X** be the point in rule space corresponding to the observed response pattern,

$$\mathbf{X}' = [\theta_X, f(X, \theta_X)]$$

The estimated Mahalanobis distance of X from the two knowledge states is

$$D_{xj}{}^2 = (X - R_j)' \sum{}^{-1} (X - R_j) \quad j = 1, 2 \tag{7.5}$$

where

$$R_1 = \begin{vmatrix} \theta_{R1} \\ f(R_1\theta_{R1}) \end{vmatrix} \quad \text{and} \quad R_2 = \begin{vmatrix} \theta_{R2} \\ f(R_2\theta_{R2}) \end{vmatrix}$$

and the covariance matrix is

$$\sum = \begin{vmatrix} \text{Var}(\theta_X) & 0 \\ 0 & \text{var}(f(X, \theta_X)) \end{vmatrix}. \tag{7.6}$$

If we use ζ (standardized $f(X, \theta_X)$) for the second variable instead of $f(X, \theta_X)$), then for $X' = (\theta_X, \zeta_{\theta_X,X})$, the Mahalanobis distance is given by $D_{xj}^2 = (X - R_j)' \Sigma^{-1}(X - R_j)$ for $j = 1, 2$, and

$$R_1 = \begin{vmatrix} \theta_{R1} \\ \zeta_{R1,X} \end{vmatrix} \quad \text{and} \quad R_2 = \begin{vmatrix} \theta_{R2} \\ \zeta_{R2,X} \end{vmatrix}$$

$$\Sigma = \begin{vmatrix} \text{Var}(\theta_X) & 0 \\ 0 & 1 \end{vmatrix} \tag{7.7}$$

To simplify the notations, $\zeta_{R1,X}$ and $\zeta_{R2,X}$ are denoted by ζ_1 and ζ_2, respectively.

$$\begin{aligned} D_{xj}^2 &= (X - R_j)' \sum^{-1}(X - R_j) \\ &= (\theta_X - \theta_{Rj} , \zeta_{\theta x, X} - \zeta_{Rj, X}) \begin{vmatrix} 1/\text{Var}(\theta_{Rj}) & 0 \\ 0 & 1 \end{vmatrix} \begin{vmatrix} \theta_X - \theta_{Rj} \\ \zeta_{\theta x,X} - \zeta_{Rj,X} \end{vmatrix} \\ &= (\theta_X - \theta_{Rj})^2/I(\theta_{Rj}) + (\zeta_{\theta x,X} - \zeta_{Rj,X})^2/\text{Var}(\zeta_{Rj,X}) \end{aligned} \tag{7.8}$$

where $\text{Var}(\zeta_{Rj,X}) = 1$, for $j = 1, 2$.

Example 7.2 shows a numerical example of computing the Mahalanobis distance using the two knowledge states of the 20-item fraction test in Example 7.1.

Example 7.2

The two knowledge states KS 17 and 33 with their rule space coordinates θ and ζ are given below. Their ideal item score patterns and corresponding attribute mastery patterns are also given. Then their rule space coordinates and the covariance matrices are given.

Knowledge States	$I(\theta)$	θ	ζ
17	25.5	0.036	2.309
33	31.2	0.6776	1.143

Ideal Item Score Patterns (20 Items)																				Attribute Mastery Patterns							
KS	1	2	3	4	5	6	7	8	9	10	11	12	13	14	15	16	17	18	19	20	1	2	3	4	5	6	7	8
17	0	1	1	0	0	1	1	1	0	0	0	1	0	0	1	0	1	0	0	0	1	1	0	1	0	1	1	0
33	0	0	0	1	0	1	1	1	1	1	1	1	0	1	1	1	1	1	1	0	0	1	0	1	1	1	1	1

Their covariance matrices in the rule space are

$$\sum_{17} = \begin{vmatrix} 0.032 & 0 \\ 0 & 1 \end{vmatrix} \quad \sum_{33} = \begin{vmatrix} 0.039 & 0 \\ 0 & 1 \end{vmatrix}$$

Suppose two students (denoted by X_2 and X_4) took this test and we would like to compute the Mahalanobis distance of between X_2 and KS 17, and KS 33. The response patterns of the students X_2 and X_4 are given below:

ID	θ	ζ	Score	1	2	3	4	5	6	7	8	9	10	11	12	13	14	15	16	17	18	19	20
2 X_2	0.463	2.356	12	0	0	0	1	0	0	1	1	0	1	1	1	0	1	1	1	0	1	1	1
4 X_4	0.054	2.978	9	0	1	1	1	0	1	1	1	0	0	0	0	0	1	1	1	0	0	0	0

Let us start from KS 33 and X_2. Substituting the numbers given above into the formula of $D^2_{(x2,ks33)}$, we get

$$D^2_{(x2,KS33)} = (\theta_{x2} - \theta_{ks33}, \zeta_{\theta x2} - \zeta_{ks33}) \begin{vmatrix} 1/\text{Var}(\theta_{ks33}) & 0 \\ 0 & 1 \end{vmatrix} \begin{vmatrix} \theta_{X2} - \theta_{ks33} \\ \zeta_{\theta x2} - \zeta_{ks33} \end{vmatrix}$$

$$= (\theta_X - \theta_{Rj})^2 / I(\theta_{Rj}) + (\zeta_{\theta x,X} - \zeta_{Rj,X})^2 / \text{Var}(\zeta_{Rj,X})$$

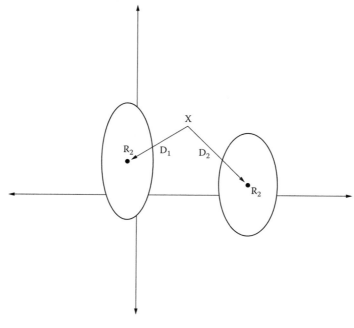

FIGURE 7.3
Decision rule using the Mahalanobis distance.

where $D_{(x2,KS33)}^2 = (0.463 - 0.678)^2/31.2 + (2.222 - 1.143)^2 = 2.948$. The Mahalanobis distance between KS 33 and X_2 is 2.948. Similarly, the distance between KS17 and X_2 is given by $D_{(x2,ks17)}^2 = (0.463 - 0.036)^2/25.5 + (2.222 - 2.309)^2 = .0147$. The decision rule is to classify X_2 as a perturbation from KS17 if $D_{(x2,ks17)}^2 < D_{(x2,ks33)}^2$, and otherwise as a perturbation from KS33 in this example.

The decision rule is depicted in Figure 7.3 with the probabilities of misclassifications, the type 1 and type 2 errors. However, the decision based on the Mahalanobis distance D_{xj}^2 does not by itself yield probabilities of misclassification.

7.2   Probabilities of Misclassifications

Let $p_j = P(\pi_j)$, $j = 1, 2$ be prior probabilities of the knowledge states π_1 and π_2. Let $p(\pi_1|X)$ and $p(\pi_2|X)$ be the posterior probabilities, and $p(X|\pi_1)$ and $p(X|\pi_2)$ be the conditional density functions of X given π_j, $j = 1, 2$. These are obtained, up to an unknown proportionality factor, by evaluating $\phi(u, \sigma)$ at the centroid (θ_j, ζ_{j}) for the knowledge states π_j, $j = 1, 2$, where $\phi(u, \sigma)$ is the density function of the bivariate normal distribution, $N(0, 1)$. Then, Bayes' decision rule is given below:

If $\dfrac{p(X|\pi_1)}{p(X|\pi_2)} > \dfrac{P(\pi_2)}{P(\pi_1)}$, then decide that $X \varepsilon \pi_1$; otherwise, decide $X \varepsilon \pi_2$.   (7.9)

It is usually convenient to take the negative log of the likelihood ratio in Equation (7.9) and rewrite the decision rule as

$$h(X) = -\ln l(X) = -\ln(p(X|\pi_1)) + \ln((p(X|\pi_2)) < \ln \frac{P(\pi_1)}{P(\pi_2)}, \text{ then decide } X \varepsilon \pi_1$$

(7.10)

Let Γ_1, Γ_2 be the regions such that if $X \in \Gamma_1$, then $p(\pi_1|X) > p(\pi_2|X)$, and if $X \in \Gamma_2$, then $p(\pi_2|X) > p(\pi_1|X)$. It then follows that the total probability of misclassification is given by Equation (7.11):

$$\varepsilon = p1 \int_{\Gamma 2} p(X|\pi_1)dX + p2 \int_{\Gamma 1} p(X|\pi_2)dX.$$ (7.11)

The integration involved here is tedious. Hence, it is customary to change the variable of integration to the likelihood ratio λ (Fukunaga, 1990):

$$\lambda = \frac{p(X|\pi_1)}{p(X|\pi_2)}$$

The density function of λ is linear. Equation 7.11 becomes

$$\varepsilon = p1 \int_0^{p2/p1} p(P \mid \pi_1)\, dP + p2 \int_0^{p2/p1} p(P \mid \pi_2)\, dP. \tag{7.12}$$

If the density function $p(X|\pi_j)$ is normal with expectations M_j and covariance matrices Σj, then decisions rule, Equation (7.10), specializes to the decision rule, Equation (6.23), in Table 6.1. In the rule space, the decision rule has to be applied often to knowledge states close together. When two knowledge states are located close to one another in the rule space, their covariance matrices become almost identical. In this case, the discriminant function becomes linear, and the error probability is given by

$$\varepsilon = p1 \int_T^\alpha p(h(X)|\pi_1)dh(X) + p2 \int_{-\alpha}^t p(h(X)|\pi_2)dh(X)$$

$$= p1 \int (2\pi)^{-1/2} \exp\,(-z^2/2)dz + p2 \int (2\pi)^{-1/2} \exp(-z^2/2)dz \tag{713}$$

$$= p1[1 - \phi((t+\eta)/\sigma_1)] + p2[1 - \phi((\eta - t)\sigma_2)]$$

where $t = \ln[p1/p2]$ and $\phi(.)$ is the unit normal distribution (Tatsuoka, 1970). Here, η is +1 or −1 times the conditional expectations of the likelihood function $h(X)$ given π_2 and π_1, respectively. In other words,

$$\eta = -E(h(X)|\pi_1) = E(h(X)|\pi_1) = 1/2(M_2 - M_1)' \sum{}^{-1} (M_2 - M_1) \tag{7.14}$$

and σ_i^2 is the variance of $h(X)$,

$$\sigma_i^2 = E[\{h(X) \pm \eta\}^2|\pi_1) = (M_2 - M_1)' \sum{}^{-1} (M_2 - M_1) = 2\eta \tag{7.15}$$

Illustration of the Model With an Example

A 40-item fraction subtraction test was given to 533 students. A computer program adopting a deterministic strategy for diagnosing erroneous rules of operation in subtracting two fractions was developed. The students' performances on the test were analyzed by the error-diagnostic program and summarized by Tatsuoka (1984a). These erroneous rules and error types were obtained from the diagnostic program and task analyses, but they were not obtained by using a Q matrix and Boolean description function. The rule space can be used for both cases as long as ideal item score patterns are uniquely identified to represent attribute mastery patterns.

In order to illustrate the rule space classification procedure, two very common erroneous rules are chosen to explain the procedure (Tatsuoka, 1984b).

Rule 8: This rule is applicable to any fraction or mixed number. A student subtracts the smaller number from the larger one in unequal corresponding parts and keeps corresponding equal parts in the answer. Examples are

$$4\frac{4}{12} - 2\frac{7}{12} = 2\frac{3}{12} = 2\frac{1}{4},$$

$$7\frac{3}{5} - \frac{4}{5} = 7\frac{1}{5}, \quad \text{and}$$

$$\frac{3}{4} - \frac{3}{8} = \frac{3}{4}$$

Rule 30: This rule is applicable to the subtraction of mixed numbers where the first numerator is smaller than the second numerator. A student reduces the whole-number part of the minuend by one and adds one to the tens digit of the numerator.

$$4\frac{4}{12} - 2\frac{7}{12} = 3\frac{14}{12} - 2\frac{7}{12} = 1\frac{7}{12},$$

$$3\frac{3}{8} - 2\frac{5}{6} = 2\frac{13}{8} - 2\frac{5}{6} = \frac{19}{24}, \quad \text{and}$$

$$7\frac{3}{5} - \frac{4}{5} = 6\frac{13}{5} - \frac{4}{5} = 6\frac{9}{5}.$$

These two rules are applied to 40 items, and two sets of responses are scored right or wrong. The binary score pattern made by Rule 8 is denoted by R8, and the other by Rule 30 is denoted by R30.

Besides the two rules mentioned above, 54 different erroneous rules are identified by task analysis. However, some erroneous rules are grouped to represent an error type. Error types do not necessarily represent micro levels of cognitive processes such as erroneous rules of operation. They are defined more coarsely, such as borrowing errors being grouped as a single error type in which several erroneous rules exist. By grouping erroneous rules to an error type, Tatsuoka (1984a) has listed 39 error types that are associated with 39 different binary response patterns. Their centroids are plotted in Figure 5.12, and their coordinates computed from 533 students are summarized in Table 5.5.

Now two students, A and B, who used Rules 8 and 30 for the 40 items are selected for this example. This was possible because their performances are diagnosed independently by the error-diagnostic system. The circles shown in Figure 5.12 represent A and B. Their estimated Mahalanobis distances $\bar{D}^2_k$, $k = 1, \ldots, 40$, to the 39 centroids are calculated respectively, and the smallest values of two distances $\bar{D}^2_A$ and $\bar{D}^2_B$ are chosen to compute probabilities of errors. Table 7.1 summarizes the results. Set 39, 19, 39, and 14 corresponds to the distributions of the knowledge states π_{39}, π_{19}, π_{39}, and π_{14}.

The $\bar{D}^2$ values of student A to sets 39 and 19 are .008 and .119, respectively, and both the values are small enough to judge that A may be classified to either set. Because $\bar{D}^2$ follows the χ^2 distribution with two degrees of freedom (Tatsuoka, 1971), the null hypotheses that $\bar{D}^2_{(A,\,set\,39)} = 0$ and $\bar{D}^2_{(A,\,set\,39)} = 0$ cannot be rejected at, say, a given criterion $\alpha = .25$. The error probabilities ε_1 and ε_2 are .581 and .266, respectively. Therefore, we conclude that A belongs to Rule 19, even though $\bar{D}^2_{(A,\,set\,39)}$ is smaller than $\bar{D}^2_{(A,\,set\,39)} = 0$. This is because the prior probability, prob(A|Rule 39), is estimated to be much smaller than prob(A|Rule 19), from calculations based on the following equations for a given X:

$$\text{Prob}(X|\pi_{19}) \propto \frac{1}{2\pi|\Sigma|^{1/2}} \exp\left[-(\theta_k, \zeta_k)' \sum_k (\theta_k, \zeta_k)^{-1}\right] \qquad (7.16)$$

TABLE 7.1

Summary of Classification Results
of Students A and B

	Student A	Student B
D^2	D^2_A, Set 40 .008	D^2_B, Set 39 .021
	D^2_A, Set 19 .119	D^2_B, Set 14 .135
ε_1	.581	.979
ε_2	.266	.010
η	.088	.040
T	−.174	−.613

and

$$t = -\ln\left[\frac{\text{prob}(X|\pi_{40})}{\text{prob}(X|\pi_{19})}\right] \qquad (7.17)$$

The classification rule used for the above example may be applicable to the case when the number of predetermined knowledge states is only about 30 or 39 at most. When the number of attributes increases to 10 or 15 for a 40-item test, the number of knowledge states easily increases to a few thousand or more. Several knowledge states can be located within a circle of radius $D^2 = 1.0$ from (θ_x, ζ_x). We need a multigroup classification procedure for such cases.

7.3 Classification of Observed Response X Into One of Many Predetermined Knowledge States

The situation of having multiple numbers of classification groups is discussed in Chapter 6. However, the number of groups is usually very small (say, at most, several), and the traditional Bayes' rule has a problem with computing error probabilities or the probabilities of misclassifications for several groups. The problem of how to estimate the error probability in two-group discriminant analysis has been addressed by many researchers, and many reliable estimators have been proposed. One of the most elegant methods was introduced in Section 7.2 and applied to the classification of responses to 40 error types of fraction subtraction problems. However, the multiple group problems have very rarely been addressed, and most of the methods proposed for two groups cannot generally be used with several groups. Most reliable estimators in the two-group situation cannot be generalized to the several-group situation. The traditional, straightforward classification procedures do not work in cognitive diagnosis unless we reduce the number of knowledge states to a manageable number. What would be a manageable number? Can we reduce the number without losing the power of reasonable cognitive diagnosis? The answer is "No." We need new approaches.

Error Probability for Multigroup Classification

Suppose the number of knowledge states is reduced to a manageable size (say, 30 or 40). In the previous example, the error probability is computed using two groups in which we have ignored the remaining 38 groups.

For multigroup classification problems, the posterior probability of group j is given by

$$p(\pi_j|X) = \frac{P_j p(X|\pi_j)}{p(X)} = q_j(X) \qquad \text{where } p(X) = \sum_{j=1}^{L} P_j p(X|\pi_j). \qquad (7.18)$$

The Bayes decision rule based on the posterior probabilities of knowledge states is given by the following:

$$\text{If } q_l(X) = \max (q_1, q_2, \ldots, q_j, \ldots, q_L), \text{ then X is classified to } \pi_l. \qquad (7.19)$$

When X is known to come from L knowledge states, we choose the one having the largest posterior probability, $q_l(X) = p_j (\pi_l|X)$ among L groups. The conditional probability of error for a given X is given by $r(X) = 1 - q_l(X)$, and the Bayes error is defined as the expected value of $r(X)$ over X.

$$r(X) = 1 - q_l(X),$$
$$\varepsilon = \text{Expectation of } r(X) \text{ over } X \qquad (7.20)$$

Selection of Prior Probabilities for Knowledge States

In reality, one knowledge state may have a greater chance of happening than another because the sizes of two populations are different. For example, a man walking on a street in a small town in the United States is more likely a White man than an Asian because the White population is larger than the Asian population in the Unites States. The knowledge states that lie in the area closer to the horizontal axis in the rule space are observed more frequently than those located in the upper part of the space. The index ζ measures atypicality of happenings for the knowledge states mapped in the rule space. However, the optimal classification rule should have the minimum chance of misclassifications, and probabilities of misclassification should be small. The optimum classification rule should take these prior probabilities of happenings into account.

After the likelihood function and the prior distribution have been determined, the posterior distribution can easily be determined conceptually. If the prior distribution is a poor reflection of the prior information available for our classification, the results may not be very meaningful. The prior distribution is supposed to represent the information before the new information (or new sample) is observed. If the past information consists exclusively of past data obtained from the previous sample, then the combination of the prior and sample information is analogous to the pooling of information from different samples. Often, however, much of the prior information will be of a more subjective nature, and assessment of the prior information will involve the elicitation of subjective probabilities.

Various methods have been proposed for the assessment of subjective probability distributions. The more convenient methods include assigning possible values to prior probabilities, and assessing cumulative probabilities to the prior distributions. This assessment can be graphed and used as the basis for cumulative distribution functions. Then, a parametric model to represent a cumulative distribution can be sought. If the prior information is viewed as equivalent to the information that would be provided by a sample with certain sample statistics, then those sample statistics can be taken as the prior parameters. The other way to do this is numerically because the posterior distribution can be determined numerically. If no member of the conjugate family of distributions fits the assessed prior probabilities, then the best option is to proceed numerically. Ultimately, inferences about a parameter are based on its posterior distribution. Therefore, questions concerning the goodness of certain approximations in terms of the prior distribution should be evaluated in terms of the impact of the approximation on the posterior distribution.

When sample information overwhelms the prior information, the posterior distribution is relatively insensitive to changes in the prior distribution. This situation occurs when a large sample is taken and the prior information is quite limited. The prior distribution then has very limited impact on the posterior distribution.

The uniform prior distribution is recommended when we do not have prior information about which of the particular knowledge states would be most commonly observed. However, the number of students previously classified into each knowledge state can be used as the empirical prior probability for the subsequent classification procedure. We know the distribution of the squared Mahalanobis distance, and this information can be used as the prior probability as will be shown in Chapter 8.

Determination of Cost

Cost is another aspect of considerations for the optimum classification. For example, an advanced calculus course requires students to get a minimum score of 75 out of a 100-item placement test. The test contains 40 algebra, 40 geometry, and 20 trigonometry items. The students who get scores of 30, 30, and 15 for the three respective content areas can be placed in this course, but those who get 40 from algebra, 35 from geometry, and 0 from trigonometry should not be placed in this course despite getting the minimum requirement score of 75. Such students are more likely to drop out of the advanced calculus course because they have never studied trigonometry or do not have enough knowledge to understand instructions. Failing

TABLE 7.2

Cost Matrix

		π_1	π_2
True State	π_1	0	$c(2|1)$
	π_2	$c(1|2)$	0

to diagnose a fatal case of cancer is more costly than misplacing students in a class mismatched to their backgrounds. The optimum classification procedure should consider the costs associated with misclassification. Suppose p $(1|2)$ is the probability of observed student X coming from π_2 but being misclassified into π_1, and p $(2|1)$ is the probability of observation X coming from π_1 but being misclassified into π_2. $c(1|2)$ is the cost of misclassification that X is coming from π_2 but is misclassified into π_1, $c(2|1)$ is the cost of misclassification that X comes from π_1 but is misclassified into π_2. Summarizing the information into a table, we get a cost matrix and a probability matrix (the cost matrix and the probability matrix are given in Tables 7.2 and 7.3).

The expected cost of misclassification (ECM) is given by multiplying the off-diagonal entries by their probabilities of occurrence,

$$ECM = c(2|1)p(2|1)p_1 + c(1|2)p(1|2)p_2 \tag{7.21}$$

The optimum classification rule should have the smallest possible ECM. This rule leads to the relationship shown in Equation (7.22):

If $p_1 = p_2$ (equal prior probabilities), then

$$\text{for } X \in \pi_1, \quad \frac{p(X|\pi_1)}{p(X|\pi_2)} \geq \frac{c(1|2)}{c(2|1)}, \text{ and for } X \in \pi_2, \quad \frac{p(X|\pi_1)}{p(X|\pi_2)} < \frac{c(1|2)}{c(2|1)}. \tag{7.22}$$

For example, if $p(X|\pi_1) = .8$ and $p(X|\pi_2) = .2$, then $c(1|2) = 4 * c(2|1)$. That is, the cost of misclassification that X is coming from π_2 but is misclassified into π_1 is four times as much as the cost of misclassification that X is coming from π_1 but is misclassified into π_2.

TABLE 7.3

Probability Matrix

		π_1	π_2
True State	π_1	0	$p(2|1)p_1$
	π_2	$p(1|2)p_2$	0

7.4 Attribute Mastery Probabilities

In a short description, the cognitive diagnosis by the rule space methodology matches test takers' item response patterns with the predetermined ideal response patterns. Knowledge states are determined by a systematic analysis of examinees' performances on a test, as well as by domain experts' cognitive hypotheses. Most aberrant patterns generated by cheating or memorizing some items from an item pool are unlikely to match these ideal response patterns. Harnisch (1996) interviewed the examinees whose response patterns were different from those in the predetermined knowledge states, and found that most of them confessed to the interviewers that they cheated on some test items. This study warns that an observed response differing from any predetermined knowledge states should not be forced into a classification. Rather, it should be carefully investigated by teachers and parents. Unclassified patterns may result from cheating or come from very unique knowledge states not included in the experts' cognitive models.

Traditional classification procedures assume that the classification groups are mutually exclusive and totally together. Therefore, every observed vector is forced to be classified into one of these mutually exclusive groups. Moreover, in traditional classification settings, the means and covariance matrices of population groups are often unknown. Thus, the estimation of unknown parameters is considered an important task.

In our setting, however, parameters of the density functions corresponding to the knowledge states, population means, and covariance matrices are known. The population means (called *centroids*) are the images of ideal item score patterns, and the covariance matrices are obtained from the information functions of the item response theory given by Equation (7.7).

As long as the item parameters of an item response model are estimated, then the centroids and the covariance matrices of predetermined knowledge states can be computed by using estimated IRT item parameters and the information functions. In latent class modeling, the centroids and covariances of the state density functions are assumed to be true and must be estimated. There are obviously some advantages and disadvantages in developing a sound classification procedure as long as IRT is used to compute the coordinates of a classification space. In other words, we have inherited some technical problems from IRT.

Unique Conditions in Rule Space Classification

This section summarizes problems, advantages, assumptions, and conditions required in the rule space classification procedures.

1. Traditionally, the number of groups handled in the Bayes decision rules for classification has been very few, mostly from two to several groups. However, the number of predetermined knowledge states derived from a given Q matrix is usually a large number. This means that the number of classification groups becomes a large number, not just several groups. For example, a Q matrix of a 60-item SAT Mathematics test with 17 attributes generated around 7,000 knowledge states.

2. It is not desirable to force all of the observed response patterns X to be classified into one of the predetermined knowledge states. We do not assume classification groups to be mutually exclusive and totally together. *Totally together* means the union set of all classification groups covers the data. Therefore, those who are not classified will be left for further study for investigating the possibility of adding more attributes to the current list of attributes.

3. Density functions of knowledge states are assumed to be multivariate normal.

4. The means and covariance matrices of knowledge state populations are known.

5. Similar item score patterns are usually mapped into points neighboring from one another in the rule space, and their covariance matrices of similar (close in terms of cognitive distance) knowledge states are very alike in terms of the corresponding values in the entries.

6. Several knowledge states are found within a region of $D^2 < 1.0$ from **X**, as shown in Figure 7.4.

The characteristics listed above guide us to develop a new classification procedure that is the best for achieving our goal, cognitive diagnosis. First, it is possible to find a cluster of several ideal item score patterns

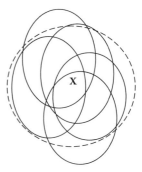

FIGURE 7.4
Several ellipses corresponding to the distribution of knowledge states cover X within the circle of $D^2 < 1.0$.

{**R1**, **R2**, …, **Rk**} around the observed response pattern **X** by computing their Mahalanobis distances to the rule space coordinate (θ_X, ζ, …, ζ_m) of **X**. Then, we choose this cluster of ideal item score patterns as a group from which the observed response would be drawn. This means that a cluster of knowledge states is considered a classification category for a given observed response pattern **X**.

Some pattern classification problems have cases in which each group consists of several clusters (Fukunaga, 1990). Therefore, our decision is based on a set of several knowledge states located in the neighborhood of **X**. The Bayes decision rule for multigroup cases in the rule space context is that **X** belongs to one of the knowledge states having the minimum distance from **X**. Because we have large numbers of classification groups, we must now modify the original Bayes' decision rule to select the knowledge states whose distances between **X** and their centroid are less than a given criterion α (say, $D^2 < \alpha$). With this condition, some observed responses may not find any knowledge state located in their vicinity points. Some observed responses can be isolated and cannot be classified into any of the predetermined knowledge states. Consequently, this classification rule enables us to spot a cheater of a test because aberrant response patterns are unlikely forced to be cassified into one of the predetermined knowledge states. Moreover, this property can be used for searching a new attribute not included in the original Q matrix. Buck and Tatsuoka (1998) in their analysis of an English Listening Test have identified quite a few valuable attributes by investigating response patterns not classified into any of the existing knowledge states.

Definition of Attribute Mastery Probabilities

Suppose X is an observed response, and we would like to find its corresponding vector of attribute mastery probabilities—the probability of applying each attribute correctly to answer the items in a test. The procedure for determining the attribute mastery probabilities is summarized in five steps:

> *Step 1.* For an observed vector (a student item response vector), we rank the knowledge states by the generalized distances between their centroids and **X**, and select the L closest groups whose distances are smaller than a given criterion α. Let us denote the generalized distances between **X** and group π_i by $D(\pi_i)$, then

$$\alpha > D(\pi_L) \geq D(\pi_{L-1}) \geq \cdots D(\pi_2) \geq D(\pi_1) \qquad (7.23)$$

> From now on, we will focus on the L groups in this circle of $D^2 < \alpha$.

> *Step 2.* Compute the posterior probability for the L groups. Let us denote them by $q_l = p(\pi_l | X)$, for $l = 1, …, L$. The posterior

probability of π_L, $p(\pi_L|X)$ is given by

$$q_1 = p(\pi_1|x) = \frac{P_1 p(x|\pi_1)}{\Sigma_{k=1,L} \, P_k P(x|\pi_k)} = \frac{P_1 \exp(-.5D_1^2)}{\Sigma_{k=1,L} \, P_k \exp(-.5D_K^2)} \qquad (7.24)$$

where

$$D_I^2 = (X - R_1) \sum_1^{-1} (X - R_1), \qquad \sum_1 = \begin{vmatrix} \sigma_{11} & \sigma_{12} & \cdots & \sigma_{1L} \\ \cdot & & & \cdot \\ \cdot & & & \cdot \\ \sigma_{L1} & \sigma_{L2} & \cdots & \sigma_{LL} \end{vmatrix}$$

If student response is classified into π_1, then the expected loss is

$$r(1) = \sum_{\substack{l=1 \\ l \neq k}}^{L} \frac{P_1 \exp(-.5D_1^2)}{\Sigma_{k=1,L} P_k P(x|\pi_k)} C(j|l) \qquad (7.25)$$

where $C(j|l)$ is the cost of misclassification. From Equation (7.23), we have that the closer the knowledge states, the larger their posterior probabilities:

$$q1 \geq q2 \geq \cdots \geq qL \qquad (7.26)$$

Step 3. Let $X_1, X_2, \ldots, X_L$ be L ideal item score patterns and $A_1, A_2, \ldots, A_l$, be L attribute mastery patterns associated with the knowledge states $\pi_1, \ldots, \pi_L$.

Step 4. If we use the Bayes decision rule described above, X belongs to π_1 to get the posterior probability q_1. However, our purpose is not to select the one group from which X most likely comes. Rather, we would like to have the probability of mastering each attribute. Because these groups in our final list are cognitively close and not separated well, we take L knowledge states into account for computing attribute mastery probability. Their posterior probabilities are used as their weights.

Step 5. Minor considerations on improvement of the classification procedure:

1. If the Hamming distance of X to the ideal item score patterns is large (say, 25% of items), then we do not consider this ideal item score pattern for L knowledge states. It happens when the dimension of the classification space is not large enough.

2. If an ideal item score pattern deviates from an observed response X by, say, 25% of the number of items, then we do not include this ideal item score pattern.

3. When we make higher dimensions of the rule space classification (say, 6 dimensions), the knowledge state R with a substantially large value of $\theta_X - \theta_R$ may be selected in one of the L closest groups. Because additional dimensions are made by adding generalized ζs, the influence of ζs on the Mahalanobis distance (or generalized distance) gets relatively larger as compared with the influence of θ. So set a bound for θ_R values—say, $|\theta_R - \theta_X| < 1.0$. By setting the condition of $|\theta_R - \theta_X| < 1.0$, the knowledge states whose θ_R is closer to θ_X will be selected.

4. Delete the knowledge states whose corresponding attribute mastery patterns are very different from the knowledge states within the criterion α. This goal will be accomplished by computing NCI values for attribute mastery patterns and deleting aberrant ones.

Let us define an attribute mastery probability for an attribute and for an individual. At this point, we have L attribute patterns associated with L closest knowledge states $\pi_1, \ldots, \pi_L$ and their posterior probabilities q_1, $q_2, \ldots, q_L$. L attribute patterns are written by a matrix (a_{lk}) of L times K in a Q matrix, where K is the number of attributes.

Definition of the attribute mastery probability: Let us denote the attribute mastery probability of attribute A_k for a given response pattern X by $p(A_k = 1|X)$. Then, $p(A_k = 1|X)$ is given by the weighted average of the kth component of L attribute mastery patterns.

In other words, the probability of attribute A_k is applied correctly to the items in a test for a given X is given by Equation (7.27):

$p(\text{Attribute } A_k \text{ is correctly applied to the items involving } A_k | X)$

$$= p(A_k = 1|X) = \sum_{l=1}^{L} q_l a_{lk}. \tag{7.27}$$

Attribute Space, Space of Ideal Item Scores, and Space of Knowledge States

In Chapter 4, we have discussed that the Boolean descriptive function (BDF) is a link between the item space and attribute space. With this BDF, an attribute mastery pattern corresponds to each ideal item score pattern. Each attribute mastery pattern is called a *knowledge state*, as discussed in

Chapters 3 and 4. Therefore, a set of ideal item score patterns forms an item space, and a set of corresponding attribute mastery patterns forms an attribute space. In other words, each ideal item score pattern has interpretable psychological meaning such as which knowledge and cognitive skills a student lacks. Let us denote $R_l = (R_{l1}, ..., R_{lP})$ by ideal item score pattern l, and let $\Lambda_l = (A_{l1}, ..., A_{lK})$ be its corresponding attribute mastery pattern.

We now have the posterior probabilities $p(\pi_l|x)$, $l = 1, ..., L$, and the expected losses $r(l)$, $l = 1, ..., L$. The ideal item score patterns are used to determine the L closest knowledge states $\pi_1, ... , \pi_L$; their ideal item score patterns $R_1, R_2, ..., R_L$ and corresponding attribute mastery patterns $A_1, A_2, ..., A_L$; and the Mahalanobis distances between a student's response pattern X and the L ideal item score patterns $D_1, D_2, ..., D_L$. Let us denote K attribute mastery patterns by a matrix, A:

$$A = \begin{vmatrix} A_1 \\ A_2 \\ \cdot \\ \cdot \\ A_L \end{vmatrix} = (A \text{ binary matrix, the order of } L \times K) = (a_{lk}) \qquad (7.28)$$

where K is the number of attributes and L is the number of closest knowledge states. Then the weighted column sum of the product of q_l and A is the attribute mastery probability for attribute A_k,

$$p(A_k = 1|X) \equiv \sum_{l=1}^{L} q_l a_{lk}. \qquad (7.29)$$

Example 7.1

Figure 7.5 lists the summary of rule space analyses for the two parallel forms of SAT Reading comprehension tests. The attribute mastery probabilities for 16 attributes are listed at the end of the listing of knowledge states with boldface. For the posttest, the mastery probability of attribute 1 was obtained by making a weighted sum of the first column and the posterior probabilities of 10 knowledge states, $1x \cdots 0495 + 1x \cdots 6681 + \cdots 1x \cdots 0065 = 1.0000$. Similarly, the mastery probabilities of the rest of the attributes were computed. The boxes represent knowledge states characterized by the most right column of *cannot do attributes*. The shaded boxes are the knowledge states closer to the attribute mastery vectors. Note that the values of the posterior probabilities decrease as the Mahalanobis distances increase.

SAT Reading Comprehension Pretest Results

KS	Mahalanobis Distance	Posterior Probability	NCI Value on Atts.	1234567890123456	Cannot Do Attributes
1	0.836	0.0245	0.60	1*11010111001110	5 7 11 12 16
2	1.106	0.0434	0.58	1*10110111001110	4 7 11 12 16
3	1.229	0.0128	0.62	1*11110111001010	7 11 12 14 16
4	1.439	0.0115	0.45	1*01111110000111	3 10 11 12 13
5	1.439	0.0092	0.51	1*01110111000110	3 7 11 12 13 16
6	1.439	0.0069	0.46	1*01110101001110	3 7 9 11 12 16
7	1.490	0.0090	0.55	1*11110111001110	7 11 12 16
8	1.490	0.0090	0.56	1*11110110001110	7 10 11 12 16
9	1.670	0.0246	0.58	1*11111101001110	9 11 12 16
10	1.787	0.2760	0.62	1*10111101001110	4 9 11 12 16

Atts. Mast. prob.=[1.0 * .94 .58 .81 1.0 .43 .93 .28 .91 .02 .04 .95 .92 1.0 .21]

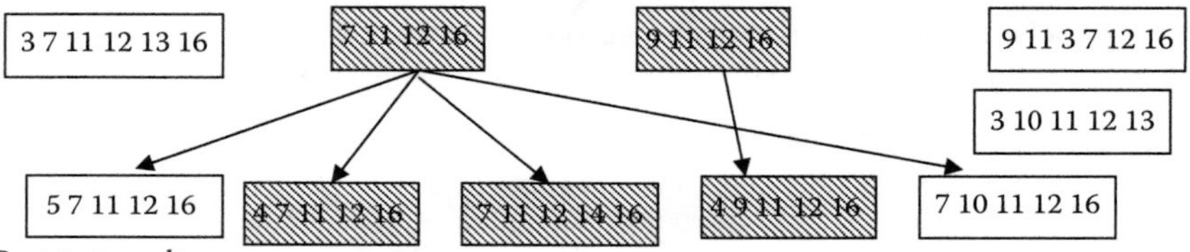

3 7 11 12 13 16   7 11 12 16   9 11 12 16   9 11 3 7 12 16

3 10 11 12 13

5 7 11 12 16   4 7 11 12 16   7 11 12 14 16   4 9 11 12 16   7 10 11 12 16

Post-test results

KS	Mahalanobis Distance	Posterior Probability	NCI Value on Atts.	Atts Mastery Patts	Cannot do Atts.
436	1.114	0.0495	0.70	1*10111111001010	4 11 12 14 16
680	1.456	0.6681	0.70	1*10111110001010	4 10 11 12 14 16
417	2.398	0.0087	0.55	1*10110111001011	4 7 11 12 14
319	2.777	0.0072	0.45	1*11110011001111	7 8 12 13
356	2.778	0.0216	0.42	1*11110011001111	7 8 11 12
667	2.779	0.0096	0.48	1*11110011000111	7 8 11 12 13
724	2.838	0.1093	0.59	1*10111110001010	4 11 12 13 14 16
231	2.866	0.0115	0.60	1*10111111001011	4 11 12 14
885	2.967	0.0065	0.67	1*10111010001010	4 8 10 11 12 14 16
878	2.967	0.0065	0.63	1*10111010000011	4 8 10 11 12 13 14

Att. mast prob.=[1.0 * 1.0 .03 1.0 1.0 .96 .82 .81 .23 .12 .02 .91 .19 1.0 .21]

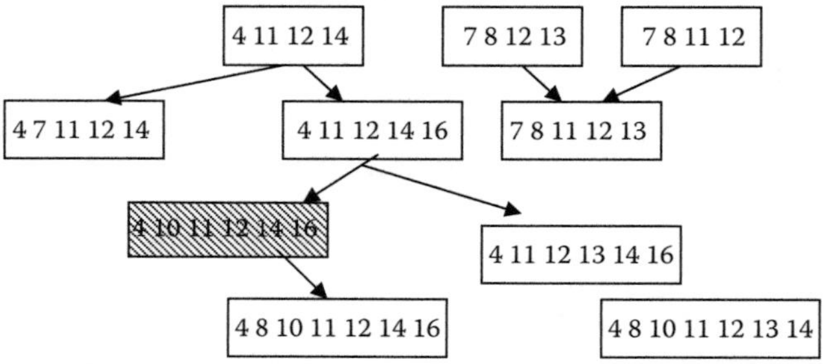

4 11 12 14   7 8 12 13   7 8 11 12

4 7 11 12 14   4 11 12 14 16   7 8 11 12 13

4 10 11 12 14 16   4 11 12 13 14 16

4 8 10 11 12 14 16   4 8 10 11 12 13 14

FIGURE 7.5
Results of analysis for repeated measures of a subject.

7.5   Reduction of Irrelevant Knowledge States

Application of BDF to a Q Matrix

When test items involve K attributes, the possible knowledge states are computed by taking 1 or 0 combinations of K attributes. Therefore, we get the number of possible patterns, 2^K. This means that for K = 10, there are $2^{10} = 1,024$ patterns, and for K = 15, $2^{15} = 32,768$ patterns, which are huge numbers. The rate of increase in the number of knowledge states becomes exponentially larger as the number of attributes increases. If we can eliminate one attribute from a list of attributes, then the number of possible knowledge states decreases dramatically. For example, if we reduced one attribute so that K = 14, then $2^{14} = 16,384$, which is one half of 32,768. Because the issue of deleting attributes is discussed in the task analysis section in Chapter 3, our discussion here will focus on the reduction of the number of knowledge states.

When the domain of a test is complex, the number of attributes increases to a larger number. A large-scale assessment usually requires a larger number of attributes to explain the variance accounted for in total scores or item difficulties. Tatsuoka and Boodoo (2000) showed that the 60-item GRE Mathematics test involved 18 attributes, and a BDF generated 6,000 to 7,000 possible knowledge states. Because 2^{18} yields 262,144 different patterns, roughly 98% of patterns were eliminated by the BDF to get 6,000 patterns. However, 6,000 is still a very large number for a classification problem.

How to Reduce the Number of Knowledge States

We can reduce the number of predetermined knowledge states generated from a Q matrix in two stages: (a) Stage 1 is before rule space classification is applied, and (b) Stage 2 is after the rule space classification is applied.

Stage 2 is always necessary and effective, but Stage 1 makes the computational burden much more manageable. When the number of knowledge states does not cause too much of a computational burden, Stage 1 can be omitted.

Before Rule Space Classification Is Applied

Step 1

There are three steps at this stage. First, the ζ and generalized ζs are computed for all possible knowledge states. ζ and generalized ζs are indices to measure the unusualness of patterns. When these values are not close to zero, they are considered atypical. In real data, these indices are

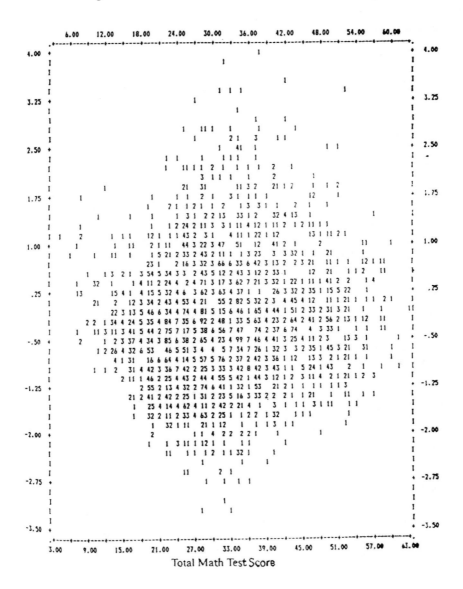

FIGURE 7.6
The scatterplot of students' points in the rule space, total score against ζ values.

usually close to zero (say, ζ < 4.0), as can be seen in Figure 7.6, which shows the plotting of ζ values over the total scores of an SAT Mathematics test. By looking into the shape of the plot and frequencies of the points, one can conclude the most observed response falls in the region close to the expectation of ζ values at each score point, $E(\zeta|\text{score of s}) = 0$. Using this property, when ideal item response patterns have, for example, $\zeta > 5.0$, they are very unusual and can be safely deleted. Thus, the final step at this stage is to delete knowledge states with at least one generalized ζ value and/or ζ values larger than 5.0.

After Rule Space Classification Is Applied

Step II

Perform the two-dimensional rule space classification on a sample, and determine the stronger attributes. Then compute generalized ς values for these strong attributes, and then apply Step I and delete knowledge states with high values.

Step III

Use of prior information, frequencies of classified subjects in knowledge states will give us more accurate information when our sample size is samll. Because a majority of predetermined knowledge states will not get any subject classified, and only several hundred are populated by at least one subject, it is desirable to delete such empty knowledge states from the beginning. However, we do not know any effective simple method for selecting populated knowledge states without performing a rule space analysis.

Step IV

Delete the knowledge states with empty or low frequencies.

After applying these steps, approximately 300 to 500 knowledge states will remain in a large-scale assessment such as the SAT, TOEFL, TOEIC, ACT, or GRE, or a state assessment.

8

Posterior Probabilities With Different Prior Probabilities and Their Effect on the Attribute Mastery Probabilities

---

One of the features of cognitive diagnosis is that we have to deal with a large number of knowledge states. The number of knowledge states goes up often from a few hundreds to several thousands for a large-scale assessment. This phenomenon is quite natural because when we think about individual differences, our common sense tells us everybody is different. We often come from different cultures, different school systems with a wide variety of curricula, and different families with several levels of educational and socioeconomic backgrounds. Most of all, each student has his or her unique experience and learning style. It is natural to assume that a larger number of knowledge state exists when thousands of students take a test, especially a large-scale assessment.

For a given person **X,** the weighted average of the several closer knowledge states are used for computing posterior probabilities of attributes. The weights are determined by their posterior probabilities. This turns out to be a plausible solution to solve the problem of having more than several hundred classification groups. Because the coordinates of the rule space, θ and ζ, $\zeta_{k,}$ $k = 1, \ldots K$, have the property that similar item patterns are located in the vicinity of each other (as can be seen in Figures 5.9 and 10.4.1), the weighted sum may provide a robust property to the estimated attribute mastery probabilities for **X**. Im (2007) studied the robustness of estimated attribute mastery probabilities by simulating Q matrices by adding errors to the true Q matrix, and found the weighted sum method could give robust estimates.

In Chapter 7, we have discussed a five-step procedure for determining attribute mastery probabilities for individuals. In this chapter, we discuss the computation of posterior probabilities by using different prior probabilities and their effects on attribute mastery probabilities in two- and three-dimensional rule space.

8.1 Two or More Higher Dimensional Rule Space and Density Functions of Knowledge States

Weights Derived From the Posterior Probability of L Closest Knowledge States

The distance (referred to as *distance* instead of *Mahalanobis distance* or the *generalized distance* hereafter) between two knowledge states increases when the dimensionality of the space becomes higher and the distances from X to the L closest groups in the two-dimensional space are generally smaller than those in the three-dimensional space, as is shown in Table 8.1. The table shows the squared distance D^2 of 14 knowledge states deviating from R_{45} (knowledge state 45, or KS 45) in the fraction test. The third coordinate ζ_1 is selected so that it is uncorrelated with the second coordinate ζ (see Chapters 3 and 4; and see K. K. Tatsuoka, 1996). Hence, the three coordinates in this example are orthogonal. Various values of $f(D^2)$, the exponential function of $-D^2/2$ given in Equation (8.1), are computed and listed in the fifth column for the two dimensional rule space coordinates, and in the eleventh column for the three dimensional coordinates. The multivariate normal

TABLE 8.1

Squared Mahalanobis Distances and $f(D^2)$ From KS 45 to 14 Other Knowledge States in Two- and Three-Dimensional Rule Space

Two-Dimensional Space				Three-Dimensional Space			
KS	D^2	$(\theta\ \zeta_0)$	$f(D^2)$	KS	D^2	$(\theta\ \zeta_0\ \zeta_1)$	$f(D^2)$
45	.00	(−.96 −1.33)	1.0	45	.00	(−.96 −1.33 .33)	1.0
47	.37	(−.87 −.85)	.9338	47	.37	(−.87 −.85 .29)	.8095
48	.65	(−1.12 −.88)	.8095	48	.65	(−1.12 −.88 .40)	.7989
46	.67	(−1.13 −.92)	.7989	46	.67	(−1.13 −.92 .92)	.4926
28	.77	(−.77 −1.23)	.7434	49	1.19	(−1.03 −.28 .36)	.0241
49	1.19	(−1.03 −.28)	.4926	17	2.73	(−.61 −1.20 .47)	.0232
18	1.64	(−.74 −.55)	.2606	20	2.74	(−.73 −.55 1.34)	.0216
20	1.72	(−.73 −.55)	.2278	18	2.77	(−.74 −.55 1.40)	.0179
22	2.12	(−.87 .07)	.1057	50	2.98	(−1.31 −.36 .47)	.0092
27	2.48	(−.64 −1.79)	.0461	21	3.06	(−.67 −.40 .90)	.0014
17	2.71	(−.61 −1.20)	.0254	28	3.62	(−.77 −1.23 −1.35)	.0002
21	2.74	(−.67 −.40)	.0234	19	4.15	(−.55 −1.16 −.09)	.0000
50	2.96	(−1.31 −.36)	.0125	22	5.15	(−.87 .07 2.07)	.0000
19	3.97	(−.55 −1.16)	.0004	27	5.47	(−.64 −1.79 −1.40)	.0000
12	8.12	(−.40 −1.94)	.0000	12	9.16	(−.40 −1.94 −.25)	.0000

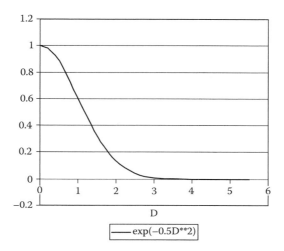

FIGURE 8.1
Plot of $\varphi(D^2) = \exp(-D^2)$ on D.

distribution $\varphi(D^2)$ is give below, where exp $(-D^2/2)$ is expressed by $f(D^2)$ in Table 8.1.

$$\varphi(D^2) = \frac{1}{\sqrt{(2\pi)^{m/2} |\Sigma|^{1/2}}} e^{\frac{-1}{2}(X-M)'\Sigma^{-1}(X-M)} = \frac{1}{\sqrt{(2\pi)^{m/2} |\Sigma|^{1/2}}} e^{-D^2/2} \tag{8.1}$$

Then the graph of $\varphi(D^2)$ is given in Figure 8.1. When D^2 gets larger—say, 5—the value of the function becomes very small. Because the curve is an exponential function, $\varphi(D^2) = \exp(-D^2/2)$ over D^2, its value decreases sharply as D^2 increases. For $D^2 = 0, 0.5, 1, 1.5, 2, 2.5, 3, 4$, and 5, the values of $\varphi(D^2) =$ 1.00, 0.882, 0.606, 0.325, 0.135, 0.044, 0.011, 0.002, and 0.000, respectively.

Posterior Probability $p(\pi_1|X)$

Let us compute the posterior probability for the L knowledge states, and denote them by $q_l = p(\pi_l|X)$, for $l = 1, ..., L$. The posterior probability of $\pi_{l,}$ $p(\pi_l|X)$ is given by

$$q_1 = p(\pi_1|X) = \frac{p_1 p(X|\pi_1)}{\sum_{k=1,L} p_k p(X|\pi_k)} = \frac{p_1 \exp(-.5D_1^2)}{\sum_{k=1,L} p_k \exp(-.5D_k^2)}$$

where

$$D_l^2 = (X - R_1)\sum_1^{-1}(X - R_1), \qquad \sum_1 = \begin{vmatrix} \sigma_{11} & \sigma_{12} & \cdots & \sigma_{1L} \\ \cdot & \cdot & \cdots & \cdot \\ \sigma_{L1} & \sigma_{L2} & \cdots & \sigma_{LL} \end{vmatrix} \tag{8.2}$$

and pl is the prior probability of membership in π_1 (Tatsuoka, 1988).

The assumption used in Equation (8.2) is that L knowledge states are mutually exclusive and totally together. In the rule space context (M–L, or M minus L), KSs are judged as having a squared Mahalanobis distance larger than a given criterion value α. The posterior probability q_l must be computed by considering all the knowledge states M that are initially generated by BDF from the Q matrix. Equation (8.3) is the posterior probability when we consider all M knowledge states generated from a given Q matrix.

$$q'_1 = p(\pi_1|X) = \frac{p_1 \exp(-.5D_1^2)}{\sum_{k=1,M} p_k \exp(-.5D_k^2)} \quad \text{for } p_k = 1 \qquad (8.3)$$

However, $\varphi(D^2)$ will be very small for the KS far from π_1 so that we can ignore them in the practice.

8.2 Classification Criterion: Cutoff and Errors

The denominator of q_1' in Equation (8.1.3) is divided into two components: $k = 1, L$ when $D_k^2 < \alpha$, and $K = L + 1, M$ when $D_k^2 > \alpha$. If the prior probability is uniform, then the denominator of q_l' becomes

$$\sum_{k=1,L} \exp(-.5D_k^2) + \sum_{k=L+1,M} \exp(-.5D_k^2) < \sum_{k=1,L} \exp(-.5D_k^2) + (M-L)*\exp(-.5\alpha^2)$$

$$(8.4)$$

From Table 8.1, $\exp(-.5D_1^2)$ decreases sharply as D_1^2 increases. So the second term of the above inequality will be smaller if we select the cutoff criterion α large enough. Let us denote the second term of the left of Equation (8.4) by $\varepsilon(x)$; then we have Equation (8.5):

$$\varepsilon(\alpha) = \sum_{k=L+1,M} \exp(-.5D_k^2) < \int_\alpha^\infty \exp(-D^2/2) \qquad (8.5)$$

Since the most right term equals $2 \exp(-\alpha/2)$,

$$\varepsilon(\alpha) = 2 \exp(-\alpha/2) \qquad (8.6)$$

Suppose we take α to be 5.0; then the value of integration of $f(5.0)$ is 0.0820, so we get $\varepsilon(\alpha) < 0.164$.

We have the relation of q_1' and q_1 below and by elimination, $\varepsilon(\alpha) > 0$ in the denominator of the second term,

$$q'_1 = p(\pi|X) = \frac{p_1 \exp(-.5D_1^2)}{\sum_{k=1}^L p_k \exp(-.5D_1^2) + \varepsilon(\alpha)} < \frac{p_1 \exp(-.5D_1^2)}{\sum_{k=1}^L p_k \exp(-.5D_k^2)} = q_1 \qquad (8.7)$$

By dividing both sides by q_1', we get equation (8.8),

$$q_1/q_1 = 1 + \varepsilon(\alpha)/\left(\sum_{k=1}^L p_k \exp(-.5_k^2)\right) \qquad (8.8)$$

If we denote the universe of knowledge states, U; those D^2 smaller than α, U_1; and those D^2 larger than or equal to α, U_2; then $U = U_1 + U_2$. Our classification task will be reduced to the two-group case. The error probability can be computed by applying the two-group classification case.

When the number of knowledge states generated from a given Q matrix becomes an extremely large number, then we have to reduce the number of attributes to a manageable size or divide the domain of concern to small subsets of the domain, in addition to performing some reduction procedures of the number of generated knowledge states described in Chapters 3 and 4. When either method discussed above does not work well, then dimensions of a classification space can be increased.

Suppose, for a given X, the L(2) closest knowledge states whose distances are less than α are identified in a two-dimensional classification space. Next, we create a three-dimensional classification space by adding the third coordinate to the first two coordinates, and find L(2) closest knowledge states for X. Then L(3) is, most likely, smaller than L(3). Because there are many different ways to choose the third coordinate to add to the original two-dimensional coordinates, the optimum selection of a new coordinate will give us the best classification results. However, this optimization algorithm has not been developed at this point, and is left for future research.

Meanwhile, we ignore the second term of Equation (8.5), and think as if we have only M knowledge states in the universe. If we choose α to be sufficiently large enough, then the second term will be a very small number, as discussed earlier.

8.3 Prior Probabilities: Gamma Function, Uniform Function, and Observed Frequencies

Prior Information From Uniform, Gamma Distributions

Let us examine the relationship between D^2 and the exponential function, $\exp(-.5D_1^2)$, with an example. The first, second, and third columns in Table 8.2 are the knowledge states used in Table 8.1, their frequencies classified (N = 595), and the ratio of frequencies, respectively. The fourth column shows the squared Mahalanobis distance D^2 for 14 knowledge states from KS 45 (π_{45}), and the fifth comprises corresponding $f(D^2)$ values. The relation between D^2 and $f(D^2)$ is plotted in Figure 8.2. The bars indicate the squared Mahalanobis distances, and the connected line shows the scaled probabilities of 14 knowledge states. The bar graph is monotonically

TABLE 8.2

Posterior Probabilities With Gamma and Uniform Priors for the 15 Closest Knowledge States From an Individual X on R_{45} for a 38-Item Fraction Addition Test in the Three-Dimensional Rule Space

Knowledge States	Frequency N = 595	Ratio of Frequencies p Value	D²	q1 When Gamma	q1 When Uniform	q1 When Frequency
45	3	.005	.000	—	.183	.144
47	3	.005	.370	.193	.152	.120
48	3	.005	.651	.193	.132	.104
46	1	.002	.673	.192	.130	.041
49	7	.012	1.19	.152	.101	.190
17	4	.007	2.73	.049	.048	.052
20	5	.008	2.74	.049	.046	.058
18	1	.002	2.77	.048	.046	.014
50	13	.022	2.98	.041	.041	.143
21	2	.003	3.06	.038	.040	.019
28	5	.008	3.62	.024	.030	.038
19	7	.012	4.15	.015	.023	.043
22	2	.003	5.15	.006	.014	.007
27	4	.007	5.47	.0005	.012	.013
12	31	.052	9.16	.0001	.002	.015

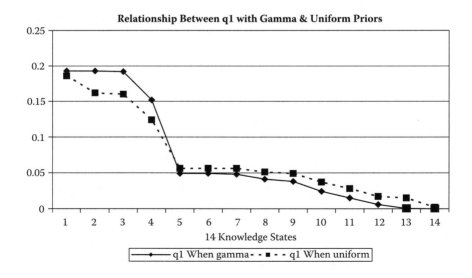

FIGURE 8.2

The relationship between the posterior probabilities of 14 knowledge states using gamma and uniform distributions as a prior.

increasing, while solid line is monotonically decreasing. The smaller D^2 is, the larger the probability becomes. For a gamma prior, column 6 in Table 8.2 gives the values of the gamma distribution for 14 KSs, and the seventh column is the product of gamma and $\exp(-.5D^2)$. The gamma density function is given in Equation (8.9) (Box & Tao, 1975; Fukunaga, 1990). The eighth column is the scaled posterior probabilities using the gamma function as a prior information (or a prior), and the ninth column is the scaled posterior probabilities using the uniform distribution as a prior by setting p_1 to p1.

$$\text{Gamma } (D^2) = \frac{1}{2^{n/2}\Gamma(n/2)}(D^2)^{\frac{n-2}{2}}e^{\frac{-D^2}{2}} = \frac{1}{2^{\frac{3}{2}}\Gamma\left(\frac{3}{2}\right)}(D^2)^{\frac{3-2}{2}}e^{\frac{-D^2}{2}}$$

$$= \frac{1}{2.5066}Df(D^2)$$

$$\tag{8.9}$$

The Relationship Between D^2 and Posterior Probabilities

Figures 8.3 and 8.4 indicate their differences in the changes of probability values. When we use gamma as the prior distribution, the knowledge states closer to R_{45} do not show much difference. When D^2 is around 3,

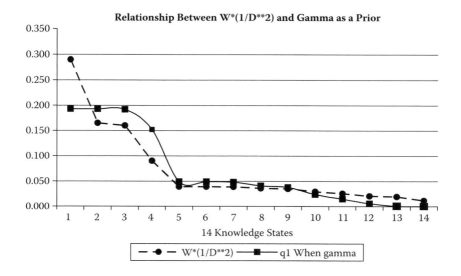

FIGURE 8.3
The relationship between rescaled D^{-2} and posterior probabilities of 14 knowledge states using gamma distribution as a prior.

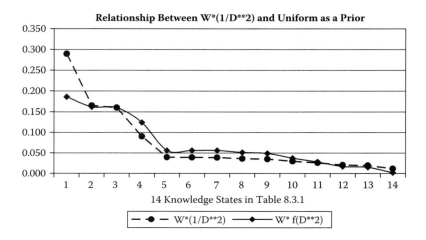

FIGURE 8.4
The relationship between rescaled D^{-2} and posterior probabilities of 14 knowledge states using uniform distribution as a prior.

which is the expected mean value of the gamma distribution for the three-dimensional space, the posterior probability decreases sharply to smaller values. In other words, the posterior probabilities of the knowledge states whose D^2 values are larger than 3 start decreasing sharply to very small values. This relation indicates that the knowledge states that are located in some remote distances from the centroid of R_{45} will not influence the values of attribute mastery probabilities much.

Because the exponential function of squared Mahalanobis distance D^2, $\varphi(D^2)$ in Equation (8.1), decreases sharply as D^2 increases, the posterior probabilities of most knowledge states with larger D^2 values become very small numbers, mostly less than .001. Therefore, one can safely consider only the knowledge states within a small circle of a given D^2 value to estimate attribute mastery probabilities.

A Prior as Classified Frequencies of Observed Responses

When an observed response X is known to come from one of the L knowledge states, the decision rule based on their posterior probabilities is to take the knowledge state that has the maximum posterior probabilities q1. From the previous study, the frequencies of classified subjects based on the maximum q1 rule are listed in the second column in Table 8.2. These p values obtained by dividing the frequency by N = 595 can be used as prior information and are called the *empirical Bayesian priors*. The posterior probability q1 when using the frequency p values will be given in the last column in Table 8.2.

It is interesting to note that the gamma prior gives the most advantage to the KS whose distance D^2 is closer to its expected mean value of 3 for this case, whereas the uniform prior gives the most advantage to the KS with the smallest D^2. The prior from the frequencies gives the most advantage to the KS with the larger frequency value. It is hard to tell which prior is the best choice from the information we currently have. Figure 8.5 shows the graphs of three posterior probabilities with gamma, uniform, and empirical priors. Because the sample size of these data is only 537, relying on the empirical frequencies as the prior information to compute the posterior probabilities is not stable.

We try to compute attribute mastery probabilities and compare the results with true mastery score patterns in Section 8.4.

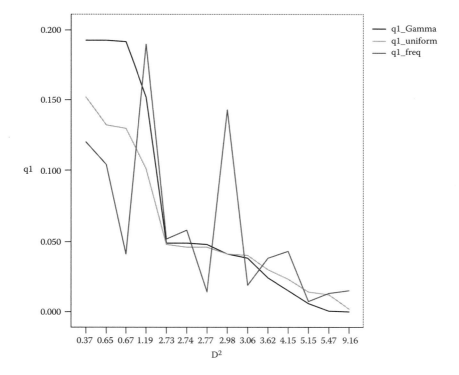

FIGURE 8.5
Comparison of the posterior probabilities using gamma uniform distributions and empirical base priors.

8.4 Attribute Mastery Probabilities and the Effects From Different Priors as the Classification Criterion α Becomes Larger

The rule "If q1(X) = max(q1, q2, ..., q j, ..., q L), then X is classified to π_1" is the traditional Bayesian decision rule for the multigroups case. However, the decision rule in the RSM does not restrict the choice to a single group from L groups. The methodology utilizes the computed posterior probabilities of L groups for X as the weights of computing the attribute mastery probabilities for X.

The probability that attribute A_k is applied correctly for X is denoted by $P(A_k = 1 | X)$ and defined by the weighted average of a_{lK}, 1, ..., L.

$$P(A_k = 1 | X) = \sum_1^L q l a_{lk} \qquad (8.10)$$

where a_{lk} is the kth element of the attribute mastery pattern A_k for knowledge state π_k.

Table 8.3 shows an example from a test of the 38-item fraction addition problems introduced in Table 5.1 in Chapter 5 and the 14 knowledge states

TABLE 8.3

Fourteen Attribute Mastery Patterns and Corresponding 14 Ideal Item Score Patterns for 14 Knowledge States That Are Closely Located to π_{45}, With Gamma, Uniform, and Empirical Priors

	Weights				
π	L = 14 Gamma	14 Uniform	14 Frequency	Attribute	Ideal Item Score Patterns
45				110011100	00000000010101001010000000001010100101
47	.193	.152	.120	110010110	00000000010001011010000000001000101101
48	.193	.132	.104	100010100	00000000010001001010000000001000100101
46	.192	.130	.041	110001100	00000000010100001010000000001010000101
49	.152	.101	.190	010000110	00000000010000110100000000001000001101
17	.049	.048	.052	110111100	00100010010101001010010001001010100101
20	.049	.046	.058	000111100	00100010010001001010010001001000100101
18	.048	.046	.014	110101100	00100010010100001010010001001010000101
50	.041	.041	.143	000000100	00000000010000010100000000001000000101
21	.038	.040	.019	010101100	00100010010000110100100010001000000101
28	.024	.030	.038	110001110	00000100010001101000001000101010001101
19	.015	.023	.043	010111110	00100010010001011010010001001000101101
22	.006	.014	.007	000101100	00100010010000010100100010001000000101
27	.001	.012	.013	110011110	00000100010101011010000010001010101101
12	.000	.002	.015	110101110	00100110110100011010010010110110100110101

TABLE 8.4

Estimated Attribute Mastery Probabilities for π_{45} With $\alpha = 9$, With Three Priors, and Applying the Cutoff Rule, 1 if Probability >.5

Attributes	True	Gamma	Cutoff	Uniform	Cutoff	Empirical	Cutoff
a1	1	.700	1	.736	1	.541	1
a2	1	.711	1	.767	1	.689	1
a3	0	.000	0	.000	0	.000	0
a4	0	.204	0	.218	0	.208	0
a5	1	.501	1	.596	1	.533	1
a6	1	.422	0	.573	1	.443	0
a7	1	1.000	1	1.000	1	1.000	1
a8	0	.421	0	.359	0	.437	0
a9	0	.000	0	.000	0	.000	0

are the same as those listed in Table 8.4. The fifth and sixth columns are the 14 attribute mastery patterns and the 14 ideal item score patterns corresponding to these 14 knowledge states, respectively. By computing the attribute mastery probabilities, we took the two criteria, D^2, to be smaller than 9 and 2, respectively. The attribute mastery probabilities in Table 8.4 are computed from the posterior probabilities of knowledge states satisfying $D^2 < 9$, and those in Table 8.5 are computed from the knowledge states with $D^2 < 2$. The third column in Tables 8.4 and 8.5 is obtained from a gamma prior, the fifth column in both tables is from the uniform prior, and the seventh is from an empirical prior.

For this hypothetical individual who belongs to knowledge state R_{45}, his or her true mastery score is the same as the attribute mastery pattern of R_{45} (110011100) in both tables. Therefore, the estimated attribute mastery probabilities are compared with this pattern as his or her true scores of attributes. In this table, we applied a cutoff score of 1 if the attribute mastery probability is

TABLE 8.5

Estimated Attribute Mastery Probabilities for π_{45} With $\alpha = 2$, With Three Priors, and Applying the Cutoff Rule, 1 if Probability >.5

Attributes	True	Gamma	Cutoff	Uniform	Cutoff	Empirical	Cutoff
a1	1	.792	1	.856	1	.675	1
a2	1	.736	1	.811	1	.818	1
a3	0	.000	0	.000	0	.000	0
a4	0	.000	0	.000	0	.000	0
a5	1	.530	1	.669	1	.607	1
a6	1	.264	0	.448	0	.306	0
a7	1	1.000	1	1.000	1	.989	1
a8	0	.471	0	.362	0	.512	1
a9	0	.000	0	.000	0	.000	0

larger than .5, and 0 otherwise. Columns 4, 6, and 8 are his or her attribute cutoff scores. The uniform prior gives exactly the same attribute cutoff scores as that of the true attribute scores given in the second column.

Concept of the True Attribute Mastery Probability of Attribute A_k

Table 8.5 shows that none of the prior cases gives the exact same attribute cutoff scores. This example shows that the uniform prior is the best with the criterion of $D^2 < 9$. We can assume that when we take larger α values, then the estimation of attribute mastery probabilities improves, and eventually converges to an individual's true attribute scores or true attribute mastery probabilities. However, a further research with Monte Carlo data will be needed.

Definition 8.1: The true attribute mastery probability for an individual is defined as the limit of Equation (8.10):

$$T_k = \text{limit of } L \Rightarrow M; \quad T_k = P(A_k = 1 | X) = \lim_{L \to M} \sum_1^L qla_{lk} \qquad (8.11)$$

8.5   Slippage Probabilities

Slippage Probabilities When True Attribute Mastery Patterns Are Known

Suppose X is a simulated response pattern randomly drawn from the population of knowledge state π_3. This simulated pattern X shares the attribute mastery pattern of (110111110) of knowledge state π_3 and has an item pattern very similar to the ideal item score pattern of π_3. The four closest knowledge states to X are listed in Table 8.6.

TABLE 8.6

Four Closed Knowledge States From π_3 Using Simulated Data X in the Three-Dimensional Rule Space for a 38-Item Fraction Addition Test

Knowledge States	D^2	exp (−.5 * D^2) $p(x \mid \pi_l)$	Gamma $p_1 = \Gamma(D^2)$	Scaled Post $W = p_1 p(x \mid \pi_l)$	Probability Error 1−W	Attribute Pattern A
3	1.05	.595	3.056	.506	.494	110111110
12	2.83	.243	2.049	.340	.660	110101110
19	6.41	.041	.520	.086	.914	010111110
17	6.92	.031	.409	.068	.932	110111100

TABLE 8.7

Summary Statistics of Knowledge State π_3 and a Simulated Response Pattern Drawn From π_3

Ideal Item Score Pattern of π_3 and Pattern of X	Point in Rule Space	Attribute Pattern
R_3　101001101101010110110100110110101101	(−.28, −3.11, .24)	110111110
X　　100101101101010110110100110110101101	(−.24, −2.43, .95)	110111110

Attribute Mastery Probabilities for 9 Attributes

$$A = (p_{a1}, p_{a2}, p_{a3}, p_{a4}, p_{a5}, p_{a6}, p_{a7}, p_{a8}, p_{a9})$$
$$= (.914, 1, 0, 1, .66, 1, 1, .932, 0)$$

Slippage Probability for 9 Attributes

$$ST = (S_{a1}, S_{a2}, S_{a3}, S_{a4}, S_{a5}, S_{a6}, S_{a7}, S_{a8}, S_{a9})$$
$$= (.086, 0, 0, 0, .34, 0, 0, .068, 0)$$

Because the weighted sum of A_3, A_{12}, A_{19}, and A_{17} with the scaled posterior probabilities q3, q12, q19, and q17 gives the attribute mastery probabilities, P_A, each attribute mastery probability is computed as follows:

$$W^T A = P_A \tag{8.12}$$

Each element of nine attributes in $W^T A$ can be computed as follows:

$a_1 = .914$,　$a_2 = 1.0$,　$a_3 = 0$,　$a_4 = 1.0$,　$a_5 = .66$,　$a_6 = 1.0$,　$a_7 = 1.0$,
$a_8 = .932$,　and　$a_9 = 0$

Table 8.7 summarizes the results. The notion of slippage probabilities is discussed in Property 8.1.

Property 8.1: Definition of slippage probability for attribute A_k is given by Equation (8.13):

$$ST_k = (1 - a_k)\, p_{ak} + a_k * (1 - p_{ak}) \tag{8.13}$$

where if $a_k = 1$, then the slippage probability of attribute A_k is $1 - p_{ak}$, and if $a_k = 0$, then it is given by p_{ak}.

Slippage Probabilities When True Attribute Mastery Patterns Are Not Known

In reality, it is impossible to have the true mastery pattern for X, and thus we have to introduce alternative ways to define slippage probabilities of attributes.

Property 8.2: Let us define the slippage probability of attribute A_k as the average of slippage probabilities of L attribute mastery patterns. That is,

$$S_k = \left[\sum_{1}^{L} \{(1 - a_{Lk}) p_{aLk} + a_{Lk}(1 - p_{aLk})\} \right] / L \quad k = 1, \ldots, K \tag{8.14}$$

TABLE 8.8

The Slippage Probabilities for Nine Attributes When the True Attribute Mastery Pattern for X Is Not Known for the Example in Table 8.6

3	110111110	.086	0	0	0	.34	0	0	.068	0
12	110101110	.086	0	0	0	.66	0	0	.068	0
19	010111110	.914	0	0	0	.34	0	0	.068	0
17	110111100	.086	0	0	0	.34	0	0	.932	0

Note: S = (.293 0 0 0 .42 0 0 .284 0), where A = $(p_{a1}, p_{a2}, p_{a3}, p_{a4}, p_{a5}, p_{a6}, p_{a7}, p_{a8}, p_{a9})$ = (.914, 1, 0, 1, .66, 1, 1, .932, 0).

where knowledge state π_l has the attribute mastery pattern of $A_l = (a_{l1}, \ldots, a_{lk}, \ldots, a_{lk})$ for $l = 1, \ldots, L$; and p_{ak} is the attributes mastery probability for X. Then the average slippage probability for attribute A_k is computed by applying Equation (8.14), and summarized in Table 8.8.

The slippage probabilities for nine attributes for X are given by the average of each column; therefore, we get S = (.293 0 0 0 .42 0 0 .284 0). Now the comparison of the slippage probabilities of both of the cases, ST and S, will show us that ST is generally larger than S.

$$ST \geq S \qquad (8.15)$$

The relation ST ≥ S is generally true because the elements in S are determined by considering approximations using erroneous information contained in the attribute patterns close to the true attribute pattern of X.

8.6 The Length of Tests, the Size of Sets of Attributes, and a Sample Size

First, the numbers of test items and attributes affect the size of a Q matrix, and the number of knowledge states generated from a given Q matrix increases exponentially as the numbers of items and attributes increase. For example, a 60-item SAT Mathematics test with 18 attributes usually has around 8,000 knowledge states (Tatsuoka, 1995), a 27-item and 14-attribute placement test in Japan has 727 knowledge states (Hayashi & Tatsuoka, 2008), and a 20-item and 17-attribute placement test for mathematics at Illinois has 780 knowledge states. A 20-item fraction subtraction test (Figure 5.6) with 7 attributes generated 39 knowledge states, and a 38-item fraction addition test with 8 attributes generated 56 knowledge states (Tatsuoka & Tatsuoka, 2005). The 45 items with 18 attributes for TIMSS Booklet 1 had 3,527 knowledge states (Tatsuoka & Corter, 2003). RSM could handle most large-scale assessments as long as the number of items would be less than or equal to around 60 items, and the number of attributes would be less than or equal to around 18. The limit of the numbers of test items and attributes that RSM could handle would be interesting to know. If researchers wanted to use 30 or even 40 attributes for a 50-item test, then they would want to know if it would be possible to estimate such a large number of attribute mastery probabilities. This issue will be further discussed in Chapter 10, but in this section we will explore the possibilities of splitting a set of attributes or items into smaller subsets, and estimate mastery probabilities separately. Whether or not divided subsets of attributes or items can produce acceptably robust estimates of attribute mastery probabilities is a good question. If the answer were yes, then one of the future research topics might be how one could divide items and attributes in a given Q matrix. Of course, we would like the estimated mastery probabilities of desired attributes to be as many as possible for a given test, and we would want to know the optimum way to split a Q matrix to get the maximum amount of information. The next section will introduce some cases of splitting sets of items and attributes.

Dividing a Set of Attributes Into Two Subsets Without Dividing the Items in a Q Matrix

TIMSS (Tatsuoka, Corter, & Tatsuoka, 2004) has 27 attributes for each booklet with the number between items 39 and 45 items. It is possible to use the original Q matrix (45 × 27) for RSM analysis, but Tatsuoka et al. (2007) showed that the original Q matrix can be decomposed into two sub-Q matrices with several attributes in common. The final outcomes of attribute mastery probabilities from sub-Q matrices 1 and 2 are compared, and the results are given in Figure 8.6. The attributes are divided into the content plus the process (mathematical thinking skills) variables, and the special skills variables plus the thinking variables, and their attribute involvement is described in Table 8.9. Table 8.10 provides a list of attributes in the three categories: (a) the contents, (b) the special skills often unique to item types, and (c) the mathematical thinking skills. RSM was performed eight times using eight different Q matrices, and their means of attribute mastery probabilities were compared. Figure 8.6 shows that the mean values of the content and process attribute Q matrix for four booklets and those of the special skills

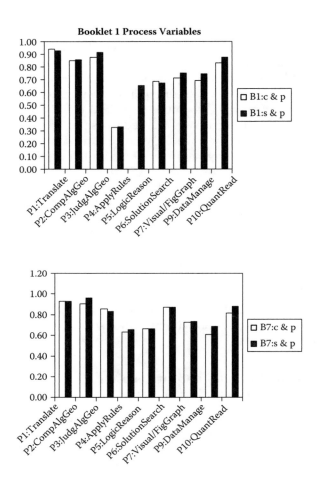

FIGURE 8.6
Comparison of estimated attribute mastery probabilities from the two subsets of attributes
(content and process variables, and special skills and process variables) across Booklets 1
and 7, with sample sizes of N1 = 1,132 and N7 = 1,110.

and process attribute Q matrix are almost identical, except for p10 in
booklet 3.

The conclusion that we may split a set of attributes into a few subsets
without changing the estimated attribute mastery probabilities is a prom-
ising property in RSM, but further investigation may be necessary because
it has not been mathematically proven yet.

TABLE 8.9

Attribute Involvement of Five Booklets and the Splited Two Subsets of the Content and Process Variables and the Special Skills and Process Variables

Booklet Attribute Set	Booklet 1		Booklet 3		Booklet 5		Booklet 7		Booklet 8	
	c&p	s&p	c&p	s&p	c&p	s&p	c&p	s&p	c&p	s&p
Attribute	*Mapping of Attributes to Analysis Variable Number in Each Booklet*									
C1:integer	1		1		1		1		1	
C2:fraction	2		2		2		2		2	
C3:algebra	3		3		3		3		3	
C4:geometry	4		4		4		4		4	
C5:statistics	5		5		5		5		5	
C6:measurement			6		6				6	
S1:UnitConvert				1		1				1
S2:Number		1		2		2		1		2
S3:FigTableGraph		2		3		3		2		3
S4:Approx/Est		3		4		4		3		4
S5:Evaluate/Verify		4		5		5		4		5
S6:RecogPatterns		5				6		5		
S7:ProporReason		6		6		7		6		6
S8:Novel/Unfamiliar		7		7		8		7		7
S9: Comparison										
S10:Open ended		8		8		9		8		8
S11:Communicate		9		9		10		9		9
P1:Translate	6	10	7	10	7	11	6	10	7	10
P1:Translate	7	11	8	11	8	12	7	11	8	11
P2:CompAlgGeo	8	12	9	12	9	13	8	12	9	12
P3:JudgAlgGeo	9	13	10	13	10	14	9	13	10	13
P4:ApplyRules	10	14	11	14	11	15	10	14	11	14
P5:LogicReason	11	15	12	15	12	16	11	15	12	15
P6:SolutionSearch	12	16	13	16	13	17	12	16	13	16
P7:Visual/FigGraph			14	17	14	18	13	17	14	17
P9:DataManage	13	17	15	18	15	19	14	18	15	18
P10:QuantRead	14	18	16	19	16	20	15	19	16	19

Splitting the Items in a Q Matrix Into Two Subsets Without Splitting Attributes

A 38-item fraction addition test whose items are listed in Table 10.9 was analyzed by splitting items in its Q matrix in half into the first 19 items and the remaining 19 items, and their two sets of the nine attribute mastery probabilities were estimated, respectively. Then their means and correlation values between two corresponding attribute mastery probabilities were computed. Table 8.11 shows that their means for seven attributes are very close and highly correlated. Again, it may be possible to split

TABLE 8.10

A List of Knowledge, Skill, and Process Attributes Derived to Explain Performance on the TIMSS-R (1999)* Math Items, Population 2 (Eighth Graders)

Content Attributes

C1	Basic concepts and operations in whole numbers and integers
C2	Basic concepts and operations in fractions and decimals
C3	Basic concepts and operations in elementary algebra
C4	Geometry
C5	Data, probability, and basic statistics
C6	Using tools to measure (or estimate) length, time, angle, and temperature

Skill (Item Type) Attributes

S1	Unit conversion
S2	Understanding number properties and relationships; number sense and number line
S3	Using figures, tables, charts, and graphs
S4	Approximation and estimation
S5	Evaluate, verify, and check options
S6	Recognize patterns and relationships
S7	Using proportional reasoning
S8	Solving novel or unfamiliar problems
S9	Comparison of two or more entities
S10	Open-ended type item
S11	Understanding verbally posed quetions

Process Attributes

P1	Translate and formulate equations and expressions to solve a problem
P2	Computational applications of knowledge in arithmetic and geometry
P3	Judgmental applications of knowledge in arithmetic and geometry
P4	Applying rules in algebra
P5	Logical reasoning—includes case reasoning, deductive thinking skills, if-then, necessary and sufficient, and generalization skills
P6	Problem search, analytic thinking, problem restructuring, and inductive thinking
P7	Generating, visualizing, and reading figures and graphs
P8	Recognize and evaluate mathematical correctness
P9	Management of data and procedures
P10	Quantitative and logical reading

* Mullis, I. V. S., Martin, M. O., Gonzales, E. J., Gregory, K. D., Garden, R. A., O'Conner, K. M., Chlrostowski, S. J. & Smith, T. A. (2000). *TIMSS 1999 International Mathematics Report.* Chestnut Hill, MA: International Study Center, Boston College.

the items into two subsets without altering estimated attribute mastery probabilities.

Note that the TIMSS example does not have the same sample across the four booklets, and each booklet has its unique sample and items. The fraction addition test has the identical sample and the same attribute set, but the items are different.

TABLE 8.11

The Means of Attribute Mastery Probabilities Estimated From Two Subsets of Items and Their Correlation Values (N = 595)

Attribute	Mean1	Mean2	Correlation
1	.44	.49	.80
2	.77	.73	.82
3	.71	.69	.78
4	.67	.60	.80
5	.55	.52	.83
6	.50	.47	.84
7	.76	.71	.82

Further, two parallel forms of SAT Mathematics tests that were developed in the 1990s were examined by comparing their estimated mastery probabilities. As can be seen in Figure 8.7, some attributes have noticeable differences, but when predicting IRT θ values from estimated attribute mastery probabilities, the results are very similar to each other, and their adjusted multiple Rs are .8969 and .9094, respectively. The following chart summarizes the results and their conditions:

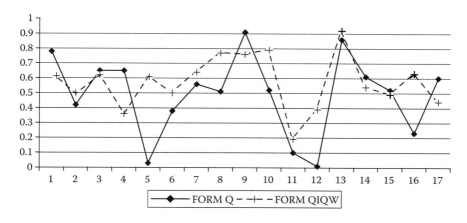

FIGURE 8.7

Comparison of the trend of attribute mastery probabilities estimated from the two forms of SAT Mathematics tests, N = 5,000.

		TIMSS	Fraction Addition	SAT Mathematics
Students	Same sample	No	Yes	No
	Share a part in common	No	No	No
	Totally different sample	Yes	No	Yes
Items	Share a part in common	Yes	No	No
	Totally different items	No	Yes	Yes
Attributes	Same attributes	No	Yes	Yes
	Share a part in common	Yes	No	No
Results		Very similar	Very similar	65% similar

Estimated attribute mastery probabilities from different booklets in TIMSS are fairly robust, even when the total set of 27 attributes is divided into the two subsets of attributes for RSM analyses. By so doing, Tatsuoka et al. (2004) successfully analyzed 27 attributes of 20 countries in the world.

Sample Size

The Q-matrix theory is the most important part of RSM, and it determines all possible knowledge states for the classification of student response patterns. The classification space, called *rule space*, is constructed from the person parameter θ of item response theory and the standardized covariance of two residuals X and $P(\theta)$ denoted by ζ, generalized ζs; therefore, necessary sample size could be at least a few hundred.

RSM is an analytic approach to diagnose students' latent knowledge states by applying the Bayesian decision rules for classification of item responses in a vector space called *rule space*. Recently, the statistical modeling approach has been applied to develop diagnostic techniques by several researchers, but their models do not have an equivalent feature to the Q-matrix theory except for the POSET model (C. Tatsuoka, 2002). In the next section, several models will be introduced.

8.7   Latent Class Models, the Hybrid Model, the Mixture Distribution Diagnostic Model, and the POSET Model

Latent Class Models

Latent class modeling was initiated by Lazaresfeld and Henry in 1968, and they tended to emphasize the difference between factor analysis and latent structure analysis rather than integrating all latent variable models into the common approach. Goodman (1974) advanced this common approach further by introducing efficient parameter estimation techniques using computer technologies. Bartholomew (1987) elegantly summarized latent variable models in his book, *Latent Variable Models and Factor Analysis*; however, the interpretation of the results from their analysis remained a difficult task, and did not provide definite and clear explanations. Statistical tendencies cannot help students' individualized learning; therefore, they are not usable for diagnostic purposes. The mathematical aspect of latent class models is mostly consistent among Lazaresfeld and Henry (1968), Goodman, Dayton and Macready (1976), and others. In educational applications, dichotomous item scores are used for modeling. The latent class models assume that the classes are mutually exclusive and totally together, and the number of classes is usually predetermined arbitrarily. That means everybody in a sample will be forced to belong to one of the classes and all classes together equal to the total sample. This is why fit statistics is important, and why the interpretation of statistically formulated classes becomes difficult. Likewise, this is why the traditional latent class models are difficult to use in cognitive diagnosis. The results from cognitive diagnostic methodologies must provide test takers with accurate and descriptive information about what knowledge they lack and which skills they cannot do. Moreover, the number of latent variables involved in a large-scale assessment such as the SAT and TIMSS is usually 20 to 30, so the number of latent classes (knowledge states) can be more than several thousand and over 10,000 easily. The estimation of parameters of the models could be tremendously difficult.

Modified Latent Class Model

Paulison (1986) developed a modified latent class model in which the distribution of each latent class is expressed by slippage probabilities from some fixed ideal item score pattern and with slippages having random variables of $1 - \varepsilon$ or ε. If an ideal item score pattern represents the correct rule, then the slippage vector of n items is $(1 - \varepsilon_1, 1 - \varepsilon_2, ..., 1 - \varepsilon_n)$, and if an ideal pattern is $(1\ 1\ 1\ 0\ 0\ , ..., 0)$, then the slippage vector becomes $(1 - \varepsilon_1, 1 - \varepsilon_2, 1 - \varepsilon_3, \varepsilon_4, ..., \varepsilon_n)$. Paulison's latent class model assumes that a set of ideal item scores will be a priori known, so the results can provide test takers with clear information on how they can improve their learning.

Hybrid Model and Mixture Distribution Diagnostic Model

Yamamoto's hybrid model (1987) is the combination of Paulison's latent model and item response theory models. In other words, he separated knowledge states in the rule space into two groups: the ones located near the IRT θ axis, and the ones with very high ζ values. Figure 8.8 shows the two-dimensional rule space coordinates of the 728 ideal item score patterns

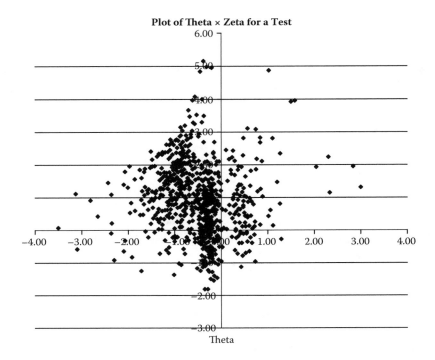

FIGURE 8.8
The rule space coordinates of 728 ideal item score patterns (knowledge states) generated from the 27×14 Q matrix of the Japanese Mathematics Placement Test.

generated from the Q matrix of a mathematics placement test developed at the Institute of Japanese Entrance Examination. The hybrid model takes points closer to the θ axis as the *IRT group*, takes upper and lower parts of clusters far away from the θ as the *latent class model group*, and estimates parameters of the combined likelihood function given below:

$$P(x_j \mid \theta_j, \zeta, \Gamma) = \prod_i^I P_{1i}(\theta_j, \zeta_i)^{x_{ij}} Q_{1i}(\theta_j, \zeta_i)^{1-x_{ij}} \quad \text{if } \Gamma_{j1} = 1$$

$$\prod_i^I P_{kij}{}^{x_{ij}} Q_{kij}{}^{1-x_{ij}} \qquad\qquad \text{if } \Gamma_{jk} = 1$$

(8.16)

where x_{ij} is the response of person j to item i, I is the number of items, K is the number of groups (latent classes), Γ_{jk} is class membership for person j, and ζ is latent class parameters. In this model, the number of latent classes K—that is, a set of ideal item score patterns—was generated from a given

Q matrix. This mixture model gives interpretable information for the latent classes for which their true item patterns are implanted as the kernels in the model, but the IRT subsample group gets only estimated θ values and not explicit diagnostic information. Von Davior (2007) developed a similar model to the hybrid model by utilizing a Q matrix and called it a *mixture distribution diagnostic model*.

POSET Model

One of the most mathematically and statistically elegant diagnostic models has been developed by C. Tatsuoka (1996, 2002; Tatsuoka & Ferguson, 2003, 2006) and is called the POSET model. The POSET model is essentially a sequential analysis defined on a partially ordered knowledge state generated from a given Q matrix. The partially ordered knowledge states introduced in Chapter 4 actually satisfy the lattice condition, and POSET exploits the properties of lattice. The item selection method uses Kullback–Leibler (K–L) information, which measures the distance between the two response distributions $f_e(x)$ and $g_e(x)$. The response distributions are defined by separating the network of knowledge states generated from a given Q matrix. In Figure 8.9, we consider three independent attributes (A1, A2, and A3) and their knowledge states (000), (100), (010), (001), (101), (110), (011), and (111). The knowledge states written in boldface and connected by boldface arrows are called "upshot" knowledge states. They involve the current state (100) as their subset, and all include *can do A1*. C. Tatsuoka named the distribution of upshot knowledge states by $f_e(x)$ and its complement set of knowledge states by $g_e(x)$ that are characterized by *cannot do A1*. Each distribution that is Bernoulli is expressed by the conditional probability of success given the current state and without mastery of the required attribute(s). For each student, the posterior state membership probability of knowledge state j after answering n items $\pi_n(j)$ is defined by

$$\pi_n(j) = \frac{\pi_0(j)\Pi_{i=1}^n f(x_i|e_i, j, \lambda)}{\Sigma_{u \varepsilon \{states\}}\pi_0(u)\Pi_{i=1}^n f(x_i|e_i, u, \lambda)} \tag{8.17}$$

where λ is item parameters, e_i is the ith state, and $\pi_0(j)$ is the prior probability of state j.

Item parameter estimation uses the Gibbs sampling algorithm, or, in other words, the Markov Chain Monte Carlo (MCMC) estimation methods. Detailed information is given in C. Tatsuoka (2002). The advantage of using Gibbs sampling is that it generates observations having Markov Chain using the condition of the probability of occurrence of r + 1th observation, which is dependent only on the most recent, rth, observation:

$$P(X_{r+1}|X_1, X_2, ..., X_r) = P(X_{r+1}|X_r)$$

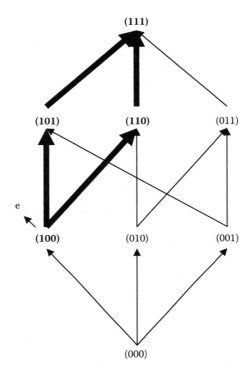

FIGURE 8.9
"Upshot" knowledge states with boldface arrows and binary vectors of the current state e = (100) in POSET generated from three attributes.

Thus, a sample from the desired posterior distribution of item parameters can be generated without calculating the posterior distribution density directly, and the posterior mean and variance can also be easily estimated from very large simulated data. This property is a great advantage for latent variable modeling approaches.

The item selection algorithm in the POSET model is proved to have the optimal rate of convergence when items have unique response distributions, as is the case here. For continuous variable X, the Kullback–Leiber information function is given by Equation (8.18):

$$K(f_e, g_e) = \int f_e(x) \cdot \log \frac{f_e(x)}{g_e(x)} dx \qquad (8.18)$$

where $f_e(x)$ is the true distribution. For discrete random variables, it is given by Equation (8.19):

$$K(f_e, g_e) = \sum f_e(x) \cdot \log \frac{f_e(x)}{g_e(x)} \tag{8.19}$$

Like Fisher's maximum likelihood information function, an item with a high K-L value is considered to be a very informative item, which can distinguish those who have the knowledge from those who do not. Posterior probabilities to knowledge states are also changed greatly when the K-L value is high (Tatsuoka & Ferguson, 2003). POSET selects the next item by computing the K-L value among the remaining items first, selects the item giving the highest value of K-L, and also gives the posterior probabilities of the two partitions of classes that are close. Testing will be terminated when updated probability to the most plausible KS satisfies a given threshold value.

RSM also developed an adaptive testing algorithm that is a direct application of the Cauchy–Schwartz convergence theory in a vector space, because rule space is a vector space with the Mahalanobis distance (Baillie & Tatsuoka, 1984; Tatsuoka, 1983b). Yamada (2008) compared the efficiency of the POSET and RSM adaptive testing algorithms and found that the POSET algorithm is more efficient and produces more accurate attribute mastery probabilities than the RSM algorithm.

9

Reliabilities of Item Score, Person's Score, and Attribute Mastery Probability, and Their Relationship to the Classical Test Theory

In the classical test theory, the observed score X is defined as the sum of the true score T and the error of measurement E, where the covariance of T and E is 0, and the variances are not zero. The reliability of score X is defined by the ratio of the variances of T and X, $\rho = \sigma^2(T)/\sigma^2(X)$. When X is the sum of n item scores, $X = X_1 + X_2 + \cdots + X_n$, then the lower bound of the reliability, Cronbach's α, is given by the following equation, which is expressed by the observed item score variances of X and item scores X_i:

$$\alpha \geq \frac{n}{n-1}\left\{1 - \frac{\Sigma_{i=1}^n \sigma^2(X_i)}{\sigma^2(X)}\right\} \tag{9.1}$$

Because it is not possible to measure the true scores directly, the reliability of a test must be inferred from the observed scores. Cronbach derived a lower bound of the test reliability using total scores and item scores. Since then, Cronbach's α has been used as the lower bound of the reliability of scores, but the relationship (Equation [9.0.1]) will not provide the reliability of a single item because the denominator $n - 1$ becomes 0 for $n = 1$; however, the information from attributes has never been utilized in any psychometric theory. Use of such information enables us to obtain the reliability of a single item. In this chapter, we introduce the reliability of attributes and an item, and then relate them to Cronbach's α (Lord & Novick, 1968; Tatsuoka, 1975). Then, we introduce *attribute characteristic curves* and relate them to item response curves and observed item difficulties.

9.1 Summary List of the Information Obtainable from a Rule Space Analysis

In Chapter 8, we discussed how to get the attribute mastery probability for each attribute from the posterior probabilities of several closest knowledge states for a given student X. We also discussed the upper bound of errors associated with a given classification criterion α; however, the

Response pattern and the corresponding Rule Space Coordinates of student X:
X = (10010110110101011011010011011010101101) X_{RSC} = (-.24, -2.43, .95)

Four closest ideal item score patterns, and their corresponding Rule Space Coordinates, Posterior probabilities and the four attribute patterns corresponding to the ideal item score patterns:

	Ideal item score patterns	Rule space points	W	Attribute patterns
R_3 =	(10100110110101011011010011011010101101)	(-.28, -3.11, .24)	.60	(110111110)
R_{12}=	(00100110110100011011001001011011010001101)	(-.40, -1.94, -.25)	.24	(110101110)
R_{19} =	(00100010010001011010010001001000101101)	(-.55, -1.16, -.09)	.04	(010111110)
R_{17}=	(00100010010101001010010001001010100101)	(-.61, -1.20, .47)	.03	(110111100)
		Total of W_k	= .91	
		Errors $\varepsilon_X(\alpha)$	= .09	

where item response pattern of X; rule space coordinate X_{RSC}= $(\theta_x, \zeta_0, \zeta_1)$; the posterior probability of X belonging to $\pi_k W_k = p(\pi_k | X)$; Attribute pattern of A

FIGURE 9.1
The information obtainable for individual X in an 38-item fraction addition test where the prior probability is uniform distribution.

discussion in Chapter 8 focused on dealing with the information for individuals. In this chapter, we will introduce attribute test theory and discuss the reliabilities of attributes.

Let us summarize the individualized information we have obtained in the previous chapter using a 38-item fraction addition test. For each individual student, Figure 9.1 has a 38-item response pattern, X; four ideal item score patterns or, equivalently, four knowledge states that are closest to X; and their corresponding rule space points denoted by X_{RSC} and R_3, R_{12}, R_{19}, and R_{17}. However, Tatsuoka and Tatsuoka (1989) showed that an erroneous rule R_k can be considered as a knowledge state π_k, so we use the notation π_k instead of R_k. Their corresponding rule space coordinates are given by $X_{RSC} = (\theta_x, \zeta_0, \zeta_1)$, $\pi_{3RSC} = (\theta_{R3}, \zeta_{0R3}, \zeta_{1R3})$, $\pi_{12RSC} = (\theta_{R12}, \zeta_{0R12}, \zeta_{1R12})$, $\pi_{19RSC} = (\theta_{R19}, \zeta_{0R19}, \zeta_{1R19})$, and $\pi_{17RSC} = (\theta_{R17}, \zeta_{0R17}, \zeta_{1R17})$, respectively. The posterior probability of X (i.e., X is coming from each knowledge state π_k) is given by $p(\pi_k | X)$ and $W^T = (p(\pi_3 | X), p(\pi_{12} | X), p(\pi_{19} | X),$ and $p(\pi_{17} | X))$. The matrix of the four ideal item response patterns—$\pi_3, \pi_{12}, \pi_{19},$ and π_{17}—is expressed by $C_I = (CI_{ij})$, and the matrix of attribute patterns for the four knowledge states is given by $C_A = (CA_{ij})$. This information is summarized in Figure 9.1.

When the populations of knowledge states $\pi_3, \pi_{12}, \pi_{19},$ and π_{17} are mutually exclusive and totally together, and we choose one knowledge state from the four, then the error probability is given by the complement of the posterior probability of our choice (Fukunaga, 1990; Riply, 1996). Usually the knowledge state having the maximum value of the posterior probability among L closest states would be selected based on Bayes' decision rule (Riply).

Therefore, in this example, if we follow the conventional selection rule, we select π_3 and get the error probability of $1 - .503 = .497$. But, in reality, there are 56 knowledge states in this example, and several protocol analyses (Shaw, 1986; Shaw & Birenbaum, 1985; Tatsuoka, 1984a) indicate that it is rare that students belong to only one knowledge state. They are exploring how to apply correctly the attributes that have not yet completely been mastered, and often their applications are unstable (Shaw, 1986). Therefore, the rule space method does not follow the traditional decision rules; we take the weighted sum of the four ideal item score patterns where the weights are the four posterior probabilities of π_3, π_{12}, π_{19}, and π_{17}. The classification rule we used in these data is knowledge states π_k with the centroid C_k whose squared distance from the point X_R in the rule space is less than 5:

$$D^2(X_R, C_k) < 5.0 \quad \text{for } k = 1, \ldots, 56$$

The person X's attribute mastery probabilities and error probability are given by

$$\text{Prob}(A = 1 \mid X) = \mathbf{W}^T \mathbf{C_A} = (.60, .24, .04, .03) * \begin{vmatrix} 1 & 1 & 0 & 1 & 1 & 1 & 1 & 1 & 0 \\ 1 & 1 & 0 & 1 & 0 & 1 & 1 & 1 & 0 \\ 0 & 1 & 0 & 1 & 1 & 1 & 1 & 1 & 0 \\ 1 & 1 & 0 & 1 & 1 & 1 & 1 & 0 & 0 \end{vmatrix}$$

$$= (.87, .91, 0, .91, .67, .91, .91, .88, 0)$$

$$= \text{attribute mastery probabilities for } X$$

Let us denote this vector by $(AP)_X$, where $\varepsilon_X(\alpha)$ is .09.

The results from the rule space analysis consist of the attribute mastery probability vector of $(AP)_X$; the upper bound of the error probability, $\varepsilon_X(\alpha)$, and K attribute patterns (or, equivalently, knowledge states) closest to X; and their ideal item score patterns for X.

Any other examples will produce the same information with different coordinates and probabilities. Based on this rich information, we introduce pseudotrue and true scores of item j for person i in the next section.

9.2 True Score and Pseudotrue Score of Item j for Person i and the Reliability of Observed Item Score X_i and Attribute Mastery Probability for an Individual

If X is an individual X's item response pattern in Figure 9.1, then the jth component of X is the score of item j for this student. As can be seen in Figure 9.1, this student has the component score of X_j for item j and $(CI)_{ij}$ for $i = 4, 12, 19,$ and 17. Now let us define the pseudotrue score for Xj and develop a theory parallel to the classical test theory. We call this new test theory the *attribute test theory*.

The Pseudotrue Score τ_j of Item j for X

The pseudotrue score of item j for X will be introduced, and it will be referred to as the RS pseudoscore τ_j. The definition of the pseudotrue scores for item j, τ_j, is given by the weighted sum of the column vector j of the matrix (CI_{ij}) that is of four ideal item score patterns, where the weights are the posterior probabilities of knowledge states, W.

The definition of τ_j is given by Equation (9.2):

$$\tau_j = \sum_{k=1}^{L} w_k (CI)_{kj} = W'(CI) \tag{9.1}$$

where L is the number of closest knowledge states that satisfy $D^2 < \alpha$ for a given α, and w_k is the scaled posterior probabilities of knowledge states and $\sum_{k=1,L} w_k = 1$.

The True Score t_j of Item J for X

The true score t_j of item j for X will be introduced, and it will be referred to as *RS true score* hereafter. The true item score for X_j is given by the weighted sum of the ideal item score for the jth column in the matrix CI, where the weights are defined by the scaled posterior probabilities of M ($L < M$) knowledge states, where M is the total number of knowledge states generated from a given Q matrix, and $\sum_{k=1,M} V_{kj} = 1$.

The definition of the RS true score for item j, t_j, is given by Equation (9.2):

$$t_j = \sum_{k=1}^{M} V_k (CI)_{kj} = V'(CI) \tag{9.2}$$

Note that the definitions, Equations (9.1) and (9.2), are still at the individual level. Figure 9.2 gives the estimated RS pseudotrue and RS true scores τ_j and t_j of item j for individual X. Because the 38-item test consists of two parallel subtests—such that item 1 in subtest 1 and item 20 in subtest 2, item 2 in subtest 1 and item 21 in subtest 2, and so on to item 19 in subtest 1 and item 38 in subtest 2 are parallel in terms of cognitive processes—the first-half patterns of the ideal item score patterns are repeated in the second half. Therefore, the first 19 elements in the attribute mastery vector are repeated in the second-half elements. For the same reason, the estimated pseudotrue and true scores have repeated elements in this case; however, this is not true in general cases. Note that in Figure 9.2, the numerals "1" are set to the probability of .91;

X   1001011011010101101 1010011011010101101

KS	Ideal item score patterns $C_l = (CI)_{ij}$	W	$C_A = (CA)_{ij}$
R_3	$=(1010011011010101101\ 1010011011010101101)$	.60	110111110
R_{12}	$=(0010011011010001101\ 0010011011010001101)$	.24	110101110
R_{19}	$=(0010001001000101101\ 0010001001000101101)$	.04	010111110
R_{17}	$=(0010001001010100101\ 0010001001010100101)$	.03	110111100

Total of W_k = .91
Errors $\varepsilon_X(\alpha)$ = .09

Attribute probability vector = (.87, .91, .09, .91, .67, .91, .91, .89, .09) with errors
τ_j (.60, .09, .91, .09, .09, .84, .91, .09, .84, .91, .09, .87, .09, .67, .09, .88, .91, .09, .91
.60, .09, .91, .09, .09, .84, .91, .09, .84, .91, .09, .87, .09, .67, .09, .88, .91, .09, .91)

FIGURE 9.2
Estimated pseudotrue score τ_j and true score t_j for item j.

zeroes are set to .09, which is the complement of .91; and the error probability associates with the classification criterion $D^2 < 5.0$.

The person X's attribute mastery probabilities (denoted by $(AP)_x$) are given by Equation (9.1) as the multiplication of the weights vector **W** in Figure 9.1 and attribute mastery patterns. The discussion about the pseudo true score τ_j and true score tj of item j for person X can be applied to attribute k for person X without loss of generality and get the attribute pseudo true score $(\tau a)_k$ and attribute true score $(\tau a)_k$, for Attribute k, respectively.

Example of a Large-Scale Assessment

The following Figure 9.3 provides an example of student performance on a 60-item large-scale mathematics test. The student received the total score of 50, and his response pattern is given at the second row from the top right below the student ID. The student missed items 15, 20, 24, 25, 40, 47, 49, 50, 55, and 60. By looking into the patterns of items as well as those of attributes, KSs 11 through 9 have very similar patterns, the distance D^2 is less than 5.00, and the posterior probability values are significantly larger than the rest of the knowledge states; however, KSs 7 through 10 are located pretty far from X, and their patterns are different from those of the first six knowledge states.

By looking into the pseudotrue score vector, these items have low estimates of the pseudotrue scores. Six more items, not included in the set of items with the observed score of zero, are found having lower pseudotrue scores than .91. This student mastered attributes 1, 2, 3, 4, 7, 8, 9, 10, 11, 12, 13, 14, 15, 16, and 17, but not attributes 5, 6, 18, and 19.

Student ID = 6781   Total score = 50
Item Response Patterns for the Student X:
    1111111111 1111011110 1110011111 1111111110 1111110100 1111011110

KS*		Ideal-item score Patterns of 10 closest KS to X denoted by CI = (CIkj) k = 1, 10; j = 1,60
KS1	11	1111111111 1111111010 1101011111 1111111110 1111111010 1111011110
KS2	13	1111111111 1111111010 1100011111 1110111111 1111111010 1111011110
KS3	19	1111111111 1111011111 1110011111 1100111110 1111010100 1111111110
KS4	15	1111111111 1111111010 1100011111 1110111110 1111111010 1111011110
KS5	17	1111111111 1111011111 1111011111 1101111110 1111010101 1111111110
KS6	9	1111111111 1111111010 1101111111 1111111111 1111111010 1111111111
KS7	1156	1001111111 1111011111 1110011111 1101111110 1111010101 1011111110
KS8	1148	1001111111 1111111010 1100011111 1111111111 1111111010 1011011111
KS9	1146	1001111111 1111111111 1110011111 1110111110 1111111110 1011111110
KS10	1144	1001111111 1111111111 1110011111 1110111111 1111111110 1011111110

KS		Attribute Mastery Patterns for 10 closest KS CA = (CAkj)	Distance D2	post.prob (θ ξ1 ξ2) W RMS coordinate
		1 2 3 4 5 6 7 8 910111213141516171819		
KS1	11	1 1 1 1 0 1 1 1 1 1 1 1 1 1 1 1 1 0 1	0.07	.28	(1.40 0.22 0.30)
KS2	13	1 1 1 1 0 1 1 1 1 1 1 1 1 1 1 1 1 1 0	0.30	.25	(1.32 -0.78 -0.69)
KS3	19	1 1 1 1 1 0 1 1 1 1 1 1 1 1 1 1 1 0 0	1.21	.14	(1.24 -0.74 -0.63)
KS4	15	1 1 1 1 0 1 1 1 1 1 1 1 1 1 1 1 1 0 0	1.44	.12	(1.21 -0.78 -0.68)
KS5	17	1 1 1 1 1 0 1 1 1 1 1 1 1 1 1 1 1 0 1	1.88	.10	(1.60 0.09 1.05)
KS6	9	1 1 1 1 0 1 1 1 1 1 1 1 1 1 1 1 1 1 1	4.40	.01	(1.71 2.06 2.12)
KS7	1156	1 1 1 1 0 1 1 1 1 1 0 1 1 1 1 1 1 0 1	12.97	.00	(1.25 2.63 1.89)
KS8	1148	1 1 1 0 1 1 1 1 1 1 0 1 1 1 1 1 1 1 1	13.52	.00	(1.17 1.72 0.95)
KS9	1146	1 1 1 1 1 1 1 1 1 1 0 1 1 1 1 1 0 0	13.71	.00	(1.53 -0.15 -0.86)
KS10	1144	1 1 1 1 1 1 1 1 1 1 0 1 1 1 1 1 1 0	16.34	.00	(1.67 -0.31 -0.98)

Total = .91
ε(α) = .09

Attribute probability vector =(.91 .91 .91 .91 .24 .67 .91 .91 .91 .91 .91 .91 .91 .91 .91 .91 .26 .39)

Pseudo-true score vector .91= i1~14; i16~17; i19; i21~22; i26~32; i35~39; i41~44; i46; i51~54; i56~59
else is   i15=.67, i18=.24, i20=.24, i24=.39, i25=.01, i33=.67, i34=.39, i40=.26, i45=.67, i47=.67, i48=.24,
i49=.67, i40=.01, i55=.24, i60=.01.

FIGURE 9.3
An example of the 10 closest ideal item score patterns and the corresponding attribute mastery patterns, and their points in the three-dimensional rule space for a old SAT mathematics test.

9.3   True Scores of Item j for Person i

Relation Between the True Score T in the Classical Test Theory and RS True Score T

In the classical test theory, the true score is defined as a random variable representing a person's true score for test items (Lord & Novick, 1968; Tatsuoka, 1975). The error score is defined as a random variable that is independent from the true score and has a nonzero variance.

For a person i, an observed score, X_{ij} for item j, is expressed by the sum of the true score, T_{ij}, and error score, E_{ij}:

$$X_{ij} = T_{ij} + E_{ij} \tag{9.3}$$

And the covariance of T_{ij} and E_{ij} is zero:

$$cov(T_j, E_j) = 0, \quad var(E_j) \neq 0 \quad for\ j = 1, ..., n \tag{9.4}$$

Let us extend this definition to the attribute test theory. The true score T_{ij} is replaced by the RS true score t_{ij} from the rule space, and e_{ij} is the errors due to the classification procedure:

$$T_{ij} = t_{ij} + e_i \tag{9.5}$$

Substituting Equation (9.5) into (9.3), we get (9.6):

$$X_{ij} = t_{ij} + e_i + E_{ij} \tag{9.6}$$

where we assume that the RS true score of item j for person i is uncorrelated with error scores (error of measurement) of item j for a person E_{ij} and classification errors e_i for person i. The classification error for a person e_i and the measurement of error E_{ij} are assumed not to be correlated. We also assume that the variances of errors are not zero. Equation (9.7) summarizes our assumptions.

$$cov(t_j, e_j) = 0, \quad cov(t_j, E_j) = 0, \quad and \quad cov(e_j, E_j) = 0; \quad var(e_j) \neq 0$$
$$and \quad var(E_j) \neq 0 \tag{9.7}$$

The discussion in this section is applicable to contributes. However, we assume attributes are latent variables and impossible to measure directly. The attributes mastery probabilities introduced in Chapter 8 are actually RS pseudo-true score of attributes.

Reliability of Estimated RS True Scores of Items for Each Person

The conventional reliability of item j denoted by ρ_j is given by the ratio of the variances of the true score and observed score for item j. We now define the reliability of the estimated RS true score, and error variances, in a similar manner to the reliability of items in the classical test theory. The variances are obtained by summing up the number of subjects for each item.

$$\rho_j = \frac{var(t_j)}{var(X_j)} \tag{9.8}$$

Let us denote the ratio of $var(e_j)$ and $var(X_j)$ by ε_j, and the ratio of $var(E_j)$ and $var(X_j)$ by δ_j:

$$\varepsilon_j = \frac{\text{var}(e_j)}{\text{var}(X_j)}. \tag{9.9}$$

$$\delta_j = \frac{\text{var}(E_j)}{\text{var}(X_j)}. \tag{9.10}$$

The new indices ε_j and δ_j indicate that they are different kinds of measurement errors affecting observed scores X: ε_j is due to the procedure to get the RS true scores t_{ij} estimated in the rule space method, and E_j is due to measurement error in the classical test theory sense. RS true score t_j for item j can be replaced by RS pseudoscore τ_j in practice, and the reliability of item j can be approximated by ρ_j':

$$\rho_j' = \frac{\text{var}(\tau_j)}{\text{var}(X_j)}. \tag{9.11}$$

Reliability of Persons, and Error Variances for Measurement Errors and Classification Errors

In Equations (9.8), (9.9), (9.10), and (9.11), the variances are obtained by summing up persons in the variables X_{ij}, t_{ij}, e_{ij}, and E_{ij} for each item; however, we can get similar measures for each person by summing up items. They are the reliability of person i, and two kinds of errors of measurement due to the classification procedure in the rule space method and the measurement procedure due to the assessment environment.

$$\rho_i = \frac{\text{var}(t_i)}{\text{var}(X_i)} \tag{9.12}$$

$$\varepsilon_i = \frac{\text{var}(e_i)}{\text{var}(X_i)} \tag{9.13}$$

$$\delta_i = \frac{\text{var}(E_i)}{\text{var}(X_i)} \tag{9.14}$$

$$\rho_i' = \frac{\text{var}(\tau_i)}{\text{var}(X_i)}. \tag{9.15}$$

The Reliability of Composite Scores

Suppose total scores are now our interest. The total score of person i for X and the true score are $s_i = \Sigma_{j=1}^n X_{ij}$ and $t_i = \Sigma_{j=1}^n t_{ij}$, respectively. The reliability of total scores ρ is defined by the ratio of the variance of the total of the estimated RS true score and the observed total scores, s.

$$\rho = \frac{\text{var}(t)}{\text{var}(s)} \tag{9.16}$$

Because the true score defined in the classical test theory is replaced by $T_{ij} = t_{ij} + e_i$, ρ is smaller than the ratio of variances of T and s.

$$\rho = \frac{\text{var}(t)}{\text{var}(s)} \le \frac{\text{var}(T)}{\text{var}(s)} = \frac{\text{var}(t+e)}{\text{var}(s)} = \text{reliability} \tag{9.17}$$

Let us denote the reliability in the classical test theory η, then we have

$$\frac{\text{var}(e)}{\text{var}(s)} = \eta - \rho \tag{9.18}$$

Therefore, the variance of classification errors is the product of the variance of the total score s and the difference between the classical reliability and the rule space reliability.

$$\text{var}(e) = (\eta - \rho)\,\text{var}(s) \le (\alpha - \rho)\,\text{var}(s) \tag{9.19}$$

where α is Cronbach's alpha (Lord & Novick, 1968). Equation (9.19) shows that the variance due to classification procedure is less than the difference of Cronbach's α and the reliability ρ.

Example 9.1

In Figure 9.3, the RSM analysis results of a student, ID = 6781, who took a large-scale 60-item mathematics test is summarized.

The matrix of attribute patterns, (CA_{mk}), where m = 1, …, L (10) and k = 1, …, K (19), is further analyzed by their partial order and expressed in a network given in Figure 9.4. The observed test scores of this student are listed in the top portion of Figure 9.3. The analysis has judged that this student is more likely to be coming from either of the 10 populations of the knowledge state, $\pi_{11}, \pi_{13}, \pi_{19}, \pi_{15}, \pi_{17}, \pi_9, \pi_{1156}, \pi_{1148}, \pi_{1146}$, and π_{1144}. Ten ideal item score patterns associated with the 10 knowledge states, their corresponding attribute mastery patterns, the Mahalanobis distance between the student's point and the 10 rule space points, the posterior probabilities of knowledge states given X, and their rule space coordinates are given in the Figure. For the reliability of an item, we chose item 15 and got the estimated RS pseudo-true score τ_{15} from Figure 9.3, $\tau_{15} = .67$. RS true total score for this student is .8526. True score variance = .0784, and the observed variance = .13; therefore, the reliability of the observed score is .62 for this student.

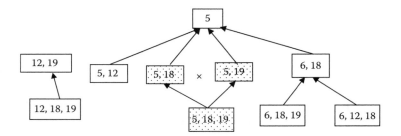

FIGURE 9.4
The structure of knowledge states for Student ID=6781. White boxes have the higher possibilities of membership. Dotted box is his first; most likely, he is from this box.

Partially Ordered Network of Knowledge Stated by an Individual

The structure of 10 knowledge states for the student ID = 6781 is given in Figure 9.4. The numbers in a box are the attributes this student cannot do. The closest knowledge state, KS1 (ID = 11) with the posterior probability of .28 is designated by *cannot do attributes 5 and 18,* and the second most likely knowledge state of this student is KS = 13, with *cannot do attributes 5 and 19* with the probability of .25. The third KS is KS = 19, with *cannot do 5, 18, and 19;* therefore, X can be located in the triangle of three boxes, [5, 18], [5, 19], and [5, 18, 19]. This relationship suggests that remediation of attribute 18 could be the most effective way to bring this student to the higher knowledge state [5].

9.4   Relationship Between the RS True Scores Estimated From a Set of Ideal Item Score Patterns and Those From Attribute Mastery Probabilities

The Q-matrix theory introduced in Chapters 3 and 4 generates all possible knowledge states from a given Q matrix and expresses each knowledge state by its corresponding ideal item score pattern and attribute mastery pattern. Attribute Test Theory parallel to the Classical Test Theory has been introduced in the previous sections of Chapter 8. We defined a new concept of reliabilities and true scores (called RS true scores) for items, attributes, and individuals from ideal item-score patterns and attribute mastery patterns. In this section we further investigate their relationships.

Can We Estimate Pseudotrue Scores From Attribute Mastery Probabilities for Person I?

Suppose we have nine attribute vectors generated from a given Q matrix, where the Q matrix (q_{kj}) is of the order of 4×5. Let us replace the element of zero, $q_{kj} = 0$, to "b" in the Q matrix, in which b indicates attribute k is not involved in item j. If we treat element 1 in the Q matrix as probability of 1, and b is a quantity representing answers that are missing, then the elements in the Q matrix are no longer Boolean variables representing involvement, and we can apply regular matrix algebra to the Q matrix.

Attribute mastery pattern

$A_k = (a1, a2, a3, a4)$ $\qquad$ Q matrix (q_{kj}) $\qquad\qquad$ Q_b

$$
\begin{array}{c|cccc}
A_1 & 1 & 1 & 1 & 1 \\
A_2 & 1 & 1 & 1 & 0 \\
A_3 & 1 & 1 & 0 & 0 \\
A_4 & 1 & 0 & 1 & 1 \\
A_5 & 1 & 0 & 1 & 0 \\
A_6 & 1 & 0 & 0 & 0 \\
A_7 & 0 & 0 & 1 & 1 \\
A_8 & 0 & 0 & 1 & 0 \\
A_9 & 0 & 0 & 0 & 0
\end{array}
$$

$$
Q = \begin{array}{c|ccccc}
 & i1 & i2 & i3 & i4 & i5 \\
\hline
a1 & 1 & 1 & 1 & 0 & 0 \\
a2 & 1 & 1 & 0 & 0 & 0 \\
a3 & 1 & 0 & 0 & 1 & 1 \\
a4 & 1 & 0 & b & 1 & 0
\end{array}
$$

$$
Q_b = \begin{array}{c|ccccc}
 & i1 & i2 & i3 & i4 & i5 \\
\hline
a1 & 1 & 1 & 1 & b & b \\
a2 & 1 & 1 & b & b & b \\
a3 & 1 & b & b & 1 & 1 \\
a4 & 1 & b & b & 1 & b
\end{array}
$$

For example, if we randomly choose A_5 and perform the element-wise multiplication of A_5 and column vectors i1, i2, i3, i4, and i5 with the operation defined by $1 * 0 = 0$, $1 * b = b$, and $0 * b = b$, then we get the matrix Q′:

$$
Q' = \begin{array}{c|ccccc}
 & i1 & i2 & i3 & i4 & i5 \\
\hline
a1 & 1 & 1 & 1 & b & b \\
a2 & 0 & 0 & b & b & b \\
a3 & 1 & b & b & 1 & 1 \\
a4 & 0 & b & b & 0 & b
\end{array}
$$

As discussed in Chapters 3 and 4, our assumption is that item score j is correct only when all of the attributes involved in item j are applied correctly; therefore, the rule space method is a multiplicative model. This assumption is an important difference from the other psychometric models and test theories.

Assumption: The item score j is correct only when all the attributes involved in item j are applied correctly.

When attribute k is not mastered, the scores of the items involving attribute k become zero. The entries of matrix Q′ are treated as probabilities—indeed, probabilities of 1 or 0—so multiplying the element in column 1 without blanks gives the expected item difficulty of item j; for example, for item 1, $1 * 0 * 1 * 0 = 0$; similarly, for items 2, 3, and 4, we get $1 * 0 = 0$, $1 = 1$, and $1 * 0 = 0$; and we get 1 for item 5. The resulting vector is (0, 0, 1, 0, 1), which is the ideal item score pattern corresponding to A_5. The ideal item pattern of A5 can be obtained by applying the rule space assumption to the original Q matrix; however, the attribute mastery probabilities are not always 1.

If an individual has attribute mastery probabilities $p_1, \ldots, p_4$ for four attributes and denotes it $A_i = (p_1, \ldots, p_4)$, and element-wise multiplication of A_i and Q with the same rules as described above yields Q′:

$$Q' = \begin{vmatrix} p_1 & p_1 & p_1 & b & b \\ p_2 & p_2 & b & b & b \\ p_3 & b & b & p_3 & p_3 \\ p_4 & b & b & p_4 & b \end{vmatrix}$$

then, for this individual, we get the estimated item scores of five items, $(p_1p_2p_3p_4,\ p_1p_2,\ p_1,\ p_3p_4,$ and $p_3)$ by applying the assumption of the rule space methodology given in Chapter 2.

Property 9.1: For a given person i, the estimated item scores obtained from attribute mastery probability vector $A_i = (p_1, \ldots, p_4)$ for item j are given by $(p_1p_2p_3p_4,\ p_1p_2,\ p_1,\ p_3p_4,$ and $p_3)$. The item difficulty for item j will be obtained by taking the average of test takers.

When we estimate the RS pseudotrue score for item j from L ideal item score patterns and the vector of L posterior probabilities for person i, we perform their element-wise multiplication of A_i and Q first, and then add them up over L. Instead, according to Property 9.1, we take multiplication of the elements of each column vector in the Q matrix in a special case, A_4, in which the elements consist of the probabilities of 1 or 0, and then it gives us the RS pseudotrue scores of items, $\tau_4 = (0\ 0\ 1\ 0\ 1)$; however, the BDF produces independently Y_4, ideal item score patterns corresponding to A_4. Note that $Y_4 = (0\ 0\ 1\ 0\ 1)$ is identical to t_4. The following example shows that this relationship is true for other cases, and indeed it is true in general.

Example 9.2

The 20-item fraction subtraction test used in Chapters 5 and 8 is used here again. This test has a Q matrix (20 items with 8 attributes). Rule space analysis for an individual, Student S, is used as an example; the RSM analysis selected the six closest knowledge states within $D^2 < 5$, and their posterior probabilities are provided in Figure 9.5, which also gives the student's observed scores X_j, RS pseudotrue scores τ_j, and estimated item scores w_j from the Q matrix and attribute mastery probabilities. The correlation values of three scores computed as follows: X and w have .643, X and τ have .688, and τ and w have .981. Their means and standard deviations are computed as follows: X is .55, τ is .43, and w is .39, respectively. The reliability for this student is given by the ratio of the variances of τ and X, $\rho_i = var(\tau)/var(X) = .1548/.2605 = .5942$.

Let us repeat Property 9.1 in more general terms.

| | Q-matrix, items × attributes | | Estimated Item Scores for Student S | | |
---	items	attributes 1 2 3 4 5 6 7 8	Pseudo true scores τ	Observed scores	Estimated item scores from attribute mastery probabilities
Q =	1	0 0 0 1 1 1 0 1	.12	1	.08
	2	0 0 0 0 1 0 0 1	.84	1	.76
	3	0 0 0 0 1 0 0 1	.84	1	.12
	4	0 1 1 1 0 0 0 1	.00	0	.04
	5	0 1 1 1 1 1 1 1	.00	0	.91
	6	0 0 0 0 0 0 0 1	.91	1	.75
	7	1 1 0 0 0 0 0 1	.91	1	.91
	8	1 0 0 0 0 0 0 1	.91	1	.91
	9	1 1 0 0 0 1 1 1	.45	1	.31
	10	0 1 1 1 0 0 1 1	.00	0	.11
	11	0 1 1 1 0 0 1 1	.00	0	.11
	12	0 0 0 1 0 0 1 1	.24	1	.20
	13	0 1 1 0 1 1 0 1	.21	0	.19
	14	0 1 1 0 0 0 0 1	.61	1	.51
	15	1 0 0 0 0 0 1 1	.91	1	.75
	16	0 1 1 0 0 0 1 1	.61	1	.46
	17	0 1 0 0 0 0 1 1	.91	0	.75
	18	0 1 1 1 0 1 1 1	.00	0	.02
	19	1 1 0 1 0 1 1 1	.12	0	.07
	20	0 1 1 1 0 1 1 1	.00	0	.05

RSM results for Student S

KS	Ideal patterns	attribute pattern	post prob
19	0 1 1 0 0 1 1 1 0 0 0 0 1 1 1 1 0 0 0	1 1 1 0 1 0 1 1	.333
15	1 1 0 0 1 1 1 1 0 0 0 1 1 1 1 1 0 0 0	1 1 1 0 1 1 1 1	.209
17	1 1 0 0 1 1 1 0 0 0 1 0 0 1 0 1 0 0 0	1 1 0 1 1 0 1 1	.122
5	1 1 0 0 1 1 1 1 0 0 1 0 0 1 0 1 0 1 0	1 1 0 1 1 1 1 1	.117
40	0 0 0 0 1 1 1 1 0 0 0 0 1 1 1 1 0 0 0	1 1 1 0 0 1 1 1	.072
16	1 1 0 0 1 1 1 1 0 0 0 0 0 1 0 1 0 0 0	1 1 0 0 1 1 1 1	.056

FIGURE 9.5
The Q matrix for Method A in a fraction subtraction test, rule space results for Student S, S's observed item scores, and estimated item scores W_j RSM pseudotrue score τ.

Property 9.2: If attribute mastery probabilities for K attributes are given and denoted by $A_k = (p_{a1}, ..., p_{ak}, ..., p_{aK})$, and an $(K \times N)$–incidence matrix $\mathbf{Q}$ is also given, then, parallel to the case when A_k is a binary vector, we can create the matrix $\mathbf{Q}'$ by replacing "0" by "b" in the $\mathbf{Q}$ matrix. And, performing the element-wise multiplication of all the columns in $\mathbf{Q}'$ with A_k, with the same rule applied to the binary attribute vector, the rule in Equation (9.4.1),

$$p_k*1 = 1*p_k = 1, \quad p_k*0 = 0*p_k = 0, \quad p_k*b = b*0 = b, \quad 1*1 = 1 \qquad (9.20)$$

and we get the matrix $\mathbf{Q}'$. In $\mathbf{Q}'$, $q_{kj} = p_{ak}$ for when item j involves attribute Ak, and $q_{kj} = b$ when item j does not involve attribute A_k. From $\mathbf{Q}'$, we estimate item difficulties from a given attribute mastery vectors by multiplying pak for item j.

$$l_j = \prod p_{ak}$$

$$p_{ak} \neq b \text{ for item } j \tag{9.21}$$

Comparison of the Means of the Observed Score X and the Estimated Item Difficulties From Attribute Mastery Probabilities

In this section, we explore the relationship between the observed score X and the estimated item difficulties from attribute mastery probabilities. Figure 9.6 shows an example of such a relationship obtained from the SAT I Verbal test, Sentence Completion Section. The proportion correct values of 19 items are computed from a sample of N = 5,000. The second column is the proportion correct values computed from observed scores X. The third column shows the attribute involvement to each item, and the fourth column shows the operation described in Equation (9.21) and Properties 9.1 and 9.2.

Predicting item difficulties from the means of attribute mastery probabilities

Item No.	item difficulty	attributes involved in item	product of attribute mastery probabilities=predicted difficulty	predicted difficulties
1	0.95	2, 6, 9	.98x.99x.96	0.95
2	0.85	4, 7, 9, 10, 11	.94x.97x.98x.96x.94	0.81
3	0.81	2, 7, 10, 16	.98x.97x.96x.87	0.79
4	0.96	6, 7	.99x.97	0.98
5	0.52	4, 6, 15,17,18, 20, 23	.94x.99x.94x.81x.91x.84x.80	0.43
6	0.57	2, 3, 4, 7, 9, 16, 18, 20,	.98x.83x.94x.97x.98x.87x.91x.84	0.48
7	0.34	2,6,13,14,17	.98x.99x.57x.81x.81	0.36
8	0.2	2,3,4,8,11,13,14	.98x.83x.94x.77x.94x.57x81	0.26
9	0.05	1,3,4,5,6,8,9,11,16,21,22,23	.45x.83x.94x.74x.99x.77x.98x.94x.87x.75x.65x.80	0.06
10	0.6	2, 3, 4, 7, 19	.98x.83x.94x.97x.82	0.61
11	0.77	6, 15, 18, 19	.99x.94x91x.82	0.69
12	0.79	6, 7,19	.99x.97x.82	0.79
13	0.46	2,3,5,11,15,16	.98x.83x.74x.94x.94x.87	0.46
14	0.52	3,7,9,10,11,12	.83x.97x.98x.96x.94x.75	0.53
15	0.21	1,6,19,21	.45x.99x.82x.75	0.27
16	0.43	6,13,18,19	.99x.57x.91x.82	0.42
17	0.83	7,11,18	.97x.94x.91	0.83
18	0.28	3,4,7,9,11,15,18,20,22	.83x.94x.97x.98x.94x.94x.91x.84x.65	0.33
19	0.27	1,7,15,17,20	.45x.97x.94x.81x.84	0.28

FIGURE 9.6
Comparison of the observed item score means and the estimated item difficulties obtained from attribute mastery probabilities in a sentence completion test in a large-scale verbal test.

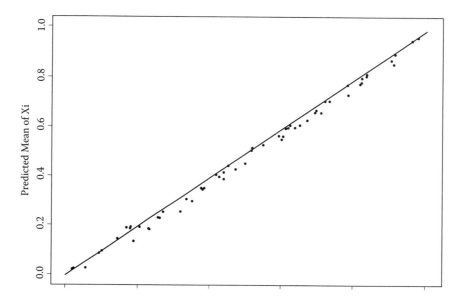

FIGURE 9.7
Comparison of the observed item score means and the estimated item difficulties obtained from attribute mastery probabilities in a SAT Mathematics test.

The last column shows the multiplication results obtained from the fourth column. Comparing the values in the last column and those in the second column reveals strikingly similar values of item difficulties.

A similar relationship is seen in the 60-item SAT Mathematics test. Figure 9.7 is the scatterplot of the two variables, with the proportion correct computed from observed scores X and the estimated item difficulties from the attribute mastery probabilities. The estimated difficulties are slightly less than actual item difficulties, but they fit extremely well within the line of assuming the equal values.

Can We Estimate Attribute Mastery Probabilities From Pseudotrue Scores?

The converse of Property 9.1 is not true. If item j has an observed score of 1, then the assumption of the rule space method requires that every attribute involved in item j must be used correctly; however, if the score of item j is 0, then there are many different ways to get the score of 0. If item j involves K attributes, then the number of ways to get the score of 0 will be $\binom{k}{k-1} + \binom{k}{k-2} + \cdots \binom{k}{1} + \binom{k}{0}$ ways (Tatsuoka, 1991). We do not have enough and sufficient conditions to determine attribute mastery probability of item j even if the difficulty of j, regardless of the observed or the true score of j, is known.

9.5   Nonparametric Attribute Characteristic Curves (ACCs)

Nonparametric Regression

Because a rule space analysis transforms item response data to attribute mastery probability data, test takers' responses collected from several forms of parallel tests having different sets of items can be merged in a single dataset as long as we use the same set of attributes across parallel forms of tests. This property is used in an analysis of TIMSS data (Tatsuoka, Corter, & Tatsuoka, 2004). We define a curve by expressing the conditional attribute mastery probability on a given parameter q or total scores by using a cubic spline smoothing function, and call it an *attribute characteristic curve* (Eubank, 1988; Tatsuoka, Birenbaum, Lewis, & Sheehan, 1993).

The ACCs shown in Figure 9.8 are estimated from the attribute mastery probabilities estimated from a sample of 10,000 in the Test of English for International Communication (TOEIC). For TOEIC attributes, for example, Attribute 23, *the ability to remember recent word matches when the relevant sections of text are longer*, is a very easy skill throughout the 800 scale scores. Attribute 20 (PR26), *the ability to process longer amounts of relevant text with a high information load*, is also an easy skill for all levels of scale scores; however, Attribute 17 (N12*N16), *the ability to process longer amounts of relevant text when it contains low frequency vocabulary*, is very difficult, so that students at a higher scale have the probability of success only below .7. Attributes 14 (TE4*PR15) and 9(PR21) have curves with steeper slopes than the remaining attributes. These skills are harder for lower scale score levels but easier for higher scale levels Attributes 17(N12*N16), Attribute 14(TE4*PR15) and Attribute 15(N13*PR27) are the interaction of two attributes. (Buck, Tatsuoka, & Kostin, 1997).

Use of ACCs for Investigating the Stability of Attributes

Two forms of the 60-item SAT I Mathematics test are analyzed, and the stability of using 17 attributes is tested by comparing the two sets of ACCs. These ACCs are obtained by fitting the attribute mastery probabilities to cubic spline smoothing functions (Tatsuoka, 1995). Figure 9.9 shows the results. The ACCs in the panels of the left column in the figure are from Form QQQ (N = 5,000), and those in the right column are from Form QQQR (N = 5,000) in the SAT Mathematics tests. Each ACC is wrapped by the 95% confidence interval obtained by the boothtrap method. Most ACCs have very narrow bands, especially the attributes *arithmetic, intermediate algebra, elementary algebra, geometry and analytic geometry, application of knowledge, reasoning and logical thinking,* and *working with figures*, which also have identical ACCs; however, the attribute *mathematical insight* has wider confidence intervals, and the ACCs from the

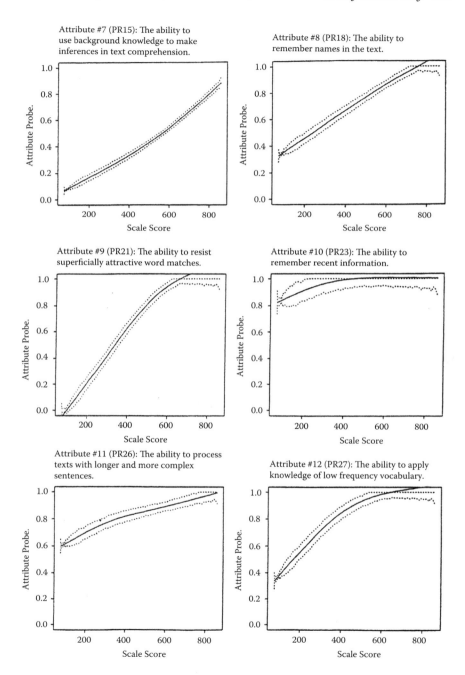

FIGURE 9.8
Attribute characteristic curves in the Test of English for International Communication.

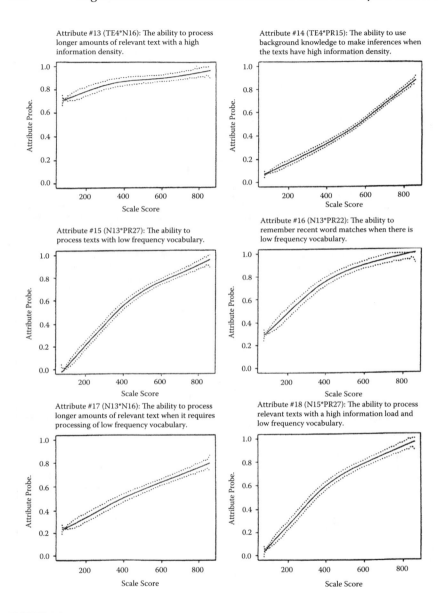

Attribute #13 (TE4*N16): The ability to process longer amounts of relevant text with a high information density.

Attribute #14 (TE4*PR15): The ability to use background knowledge to make inferences when the texts have high information density.

Attribute #15 (N13*PR27): The ability to process texts with low frequency vocabulary.

Attribute #16 (N13*PR22): The ability to remember recent word matches when there is low frequency vocabulary.

Attribute #17 (N13*N16): The ability to process longer amounts of relevant text when it requires processing of low frequency vocabulary.

Attribute #18 (N15*PR27): The ability to process relevant texts with a high information load and low frequency vocabulary.

FIGURE 9.8
(Continued)

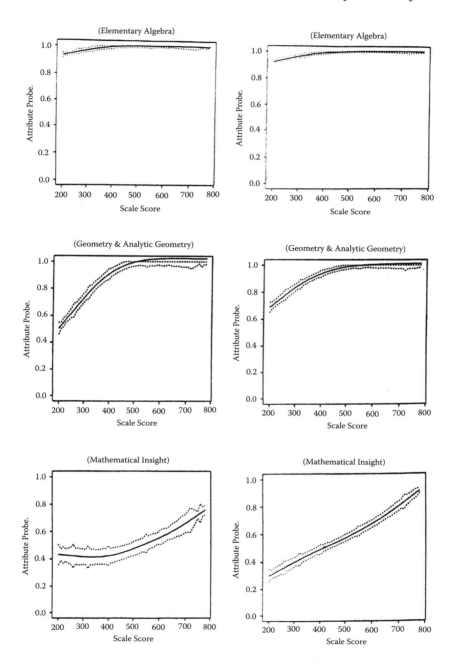

FIGURE 9.9

Comparison of attribute characteristic curves for the attributes estimated from two parallel forms of SAT Mathematics tests.

A2   (Elementary Algebra):
Can work with variable (addition and subtraction only), linear equations, linear algebraic expressions, signed-numbers, absolute values, irrational numbers such as 3.

A4   (Geometry and Analytic Geometry):
Can work with perimeter, area and volume for triangles, circles, rectangles, and other geometric objects. In analytic geometry, can work with points, lines, and their expressions in terms of a coordinate system.

A6   (Mathematical Insight):
Can reject the "wrong structure" which is given, and find a new one. The new structure is a solvable form. When two or more strategies exist, one can choose a better, simpler or the quickest strategy. When two or more rules, properties, theorems are available, can choose a better, simpler, or the quickest one. Simple computations or operations of the numbers are not included.

A7   (Application of Knowledge):
Can recall and interpret knowledge about the basic concepts and properties in arithmetic, elementary algebra, advanced algebra, geometry, and analytic geometry. Can perform computations in arithmetic (ratio, powers), geometry, signed-numbers, absolute values, median, and mode.

A9   (Reasoning and Logical Thinking):
Can reason from cause to effect, make judgement on "number sense," identify and understand necessary and sufficient conditions, and apply them appropriately to solve problems, check that the solutions hold true in the general case as opposed to simply a specific case. Spatial reasoning skills.

A11   (Working With Figures, Tables, and Graphs):
Can comprehend tables, figures, and graphs. In the statement of the problem, the student can relate the geometric terms with figures, graphs, and charts. Can generate figures for using external representation to facilitate problem-solving activities.

FIGURE 9.10
A short list of six prime attributes for a large scale mathematics test.

two forms have different shapes. There are two reasons why these ACCs have different shapes: Either (a) these attributes are difficult to code consistently, and/or (b) these attributes need to be improved and redefined. Because SAT items were developed in the 1980s and early 1990s without considering cognitive thinking skills, it would be difficult to focus narrowly on these thinking skills and obtain consistent coding across the different forms of such tests. Figure 9.10 lists the six attributes of 17 attributes used in Figure 9.9.

The list of attributes in the original study includes interaction attributes, such as A_6A_{10} or A_9A_{10}, which are combinations of two or three attributes. The probabilities of getting the interaction attributes correct will be the product of the mastery probabilities of single attributes such as A_9, A_{10}, or A_6. Table 9.1 gives the norm table of the SAT Mathematics test. The

TABLE 9.1

Norm Table of Attributes Performance on the Items in a Large-Scale Mathematics Test, Form ZZZ

Scale Attributes	Scores (200–800)													
	200	250	300	350	400	450	500	550	600	650	700	750	800	Mean
Elementary algebra	.86	.90	.93	.95	.97	.98	.99	.99	.99	.99	.99	.99	.99	12.52
Straight translation	.85	.88	.92	.94	.96	.98	.99	.99	.99	.99	.99	.99	.99	12.46
Arithmetic	.83	.86	.88	.91	.93	.95	.97	.98	.99	.99	.99	.99	.99	12.26
Figure, table	.72	.77	.83	.88	.92	.95	.97	.99	.99	.99	.99	.99	.99	11.98
Apply knowledge	.61	.70	.78	.85	.90	.95	.98	.99	.99	.99	.99	.99	.99	11.71
Geometry	.59	.68	.76	.83	.89	.94	.97	.99	.99	.99	.99	.99	.99	11.60
Apply rules	.68	.73	.79	.83	.87	.90	.93	.96	.97	.99	.99	.99	.99	11.62
Test-taking skills	.65	.72	.79	.84	.88	.92	.94	.95	.96	.97	.97	.98	.99	11.56
Complex problem	.58	.65	.72	.78	.84	.89	.93	.96	.99	.99	.99	.99	.99	11.30
Management	.70	.71	.73	.75	.78	.82	.86	.90	.94	.97	.99	.99	.99	11.13
Reasoning	.50	.56	.63	.69	.75	.81	.87	.92	.95	.98	.99	.99	.99	10.63
Open-ended	.41	.49	.57	.64	.71	.77	.81	.85	.88	.91	.95	.98	.99	9.96
Intermediate algebra	.42	.47	.53	.58	.63	.68	.73	.79	.84	.90	.95	.99	.99	9.50
Problem search	.39	.44	.49	.53	.58	.63	.68	.73	.79	.86	.92	.98	.99	9.01
Logical reading	.42	.46	.50	.53	.57	.61	.66	.71	.78	.84	.91	.97	.99	8.95
Mathematical insight	.25	.30	.36	.41	.45	.50	.55	.60	.66	.72	.79	.87	.99	7.45
Translate, model	.09	.13	.18	.22	.26	.32	.37	.43	.50	.57	.66	.76	.86	5.35

interaction attributes can be added to the norm table by multiplying appropriate entries of the table at any level. For example, if an admissions office would like to select National Merit Scholars among high-ability students, and would like to select somebody who is strong in reasoning skills and innovative thinking skills such as A_6, then it can make a supplementary norm table for the interaction attribute $A_9 * A_6$: At scale of 650 we get $A_9 * A_6 = .70$; at 700, $A_9 * A_6 = .78$; at 750, $A_9 * A_6 = .86$, and at 800, $A_9 * A_6 = .98$.

9.6 Nonparametric Item Response Curves

The Norm Table of Attributes Over Scale Scores of a Large-Scale Mathematics Assessment

Because ACC is computed by estimating conditional expectations on the scale score, one can rewrite these curves into a norm table. The following Table 9.1 is obtained from the SAT Mathematics test, Form QQQ. The entries in the table are average conditional probabilities at SAT scale score levels, and are obtained from ACCs. The order of attributes is sorted by the mean of attribute probabilities given at the far-right column, so that the most difficult attribute is located at the bottom and the easiest attribute is located at the top. The attribute *translating word expressions into algebraic equations and/or arithmetic formulas* is the most difficult followed by *mathematical insight*. As we have expected, content attributes except for *intermediate algebra* are pretty easy. *Straightforward translation of word expressions, application of knowledge,* and *application of rules for solving equations* are also easy attributes.

If we consider a student whose scale score is 500, we can find this student's expected performances on the 17 attributes by looking at the column for 500.

Estimating Item Difficulties From Attribute Mastery Probabilities

One of the assumptions for the rule space methodology is that for any item, one must apply all attributes involved in the item correctly. If item j has attributes A1, A2, and A3 required in answering item j, and they have mastery probability of p1, p2, and p3, then we have the compound binomial distribution of $\phi = (p_k + q_k)^3$, and thus the following rule:

> The score of 1 for item j: If and only if A1 = A2 = A3 = 1 and its probability is $p_1 p_2 p_3$.

> The score of 0 for item j: A1 = A2 = 1, A3 = 0;
> A1 = 0, A2 = A3 = 1;
> A1 = A3 = 1, A2 = 0;
> A1 = 1, A2 = A3 = 0;
> A2 = 1, A1 = A3 = 0; and
> A3 = 1, A1 = A2 = 0,

and the probability of getting the score of zero is $1 - p_1 p_2 p_3$.

Property 9.3: The conditional probability of answering item j correctly at a given score level can be estimated from the norm table (Table 9.1) by multiplying the expected attribute mastery probabilities of the attributes involved in item j.

Estimation of Item Response Curves From Attribute Characteristic Curves

Table 9.2 gives a partial list of the attributes involved in the items of the SAT Mathematics test, and Figure 9.1 has six small panels in which two item characteristic curves are drawn: One is the item response curve obtained from the two-parameter logistic model, and the other is a non-parametric item characteristic curve obtained from the attribute mastery probabilities by applying Property 9.3 Items 8, 15, 45, 54, 56, and 57 have

TABLE 9.2

The Estimated Item Parameters From the Two-Parameter Logistic Model, Some Large-Scale Mathematics Test, Form ZZZ (N = 5,000)

Items Selected	A Values	B Values	Attribute Involvement
8	1.0688	−0.2588	2 8 12
15	1.0131	0.4020	1 2 7 9 13 16 17
45	0.7018	−0.2440	1 6 9 10 13 14 16 17 18 19
54	0.7520	−0.7232	16 17
57	0.7090	0.7488	2 4 7 8 11 13
58	0.5055	0.7784	2 7 9 10 12 13 14 19

been chosen to show the contrast of the two curves. The estimated item parameters of these six items are as follows.

The item response curves are defined over the variable q, whose mean is zero and standard deviation is 1, and the nonparametric item characteristic curves obtained from the expected conditional attribute mastery probabilities in Table 9.1 have been defined over the SAT scale scores of 200 to 800. Table 9.3 provides the equivalent values between the IRT q and the SAT scale scores.

Now we are ready to apply Property 9.3 and plot the nonparametric item characteristic curves and item response curves of a two-parameter logistic model using a and b values obtained from BILOG (1995). Figure 9.11 shows the results of plotting. Items 15, 45, and 8 have parametric logistic curves below the nonparametric curves, whereas item 57 has the nonparametric curves consistently below the parametric logistic curves. Item 58 is the most difficult item among six items, followed by item 57. Item 45 has item difficulty of −.2440, but the number of attributes involved in this item is the largest, 10 attributes. Item

TABLE 9.3

Equivalent Scale Between IRT θ and Some Large-Scale Test Scale Scores

1	200	−4
	201–250	(−3.999 −2.330)
2	260–300	(−2.32 −1.570)
	310–350	(−1.560 −1.030)
3	360–400	(−1.020 −0.550)
	410–450	(−0.540 −0.180)
4	460–500	(−0.170 0.170)
	510–550	(0.180 0.580)
6	560–600	(0.590 0.919)
	610–650	(0.920 1.284)
7	660–700	(1.286 1.702)
	710–750	(1.710 2.480)
8	760–800	(2.500 4.000)

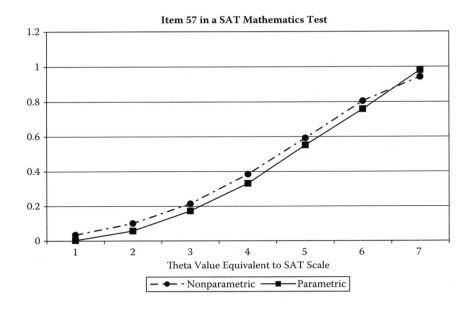

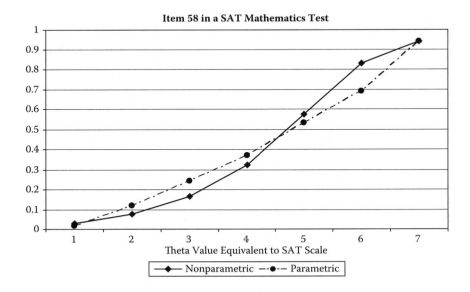

FIGURE 9.11

Nonparametric item characteristic curves estimated from attribute mastery probabilities and two-parameter logistic curves plotted on the common scale of IRT θ and SAT scale scores given in Table 9.3.

TABLE 9.4

A List of Attribute Involvement in SAT Mathematics, ZZZ Form

Item	Attributes Involvement	Item	Attributes Involvement
1	13 17	26	1 2 14
2	1 2 7 9 12	27	2 8 14
3	2 8 12 13	28	4 7 11 41
4	1 7 14 16	29	3 7 8 9 14 16
5	4 7 11	30	4 9 11 14
6	1 13 14 16 17	...	
7	2 17	...	
8	3 7 9 13 16	40	1 2 5 7 9 10 13 14 16 19
9	2 4 7 11 13	41	1 15 17
10	4 7 9 11 13 17	42	1 5 7 15
11	2 3 8	43	2 8 15 16 17
12	1 7 9 13 16	44	7 15
13	4 7 10 11 13	45	2 4 7 9 11 15
14	1 7 13 17	...	
15	2 3 6 8 9	...	
16	1 7 9 16 17	54	1 16 17
17	1 2 7 8 13 16 17	55	3 5 9 11 16
18	1 5 7 13 14 16	56	3 7 8 9 16
19	2 4 7 8 9 11 13	57	2 4 7 8 11 13
20	2 5 7 8 14 16	58	2 7 9 10 12 13 14 19
21	1 2 4 7 11 13 16	59	1 2 8 9 12 13 14 16 17
22	2 3 8 9 17	...	

58 is much harder than item 45, but involves a lesser number of attributes, eight. It may be necessary to check the attribute involvement in item 45.

9.7 Test–Retest Reliability

Test–Retest Reliability

One of the methods to measure the reliability of attribute mastery probabilities is to investigate the test–retest reliability of attribute mastery probabilities. The fraction tests were carefully constructed so that the test–retest is perfectly parallel with respect to the attribute level. *Perfectly parallel* means their underlying constructs were cognitively parallel. The following work is based on Tatsuoka and Tatsuoka (2005).

Each parallel pair of items in two sets of fraction tests (Klein, Birenbaum, Standiford, & Tatsuoka, 1981; Tatsuoka, 1985) requires the exactly identical set of processing tasks. Their mean values of items and attributes between the test and retest of fraction subtraction problems are not statistically different with $p < 0.001$ and are given in Table 9.5.

TABLE 9.5

Mean Responses of 20 Items for Two Subtests for Two Parallel Subtests of a Fraction Test

Item	Mean 1	Mean 2	Item	Mean 1	Mean 2	Attributes	Mean 1	Mean 2
1	.50	.45	11	.49	.45	1	.44	.49
2	.55	.51	12	.71	.67	2	.77	.73
3	.50	.48	13	.30	.29	3	.71	.69
4	.55	.57	14	.71	.70	4	.67	.60
5	.56	.48	15	.44	.43	5	.55	.52
6	.79	.77	16	.68	.67	6	.50	.47
7	.39	.40	17	.46	.43	7	.76	.71
8	.76	.81	18	.46	.46			
9	.64	.57	19	.31	.32			
10	.39	.38	20	.41	.37			

Note: Total score of test 1 is 10.62 and of test 2 is 10.23.

TABLE 9.6

Test–Retest Reliability for Two Parallel Items and Attributes, and Contingency Table of Item Scores for Two Parallel Items

Items	Correlation	Attribute Probabilities	Correlation	Classification of Item Scores (1 1)	(0 0)	(1 0)	(0 1)
(1, 21)	.63	(pa1, pb1)	.80	218	218	67	33
(2, 22)	.76	(pa2, pb2)	.82	208	263	46	19
(3, 23)	.72	(pa3, pb3)	.78	227	233	43	33
(4. 24)	.67	(pa4, pb4)	.80	202	245	38	51
(5, 25)	.44	(pa5, pb5)	.83	172	211	102	51
(6, 26)	.66	(pa6, pb6)	.84	84	391	35	26
(7, 27)	.73	(pa7, pb7)	.82	287	179	35	35
(8, 28)	.62			83	380	21	52
(9, 29)	.58			153	275	72	36
(10, 30)	.67			291	162	43	40
(11, 31)	.78			259	217	37	23
(12, 32)	.60			111	234	57	32
(13, 33)	.60			337	110	48	41
(14, 34)	.68			116	350	37	33
(15, 35)	.78			269	209	33	25
(16, 36)	.64			127	325	48	36
(17, 37)	.73			271	195	37	33
(18, 38)	.70			240	215	36	45
(19, 39)	.76			340	141	25	30
(20, 40)	.76			120	175	35	206

Note: Correlation of test–retest test scores is .99.

Estimates of the proportions (i.e., mean) of correct responses for the items and estimates of the proportion of mastery of each of the seven attributes are summarized in Table 9.5. The mean values across the pairs of parallel items are almost identical, and moreover, the mean values of seven attribute probabilities are also almost identical. The means of total scores from the two tests are 10.62 and 10.23, respectively. Table 9.6 summarizes the correlation values of item scores and the attribute mastery probabilities. It is interesting to note that the correlation values of item scores are low as compared with the correlation values of the total scores of the two parallel tests. Test–retest reliability of the total scores is extremely high at .99, whereas most items have test–retest reliability of 0.60 to 0.80. By looking into the 2 × 2 cross tabulation of item scores, one can find that the numbers in the cells (1, 0) and (0, 1) can be somewhat large (although not as large in general as for cells (1,1) or (0,0)). This implies that the reliability of total scores may not comparably measure the stability of underlying cognitive performance on a test item level. When we compute the test–retest correlation of seven attributes and get the values of .80, .82, .78, 80, .83, .84, and .82, respectively, we see that these values are higher than the correlation values of the 20 items. This may be due to each attribute being involved in several items.

10

Validation of Attributes, a Q Matrix Coded by the Involvement of Attributes to Items and a Test

The selection and identification of attributes in a test for RSM analyses are extremely important, and we have spent a great deal of time on the development of the procedure. The procedure starts with studying students' protocols, documenting interviews on how students solve given problems, creating self-protocols by several experts and researchers with various backgrounds, and finally studying the information in detail. We usually team up with domain experts, cognitive psychologists and scientists, and experienced educators, because it is necessary to develop a list of attributes that reflects educational and cognitive perspectives, and represents a majority of students' thinking skills and knowledge, which underlie the performance on a given problem. Interestingly, RSM analyses can be effectively used for the selection, identification, refinement, and validation of attributes. This chapter introduces the RSM validation procedure from different angles by using various examples, and summarizes it in a list.

In the RSM framework, the necessary knowledge states for classification are automatically generated by applying Boolean algebra to a Q matrix. They are logically derived knowledge states from a given Q matrix and not listed by experienced teachers like the BUGGY system. The knowledge states called or labeled *bugs* or *erroneous rules of operations*, which are discussed in cognitive science in the context of expert systems or "Buggy systems," were initially discovered by humans without the help of statistical computations (Brown & Burton, 1978; Tatsuoka, 1983b); therefore, the validation procedures in RSM include a validity study for the knowledge states that capture some numbers of students, and validation of RSM classification results. The validation of RSM classification results is given in Section 10.4 by using the erroneous rules of operations in the signed-number problems that are found by expert teachers in their classrooms. The nature of this validation is easy, because one can use simulation data with known, validated knowledge states.

The RSM validation procedure has three phases: validation of attributes; validation of knowledge states, or, equivalently, validation of a Q matrix, and validation of classification results. They are described in Sections 10.1 through 10.6. The last section discusses the construct validity of a test that is based on the thesis work done by Dogan (2006).

10.1   Selection of Attributes

If an item displays poor fit with its estimated item characteristic curve in Figure 9.11, then the implication is that the item and the hypothesized attributes that are involved in it need further attention; however, it is a challenge to pinpoint the cause of the misfit to the estimated item characteristic curve. Possible reasons involve an omission of one or more attributes in our list of attributes, and/or an omission of attributes involved in the item during coding a Q matrix, or coding an attribute that is not required; therefore, it is important that we begin with the right attributes with right coding. Nevertheless, Im (2007) investigated the effect of RSM classification results when miscoding one or two attributes in a Q matrix and found that RSM classification is robust in her simulation study.

One of the best ways to validate and improve the list of attributes is to study protocols and interview students. In addition to study protocols, RSM analysis results can be used to search for new attributes not included in the original list of attributes. Buck and Tatsuoka (1998) searched attributes missed by the first round of RSM analysis by sorting out the non-classified response patterns and found a number of similar patterns that were caused by the absence of a common attribute. Because RSM does not force everybody in a sample to be classified into one of the knowledge states like latent classes models do, studying unclassified subjects often provides useful information on unused attributes.

Regressing attributes in a Q matrix onto item difficulties appeals to our common sense in order to check how well a list of our attributes can explain the variance of item difficulties. But it may not be one of the best methods for the selection of attributes, because the sample size, the number of items, is usually extremely small. We discuss a method using a tree regression with Tukey's Jackknife procedure in the section 10.3.

10.2   Validation of a Q Matrix

Formulating Hypotheses for Testing

Before RSM classification procedures will be performed on observed response patterns, we have to identify and select a set of attributes in a domain and to represent them in an item attribute matrix called an *incidence matrix Q*. In other words, domain experts first generate their hypotheses about the underlying cognitive processing skills and knowledge required for correctly answering test items. Second, the experts' hypotheses should be tested by applying various statistical techniques; therefore, testing of hypotheses will be done in the second stage.

How Well Can a Q Matrix Explain Students' Knowledge States?

Plotting the generated knowledge states from a given Q matrix in the rule space can distinguish high-quality attributes and a Q matrix created by experts from that created by novices. The y-coordinate of the rule space consists of an index measuring unusualness of response patterns compared with the average, ordinary, and majority of the response patterns in a sample. Response patterns far apart from the x-coordinate of IRT q are judged as unusual patterns. As can be seen in Figure 10.1a and Figure 10.1b, novices produced knowledge states that would not have occurred in the population, whereas expert teachers produced knowledge states often seen in their classrooms. The classification results based on

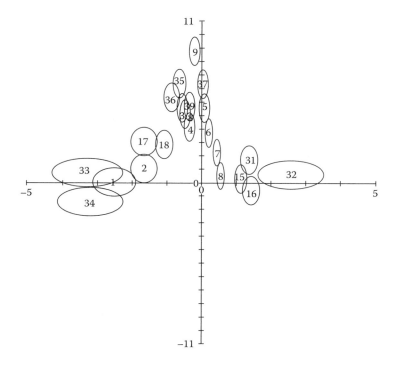

FIGURE 10.1a
Knowledge states generated from a Q matrix developed by a novice.

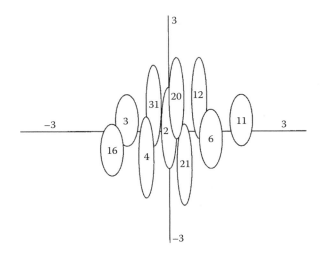

FIGURE 10.1b
Knowledge states generated from a Q matrix developed by an expert teacher.

the expert teachers' Q matrix indicated that the predetermined knowledge states from the Q matrix could explain test takers' underlying cognitive processes and knowledge used in correctly answering the items in a test.

How Well Can a Q Matrix Explain Item Difficulties?

The Q matrix displays item-level information (i.e., which attributes are involved in which items). Additional item-level information such as item difficulties can also be incorporated with the Q matrix. Additionally, we test how well the variance of the item difficulties can be explained by attribute involvement using multiple regression techniques. It is recommended that more than one hypothesized Q matrix be created involving attributes determined by investigating protocols by students, and solutions by domain experts and coders. The reliability of the Q-matrix coding should be examined before investigating the strength of the relationship between the Q matrix and the item difficulties. After the reliabilities are examined, a series of multiple regression analyses can be conducted, which treat the item difficulties as the dependent variable and the entries of the Q matrix as the independent variable. The basic idea behind this approach is that the difficulty level of a given item should be a function of the cognitive demands that it poses to the examinee; therefore, a valid Q matrix should explain a significant portion of the variance in item difficulties. If this can be proved, results of such regression analyses can be used as a source of validation for the given Q matrix.

TABLE 10.1

Model Summary of TIMSS: 164 Items Coded by 27 Attributes

Multiple R	.896	ANOVA F value	20.131
R^2	.802	Significance	< .0001
Adjusted R^2	.762		
Standard of the estimate	.093		

Table 10.1 is the summary results of a multiple regression analysis using 164 item proportion correct values obtained from 150,000 TIMSS data as a dependent variable and 27 attributes as dependent variables introduced in Tatsuoka, Corter, and Tatsuoka (2004). The squared R is .802, and the adjusted R square is .762. The high value of R squared suggests the attributes are good enough to proceed to a rule space analysis.

10.3 Selection of a Smaller Number of Attributes From a Larger Number of Attributes

Selection and identification of attributes are sometimes troublesome because domain experts may come up with a huge number of attributes for a given test. A multiple regression analysis requires the number of items to be larger than the number of attributes. In such a case, a regression tree analysis can be used for attribute selection. The regression tree method has been used often for variable selection problems, biostatistics, and drug and pharmaceutical research in chemistry.

Tree Regression Method for Attribute Selection

If our goal is to select attributes, then we should avoid using a stepwise forward or backward regression analysis, because these algorithms do not select the optimal set of attributes. The same argument will be applicable to the regression tree method. Venables and Riply (1994) stated that "almost all current tree construction methods, including those in S, use a one-step look ahead. That is, they choose the next split in an optimal way, without attempting to optimize the performance of the whole tree" (p. 332). The algorithms that can select the absolute optimal set of variables from a larger pool of variables may be very difficult and may need perform Tukey's jack-knife estimation procedure (Mosteller & Tukey, 1977); therefore, it is dangerous to rely on a single optimization technique for attribute selection. Instead, we have to use several different tools together. Many statisticians use the bootstrapping approach together with the regression tree method. It is time-consuming to generate 100 bootstrapping datasets, but this will give us the best solution that is the closest to the true model. One must be aware of the weakness in the current optimization algorithms available in model selection techniques. We do not want to select a set of attributes knowing that the statistical tools we use do not select the optimal set of attributes. We have to use several rules together for the attribute selection problem.

In recent years, a regression tree method (Breiman, Friedman, Olson, & Stone, 1984) has attracted researchers in various fields because tree-based models express knowledge and aid decision making in such a way that they encapsulate and structure the knowledge of experts to be communicable to others. The variables in a tree regression are binary: splitting continuous and/ or categorical variables. Constructing a tree may be seen as a type of variable selection. The interactions between variables are handled automatically, determining which variables are to be divided and how the split is to be achieved. The end point of a tree is a partition of the space in which all observations will be classified. The task is to find a tree that describes it succinctly.

A Large-Scale Writing Assessment

A tree regression method is used for selecting variables in the SAT Verbal writing test. The SAT Verbal writing dataset has 60 items, and each item was coded by 100-attribute involvement. The SPLUS version of CART was run 100 times on 100 bootstrap samples of the 60 items. CART only allows a binary split, so continuous variables are converted to a binary value by $x_j >$ t for 1 and $x_j < $ t to 0. If the variables are binary, such as a Q matrix, then t can be set to .5 for CART. Figure 10.2 shows the result of the tree for the SAT Verbal writing test. The number in each oval is the predicted value of *equated delta*, which is the linearly transformed item p values with a mean of 10. The end points of the tree are 10 squares with the predicted delta values.

The terminal node 8.680 can be obtained by splitting attributes of A30, A35, A33, A40, A41, and A15. The numbers below the nodes express the sum of squared regression residuals, called *deviances*, and the number of items in each classification. The smaller the deviance values, the better the equated delta values will be predicted.

Venables and Riply (1994, p. 332) stated that almost all current tree construction methods use a one-step look ahead. That is, they choose the next split in an optimal way, without attempting to optimize the performance of the whole tree. This is necessary to avoid a combinatorial explosion over future choices.

For each node i, there is a probability distribution with the probability of p_{ik}, so that for each item assigned to a node and at each node, we have a random sample n_{ik} from the multinomial distribution specified by p_{ik}:

$$\prod_{\text{item } j} p(j) y_j = \prod_{\text{node } i} \prod_{\text{class } k} p_{ik}^{n_{jk}} \tag{10.1}$$

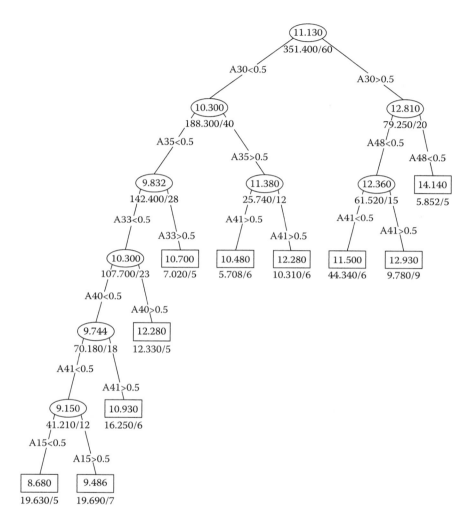

FIGURE 10.2
Output of the first Q matrix in the SAT Writing test (60 items with 101 attributes) from a regression tree program CART.

Deviance for the tree is defined as

$$D = \sum D_i, \qquad D_i = -2 \sum n_{ik} \log p_{ik} \tag{10.2}$$

where i is nodes and $\sum$ is sum over nodes.

When splitting node s to t and u, the reduction in deviance for the tree is

$$D_s - D_t - D_u = 2 \sum [n_{ik}\log(p_{ik}/p_{sk}) + n_{uk}\log(p_{uk}/p_{sk})] \qquad (10.3)$$

where $\sum$ is summed over k. We are replacing p_{ik}, p_{uk}, and p_{sk} by sample estimates,

$$p_{ik} = n_{ik}/n_i \qquad p_{uk} = n_{uk}/n_u, \qquad p_{sk} = (n_t p_{ik} + n_u p_{uk})/n_s = n_{sk}/n_s$$

so the reduction in deviance is given by

$$D_s - D_t - D_u = 2 \sum \{n_{tk}\log[n_{tk}n_s/n_{sk}n_t] + n_{uk}\log[n_{uk}n_s/n_{sk}n_u]\} \qquad (10.4)$$

The tree construction process takes the maximum reduction over all allowed splits of nodes and continues until the number of items at each node becomes small (say, 5 in this study).

Overall, the 100 trees were used to count the number of times each attribute was used to split a node. Output of the first Q matrix was given earlier in Figure 10.2. Attribute 30 split into two branches, and then Attributes 35 and 48 split in the two branches, respectively. These counts can be viewed as a measure of variable importance. Table 10.3 summarizes the numbers of appearances in 100 samples. Buck, Tutsuoka VanEssen, and Kostin

TABLE 10.3

Count of Attributes Used for Splitting a Node

Attributes	Count	Attributes	Count	Attributes	Count
1. A30	77	20. A27	17	39. A9	2
2. A103	71	21. A23	17	40. A45	2
3. A41	63	22. A104	17	41. A1	2
4. A35	41	23. A105	16	42. A72	1
5. A39	38	24. A64	13	43. A72	1
6. A33	37	25. A22	13	44. A44	1
7. A46	33	26. A5	11	45. A2	1
8. A48	31	27. A63	10		
9. A40	29	28. A21	10		
10. A16	29	29. A10	10		
11. A53	27	30. A78	8		
12. A29	27	31. A34	8		
13. A50	25	32. A28	7		
14. A24	25	33. A91	6		
15. A106	25	34. A8	5		
16. A32	21	35. A7	4		
17. A43	18	36. A62	4		
18. A15	18	37. A17	3		
19. A70	17	38. A14	3		

TABLE 10.4

Means, SDs, and Discrimination Powers for
SAT Verbal Writing Attributes

Variables	Means	Standard Diviation	Corr (Totals, Attributes)
Totals	19.57	6.12	
AT1	0.97	0.15	.20
AT2	0.99	0.08	.14
AT3	0.84	0.36	.14
AT4	0.73	0.43	−.10
AT5	0.99	0.02	.04
AT6	0.99	0.08	.11
AT7	0.98	0.12	.11
AT8	0.86	0.34	.45
AT9	0.84	0.36	.27
AT10	0.89	0.30	.19
AT11	0.64	0.47	.45
AT12	0.28	0.45	.10
AT13	0.63	0.48	.40
AT14	0.83	0.37	.04
AT15	0.85	0.35	.40
AT16	0.89	0.30	.20
AT17	0.92	0.26	.22
AT18	0.85	0.35	.31
AT19	0.93	0.24	.38
AT20	0.95	0.20	.30
AT21	0.68	0.46	.43
AT22	0.99	0.03	.04
AT23	0.38	0.48	.13
AT24	0.63	0.48	.29

Tatsuoka (2000) selected the highest 24 attributes, and performed the rule space analysis on a new Q matrix with the order of 60×24. Table 10.4 summarizes the mean and standard deviation of the selected attributes obtained from the rule space results.

In Table 10.4, attributes 1, 2, 5, 6, 7, and 22 have excessively high mean values, closer to .99, so they are deleted from the list of attributes. A multiple regression is performed to see how much the total score variance is explained by these attributes, and R^2 is found to be .86, which is satisfactory. Principal component analysis showed that Attribute 22 and 23 correlated highly; consequently, we deleted Attribute 22 from the final analysis after the domain experts agreed to do so. The linear multiple regression analysis result is summarized in Table 10.5. The R squared is .8624, and the adjusted R^2 is .8618, which is almost the same as R^2 because the sample size is a large number, N = 5,000. We have selected 22 attributes for the RSM final analysis (Buck et al., 2000).

TABLE 10.5

Regression Analysis for Total Scores as Dependent Variables and Attribute Mastery Patterns as Independent Variables

Dependent Variable: Total Scores, N = 5000
Independent variables: 22 Attribute Mastery Probabilities

Analysis fo Variance of Regression Equation: F Value = 1419.3 Prob. = 0.0001

R- square:	0.8624
Adjusted R- Square:	0.8618
R	0.7427

Use of Multiple Regression Analysis: Study of the Third International Mathematics and Science Study (TIMSS)

TIMSS 1999-study (Mullis, et al., 2000), conducted in the mid-1990s, and its database have been studied. The test consists of 8 booklets, with 163

TABLE 10.6

Summary of Multiple Regression Analyses for TIMSS Booklets 1, 3, 5, and 7[a]

	Booklet			
Content and Process Variables	**1**	**3**	**5**	**7**
R	.899	.944	.948	.841
R^2	.809	.891	.899	.708
Adjusted R^2	.805	.890	.898	.704
ANOVA p value	.0001	.0001	.0001	.0001
F	334.35	577.23	628.89	176.01
df1	14	16	16	15
df2	1117	1143	1146	1109
Classification rate with $D^2 < 4.5$	99.9%	99.9%	99.5%	99.2%

	Booklet			
Skill and Process Variables	**1**	**3**	**5**	**7**
R	.875	.931	.952	.894
R^2	.766	.867	.907	.900
Adjusted R^2	.762	.865	.905	.896
ANOVA p value	.0001	.0001	.0001	.0001
F	202.47	386.30	549.80	228.92
df1	18	19	20	19
df2	1131	1143	1146	1109
Classification rate with $D^2 < 4.5$	99.9%	99.9%	99.9%	99.9%

[a] The dependent variable is the total scores, and independent variables are the estimated attribute probabilities.

items in general mathematics, and was administered to eighth graders in 42 different countries. By analyzing students' work on the items and at the same time analyzing several protocols, researchers identified a set of attributes and coded a Q matrix. In order to validate the attributes and the Q matrix, several multiple regression analyses were performed (Corter & Tatsuoka, 2004; Tatsuoka et al., 2004). In the previous section, Table 10.1 showed or "demonstrated" the result of a multiple regression analysis on the item difficulties, and found 76% of the variance of item difficulties can be explained by the attributes we identified in our Q matrix.

After rule space analysis results are obtained, one can validate how well the attribute mastery probabilities are by regressing them onto the total scores, or estimated IRT q values. Table 10.6 summarized the results of the TIMSS study. The classification rates across booklets are 99% or above, and R^2 values are high; therefore, we concluded that our attributes used in the TIMSS study are the ones used by a majority of students.

10.4 Validation of the Rule Space Analysis Results

Using Students' Protocols or Interviews

Because the knowledge states are latent and mathematically derived, it is very difficult to confirm directly whether the examinees are classified into their true states. In several studies, the diagnosed results from the RS method were compared with protocols or students' interviews in fraction addition and subtraction problems (Shaw & Birenbaum, 1985; Shaw, Standitord, Klein & Tatsuoka, 1982; Tatsuoka, 1984a). Researchers found that the RSM method diagnoses examinees' true states well.

Experimental Approach

The second approach, *controlled remediation,* is introduced in Tatsuoka and Tatsuoka (1997). This study tried to determine empirically whether the RSM method for a sample would effectively classify examinees into their true states. Additionally, it tried to test whether diagnostic information would be useful and efficient for remediation. If a diagnosed result is correct, then carefully written remedial instruction should be able to remediate the examinees' diagnosed deficiencies. The results indicated again that the RSM method accurately diagnosed the examinees' true states.

The third approach used an experimental design approach. Gierl (1996) designed a protocol study of the verbal problems in the SAT Mathematics test. The cognitive model he used was the theory of information-processing skills. Twenty raters listened to the protocol tapes and rated their judgment as to how each examinee solved items. The results indicated that 95% of the raters' coding matched with the results of a rule space analysis.

The fourth study used a questionnaire that was given to examinees to identify the knowledge state they believe they have. The rule space results matched very well to the self-reported knowledge state (Shaw, 1986). Moreover, the teacher of the examinees who were unclassified interviewed them and found that quite a number of examinees confessed they had cheated on the test (Shaw, 1986). Possible benefits from the information obtained by the rule space analyses may be substantial. In this section, we will show evidence of how well and accurately RSM classifies Monte Carlo data and then introduce a *controlled remediation* approach.

Validation of RSM Classification Using Simulation Data and Real Data

A 40-item free-response test comprising four parallel subtests of 10 items each in signed-number subtraction problems was administered to students in a local junior high school and found 46 different knowledge states, which were identified by error analysis conducted by four experts (Birenbaum & Tatsuoka, 1982). Four knowledge states were randomly selected, and Monte Carlo data were generated by adding 1, 2, or 3 slips to their ideal item score patterns. The rule space coordinates of the signed-number test were computed, and these simulated response patterns were mapped into the rule space. Figure 10.3 shows that simulated responses that deviated by a few slips from their ideal item score patterns fell in the circles of their expected knowledge states (Tatsuoka, 1985).

Figure 10.4 shows the classification matrix of 20 knowledge states. Note that off-diagonal cells are 0's, and all simulated data from each knowledge state are classified into their original knowledge states. This shows that RSM classifies correctly.

Independently, Kim (1989) compared the rule space classification procedure with linear discriminant analysis and K's nearest method, and found that RSM and discriminant function produced the same classification results on simulated data, as long as the covariance matrices of knowledge states are nonsingular. Kim also found that the computational speed of the rule space classification was much faster than using the other two methods. Kim generated simulation data from a large-scale Illinois Placement Test by using 20 knowledge states selected from various rule space locations.

The other study, by Hayashi (2002), divided randomly a sample of 596 students into two groups. The Sample 1 students' responses to the fraction addition test were used to compute the nodes of a neural network, and the second sample was used to compare the results from the RSM and the tamed neural network. They were very close.

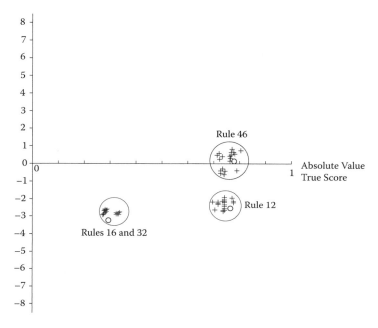

FIGURE 10.3
Four clusters of the response patterns deviated from the four ideal item score patterns of four erroneous rules (knowledge states) in a signed-numbered test.

KS (Rule)	Correct %	3	6	7	11	12	13	15	16	17	18	21	22	25	30	32	33	34	37	38	45	46
3	100	31	0	0	0	0	0	0	0	0	0	0	0	0	0	0	0	0	0	0	0	0
6	100	0	31	0	0	0	0	0	0	0	0	0	0	0	0	0	0	0	0	0	0	0
7	100	0	0	31	0	0	0	0	0	0	0	0	0	0	0	0	0	0	0	0	0	0
11	100	0	0	0	31	0	0	0	0	0	0	0	0	0	0	0	0	0	0	0	0	0
12	100	0	0	0	0	31	0	0	0	0	0	0	0	0	0	0	0	0	0	0	0	0
13	100	0	0	0	0	0	31	0	0	0	0	0	0	0	0	0	0	0	0	0	0	0
15	100	0	0	0	0	0	0	31	0	0	0	0	0	0	0	0	0	0	0	0	0	0
16	100	0	0	0	0	0	0	0	31	0	0	0	0	0	0	0	0	0	0	0	0	0
17	100	0	0	0	0	0	0	0	0	31	0	0	0	0	0	0	0	0	0	0	0	0
18	100	0	0	0	0	0	0	0	0	0	31	0	0	0	0	0	0	0	0	0	0	0
21	100	0	0	0	0	0	0	0	0	0	0	31	0	0	0	0	0	0	0	0	0	0
22	100	0	0	0	0	0	0	0	0	0	0	0	31	0	0	0	0	0	0	0	0	0
25	100	0	0	0	0	0	0	0	0	0	0	0	0	31	0	0	0	0	0	0	0	0
30	100	0	0	0	0	0	0	0	0	0	0	0	0	0	31	0	0	0	0	0	0	0
32	100	0	0	0	0	0	0	0	0	0	0	0	0	0	0	31	0	0	0	0	0	0
33	100	0	0	0	0	0	0	0	0	0	0	0	0	0	0	0	31	0	0	0	0	0
34	100	0	0	0	0	0	0	0	0	0	0	0	0	0	0	0	0	31	0	0	0	0
37	100	0	0	0	0	0	0	0	0	0	0	0	0	0	0	0	0	0	31	0	0	0
38	100	0	0	0	0	0	0	0	0	0	0	0	0	0	0	0	0	0	0	31	0	0
45	100	0	0	0	0	0	0	0	0	0	0	0	0	0	0	0	0	0	0	0	31	0
46	100	0	0	0	0	0	0	0	0	0	0	0	0	0	0	0	0	0	0	0	0	31

FIGURE 10.4
Use of Monte Carlo data to validate rule space classification.

10.5 Controlled Remediation: Cognitively Diagnostic Computerized Adaptive Testing and Remediation

The usefulness of cognitive diagnoses for remedial instruction was studied by Tatsuoka and Tatsuoka (1997). In their study, cognitive diagnoses were performed by an adaptive testing system developed on the PLATO system in the 1980s (the Computer-Based Educational Teaching System, developed at the University of Illinois). The adaptive testing algorithm in the RSM that was developed by Tatsuoka and her associates (Baillie & Tatsuoka, 1984; Tatsuoka, 1986) and that has been studied further (Yamada, 2008) was implemented on the system and connected to several instructional units aiming at removing students' diagnosed errors and teaching the correct knowledge and cognitive skills. The results of the study strongly indicate that knowing students' knowledge states prior to remediation is very effective, and that the rule space method can effectively diagnose students' knowledge states and can point out ways for remediating their errors quickly with minimum effort. It also found that the design of instructional units for remediation can be effectively guided by the rule space model, because the determination of all possible knowledge states in a domain of interest, given a Q matrix, is based on a partially ordered tree structure of knowledge states, which is equivalent to ideal item score patterns determined logically from the Q matrix.

The RSM was applied to 39 fraction addition problems and identified 33 knowledge states. Shaw et al. (1982) validated seven attributes by interviewing students. Comparing diagnosed results from the rule space analysis to protocol analyses is one way to validate whether or not the diagnosed results are really expressing the underlying cognitive processing and knowledge states required in solving the problems in the domain of interest.

Experimental Study: Controlled Remediation

An alternative approach to protocol analysis called *controlled remediation* is introduced in a paper by Tatsuoka and Tatsuoka (1979), and the results of this approach are replicated in two samples. Because knowledge states are latent, it is very difficult to confirm directly whether or not the students are classified into their true states. The controlled remediation approach tries to make indirect inferences about students' latent states from the remediated results. In other words, we diagnose students' knowledge states first, find out which cognitive attributes the student cannot do, and then remediate only the attributes diagnosed as not mastered. If the nonmastered attributes are remediated, then we expect the posttest results to indicate that these attributes are mastered. Because we assume that nonmastery attributes cannot be mastered without remediation, we make a conclusion that the rule space classification is reliable if the nonmastered attributes in the pretest are diagnosed as mastered in the posttest.

The whole series of controlled remediation programs was prepared on the PLATO system: the computer-adaptive pretest of fraction addition problems, the router to various instructional units based on the pretest results, the exercises after each instructional unit, and the adaptive post-test and retention test. The adaptive algorithm is different from the conventional adaptive testing procedure, such as the maximum information method (Lord, 1980), which measures the ability level θ defined in the IRT. The new algorithm was developed to diagnose students' knowledge states in a multidimensional rule space and includes the maximum information method as a subpart of the algorithm (Tatsuoka, 1986). In other words, the RSM adaptive algorithm is an extension of the maximum information method. Diagnosed results include students' estimated θ values.

Attributes, Knowledge States, and the Q Matrix Used in the RSM-Based Adaptive Diagnostic Testing System

Nine attributes are used on three types of fraction addition problems $a(b/c) + d(e/f)$: addition of simple fractions, F + F; addition of two mixed numbers, M + M; and addition of a fraction and a mixed number, F + M or M + F. Items are given in Table 10.9. Attributes are described below in Table 10.7

The Q matrix is given in Table 10.8 and 33 knowledge states that was not empty in an RSM analysis on the previous dataset is used in this experiment. Table 10.10 gives the most popular five KSs. KS 21 represents the state in which all answers are wrong, and KS 10 represents mastery of all attributes.

TABLE 10.7

A List of Attributes for Fraction Addition Problems

A1	Separate the whole-number part from the fraction part when a $\neq$ 0 or d $\neq$ 0 (F + M or M + F).
A2	Separate the whole-number part from the fraction part when a $\neq$ 0 and d $\neq$ 0 (M + M).
A3	Get the common denominator (CD) when c $\neq$ f.
A4	Convert the fraction part before getting the CD.
A5	Reduce the fraction part before getting the CD.
A6	Answer to be simplified.
A7	Add two numerators.
A8	Adjust a whole-number part, for example 2 8/6 + 3 10/6 = (2 + 3) + (8/6 + 10/6) = 5 + (4/3 + 5/3) = 5 + 9/3 = 5 + 3 = 8; 2 8/6 = 3 2/6.
A9	Combination of A2 and A3.

TABLE 10.8

Q Matrix of Fraction Addition Problems for 19 items and 9 attributes

Item	1 2 3 4 5 6 7 8 9	Item	1 2 3 4 5 6 7 8 9
1	1 1 0 1 1 1 1 1 0	11	0 0 1 0 0 1 1 0 0
2	0 0 1 1 1 1 1 0 0	12	1 1 0 0 0 1 1 0 0
3	0 0 0 1 0 1 1 0 0	13	1 1 1 0 0 0 1 0 1
4	1 1 1 0 1 1 1 1 1	14	0 0 0 0 1 0 1 0 0
5	0 1 1 1 0 1 1 1 1	15	0 0 1 0 0 0 1 0 0
6	1 1 0 0 0 1 1 1 0	16	0 1 0 0 0 0 1 1 0
7	0 0 0 1 0 1 1 0 0	17	0 0 0 0 0 0 1 0 0
8	0 0 1 0 0 0 1 0 0	18	0 0 1 0 0 0 1 0 0
9	1 1 0 1 0 1 1 1 0	19	0 0 0 0 0 0 1 0 0
10	0 0 0 0 0 0 1 0 0		

Remediation Instruction and Routing Method

Fourteen instructional units were written on the same computerized instructional system as that on which the tests were prepared. For example,

TABLE 10.9

Fraction Addition Problems of the Form $a(b/c) + d(e/f)$, Where $a \neq 0$ and/or $d \neq 0$ and 38 Problems

1. 2 8/6 + 3 10/6	20. 3 10/4 + 4 6/4
2. 2/5 + 1 2/8	21. 2/7 + 18/12
3. 8/5 + 6/5	22. 9/7 + 11/7
4. 2 1/2 + 4 2/4	23. 1 1/3 + 2 4/6
5. 1/2 + 1 10/7	24. 1/5 + 2 5/3
6. 3 5/7 + 4 6/7	25. 3 4/5 + 5 3/5
7. 3/5 + 7/5	26. 7/4 + 5/4
8. 1/3 + 1/2	27. 1/5 + 1/4
9. 1 4/7 + 112/7	28. 1 3/5 + 1 8/5
10. 3/5 + 1/5	29. 4/7 + 1/7
11. 3/4 + 1/2	30. 5/6 + 1/3
12. 2 5/9 + 1 1/9	31. 3 5/8 + 1 1/8
13. 3 1/6 + 2 3/4	32. 2 1/8 + 3 5/6
14. 15/35 + 10/35	33. 16/36 + 10/36
15. 1/2 + 3/8	34. 1/3 + 4/9
16. 1 2/5 + 3/5	35. 2 5/7 + 2/7
17. 1/4 + 3/4	36. 1/5 + 4/5
18. 4/15 + 1/10	37. 5/6 + 1/8
19. 4/5 + 3/5	38. 6/7 + 3/7

Note: (a) If $a = 0$, then b/c is denoted by F (e.g., 3/4 or 1/2); (b) if $a \neq 0$, then $a(b/c)$ is denoted by M (e.g., 2 ¾); and (c) $d(b/c) \rightarrow (ac + b)/c$.

TABLE 10.10

Mastery Patterns of the 11 Most Popular Knowledge States

KS	A1	A2	A3	A4	A5	A6	A7	A8	A9	Serious Description of Knowledge States
21	0	0	0	0	0	0	0	0	0	Nonmastery state
10	1	1	1	1	1	1	1	1	1	Mastery state
6	1	1	1	1	1	1	1	1	0	Cannot get common denominator (CD) for mixed numbers
9	1	1	1	0	1	0	1	0	1	Cannot simplify answers to the simplest form
16	1	1	0	0	0	0	1	0	1	Cannot do A3, A4, A5, A6, and A8
24	1	1	0	1	0	1	1	1	1	Cannot do A3 and A5
25	0	1	0	1	1	1	1	0	1	Cannot add M + F, and cannot get CD
26	0	1	1	1	1	1	1	1	1	Cannot do A1, that is, does not understand a + 0 = a
33	1	0	0	0	0	1	1	1	1	Cannot do A2, A3, A4, and A5
4	1	1	0	1	1	1	1	1	1	Cannot get the common denominator
11	0	0	0	1	0	1	1	1	1	Can add two simple fractions with c = d only

if an examinee was classified into State No. 25, then an automated adaptive routing system sends the examinee to the units *Instruction 3*, teaching what a common denominator is and how to get it, and *Instruction 1*, reminding the student that the problems of the F + M type can be separated into 0 and the whole-number part of the second number and that $0 + d = d$.

The relationships among the knowledge states can always be expressed by a tree, such as the example given in Figure 10.5. We now describe how such a tree structure is used with Mahalanobis distances to direct the remediation process.

Membership in State No. 10 means that all attributes are mastered. The state *cannot do A4* means the examinee cannot do A4 but can do the remaining attributes A1, A2, A3, A5, A6, A7, A8, and A9. If an examinee was classified into the cognitive state *cannot do A8, A4, A5, and A9*, which is shown at the bottom of the tree given in Figure 10.5, then the issue that arises is whether A8 should be remediated first followed by A5, or whether A5 should be remediated first followed by A8. If that state *cannot do A8, A4, A5, and A9* is the examinee's state X diagnosed by the pretest, then the Mahalanobis distance between X and the state *cannot do A8 and A4, and A9* is 1.2; however, if the Mahalanobis distance between X and state *cannot do A4 and A5, and A9* is 5.1, which is larger than 1.2, then a comparison of these numbers provides a plausible rule for a computerized routing system. The resulting rule indicates that remediating A5 should be chosen prior to remediating A8.

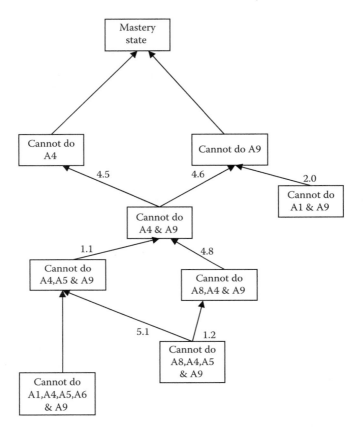

FIGURE 10.5
A learning path of nine knowledge states with the likelihood ratio of the two states connected directly.

Three fraction diagnostic tests—a pretest, posttest, and retention test—were given in 1988 to students in the seventh and eighth grades of a junior high school in a small city in Illinois. The pretest classified each student into one of 33 states. Because each state is expressed as the mastery and nonmastery of given attributes, the examinees were assigned to the instructional units that would teach them their nonmastered skills. When examinees were classified into State No. 10, the mastery state, they were allowed to skip the posttest. A majority of students did not take the posttest, and they were not asked to take the retention test either. The examinees were given a series of exercises at the end of each remediation unit. After correctly doing the exercises for all the remediation units that they had to complete, the examinees were given the posttest, which was also adaptive, and a cognitive diagnosis was carried out. Some students who could not complete the remediation units within a class hour had to come back again to their computer lab to continue their assignments. A few students had to come back several times to complete the exercises and the posttest.

Three months later, the retention test was administered to the examinees, and the retention of examinees' states was examined. The item pool for the retention test was the same as that of the posttest, and the test was also a computerized adaptive test.

In the next year, 1989, the same study was replicated with 191 students. Some of the students, who participated in the pretest in the 1988 study but could not complete their assigned remediation instruction and/or the posttest, were allowed to continue their unfinished study in the 1989 study.

The two studies show some resemblance in the classification results. In the pretest given in 1988, 57 examinees achieved the mastery state (No. 10), whereas 39 failed in all the attributes and ended up in the nonmastery state (No. 21). In 1989, 34 were classified in the mastery state, and 13 were in the nonmastery state. Throughout the six tests, State No. 26 is the most common knowledge state after No. 10. The examinees in No. 26 are also very high achievers, and their errors are *cannot do F + M type but can do all other attributes required in the other types of problems*. Their erroneous rules are often *append 1 to F type and proceed with all the computations correctly* ($2/5 + 4\,3/7$ becomes $1\,2/5 + 4\,3/7$) or *omitting the whole-number part in the answer* ($\{0 + 4\} + \{2/5 + 3/7\} = 29/35$). The frequencies of such errors were reported in Tatsuoka (1984a) and Shaw et al. (1982).

Table 10.11 (1988 data) shows that 57% of the examinees who are classified in No. 26 in the pretest moved from No. 26 to No. 10 (all tasks mastered),

TABLE 10.11

Percentages of Transition Frequencies of Students Who Are Classified in 10 States

Pretest KSs	Post Test States										
	10	26	6	9	33	25	16	24	11	21	Other States
10	—[a]	—	—	—	—	—	—	—	—	—	—
26	57	33	2	4	0	0	0	0	0	0	4
6	42	27	15	8	4	0	0	0	0	0	4
9	25	33	17	17	0	0	0	0	0	0	8
33	78	0	22	0	0	0	0	0	0	0	0
25	68	8	8	0	0	8	0	0	0	0	8
16	32	8	16	4	4	0	4	0	0	0	32
24	33	0	22	0	11	0	11	0	0	0	23
11	20	20	7	13	0	0	0	7	0	0	33
21	18	21	5	3	0	10	0	0	3	3	37

[a] Students who were classified in State No. 10 in the pretest did not take the posttest or retention test.

and 33% remained in No. 26. Sixty-eight percent from No. 25 and 32% from No. 16 moved to No. 10, respectively, and 8% and 4% remained in the same classes. Furthermore, 42%, and 27% from No. 6 moved to No. 10 and No. 26, respectively, but 15% remained unchanged. Seventy-eight percent of the examinees classified in No. 33 moved to No. 10, and the remaining 22% moved to No. 6. Eighteen percent and 21% of the examinees classified in No. 21 moved to No. 10 and No. 26, respectively. Thirty-seven percent of No. 21 examinees moved to various states that are not listed in Table 10.5.5. In the posttest, 89 examinees (39% of the 226 students who took the posttest) were classified into No. 10. Thirty-three percent of the No. 26 examinees stayed in No. 26 on the posttest; however, four examinees who were in No. 26 moved back to lower level states. The lower level states are simply defined by their lower values of estimates, and higher level states mean that they have higher values of estimates. In all, 16 examinees (7% of N = 226) moved back to lower level states, but a majority of the examinees (93%) moved to higher level states. Similar trends were found in the replication study in 1989.

Pre-, Post-, and Retention Test Results

For changes from the posttest to the retention test, quite a few examinees moved back to their pretest states. Twenty-five examinees maintained their mastery states in the retention test, whereas 23 did not take the retention test. Forty-one examinees (48%) regressed toward lower level states from their posttest state, No. 10. The examinees who were classified in No. 26 retained their skill level better than did those in No. 10; 43% stayed in either No. 10 or No. 26, whereas 34% moved back to lower level states. Overall, 48% of the examinees (N = 185) regressed toward lower level states between the posttest and retention test. Twenty-one percent of the examinees maintained their posttest states, and 31% moved up to higher level states than the posttest states.

Changes between the pretest and the retention test are encouraging. Fifty-five examinees moved from various states to the mastery state, No. 10. Thirty moved to No. 26, and 25 moved to No. 6. If we add up these numbers, 110 out of 185 examinees (59%) were classified either into No. 10 or into No. 26 or No. 6 (which are near mastery states), and only about 6% of examinees regressed toward lower level states from the pretest state to the retention state.

Serious Errors and Nonserious Errors of Knowledge States

Because 45 examinees dropped out of our experiment before taking the retention test, the sample size of some knowledge states became very small (e.g., 1 or 2); therefore, the 33 states were grouped into two categories: those

TABLE 10.12

2×2 Contingency Table of Seriousness of Error Classes in Pre- and Posttests, 1988 Data

Pretest	Serious	Nonserious	Total (%)
Serious	21	93	114 (51%)
Nonserious	1	107	108 (49%)
Total (%)	22 (10%)	200 (90%)	222

with serious versus nonserious error types. Of the 26 states that have mastery tasks prepared in the remedial instructional units, nine states (Nos. 26, 6, 7, 9, 8, 19, 33, 31, and 32) were categorized as nonserious error states, and the remaining 17 were categorized as having serious errors. Tables 10.12 and 10.13 show 2×2 contingency tables of serious versus nonserious error groups for the pre- and posttest in the 1988 and 1989 data.

Table 10.14 is the corresponding table for the pretest and retention test in 1988. Table 10.12 shows that 51% of the examinees in the pretest were classified in the serious error groups, but only 10% of the examinees in the posttest were classified in the serious error groups. Almost 90 examinees changed their states from the serious error groups to the nonserious error groups. Table 10.13 shows a similar result to that of Table 10.12.

These results imply that diagnoses using the rule space methodology are very reliable. Indeed, we carefully designed our remediation instruction so that if cognitive diagnoses by the rule space model were not correct, then remediation would not work well.

Table 10.13 shows that 38 (or 23% of) examinees moved from nonserious to serious error groups, whereas 4 moved from serious to nonserious error groups. Although the design of instructional lessons for remediating these examinees can be improved in the future, we still consider the rule space diagnoses to be reliable. The number of examinees who remained in nonserious error groups was 110, which is 68% of the examinees who participated in the retention test.

TABLE 10.13

2×2 Contingency Table of Seriousness of Error Classes in Pre- and Posttests, 1989 Data

Pretest	Serious	Nonserious	Total (%)
Serious	19	75	94 (55%)
Nonserious	1	77	78 (45%)
Total (%)	20 (12%)	152 (88%)	172

TABLE 10.14

2 × 2 Contingency Table of Seriousness of Error Classes in Post- and Retention Tests, 1988 Data

Pretest	Serious	Nonserious	Total (%)
Serious	15	4	19 (11%)
Nonserious	38	110	148 (89%)
Total (%)	20 (32%)	152 (68%)	167

Elapsed Time for Remediation

The overall average time for completing required remediation units is about 37 minutes across knowledge states. About half of the examinees reached mastery or near mastery, whereas 5% of the examinees remained in the serious error category.

This study introduced a computerized cognitive adaptive testing procedure and used the effect on remedial instruction as empirical validation of this testing procedure. This empirical study indicated that RSM can diagnose students' knowledge states effectively and remediate the students' errors quickly with minimum effort. Because RSM is a statistical method, it is possible to apply it to various domains for diagnosing students' weaknesses and strengths, and for identifying nonmastered skills. Then, appropriate, individualized instruction can be given.

Designing instructional units for remediation can be effectively navigated by RSM because the determination of all the possible ideal item score patterns from a given Q matrix is based on a tree structure of attributes, knowledge states, and items (Tatsuoka, 1990). Remediation should start with the states having the highest probability of mastery for diagnosed deficiency of skills. Previous observations in the computerized lessons, analyses of various tests on the PLATO system, and several teachers' comments resulted in our expectation that our cyclic system (i.e., pretest, diagnosed prescription, routing, remediation, exercises, and posttest), followed by diagnosed prescription, routing, remediation, and the like, would be an efficient teaching tool on computers (Tatsuoka & Edins, 1985).

10.6   An RSM Analysis as a Hypothesis Testing Method

The two stages of RSM analysis consist of (a) development of a Q matrix and its validation, and (b) classification of response patterns and finding subjects' knowledge states. RSM can be viewed as a statistical tool for testing a series of hypotheses. Domain experts may come up with subjective and obscure attributes, but this methodology helps the experts judge the quality of attributes from a statistical point of view. At the same time, it enables them to find new attributes they might never have thought of as important attributes, which explain the underlying cognitive processing skills and knowledge states used by students to achieve the correct answers. Chipman, Nichols, and Brennan (1995) stated that

> from the cognitive perspective, it is worth noting that RSM analysis might have considerable appeal as an approach to starting the analysis of a new knowledge domain. It could provide hints as to where the action is, where substantial individual differences in performance lie. It could guide the investments of research effort required to understand cognitive performance in detail. (p. 11)

The development of a cognitive model starts at testing a Q matrix utilizing simple statistical techniques. The simplest way to do this is to use a multiple regression on the item difficulties and coded attributes in a Q matrix, and to use students' total scores and attribute mastery probabilities obtained from rule space analyses (Buck, Tatsuoka, & Kostin, 1997). If a very high percentage of the variances of item difficulties is explained by the attributes used in RSM, then such attributes would actually be used by a majority of students, and they must represent students' cognitive skills and knowledge.

A Learning Progressive Network

Construction of a network of knowledge states enables us to understand how each student progresses with learning. Tatsuoka et al. (2006) used a learning progressive network to explain the various ways in which students from 20 different countries learned mathematics in the seventh grade. Dogan (2006) also used learning progressive paths to explain how students from different school systems learned differently. Analyses of the NAEP Science Performance Assessment by Yepes Baraya, Allen, and Tatsuoka (2000) have revealed that there are two distinctly different progressive paths of learning, as shown in Figure 10.6. The first progressive path discovered in the NAEP Science Assessment is that students progress by acquiring skills in manipulating equipment, recording data, and using information derived from them, numerical computation, and the use of the knowledge of experimental procedures. In contrast, other students demonstrate a different progressive path characterized by skills in interpreting data and strategic knowledge. As can be seen in Figure 10.6.1, these two progressive paths do not intersect well.

The reading comprehension part of the TOEFL test has shown that there are three progressive paths. A study of the dimensionality of TOEFL has shown that the proportion of students belonging to progressive paths is

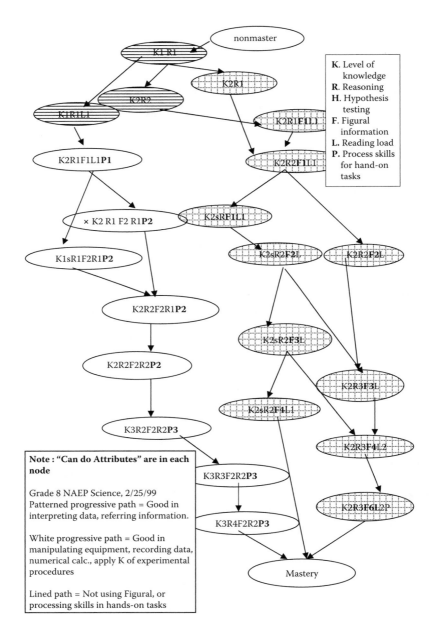

FIGURE 10.6
Grade 8 progressive paths of NAEP Science performance test: hands-on tasks.

an important factor in deciding the psychometric dimensionality of a test (Saito, 1998). If a strong majority of students belongs to the first path, then the test becomes psychometrically unidimensional. The performance scores scaled traditionally provide a reasonable description of students who belong to the main progressive path; however, those who belong to other progressive paths have acquired their skill level in quite different ways from the students in the main progressive path, even though their scaled scores can be the same as those in the main path. This finding and interpretation are supported by Birenbaum's (1981) simulation study.

For the NAEP Science case, the psychometric dimension has been found to be two, and the psychological dimension is also two, because the frequencies of the two progressive paths are about the same. It is clear that approximately half of the students in a sample tend to use inductive thinking skills, whereas the remaining students tend to use deductive thinking skills more heavily. Saito's TOEFL study, which used students with a Japanese background, showed that the main progressive path is affected by familiarity with vocabulary knowledge; however, the second progressive path is more strongly affected by various higher level thinking skills that are often found in the attribute analysis of SAT Verbal tests.

The traditional scaled scores reflect the main progressive path in a Japanese population, so that higher scale scores correspond to students with richer vocabulary. Scales constructed by assuming the unidimensionality of data cannot explain the proficiency levels of students who belong to weaker alternative progressive paths. Saito's study clearly indicates that students belonging to alternative progressive paths or unpopular progressive paths may not be properly evaluated by traditional statistical or psychometric analyses, which are based on the scores of a test. Moreover, the performance of Japanese students on reading comprehension is somewhat different from the performance of native English speakers. The performances on the TOEFL test by English-as-a-second-language speakers are affected more by their vocabulary levels than their ability to use various cognitive skills, which is unlike the situation for typical SAT test takers.

A Summary List of RSM Validation Steps

The following listing summarizes a possible procedure of RSM validation for testing cognitive modeling hypotheses:

Step 1. Before the Rule Space Analysis Is Performed

The procedure to apply the RSM is summarized in the steps that are ordered 1 through 5 below. The first action is to identify and search for attributes with or without performing task analysis or protocol analysis on a test taken by students, teachers, or researchers.

1. Domain experts identify attributes in a domain of interest.

2. Code attributes' involvement or relationship for each item, and make a Q matrix.

3. Apply regression techniques (for example, a multiple regression, tree regression, or neural network) to predict item difficulties in the Q matrix. It is important to note that the forward or backward stepwise algorithms in multiple regression analyses or the lock "one step look ahead" algorithm in tree regression analyses does not select the best set of variables, so it is recommended to use the bootstrap sampling technique. When the number of attributes is larger than the number of items, then a tree regression with bootstrap sampling can be applied to reduce the number of attributes to a manageable size.

   Criticism may arise arguing that item difficulty may not reflect subjects' performance directly, so we ought to use variables measuring subjects' performance. In order to answer this critique, we may replace item difficulty with the expectation of person response curves over θ (Tatsuoka & Linn, 1983).

4. Compute the pseudomeans of attributes from data and the Q matrix without going through the rule space procedure. The pseudomeans are obtained by computing $(1/N) X'Q$; however, it is important to notice that we assume implicitly in this computation that if item j has the score of zero, then all of the attributes involved in item j have scores of zero. Because this assumption is very unrealistic, we do not use this strong relation later in RSM. If we have too many attributes, then the number of knowledge states will be an extremely large number; therefore, we have to reduce the number of attributes. The attributes with high pseudomean values of .99 or .98 can be deleted. Furthermore, delete attributes with negative regression coefficients. Next, we go back to create a new Q matrix, and repeat the procedure until we get the multiple R^2 equal to or higher than .85.

5. Generate all possible knowledge states from the Q matrix we created. Although we used item difficulties for a model selection, it is not enough to validate our initial cognitive model. Because the sample size in a regression analysis is the number of items, regression coefficients are extremely unstable statistically. If a few entries of the Q matrix were changed from 1 to 0 or from 0 to 1, then the magnitudes of some regression coefficients that are originally significantly different from 0 could be altered to be not different.

Step 2. Validation of the Initial Cognitive Model by Examining a "Goodness of Fit" of the Generated Knowledge States From the Q Matrix

Stage 2 is to test the hypothesis created by domain experts that is represented by the Q matrix in Step 1. In this stage, we classify students' responses to their possible knowledge states by applying a classification procedure. The main steps are summarized below in 6 through 9.

6. Construct a rule space by expressing all of the knowledge states as the points in the rule space.
7. Set several classification criteria, and apply the Bayes classification procedure. A classification rate of 90% indicates that the Q matrix fits a sample well.
8. Compute attribute mastery probabilities for an examinee.
9. Apply several multivariate statistical analyses such as a principal component analysis, a factor analysis for the dimensionality test and for grouping of similar attributes, and correlational analyses for selecting attributes with high discrimination powers. Delete the attributes with high means, such as .99 or .98.
10. Go to 1. Make a new Q matrix, and generate all possible knowledge states. Repeat procedures 6 through 9.

10.7 Using RSM in Examining the Construct Validity of a Test

The most important steps in validating a test are defining the constructs that the test measures (Haladyna & Downing, 2004) and providing better score interpretation (Embretson & Gorin, 2001). Although several different types of validity (e.g., content validity, construct validity, and criterion-related validity) exist, construct validity is often used as the all-encompassing term. *Construct validity* is defined by "the extent to which the test measures the right psychological constructs" (pp. 13–103). Messick (1989) argued that a fundamental feature of construct validity is construct representation, which can be identified through analysis of cognitive processes underlying test performance, primarily by decomposing the test into requisite component processes. He discussed several aspects of construct validity and noted that a key issue for the content aspect of construct validity is the specification of the boundaries of the construct domain to be assessed, "[which] is determining the knowledge, skills and other attributes to be revealed by the assessment tasks" (1990, p. 12); therefore, before it is possible to collect evidence of construct validity, it is necessary to reveal the constructs measured by a test. Wiley (2002) pointed to the same issue: "The specifications of the constructs measured by a test seem to be a necessary prerequisite to its construct validation" (p. 214). The attribute identification and attribute validation phases in RSM can be seen as a way of achieving construct formulation or construct specification, and hence as an essential part of test validation.

In the past, traditional methods such as factor analysis and qualitative methods such as expert judgment procedures have been used to explore the constructs measured by a test to establish its validity; today, however, there is general acceptance within the psychometric community that the cognitive psychology of test performance must be understood in order to validate tests (Snow & Lohman, 1993). Analysis of the cognitive demands of a test and identification of the attributes that underlie that test are part of the effort to understand the psychology of test performance. Only with the help of this kind of analysis can our understanding of the constructs represented by the tests be improved (Gierl, 1996) and the boundaries and structure of the construct domain be revealed (Messick, 1989, 1990).

The RSM is a tool in hypothesizing and testing the cognitive and domain-specific skills and knowledge that a test measures. In fact, Dogan (2006) argued that incorporating RSM applications into the validation process addresses both *construct definition* and *score interpretation* aspects of test validation. In his 2006 study, Dogan illustrated how the RSM methodology can be used in exploring the construct structure of a high-stakes test. In this study, a set of 15 attributes that underlie the mathematics subtest of the 2004 University Entrance Examination of Turkey were developed and validated. Attribute validation was achieved using the following key results:

1. 80% of variance in item difficulties was explained by attribute involvement.
2. 100% classification was achieved, indicating that observed item response patterns were successfully matched with those derived from the Q matrix.
3. 95% of variance in IRT-based ability estimates and 96% of the variance in total scores were explained by attribute mastery levels.

The study showed that a unique advantage of using the RSM in the validation process is that with the use of this model, it is possible to study the proposed construct structure of a given test *empirically*. A hypothesis about cognitive performance in a given domain is subject to falsification if it fails to successfully classify examinees (Leighton, Gierl, & Hunka, 2004). Dogan (2006) argued that in the RSM context, it is the Q matrix that represents this *hypothesis of cognitive performance*; therefore, the performance of the RSM analysis serves as an indication as to whether this hypothesis should be retained or rejected. In other words, although qualitative methods such as task and protocol analyses are carried out in determining the list of constructs that the test measures, the mapping of these constructs onto the test, as represented by the Q matrix, can be further put to an empirical test.

Using a diagnostic testing model such as the RSM in the validation process has several other advantages. First, this model makes it possible to approach validation at the item level (Dogan, 2006). As several researchers pointed out, the inferences drawn about student test performance are stronger theoretically and empirically when individual test items are investigated for the cognitive processes they evoke in students (Embretson, 1999; Embretson & Gorin, 2001; Ercikan et al., 2004; Ferrara et al., 2003, 2004; Irvine & Kyllonen, 2002). In other words, inferences about students' skills and knowledge are expected to have greater validity when more evidence is gathered about what each test item specifically measures (Nichols, 1994). As Ferrara et al. (2004) put it, "Test scores can be construct valid only to the degree to which a test's component items are construct valid" (p. 1). Without properly defining the set of skills measured by a test and how those skills map onto specific items, the validity of scores obtained from that test cannot be established.

In short, researchers today have agreed that the knowledge, cognitive processes, and strategies used by examinees to solve problems cannot be ignored when attempting to validate the inferences made about these examinees (Embretson, 1983, 1994, 1998; Messick, 1989; Snow & Lohman, 1993). Construct meaning is elaborated upon by understanding the processes, strategies, and knowledge used to solve test items (Embretson, 1999, p. 632). Because performance is described using a specific set of cognitive competencies (Leighton et al., 2004), test scores anchored to a cognitive model such as the RSM are more interpretable and meaningful, and therefore more valid.

References

Albert, D., & Lukes, J. (1999). *Knowledge space: Theories, empirical research, and application*. Hillsdale, NJ: Erlbaum.

Anderson, J. R. (1984). Cognitive psychology and intelligent tutoring. Paper presented at the sixth annual meeting of the Cognitive Science Society, Boulder, CO.

Baillie, R., & Tatsuoka, K. K. (1980). *GETAB: A computer program for estimating item and person parameters of the one- and two-parameter logistic model on the PLATO system*. Urbana: University of Illinois, Computer-Based Educational Research Laboratory (CERL).

Baillie, R., & Tatsuoka, K. K. (1982). *FBUG: A computer program for diagnose erroneous rules of operation in fraction addition and subtraction problems*. Urbana: University of Illinois, Computer-Based Educational Research Laboratory (CERL).

Baillie, R., & Tatsuoka, K. K. (1984). *Application of adaptive testing to a fraction test* (Research Report 84-3-NIE). Urbana: University of Illinois, Computer-Based Educational Research Laboratory (CERL).

Bartholomew, D. J. (1987). *Latent variable models and factor analysis*. New York: Oxford University Press.

Bejar, I. (1980). A procedure for investigating the unidimensionality of educational measurement. *Journal of Educational Measurement, 17*(4), 283–296.

Bennett, R. E., & Ward, W. C. (1993). *Construction versus choice in cognitive measurement*. Hillsdale, NJ: Erlbaum.

Birenbaum, M. (1981). *Error analysis: It does make a difference*. Unpublished doctoral dissertation, University of Illinois at Urbana-Champaign.

Birenbaum, M. (1985). Comparing the effectiveness of several IRT-based indices of response pattern appropriateness in detecting unusual response pattern. *Educational and Psychological Measurement, 45*, 523–534.

Birenbaum, M., Kelly, A. E., & Tatsuoka, K. K. (1993). Diagnosing knowledge states in algebra using the rule-space model exponents. *Journal of Research in Teaching Mathematics, 24*(5).

Birenbaum, M., & Shaw, D. J. (1985). Task specification chart: A key to a better understanding of test results. *Journal of Educational Measurement, 10*, 167–174.

Birenbaum, M., Tatsuoka, C., & Xin, T. (2005). Large-scale diagnostic assessment: Comparison of eighth graders' mathematics performance in the United States, Singapore, and Israel. *Assessment in Education, 12*, 167–181.

Birenbaum, M., Tatsuoka, C., & Yamada, T. (2004). Diagnostic assessment in TIMSS-R: Between countries and within-country comparisons of eighth graders' mathematics performance. *Studies in Educational Evaluation, 30*, 151–173.

Birenbaum, M., & Tatsuoka, K. K. (1980). *The use of information from wrong responses in measuring students' achievement* (Research Report 80-1-ONR). Urbana: University of Illinois, Computer-Based Education Research Laboratory (CERL).

Birenbaum, M., & Tatsuoka, K. K. (1982). On the dimensionality of achievement test data. *Journal of Educational Measurement, 19*(4), 259–266.

Birenbaum, M., & Tatsuoka, K. K. (1983). The effects of a scoring system based on the algorithm underlying the students' response patterns on the dimensionality of achievement test data of the problem solving type. *Journal Educational Measurement, 20,* 17–26.

Birenbaum, M., Tatsuoka, K. K., & Nasser, F. (1997). On agreement of a diagnostic classification from parallel subtests: Score reliability at the micro level. *Educational and Psychological Measurement, 57*(4), 541–558.

Birkoff, B. (1970). *Lattice theory.* New York: Macmillan.

Box, G. E. P., & Tao, G. C. (1975). *Bayesian inference in statistical analysis.* Reading, MA: Addison-Wesley.

Breiman, L., Friedman, J. H., Olson, R. A., & Stone, C. L. (1984). *Classification and regression trees.* Monterey, CA: Wadsworth.

Brown, J. S., & Burton, R. R. (1978). Diagnostic models for procedural bugs in basic mathematical skills. *Cognitive Science, 2,* 155–192.

Brown, J. S., & VanLehn, K. (1980). Repair theory: A generative theory of bugs in procedural skills. *Cognitive Science, 4,* 379–426.

Buck, G., & Tatsuoka, K. (1998). Application of the rule-space procedure to language testing: Examining attributes of a free response listening test. *Language Testing, 15*(2), 119–157.

Buck, G., Tatsuoka, K., & Kostin, I. (1997). The skills of reading: Rule-space analysis of a multiple-choice test of second language reading comprehension. *Language Learning, 47*(3), 423–466.

Buck, G., Tatsuoka, K., VanEssen, T., & Kostin, I. (2000). *RSM analysis of SAT V writing test* (ETS Technical Report). Princeton, NJ: Educational Testing Services.

Chen, Y. H., Gorin, J. S., Thompson, M. S., and Tatsuoka, K. K. (2008). *Cross-cultural Validity of the TIMSS-1999 Mathematics test. Verification of the cognitive model. International Journal of Testing* 8:251–271. New York: Routledge, Taylor & Francis Group.

Chipman, S. F., Nichols, P. D., & Brennan, R. L. (1995). Introduction. In P. D. Nichols, S. F. Chipman, & R. L. Brennan (Eds.), *Cognitively diagnostic assessment.* Hillsdale, NJ: Erlbaum.

Cliff, N. (1977). A theory of consistency of ordering generalizable to tailored testing. *Psychometrika, 42,* 375–399.

Corter, J. E. (1995). Using clustering methods to explore the structure of diagnostic test. In P. D. Nichols, S. F. Chipman, & R. L. Brennan (Eds.), *Cognitively diagnostic assessment* (pp. 327–359). Hillsdale, NJ: Erlbaum.

Corter, J. E., & Tatsuoka, K. K. (2004). *Cognitive and measurement foundations of diagnostic assessment in mathematics* (College Board Technical Report I). New York: College Board.

Davey, B. A., & Priestley, H. A. (1990). *Introduction to lattices and order.* Cambridge: Cambridge University Press.

Davis, F. B. (1968). Research in comprehension in reading. *Reading Research Quarterly, 3,* 499–545.

Dayton, C. M., & Macready, G. B. (1976). A probabilistic model for validation of behavioral hierarchies. *Psychometrika, 41,* 189–204.

Dean, M. (2006). *Item attributes for explaining TIMSS advanced mathematics test performance*. Unpublished doctoral thesis, Columbia University.

Dibello, L. V., Stout, W. F., & Roussos, L. A. (1995, April). *Unified cognitive psychometric diagnosis foundations and application*. Paper presented at the annual meeting of the American Educational Research Association, Atlanta, GA.

Dogan, E. (2006). *Establishing construct validity of the mathematics subtest of the University Entrance Examination in Turkey: A rule space application*. Unpublished doctoral thesis, Columbia University.

Draper, N. R., & Smith, H. (1990). *Applied regression analysis*. New York: Wiley.

Drasgow, F. (1982). Choice of test models for appropriateness measurement. *Applied Psychological Measurement, 6*, 297–308.

Drasgow, F., Levine, M. V., & Williams, E. A. (1985). Appropriateness measurement with polychotomous item response models and standardized indices, *British Journal of Mathematical and Statistical Psychology, 38*, 67–86.

Easley, J. A., & Tatsuoka, M. M. (1968). *Scientific thought, cases from classical physics*. Boston: Allyn & Bacon.

Embretson, S. E. (1983). Construct validity: Construct representation versus nomothetic span. *Psychological Bulletin, 93*, 179–197.

Embretson, S. E. (1994). Application of cognitive design systems to test development. In C. R. Reynolds (Ed.), *Cognitive assessment: A multidisciplinary perspective* (pp. 107–135). New York: Plenum.

Embretson, S. E. (1998). A cognitive design system approach to generating valid tests: Application to abstract reasoning. *Psychological Methods, 3*, 380–396.

Embretson, S. E. (1999). Cognitive psychology applied to testing. In F. T. Durso (Ed.), *Handbook of applied cognition* (pp. 629–660). Chichester, UK: John Wiley.

Embretson, S., & Gorin, J. (2001). Improving construct validity with cognitive psychology principles. *Journal of Educational Measurement, 38*, 343–368.

Ercikan, K., Law, D., Arim, R., Domene, J., Lacroix, S., & Gagnon, F. (2004, April). *Identifying sources of DIF using think-aloud protocols: Comparing thought processes of examinees taking tests in English versus in French*. Paper presented at the annual meeting of the National Council on Measurement in Education (NCME), San Diego, CA.

Eubank, R. L. (1988). *Spline smoothing and nonparametric regression*. New York: Marcel Dekker.

Falmagne, J. C., & Doignon, J. P. (1988). A class of stochastic procedures for assessment of knowledge. *British Journal of Mathematical and Statistical Psychology, 41*, 1–23.

Ferrara, S., Duncan, T. G., Freed, R., Velez-Paschke, A., McGivern, J., Mushlin, S., et al. (2004, April). Examining test score validity by examining item construct validity. Paper presented at the annual meeting of the American Educational Research Association, San Diego, CA.

Ferrara, S., Duncan, T., Perie, M., Freed, R., McGivern, J., & Chilukuri, R. (2003, April). Item construct validity: Early results from a study of the relationship between intended and actual cognitive demands in a middle school science assessment. Paper presented at the annual meeting of the American Educational Research Association, Chicago.

Fukunaga, K. (1990). *Introduction to statistical pattern recognition* (2nd ed.). New York: Academic Press.

Gelman, A., Carlin, J. B., Stern, H. S., & Rubin, D. B. (1995). *Bayesian data analysis.* New York: Chapman & Hall.

Gierl, M. J. (1996). An investigation of the cognitive foundation underlying the rule-space model. *Dissertation Abstracts International, 57*(01), 5351B. (UMI No. 9702524).

Gierl, M. J., Leighton, J. P., & Hunka, S. (2000). Exploring the logic of Tatsuoka's rule-space model for test development and analysis. *Educational Measurement: Issues and Practice, 19,* 34–44.

Ginzburg, H. (1977). *Children's arithmetic: The learning process.* New York: Van Nostrand.

Glaser, R. (1981). The future of testing: A research agenda for cognitive psychology and psychometrics. *American Psychologists, 36*(9), 923–936.

Goodman, L. A. (1974). The analysis of qualitative variables when some of the variables are unobservable. Part I: A modified latent structure approach. *American Journal of Sociology, 79,* 1179–1259.

Guerrero, A. (2001). Cognitively diagnostic perspectives on English and Spanish test of mathematics aptitudes. *Dissertation Abstracts International, 62*(08), 543B. (UMI No. 3005725).

Haertel, E. H., & Wiley, D. E. (1993). Representation of ability structure: Implications for testing. In N. Fredriksen, R. Mislevy, & I. Bejar (Eds.), *Testing theory for a new generation of tests* (pp. 359–384). Hillsdale, NJ: Erlbaum.

Haladyna, T. M., & Downing, S. M. (2004, Spring). Construct-irrelevant variance in high-stakes testing. *Educational Measurement: Issues and Practice,* 17–27.

Harnisch, D. L. (1996). Perspectives on reporting proficiency scaling results to students and teachers. Organizer and presenter for the invited symposium to the annual meeting of the National Council on Measurement in Education, New York.

Harnisch, D. L., & Linn, R. L. (1981). Analysis of item response patterns: Questionable test data and dissimilar curriculum practices. *Journal of Educational Measurement, 3,* 39–87.

Harnish, D. L. & Tatsuoka, K. K. (1983) A comparison of appropriate indicies based on item reponse theory. In Hanbleton, R. K. (Ed.) *Applications of item response theory.* Vancouver, BC: Educational Research Institute of British Columbia.

Hayashi, A. (2002, December). A comparison study of rule-space method and neural network model for classifying individuals and an application. Paper presented at the fourth conference of the Asian Regional Section of the International Association for Statistical Computing (IASC), Busan, Korea.

Hayashi, A., & Tatsuoka, K. K. (2008). *RSM analysis when a Q-matrix has submatrices of Guttman scale* (Technical Report). Tokyo.

Hoffman, K. M., & Kumze, R. (1971). *Linear algebra.* Englewood Cliffs, NJ: Prentice Hall.

Hubert, L. J. (1974). Some applications of graph theory to clustering. *Psychometrika, 39,* 283–309.

Hunt, E. (2006). *The mathematics of behavior.* London: Cambridge University Press.

Im, S. (2007). *Statistical consequences of attribute misspecification of the rule space model.* Unpublished doctoral dissertation, Columbia University.

Irvine, S. H., & Kyllonen, P. C. (Eds.). (2002). *Item generation for test development.* Mahwah, NJ: Erlbaum.

Junker, B. W., & Sijtsma, K. (2001). Cognitive assessment models with few assumptions and connections with non parametric item response theory. *Applied Psychological Measurement, 25,* 258–272.

Kendall, M. G., & Stuart, A. (1973). *Advanced theory of statistics.* New York: Hafner. (Vol. 1 originally published in 1958, and Vol. 2 in 1961).

Kim, S. H. (1989). *Classification of item response patterns into misconception groups.* Unpublished doctoral dissertation, University of Illinois at Urbana-Champaign.

Kingsbury, G. G., & Weiss, D. J. (1979). *Relationships among achievement level estimates from three characteristic curve scoring methods* (Research Report 79-3). Minneapolis: University of Minnesota, Department of Psychology, Psychometric Methods Program.

Klein, M., Birenbaum, M., Standiford, S., & Tatsuoka, K. K. (1981). *Logical error analysis and construction of tests to diagnose student "bugs" in addition and subtraction of fractions* (Technical Report 81-6-NIE). Urbana: University of Illinois, Computer-Based Educational Research Laboratory (CERL).

Kogut, J. (1987). *Detecting aberrant response patterns in the Rasch model* (Report No. 87-3). Enschede, the Netherlands: University of Twente.

Kogut, J. (1988). *Asymptotic distribution of an IRT person fit index* (Report No. 88-13). Enschede, the Netherlands: University of Twente.

Kolman B., Bushy, R. C., & Ross, S. C. (2004). *Discrete mathematical structures,* 5th Ed. Upper Saddle River, NJ: Pearson & Prentice Hall.

Koppen, M., & Doignon, J. P. (1990). Theoretical note: How to build a knowledge space by querying an expert. *Journal of Mathematical Psychology, 34,* 311–331.

Krus, D. J. (1975). *Order analysis of binary data matrices.* Los Angeles: Theta Press.

Kuramoto, N. T., Scott, H. S., & Kasai, M. (2003). Validity of a Japanese vocabulary test: Cognitive analysis with rule space methodology. *Japanese Journal of Educational Psychology, 51,* 43–424.

Lachenbruch, P. A. (1975). *Discriminant analysis.* New York: Hafner.

Lazaresfeld, P. F., & Henry, N. W. (1968). *Latent structure analysis.* New York: Houghton-Mifflin.

Leighton, J. P. & Gierl, M. J. (2007). *Cognitive diagnostic assessment for education.* Cambridge: Cambridge University Press.

Leighton, J. P., Gierl, M. J., & Hunka, S. (2004). The attribute hierarchy model: An approach for integrating cognitive theory with assessment practice. *Journal of Educational Measurement, 41,* 205–236.

Levine, M. V., & Rubin, D. B. (1979). Measuring the item response patterns: Questionable test data and dissimilar curriculum practices. *Journal of Educational Statistics, 4,* 269–290.

Lord, F. M. (1980). *Application of item response theory to practical testing problems.* Hillsdale, NJ: Erlbaum.

Lord, F. M., & Novick, M. R. (1968). *Statistical theories of mental test scores.* Reading, MA: Addison-Wesley.

Macready, G. B., & Dayton, C. M. (1977). The use of probabilistic models in assessment of mastery. *Journal of Educational Statistics, 2*, 99–120.

Masters, G. (1982). A rasch model for partial credit scoring. *Psychomerika, 47*, 149–174

Mayer, R. E. (1983). *Thinking, problem solving, cognition.* New York: W. H. Freeman and Company.

Meijer, R. R. (1994). *Nonparametric person fit analysis.* Unpublished doctoral dissertation, Vrije Universiteit, Amsterdam.

Messick, S. (1989). Validity. In R. L. Linn (Ed.), *Educational measurement* (3rd ed., pp. 13–104). New York: American Council on Education and Macmillan.

Messick. S. (1989). Validity. In R. L. Linn (Ed.), *Educational measurement* (3rd ed., pp. 13–104). New York: American Council on Education and Macmillan.

Messick, S. (1990). *Validity of test interpretation and use* (Research Report No. RR-90-11). Princeton, NJ: Educational Testing Services.

Mislevy. R. J. (1995). Probability-based inference in cognitive diagnosis. In P.D. Nichols, S. F. Chipman, R. L. Brennan (Eds.), *Cognitively diagnostic assessment.* Hillsdale, NJ: Erlbaum.

Mokken, R. J. (1970). *A theory and procedure of scales analysis: With applications in political research.* The Hague: Mouton.

Molenaar, I. W., & Hoitjink, H. (1990). The many null distributions of person fit indices. *Psychometrika, 55*, 75–106.

Molenaar, I. W., & Sijtsma, K. (1984). Internal consistency and reliability in Mokken's nonparametric item response model. *Tijdshrift voor Onderwijseresearch, 9*, 257–268.

Mosteller, F., & Tukey, J. W. (1977). *Data analysis and regression.* Reading, PA: Addison-Wesley.

Mullis, I.V.S., Martin, M.O., Gonzales, E. J., Gregory. K. D., Garden. R. A., O'Connor, K. M., Chrostowski, S. J., & Smith, T. A. (2000). *TIMSS 1999 International Mathematics Report.* Chestnut Hill, MA: International Study Center, Boston College.

Nichols, P. D. (1994). A framework for developing cognitively diagnostic assessment. *Review of Educational Research, 64*(4), 575–603.

Nitko, A. J. (1980). Criterion-referencing schemes. In S. T. Mayo (Ed.), *New directions for testing and measurement: Interpreting test performance* (p. 6). San Francisco: Jossey-Bass.

Paulison, J. A. (1986). *Estimation of parameters in latent class models with constraints on the parameters* (ONR Technical Report). Portland, OR: Portland State University.

Resnick, L. B. (1976). Task analysis in instructional design: Some cases from mathematics. In D. Klahr (Ed.), *Cognition and instruction.* Hillsdale, NJ: Erlbaum.

Resnick, L. B. (1983). A developmental theory of number understanding. In H. P. Ginsbury (Ed.), *The development of mathematical thinking* (pp. 109–151). New York: Academic Press.

Riply, B. D. (1996). *Pattern recognition and neural networks.* Cambridge: Cambridge University Press.

S-Plus® 2000. (1999). Math Soft Inc. Cambridge, MA.

Saito, H. (1998). *Cognitive diagnostic perspectives of a second language reading test.* Unpublished doctoral thesis, University of Illinois at Urbana-Champaign.

Samejima, F. (1972). Estimation of latent ability using a response pattern of graded scores. *Pyschometrik a Monograph, 17*.

Sato, T. (1975). *The construction and interpretation of S-P tables*. Tokyo: Meiji Tosho (in Japanese).

Sato, T. (1978). Hierarchical display of networks of teaching elements using the interpretive structure modeling method. In *IECE transactions on educational technology, ET-78-4, 1978-06* (pp. 23–28). Tokyo: IECE (in Japanese).

Sato, T. (1990). *An introduction to educational information technology*. Kawasaki, Japan: NEC Technical College.

Shaw, D. S. (1984). Fraction subtraction errors: Case studies. In K. K. Tatsuoka (Ed.), *Analysis of errors in fraction addition and subtraction problems* (Final Report for Grant No. NIE-G-81-002, pp. 40–51). Urbana: University of Illinois, Computer-Based Education Research Laboratory (CERL).

Shaw, D. S. (1986). *Effects of adaptive diagnostic testing on two types of computerized remediation*. Unpublished doctoral thesis, University of Illinois at Urbana-Champaign.

Shaw D. S. & Birenbaum, M. (1985). Task specification chart: A key to better understanding of test results. *Journal of Educational Measurement, 22*, 219–230.

Shaw, D. S., Standiford, S. N., Klein, M., & Tatsuoka, K. K. (1982). *Error analysis of fraction arithmetic: Selected case studies* (Research Report No. 82-2-NIE). Urbana: University of Illinois, Computer-Based Education Research Laboratory (CERL).

Simmons, G. F. (1963). *Introduction to topology and modern analysis*. San Francisco: McGraw-Hill.

Sleeman, D., Kelly, A. E., Martink, R., Ward, R. D., & Moore, J. L. (1989). Studies of diagnosis and remediation with high school algebra students. *Cognitive Science, 13*, 551–568.

Snow, R. E., & Lohman, D. F. (1993). Cognitive psychology, new test design, and new test theory: An introduction. In N. Fredriksen, R. J. Mislevy, & I. Bejar (Eds.), *Test theory for a new generation of tests* (pp. 1–17). Hillsdale, NJ: Erlbaum.

SPSS® Inc. (1997). SPSS base 7.5 syntax reference guide. SPSS Inc.

Standiford, S., Tatsuoka, K. K., & Klein, M. (1982). *Decimal fraction arithmetic: Logical error analysis and its validation* (Research Report No. 82-1-NIE). Urbana: University of Illinois, Computer-Based Education Research Laboratory (CERL).

Stuart, A. & Ord, K. J. (1987). *Kendall's advanced theory of statistics originated by Sir Maurice Kendall*. Fifth Edition of Volume 1 *Distribution theory*. New York: Oxford University Press

Takeya, M. (1981). *A study on item relational structure analysis of criterion referenced tests*. Unpublished doctoral dissertation, Waseda University, Tokyo.

Tatsuoka, C. (1996). *Sequential classification on partially ordered sets*. Unpublished doctoral thesis, Cornell University.

Tatsuoka, C. (2002). Data analytic methods for latent partially ordered classification models. *Applied Statistics (Journal of the Royal Statistical Society Series C), 51*, 337–350. See also *Corrigendum* (2005), *54*, 465–467.

Tatsuoka, C., & Ferguson, T. (2003). Sequential analysis on partially ordered sets. *Journal of the Royal Statistical Society Series B, 65,* 143–157.

Tatsuoka, K. K. (1975). *Vector-geometric and Hilbert space reformulation of classical test theory.* Unpublished doctoral dissertation, University of Illinois at Urbana-Champaign.

Tatsuoka, K. K. (1981). *An approach to assessing the seriousness of error types and predictability of future performance* (Research Report No. 81-1-ONR). Urbana: University of Illinois, Computer-Based Education Research Laboratory (CERL).

Tatsuoka, K. K. (1983a). Changes in error types over learning stages. *Journal of Educational Psychology, 76*(1), 120–129.

Tatsuoka, K. K. (1983b). Rule space: An approach for dealing with misconceptions based on item response theory. *Journal of Educational Measurement, 20*(4), 345–354.

Tatsuoka, K. K. (Ed.). (1984a). *Analysis of errors in fraction addition and subtraction problems* (Final Report for Grant No. NIE-G-81-0002). Urbana: University of Illinois, Computer-Based Education Research Laboratory (CERL).

Tatsuoka, K. K. (1984b). Caution indices based on item response theory. *Psychometrika, 49*(1), 95–110.

Tatsuoka, K. K. (1985). A probabilistic model for diagnosing misconceptions by the pattern classification approach. *Journal of Educational Statistics, 50,* 55–73.

Tatsuoka, K. K. (1986). *Adaptive testing algorithm in the rule space method* (ONR Technical Report). Urbana: University of Illinois, Computer-Based Education Research Laboratory (CERL).

Tatsuoka, K. K. (1987). Validation of cognitive sensitivity for item response curves. *Journal of Educational Measurement, 24,* 233–245.

Tatsuoka, K. K. (1990). Toward an integration of item-response theory and cognitive error diagnoses. In N. Frederiksen, R. L. Glaser, A. M. Lesgold, & M. G. Shafto (Eds.), *Diagnostic monitoring of skill and knowledge acquisition.* Hillsdale, NJ: Erlbaum.

Tatsuoka, K. K. (1991). *Boolean algebra applied to determination of the universal set of misconception states* (ONR-Technical Report No. RR-91-44). Princeton, NJ: Educational Testing Services.

Tatsuoka, K. K. (1993). Item construction and psychometric models appropriate for constructed responses. In R. E. Bennett & W. C. Ward (Eds.), *Construction versus choice in cognitive measurement* (pp. 107–133). Hillsdale, NJ: Erlbaum.

Tatsuoka, K. K. (1995). Architecture of knowledge structures and cognitive diagnosis: A statistical pattern recognition and classification approach. In P. D. Nichols, S. F. Chipman, & R. L. Brennan (Eds.), *Cognitively diagnostic assessment.* Hillsdale, NJ: Erlbaum.

Tatsuoka, K. K. (1997). Use of generalized person-fit indices ζs for statistical pattern classification. *Journal of Applied Educational Measurement, 9*(1), 65–75.

Tatsuoka, K. K., & Baillie, R. (1982). *Rule space, the product space of two score components in signed number subtraction: An approach to dealing with inconsistent use of erroneous rules* (Technical Report No. 82-3-ONR). Urbana: University of Illinois, Computer-Based Education Research Laboratory (CERL).

Tatsuoka K. K., & Birenbaum, M. (1981). Effects of instructional backgrounds on test performances. *Journal of Computer-Based Instruction, 8,* 1–8.

Tatsuoka, K. K. & Birenbaum, M. (1983). The effect of a scoring system based on the algorithm underlying the students' response patterns solving type. *Journal of Educational Measurement, 20*(1), 17–26.

Tatsuoka, K. K., & Birenbaum, M. (1993). On the stability of responses to parallel items and its implications for diagnostic assessment. *Journal of Applied Psychological Measurement, 17*(1), .

Tatsuoka, K. K., Birenbaum, M. M., & Arnold, J. (1990). On the stability of students' rules of operation for solving arithmetic problems. *Journal of Educational Measurement, 26*(4), 351–361.

Tatsuoka, K. K., Birenbaum, M., Lewis, C., & Sheehan, K. S. (1993). *Proficiency scaling based on attribute regression curves* (Technical Report). Princeton, NJ: Educational Testing Services.

Tatsuoka, K. K., Birenbaum, M., Tatsuoka, M. M., & Baillie, R. (1980). *Psychometric approach to error analysis of response patterns of achievement tests* (Technical Report No. 80-3-ONR) Urbana: University of Illinois, Computer-Based Education Research Laboratory (CERL).

Tatsuoka, K. K., & Boodoo, G. (2000). Subgroup differences on the GRE Quantitative Test based on the underlying cognitive processes and knowledge. In D. Lesh & W. E. Kelly (Eds.), *Research design and methodologies for mathematics and science*. Hillsdale, NJ: Erlbaum.

Tatsuoka, K., & Corter, J. (2003). *Attribute coding manual on TIMSS 7th graders* (NSF Technical Report). New York: Teachers College, Columbia University.

Tatsuoka, K., Corter, J., & Tatsuoka, C. (2004). Patterns of diagnosed mathematical content and process skills in TIMSS-R across a sample of 20 countries. *American Educational Research Journal, 41*(4), 901–926.

Tatsuoka, K. K., & Edins, J. M. (1985). Computer analysis of students' procedural "bugs" in an arithmetic domain. *Journal of Computer-Based Instruction, 12*(2), 34–38.

Tatsuoka, K., Guerrero, A., Corter, J. E., Yamada, T., Tatsuoka, C., Xin, T., et al. (2006). International comparisons of mathematical thinking skills in TIMSS-R (NSF Technical Report III). *Japanese Journal of Research on Testing, 2*(1), 3–40.

Tatsuoka, K. K., & Hayashi, A. (2001). A statistical method for classifying individuals into their latent knowledge state. *Journal of the Society of Instrument and Control Engineers, 40*(8), 561–567 (in Japanese).

Tatsuoka, K. K., Kelly, A. E., Tatsuoka, C. M., Varadi, F., & Dean, M. (2007). *Rule space and associated analysis of the Broward County Schools Benchmark FCAT (B-FCAT) test* (Technical Report II to the National Science Foundation). Ewing, NJ: Tanar Software.

Tatsuoka, K. K., & Linn, R. L. (1983). Indices for detecting unusual patterns: Links between two general approaches and potential applications. *Applied Psychological Measurement, 7*(1), 81–96.

Tatsuoka, K. K., Linn, R. L., Tatsuoka, M. M., & Yamamoto, K. (1988). An application of the Mantel-Haenszel procedure to detect item bias resulting from the use of different instructional strategies. *Journal of Educational Measurement, 25*(4), 301–320.

Tatsuoka K. K., & Tatsuoka, C. (2005). Stability of classification results on the cognitive diagnosis for individuals. *Japanese Journal for Research on Testing, 1*(1), .

Tatsuoka, K. K., & Tatsuoka, M. M. (1980). Detection of aberrant response patterns and their effect on dimensionality (Research Report No. 80-4-ONR). Urbana: University of Illinois, Computer-Based Education Research Laboratory (CERL).

Tatsuoka, K. K., & Tatsuoka, M. M. (1982). Detection of aberrant response patterns. *Journal of Educational Statistics, 7*(3), 215–231.

Tatsuoka, K. K., & Tatsuoka, M. M. (1983). Spotting erroneous rules of operation by the individual consistency index. *Journal of Educational Measurement, 3*, 221–230.

Tatsuoka, K. K., & Tatsuoka, M. M. (1987). Bug distribution and pattern classification. *Psychometrika, 52*(2), 193–206.

Tatsuoka, K. K., & Tatsuoka, M. M. (1997). Computerized adaptive diagnostic testing. *Journal of Educational Measurement, 34*, 3–20.

Tatsuoka, K. K., Xin, T., Tatsuoka, C., & Kelly, A. E. (2005). *Patterns of attribute characteristic curves and their relationship to teachers' background questionnaire* (NSF Technical Report). New York: Teachers College, Columbia University.

Tatsuoka, M. M. (1970). *Discriminant analysis: The study of group differences.* Champaign, IL: Institute for Personality and Ability Testing.

Tatsuoka, M. M. (1971). *Multivariate analysis.* New York: John Wiley.

Tatsuoka, M. M. (1986). Graph theory and its applications in educational research: A review and integration. *Review of Educational Research, 56*, 291–329.

Tatsuoka, M. M. (1988). *Multivariate analysis.* New York: Macmillan.

Tatsuoka, M. M., & Tatsuoka, K. K. (1989). Rule space. In S. Kotz, & N. L. Johnson (Eds.), *Encyclopedia of statistical sciences.* New York: Wiley.

Trabin, B. D., & Weiss, D. J. (1979). *The person response curve: Fit of individuals to item characteristic curve models* (Research Report No. 79-7). Minneapolis: University of Minnesota, Department of Psychology, Psychometric Methods Program.

Van der Flier, H. (1977). Environmental factors and deviant response patterns. In Y. H. Poortinga (Ed.), *Basic problems in cross cultural psychology.* Amsterdam, The Netherlands: Swets & Seitlinger.

Van der Flier, H. (1982). Deviant response patterns and comparability of test scores. *Journal of Cross-Cultural Psychology, 13*(3), 267–298.

VanLehn, K. (1983). *Felicity conditions for human skill acquisition: Validating an AI-based theory* (Technical Report No. CIS-21). Palo Alto, CA: Xerox Palo Alto Research Centers.

Varadi, F., Tatsuoka, C., & Tatsuoka, K. K. (1992). *BUGLIB* (Modified version). Unpublished computer program, Trenton, NJ.

Varadi, F., & Tatsuoka, K. K. (1989). *BUGLIB.* Unpublished computer program, Trenton, NJ.

Venables, W. N., & Riply, B. D. (1994). *Statistics and computing.* New York: Springer Verlag.

Von Davier, M. (2007). *Mixture distribution diagnostic models* (Technical Report No. RR-07-32). Princeton, NJ: Educational Testing Services.

Warfield, J. N. (1973a). On arranging elements of hierarchy in graphic form. *IEEE Transactions on Systems, Man and Cybernetics, SMC-3*, 121–132.

Warfield, J. N. (1973b). Binary matrices in system modeling. *IEEE Transactions on Systems, Man and Cybernetics, SMC-3*, 441–449.

Weiss, D. (1983). *New horizons in testing*. New York: Academic Press.

Wiley, D. E. (2002). Validity of constructs versus construct validity of scores. In H. I. Braun, D. N. Jackson, & D. E. Wiley (Eds.), *The role of constructs in psychological and educational measurement* (pp. 207–227). Mahwah, NJ: Erlbaum.

Wise, S. L. (1981). *A modified order-analysis procedure for determining unidimensional items set*. Unpublished doctoral dissertation, University of Illinois at Urbana-Champaign.

Wright, B. D. (1977). Solving measurement problems with the Rasch model. *Journal of Educational Measurement, 14*, 97–116.

Wright, B. D., & Masters, G. N. (1982). *Rating scale analysis*. Chicago: Mesa Press.

Xin, T., Xu, Z., and Tatsuoka, K. (2004). Linkage between teacher quality and student cognitive development: A rule-space model. *Studies in Educational Evaluation, 30*(3), 205–223.

Yamada, T. (2008). *Comparison of cognitively diagnostic adaptive testing algorithms*. Unpublished doctoral dissertation, Columbia University.

Yamamoto, K. (1987). *A model that combines IRT and latent class models*. Unpublished doctoral thesis, University of Illinois at Urbana-Champaign.

Yamamoto, Y., & Wise, S. L. (1980). *Extracting unidimensional chains from multidimensional datasets: A graph theory approach* (ONR Research Report). Urbana: University of Illinois.

Yepes Baraya, M., Allen, N., & Tatsuoka, K. (2000). *Rule space analysis on NAEP Science Assessment* (ETS Report). Princeton, NJ: Educational Testing Services.

Author Index

Subject Index

A

Aberrant response patterns, detection of, 13–26
  aberrant response patterns, 14, 17
  branching in testing system, 17
  erroneous rules, 17
  FBUG testing system, 17
  Guttman scale, 17
  Guttman vector, 19
  Individual Consistency Index, 24–26
  Norm Conformity Index, 18–24
Ability state, 52
ACCs, *see* Attribute characteristic curves
Adjacency matrix, 64–66, 76
  equivalent, 64
  immediate prerequisite, 64
  indirect relations, 65
Analysis of variance (ANOVA), 23, 125
ANOVA, *see* Analysis of variance
Aptitude tests, difference between achievement and, 11
Associative law, 72
Attribute(s), *see also* Validation of attributes and Q matrix coded by involvement of attributes to items and test
  combinations of, 5
  fraction subtraction problems, 41
  incidence matrix, 41
  lattice
    Boolean operation, 75
    definition of Boolean algebra, 75
    identities and complement, 75
  network of, 91–93
  patterns, combinatorial combinations of, 96–97
  psychometric, 55
  Q matrix, 55
  types, 2
Attribute characteristic curves (ACCs), 256–261
  cubic spline smoothing functions, 256
  investigation of attribute stability, 256–261
  95% confidence intervals, 256
  nonparametric regression, 256
  norm table of attribute performance from SAT Math, 260

SAT Mathematics test, 256
Test of English for International Communication, 256
Attribute mastery probabilities, 204–210, *see also* Posterior probabilities with different prior probabilities and effect on attribute mastery probabilities; Rule space decision rules and attribute mastery probabilities
  attribute space, space of ideal item scores, and space of knowledge states, 208–210
  Boolean descriptive function, 208
  cheated response patterns, 204
  definition, 206–208
    application of attribute A_k, 208
    choose L closest groups, 206
    posterior probabilities for L closest groups, 208
    weighted average of kth component of L attribute patterns, 208
    weights, 207
  ideal item score patterns and, 250–255
    assumption of when item score is correct, 251
    comparison of means of observed score X and estimated item difficulties, 254–255
    comparison of observed item, 254
    estimated item difficulty obtained by taking average of test takers, 252
    estimated item scores obtained from 252
    estimation of attribute mastery probabilities from pseudotrue score, 255
    estimation of pseudotrue scores from attributes mastery probabilities for person i, 250–254
    multiplicative model, 251
    SAT I Verbal test, 254
  latent class modeling, 204
  mutually exclusive, totally together classification groups, 204
  RSM analysis for SAT Reading comprehension test, 209